MW01286180

Finding Radical Wholeness

SELECTED BOOKS BY KEN WILBER

Boomeritis: A Novel That Will Set You Free

A Brief History of Everything

The Essential Ken Wilber: An Introductory Reader

Grace and Grit: A Love Story

Integral Meditation: Mindfulness as a Path to Grow Up, Wake Up, and Show Up in Your Life

Integral Psychology: Consciousness, Spirit, Psychology, Therapy

Integral Spirituality: A Startling New Role for Religion in the Modern and Postmodern World

The Integral Vision: A Very Short Introduction to the Revolutionary Integral Approach to Life, God, the Universe, and Everything

One Taste: The Journals of Ken Wilber

The Religion of Tomorrow: A Vision of the Future of the Great Traditions—More Inclusive, More Comprehensive, More Complete

Sex, Ecology, Spirituality: The Spirit of Evolution

The Simple Feeling of Being: Visionary, Spiritual, and Poetic Writings

A Theory of Everything: An Integral Vision for Business, Politics, Science, and Spirituality

Finding Radical Wholeness

THE INTEGRAL PATH TO
UNITY, GROWTH, AND DELIGHT

KEN WILBER

SHAMBHALA

Shambhala Publications, Inc.
2129 13th Street
Boulder, Colorado 80302
www.shambhala.com

Cover art: Sunward Art/Shutterstock
Cover design: Pete Garceau
Interior design: Katrina Noble

9 8 7 6 5 4 3 2 1

First Edition
Printed in the United States of America

Shambhala Publications makes every effort to print on acid-free, recycled paper. Shambhala Publications is distributed worldwide by Penguin Random House, Inc., and its subsidiaries.

LIBRARY OF CONGRESS CATALOGING-IN-PUBLICATION DATA
Names: Wilber, Ken, author.
Title: Finding radical wholeness: the integral path to unity, growth, and delight / Ken Wilber.
Description: Boulder, Colorado: Shambhala Publications, Inc. [2024] | Includes index.
Identifiers: LCCN 2022048951 | ISBN 9781645471851 (Hardcover)
Subjects: LCSH: Spirituality. | Well-being. | Self-actualization (Psychology).
Classification: LCC BL624.W5325 2023 | DDC 204/.4—dc23/eng/20230124
LC record available at https://lccn.loc.gov/2022048951

CONTENTS

Finding Radical Wholeness

Introduction

This is a book about Wholeness. I'm capitalizing "Wholeness" because I want to give it a certain weight. In fact, I claim—and will try to convince you—that discovering a genuine Wholeness is actually the meaning of a real spirituality, and thus it can offer you a genuine meaning and purpose to your life. But this is not a spirituality that is theistic; it is not mythic; it does not rely on accepting a particular belief system; it does not postulate the existence of a supreme deity, or a supernatural being, or a transcendental reality that you should worship. It's fine if you happen to believe in any of those, but they are not what this book is about. Besides, you can believe in any of those items and still lack—or gain—a genuine Wholeness itself. But discovering this Wholeness is what a real spirituality is all about; and in this book, you will find ways to fully discover a real Wholeness in the midst of your life and see the profound difference that it can make for your own being and awareness.

You've probably heard the common phrase "I'm spiritual but not religious." In a sense, that phrase applies to this book. Its approach is spiritual, in the sense that it helps you to directly discover a real Wholeness—a genuine spirituality—right here and right now in your own life, but it does not demand any sort of belief in magical and mythic stories, miracle events, or anything like an institutional religion. In redefining a genuine spirituality as the discovery of a real Wholeness, it bypasses most of the magical and mythic belief systems that permeate so many of the world's religions—and in exactly that sense, it is "spiritual but not religious." So you won't find any beliefs such as "Moses really did part the Red Sea," "Mohammed really did fly to the moon on his horse and cut it in two with his sword," "Lao Tzu really was nine hundred years old when he was born," and so on. Mythic stories like those are the cornerstones of many—even most—of the world's great religions, and a primary factor in whether you are following those religions correctly is whether or not you actually accept and believe in those myths. Again, it's fine with me if you accept any of those mythic belief systems, but you will not be asked to do so in this book. Instead, a new form of spirituality—the discovery of a real Wholeness—will instead be laid out, along with specific exercises and practices that will help you directly and immediately realize a genuine Wholeness permeating your entire life. You will definitely be able to say, "I'm spiritual but not religious." (And by the way, a recent poll reported by *Time* magazine shows that over 70 percent of millennials say that the phrase "spiritual but not religious" applies to them, so this type of approach definitely has an audience ready to adopt it seriously.)

Immanuel Kant, writing in 1793, said that you could tell that it was definitely a modern world because if a person were on their knees praying and somebody came in and saw them, they would be profoundly embarrassed. Today we live in a world where many people, especially those highly educated, do not find the magical and mythic stories of the world's great religions to be at all believable, not anymore. And, yes, many of those people would be embarrassed if they were caught, one way or another, believing in any of those ancient mythic "unbelievable" stories. The spirituality you will find in this book will not, I believe, embarrass you, no matter how highly educated you are. It simply helps you find a genuine Unity and Wholeness in your own being and awareness, and there are many extraordinary benefits that come from finding that kind of Wholeness in your life—benefits in your work, relationships, play, parenting, career, and your simple being.

This is not to say that there is no benefit at all in any of the aspects of the original forms of the world's great religions. I will not be asking you to believe any of the magical, mythic, or miracle stories of any traditional religion. I definitely will not try to convince you of anything such as Jesus Christ really being born of a biological virgin. (The fact that Mary pulled that one off is astonishing. She's pregnant, and if her husband is not the father, then she's clearly been fooling around, and so she has to invent some sort of story as her excuse. And Joseph, her husband, is apparently so dense, he actually buys Mary's story: "Yes, I had sex, but don't worry, the real father is not from this planet.") Those are the types of "unbelievable" stories that have modern men and women scratching their heads and getting embarrassed if caught believing.

But that is not to say that, in all of Christianity (or in any other world religion), there is absolutely nothing of value. This, of course, is where we have to be very, very, *very* careful. I suggest that there is a small but important core of most of the world's religions that is truly spiritual, as I'm using the term. In other words, most traditional religions have some aspects that really do help people discover a genuine Wholeness, so the very core—and only the core—of these approaches is "spiritual but not religious."

Take Christianity, for example. Yes, there are a great number of magical and mythic beliefs and miracles that a Christian is asked to adopt—for example, the beliefs laid out in the Nicene Creed and the Apostle's Creed, all variations on the myths of the one and only biological son of the one and only creator of the universe, who died for your sins and will resurrect you on judgment day to your eternal glory. To today's educated mind, not one of these statements is believable. But, especially in early Christianity, there was something else it offered: a Waking Up to a Wholeness awareness, and it did this through a path of meditation or contemplation. Thus, for example, St. Paul says, "Let this consciousness be in you that was in Christ

Jesus, that we all may be one." This search for Oneness, this drive toward Wholeness, was a core component of Christianity, as it was in many other of the world's Great Wisdom Traditions—for example, Hinduism, Buddhism, and Sufism. What's most important is that this Wholeness is completely independent of one's beliefs. And, especially, what is not required are magic-mythic beliefs, which are what we find in religious treatises like the Bible. These are no longer needed—especially since they are holdovers from earlier, lower, and now largely outdated (and hence "unbelievable") stages of evolution or Growing Up—namely, the magic and mythic stages.

Having a near-death experience (NDE) is completely independent of whether you are a materialist, idealist, nihilist, or a faith believer. Likewise, the discovery of a real Wholeness does not in any way depend upon your believing in any sort of magical or mythic belief system (or any rational belief system, for that matter). That's just not a requirement. In addition to all the mythic stories in Christianity, there are also contemplative, meditative, or truly mystical schools of Christianity that aim directly for a genuine experience of Wholeness—for example, the approach expressed in texts like *The Cloud of Unknowing* (where "unknowing" means letting go of things like mythic beliefs so as to get into a Waking Up Awareness beyond all belief systems). That experience of Wholeness is totally independent of accepting any of the magical and mythic beliefs that usually come with a conversion to Christianity. Most of the genuine Christian mystics that I know (and by "mystic," I mean somebody who has had a direct spiritual experience of this Wholeness) don't believe any of the central Christian myths or in the supernatural miracles, including the virgin birth and the resurrection of the physical body—none of them.

So it is one thing to say that, in being a Christian, you have discovered your own Christ consciousness—meaning, you have discovered your Real Self and the fundamental Wholeness of the entire universe ("so that we all may be one")—and it is quite another to say, "I believe in the Father, the Son, and the Holy Ghost; that the Son was born of a virgin and was crucified, was dead and resurrected, ascended unto heaven, and now offers me salvation from original sin." Those are two entirely different things; one is spiritual, the other is religious.

The brilliant writer Bishop John Shelby Spong wrote numerous books—such as his 2018 work *Unbelievable*—that drive home very similar points about Christianity, and strongly. Spong starts by pointing out that there is a very big difference between *experience* and *explanation*. That is right on the mark. We often call experience a "knowledge by acquaintance" and explanation "a knowledge by description." It's an important distinction. What we will be directly exploring in this book is a knowledge by acquaintance—a direct *experience*—of Wholeness, and although this ultimate Unity consciousness will be described (an *explanation*), you will need to directly experience this Wholeness yourself to actually know what it means (and we'll be exploring exercises that let you do exactly that). Spong argues that real Christianity involves a direct *experience* of Oneness but, historically, Christianity got hijacked by an *explanation* that came from a lot of literalized first-century myths and a rather byzantine fourth-century philosophy. As for the myths and miracles in the Bible, Spong outrageously denies the reality of all of them. Spong himself certainly does not believe in any of them. And this includes every magic-mythic belief of Christianity, including the idea that Jesus literally died for your sins, the notion of a biological virgin birth, physical ascension, Moses parting the Red Sea, Elijah going straight to heaven in his chariot, and on and on. Spong denies every myth, miracle, and supernatural occasion associated with Christianity (and he's relentlessly done so in a dozen books; and remember, he was a real bishop, for heaven's sake, and I honestly don't know how he avoided excommunication). Spong wants the *direct experience* of Oneness, of pure Wholeness (which he calls a wholeness of "living, loving, and being"), and he doesn't want a single myth thrown in there as an (unbelievable) explanation of that experience, which is exactly where the title of his book comes from (*Unbelievable*). Spong was truly "spiritual but not religious," and he believed—as I do—that Jesus was, too, and that the announcement of Wholeness was the core of Christ's message.

I would add that it is also the core message of Gautama Buddha, Shankara, Plotinus, Lao Tzu, Lady Tsogyal, Chuang Tzu, and most of the other great Realizers who were the founders of the traditional religions. We find this quest for Wholeness at the center of most of the world's great religions, even though their major mythic stories differ wildly. After all, if you are truly one with the universe, you're one with the universe, no matter how you explain or frame it. One is one. If you examine the great traditions carefully, you will readily see this common core of Unity consciousness in virtually all of them. There is actually a philosophical school called the "Perennial Philosophy," which believes that this fundamental Wholeness is what all of the world's great religions are pursuing; and while their outward forms vary immensely (their mythic *explanations* vary), this inner Wholeness is essentially the same in virtually all of them (the *experience* of Oneness is similar). We have to be careful here because although there is a certain sense in which the basic Wholeness is similar in all of them, it's also true that most experiences include some degree of interpretation (which is partially based on culture), so we really don't find too many things that are truly "perennial" or unchanging. Still, the core truth of the Perennial Philosophy is that as the meditation systems became more and more sophisticated, they all tended to point to a very similar ultimate Wholeness. The discovery of that Wholeness—a direct experience of Unity consciousness—was variously called "Enlightenment," "Awakening," "Satori," "Metamorphosis," "Fana," or the Great Liberation, which is the basic aim of meditation itself.

As we will directly explore later, that Wholeness is not mythic, supernatural, or magical; rather the experience of Wholeness is that, as you are looking at the world around you, suddenly you and that world become one single experience of Unity consciousness. You feel that you are indeed one with the entire world; you are one with everything, and the entire universe is arising within you. That's typically the direct experience of Unity consciousness—and then, *after* that *experience*, you will usually come up with all sorts of *explanations* for it, most of which won't stand up to any sort of critical scrutiny and would rationally be shot down, but that won't stop you from trying. And you'll still know, however difficult the explanations might be, that the experience itself was very real. It is indeed an authentic peak experience of the Ground of All Being; it's a real Waking Up, a genuine glimpse of an ultimate Unity consciousness, a divine Oneness, what some Tibetan Buddhists call the "One Taste" of a real Wholeness.

So I maintain that the Vedanta school of Hinduism, Taoism, Kabbalah, contemplative or mystical Christianity, most forms of Neoplatonism, many earlier forms of Buddhism, all schools of Mahayana and Vajrayana, Hasidism, and Sufism, among many others, have, at their deepest core, the pursuit and discovery of this genuine nondual Wholeness. We will be looking at a Waking Up to this Wholeness and exploring ways to directly realize and experience it ourselves without having to adopt any of the mythic stories or other strange explanations that almost always came with the original forms of these religions. Spirituality is basically religion without weirdness, and that's the form we'll be pursuing.

We will also see, to anticipate another point, that human development includes several stages of growth and evolution, which brilliant researchers like Jean Gebser have described and named—for example, archaic, magic, mythic, rational, pluralistic, integrated. Humanity itself is moving through those stages (including the lower stages of magic and mythic on the way to higher stages such as rational and integrated—with humanity today just reaching the beginning of the integrated stage). We'll be looking at those stages more carefully later, but right now I note that I will claim that almost all of the magical and mythic stories in the Bible were written when humanity was at those earlier stages—the magic and mythic stages—some two thousand to six thousand years ago. Thus, at the time they were written, they were not mistakes or hallucinations or delusions, but they were written by humans at the earlier magic and mythic stages of development—and they honestly and sincerely meant what they wrote. At that point, I will soften my harsh criticism of those religious views—it's like yelling at a five-year-old—but without changing the essential point that they are indeed products of earlier, lower, and largely outmoded and outdated (and hence indeed "unbelievable") stages of human evolution and that none of these beliefs are required for a direct experience of real Wholeness. But, if you have any of those beliefs, you don't have to get rid of them—although you might choose to do so, or at least find ways to update them.

So we're looking for a genuine Wholeness. But there's a very strange thing about Wholeness—and here we come to the very central point of this book. Wholeness almost never just stands out in awareness, all by itself. Wholeness is not something that everybody automatically sees, like a rock or a tree. You actually have to know where to look for Wholeness, and then you have to go out and look for it. Otherwise, as strange as it might seem, you won't find Wholeness; you will remain partial, fragmented, and broken—or at least not nearly as Whole as you could be. Although Wholeness is literally all around you, with you, and in you—it's flooding your awareness right now—if you don't know where to look for it, it will go right past you and you won't even suspect that it's there. I will be emphasizing that point over and over and over again until we're both completely tired of it. But it's very much the truth; and, in fact, if there were one point alone that I would like you to take from this book, it would be "You have to know where to look for Wholeness." The vast majority of people in this world have very little Wholeness in their lives because nobody ever showed them where to look for it.

Just as interesting (and just as surprising) is that when we pursue ways to look for Wholeness, we find that there are several different (but equally important) types of genuine Wholeness. And there are pathways (or practices or experiential exercises) that you can explore to help you see each type. In fact, we'll be looking carefully at each of those different areas of Wholeness and explaining them clearly so you'll know exactly what to do to see them. Let me start by saying that only one of these types of Wholeness (there are five of them) has anything to do with spirituality, so if you're not interested in anything to do with spirituality, I think you can still like and enjoy this book.

For now, I'll give these 5 different types of Wholeness some names: Waking Up, Growing Up, Opening Up, Cleaning Up, and Showing Up. These are all activities you can do in your life, and each of them will show you an unbelievably profound type of Wholeness. And if you put all of these types of Wholeness together, you will have what could be called a wildly inclusive "Big Wholeness." Look through these various types of Wholeness as they are explained, and see if they make sense to you. You can always toss out the ones that don't. But most people find them incredibly illuminating; in fact, there's a worldwide professional movement devoted to this Big Wholeness called "Integral Metatheory," which just happens to be a view that I represent.

It's flat-out amazing when you first look at it, but each one of those five pathways reveals a very different type of Wholeness. You would seriously think that Wholeness being Wholeness, there would be only one of them. And this is where we stumble on a shocking realization: the Wholeness offered by authentic Waking Up paths—which formed the core of the world's Great Religions and consisted of an experience of "being one with everything"—turns out to be just one major type of Wholeness (the type that we call "Waking Up").

But, there are at least 5 major aspects, dimensions, or areas of fundamental Wholeness (namely—Waking Up, Growing Up, Opening Up, Cleaning Up, and Showing Up), and this turns out to be profoundly important, because each one of those areas shows us a very, very different type of Wholeness.

Humanity, in the East and West, North and South, has worked for thousands and thousands of years, right up to today, in order to discover all of these areas of Wholeness. And this was not an easy task, because it is still true that not one of these areas of Wholeness is totally obvious or apparent right now; none of them is just parading by in front of your awareness and loudly announcing itself. Every one of them has to be directly looked for. And you have to know it's there, or you won't even try.

This is why Integral Metatheory, where *Integral* basically means "Wholeness," had to search for nearly five decades to find all of these areas of Wholeness. And one of the first things that people often do when they find this Integral approach is sort of hit themselves in the head for not being able to see and find all these areas of Wholeness themselves, since once they see them, they all seem so incredibly obvious. In one sense, they are very obvious and they are running through your awareness right now. But it's still quite true that if you don't know where and how to look for them, they will remain mysterious unknowns in your life. In fact, of the 5 types of Wholeness that I just mentioned, three of them, Growing Up, Opening Up, and Cleaning Up, were discovered only in the last one hundred years, which means that, for almost their entire history, human beings were actually training themselves to be partial, fragmented, and broken.

There is, today, no system of growth anywhere in the world that includes all 5 of these types of Wholeness. Thus, if you want a real Wholeness, you've come to the right place. What you'll find in the following pages are simple outlines, practices, and pointing-out instructions that you can easily use and that will directly, and almost immediately, show you these 5 areas of "Big Wholeness." I myself did not invent any of them, and every one has a substantial knowledge community around the world that explores it in immense depth and detail. But I have pulled them all together and presented them in a type of superholism (or Integral Metatheory) that will help you find all of the fundamental Big Wholenesses that are lying under your own nose right now, if you know where to look.

This book was originally titled "Making Room for Everything." Given my discussion of Wholeness thus far, it might be obvious why I originally chose that title. Genuine Wholeness—Big Wholeness—makes room for everything in your life, much of which right now might not be included. You are very likely missing an enormous number of things that actually belong to you and should be included in your own life, to its huge benefit and likely improvement, but you haven't made room for them—you don't have enough Wholeness. When you really see the fundamental Big Wholeness of this world, then everything fits and you feel as if there is a superabundant fullness in your life, and no friction, no tension, no torture. But to make room for everything, you need to know exactly where to look for a complete Wholeness—and this means you need to know where and how to look for a real Waking Up, Growing Up, Opening Up, Cleaning Up, and Showing Up. Each one of those processes makes it very clear to you exactly where its own genuine Wholeness lies. One of the most shocking things to me in my entire professional life has been the realization of just how utterly hidden real Wholeness is—and it's shocking because, when you do see it, it is absolutely and staggeringly obvious. How did it take humanity hundreds of thousands of years to discover most of these things? How blind could we possibly be?

For example, when you see what Growing Up is, I think that, like most people, you will have two major reactions: (1) you will understand why this entire process was not discovered by humanity until around one hundred years ago, and (2) you will be almost stunned by what this process shows you about Wholeness, because you will see a type of Wholeness that you probably had no idea even existed. You could be a serious holist, a dedicated systems theorist, or some other believer in the real Wholeness of this world, and yet your response will likely be, "Wow, I didn't suspect that kind of Wholeness was even there!"

Like the other 5 Wholeness-disclosing processes, Growing Up will show you an aspect of Wholeness that is both easy to understand and not at all obvious (until, once again, it is pointed out, whereupon it becomes utterly apparent). We see this with all of the various aspects of Big Wholeness. For instance, with the process of Waking Up, we are indeed talking about a direct experience that most of the great religions were originally founded on and that they originally sought to transmit to others, and that was an experience of pure Wholeness. And we'll see, in the next chapter, that the evidence for this profound Waking Up experience is so overwhelming that one well-respected expert has called its existence "not disputable."

The meditation or contemplation systems of the great religions worked directly with these Waking Up realizations, and these systems didn't involve any magic or mythic stories but instead were profound consciousness-transformation psychotechnologies. All they wanted was the pure Wholeness or ultimate nondual Unity experience. This direct *experience* was then given different *explanations* by the different religions. Those religions often differed in many ways, but whenever mystics (or those who actually had this direct experience of Oneness) from different religions met and talked, they knew almost immediately that they were talking about the same basic reality—they looked in each other's eyes and simply knew; they could see it. They knew that behind, beyond, or under this relative world of separate things and events there is a profound Oneness or true Wholeness, and those who have not realized this ever-present

Unity are still caught in the conventional world of perpetual human suffering and misery, a world that is universally said to be a fallen world—dualistic, fragmented, full of original sin, alienated, and broken—but a world that, in the "twinkling of an eye," could be totally seen through and released with a real Waking Up to an ever-present genuine Wholeness.

Many people today are familiar with a Buddhist version of these Waking Up practices known as "mindfulness." They use mindfulness for reducing stress, improving sleep, relieving depression and anxiety, increasing health, improving productivity, bettering relationships, and various other self-improvements, and that's fine—there is much scientific evidence that mindfulness will do all of those things. But mindfulness was not originally invented to do any of those things. It was originally invented as a way to directly experience God. That is—to drop the old mythic God terms—mindfulness was a way to immediately realize a pure nondual Wholeness, a direct Unity consciousness, a fundamental groundless Ground of All Being, a nirvana of limitless unbrokenness and no suffering instead of an illusory and perpetually painful world of fragmented and disjointed samsara.

These Waking Up systems maintain two things about the ultimate goal of Awakening: (1) everybody *fully possesses* right now the already Enlightened or fully Awakened Mind (of pure Wholeness), but (2) virtually nobody is aware of it. Most of these great meditation traditions therefore maintain that there is nothing you can do to achieve Waking Up, Enlightenment, or Liberation because it is always already completely present right now, and you can't achieve something that already is (attaining Enlightenment makes no more sense than attaining your lungs or acquiring your feet). But you can immediately recognize this ever-present Enlightened Mind if somebody simply points it out to you (these are known as "pointing-out instructions," and we'll directly give many of those below so you can see this—and experience it—directly for yourself).

The utter obviousness of the actual Wholeness of each of these 5 areas is simply astonishing—if, indeed, they are pointed out. But it's also astonishing that none of them includes the others. That is, you can fully discover the Wholeness of one but not see the Wholeness offered by the others. This applies even to the ultimate Unity consciousness of Waking Up. You can have a major Waking Up experience and still not see anything about Growing Up, Cleaning Up, Opening Up, or Showing Up. Likewise, you can fully Show Up and not have a clue about Waking Up; or you can practice Cleaning Up and know absolutely nothing about Growing Up. What's more, all 5 of these types of Wholeness grow and develop through different pathways, and they do so in almost completely independent ways, so that you can be very advanced in one and still be very low in the others, or in any combination. All of these things are like apples and oranges (and pears and limes and peaches)—that is, 5 quite different realities—although they all add up to one astonishingly Big Wholeness.

But there are also a few things that you have to do in order to be able to see any of these Wholenesses. Even though a good deal of it might be laid in your lap the moment you are born, an actual awareness of it is not. You will indeed almost certainly have to have them pointed out. If you haven't, the chances are quite high that there is relatively little Wholeness in your life, and what's more, you almost certainly know this. And even if there is a bit of Wholeness present, it's fairly likely that it's not that much and that it could be increased enormously.

That's what this book is intended to help you do. It's going to point out these 5 versions of Wholeness, a Wholeness that is drenching you right now. We'll go through the types of Big Wholeness that you can find by Waking Up, Growing Up, Opening Up, Cleaning Up, and Showing Up (and we'll add one area that will directly help you see this, an area called "Integral sexual Tantra," where you'll be using sex to directly Wake Up). In each case, there is a significant type of Wholeness awaiting you. What's so amazing about this is indeed how absolutely ever-present real Wholeness is yet how utterly non-obvious it almost always is. It really is *Deus absconditus* ("God hidden")—Spirit or Wholeness hidden, not showing itself, not apparent or obvious, as if God were seriously trying to avoid being seen.

In today's world, virtually all 5 types of Wholeness remain great hidden secrets, which is why the world lacks so much Wholeness—and is indeed fractured, fragmented, broken, and massively polarized. The world is not consciously acting on a single one of the 5 major types of Wholeness. We can say that today's world has a great lack of Wholeness, or we can say that today's world has a great lack of Spirit. Those two words—*Wholeness* and *Spirit*—are essentially synonymous the way that I am using them.[1] And though today's world, by almost any standard, is in some places very religious, it is almost never very spiritual. There just isn't enough Wholeness to go around.

This lack of Wholeness, this lack of Spirit, is why today's world has such a hard time making room for everything—or, in some cases, making room for anything. You might feel this way about your own life. Today's world is cramped, crowded, clawing, claustrophobic. Everything is smashed into everything else, and people everywhere are elbowing each other, trying to find more space for their own opinions, views, and ideas. Social media are especially cramped, with people in each other's faces in the loudest, nastiest, most virulent fashion possible. Making room for everything is exactly what people today have the most difficult time doing. Their space is small, their territory crowded, their backyards full of invaders, all yelling and screaming for a little more space.

But when you see all of these types of Wholeness lying under your nose right now, your world becomes vastly roomier, more spacious. It's as if your being and awareness simply open up and suddenly there is room for everything in your life. A profound meaning and purpose will open up for you in the very midst of your life, drenching it to the core. Once you see the Big Wholeness in your own world, you will know exactly where you fit and where you belong, and your meaning in this Wholeness will become very apparent and obvious—and your meaning is that you are ultimately one with all of this Wholeness. Until that point, all of this otherwise hidden Wholeness is lying all around you but is totally unnoticed, and thus it is not active enough to actually offer you any of its roominess for your own being.

The world indeed seems totally cramped and crowded, closed and constrained, and you are caught in the crush. But when you discover this vast Wholeness—a truly Big Wholeness—lying right in your own backyard, it's a new world altogether. And this world does indeed make room for everything. There's nothing artificial or make-believe about it. The deep and vast Wholeness that you have discovered—and when seen, it's as real and vivid as a ride on a Ferris wheel—reaches out and embraces everything that is arising in you and your world, and opens you fully to all of it, with no stress, no strain, no friction, no restraint. One of the things that I have heard most often from people who have made this astonishing discovery is "Being one with everything, I felt like I could breathe, really breathe, as if for the very first time, even though this had been staring me in the face my entire life." I believe that is what making room for everything will do for you too. It will give you enough room to move around in a free and unencumbered way, embracing everything in your life with joy and meaning. You will no longer be pushed or pulled by things and events that seem outside of your control but rather you will find yourself one with the entire universe, embracing it all as if it were God itself—because, with our new meaning of "God" as total Wholeness, that's exactly what it is. You will be about as "spiritual but not religious" as you could possibly be, or, in other terms, as Whole as you could ever want.

If you like, we can start right now on this remarkable discovery.

1

Introduction to Waking Up

We start with the dramatic Wholeness offered by Waking Up.

Waking Up is a baseline position for those who want a deep, extensive, and even absolute experience of Wholeness (we'll see what *absolute* means in just a moment), and it has probably had a more profound impact on human history than any other experience that has ever occurred. While ordinary people "lead lives of quiet desperation" (and pain and suffering), Waking Up has been the fallback position for anyone, whether in the East or the West, who wanted a more authentic, vital, enlightened, and "awakened" life, one that did indeed have an "absolute" or "ultimate" meaning, because it was plugged directly into the ultimate Ground of All Being (and that is not a myth but an immediate and direct experience).

Waking Up has been known to human beings for thousands of years, possibly going back in its earliest forms as far as twenty thousand years ago to the ancient shamans, whose voyages to the upperworlds and underworlds involved various forerunners to these types of Waking Up spiritual (or nondual Wholeness) experiences. And as humanity evolved, and as their spiritual realizations seemed to become more and more evolved as well, the depth of this spirituality seemed to increase or become even more sophisticated.

Now what I'm about to say concerning various spiritual experiences (or "religious experiences"—to use the term in its old-fashioned way—or simply experiences of a massive Wholeness) might sound very far out and perhaps silly or even crazy to you, and so I'll just ask that you suspend any suspicion or even revulsion you might have about these notions and simply play along for now. Humanity has discovered some very profound ways to validate these various Waking Up experiences—to either confirm or reject them. These "spiritual but not religious" experiences can ground a type of interior science, which takes nothing on belief or as dogma but rather bases its claims on direct experience and evidence, and asks you to believe nothing that you haven't verified for yourself. So please keep that in mind, and I'll give examples of these types of scientific verifications as we proceed. You'll be asked to accept nothing that you haven't directly experienced yourself.

For now, by way of introduction to the topic of Waking Up, notice that, over the centuries and millennia, various spiritual systems around the world pressed into increasingly deeper and deeper, or wider and wider, or higher and higher spiritual experiences. There was a progressive discovery of ever-greater and more inclusive spiritual states of consciousness, and any human being could, if they took up the requisite interior scientific experiments and practices, find out for themselves what these higher and higher states were.

Generally speaking, the path of Waking Up had a single major goal. It started with the average state of consciousness of a typical human being, which was said to be narrow, limited, fragmented, and marked by inherent suffering, anxiety, and torment—a state that generally was said to involve what is called the "separate-self sense," "self-contraction," the "illusory self," the "fallen self," the "dreaming self," or simply the "ego" (none of them complimentary terms). The goal of Waking Up was, through the direct experimental practices of meditation, contemplation, or yoga, to transform consciousness from that limited and contracted state through several much more inclusive, open, and free states, to a genuine Wholeness, a pure Nonduality, an ultimate Unity consciousness or Kosmic consciousness,[1] an absolute Oneness with the entire universe. This Wholeness wasn't just a religious belief or theological dogma or something to be taken on mere faith but a direct and immediate personal experience, a datum or real evidence given to anybody who successfully carried out the interior experiment of meditation or contemplation. (Since meditation is primarily a practice of direct awareness and not a mythic belief system, I will take meditation as an example of something that is "spiritual but not religious"—and it is definitely interested in experience not explanation, which most meditation systems take to be part of the problem, not the solution.)

If we look at any of these many meditation or contemplation systems around the world, we find that most of them left quite detailed maps of these higher spiritual territories, and they left very specific experiments for a seeker to perform in order to progress to, and directly experience, these higher states. This process of spiritual growth, development, and realization—Enlightenment, Awakening, or simply Waking Up—is a profound Wholeness-revealing process and is found in virtually all of the major systems of meditation, contemplation, yoga, or contemplative prayer presented in the Great Wisdom Traditions.

Notice that we are not talking about any sort of deity form, like an old man sitting on a throne in the sky and watching over your every thought and action. We're not talking about any magic or mythic stories, any religious beliefs or miracles—nothing like that. We're talking about a state of consciousness—a direct and immediate experience (not explanation)—in which you deeply feel one with the entire universe, one with everything, finite and infinite, manifest and unmanifest.

This is the direct experience that we're calling "Waking Up," "ultimate Unity consciousness," "Nondual awareness," "divine Oneness," or "One Taste" (Zen calls it "satori," a term you might have heard; it's a term I'll also often use). And—as incredibly strange as this will sound to the average Westerner, most of whom have never even heard of this kind of thing—the evidence for the existence of this type of absolute consciousness is utterly overwhelming and virtually undeniable. (I'll give some evidence below.) If you want to ground your spiritual beliefs—or just your beliefs in general—in anything that seems to have an ultimate proof for its existence, this is it.

What's more, the path of Waking Up is the only major discipline anywhere in the world's history that has claimed it was dealing with an *ultimate Truth*. There were lots of *relative truths* all over the place, and the Paths of Liberation (the Wisdom Traditions that directly and explicitly dealt with Waking Up) denied none of these relative truths. The truths of things that would later be established by science—the truths of physics, chemistry, biology, astronomy, and so on—were all respected and accepted. But those were all relative truths (and their believers never claimed that these truths were anything but that); they dealt with reality in the relative realm of space and time, a reality that changes and evolves over time. But Waking Up, the claim went, deals not with relative truth but with ultimate Truth. Ultimate Truth does not deal with a particular being or group of beings; it deals with Being itself, with a capital *B*—the Ground of All Being, spaceless and therefore infinite, timeless and therefore eternal, and a groundless Ground that underlies every relative truth in existence but is not itself a relative truth (and thus is not detectable by ordinary, external science but only by an interior, meditative science). This radical Waking Up experience was universally and unanimously claimed to be disclosing a genuinely ultimate Truth not a relative truth.

This is a bit of a sidebar, but of the people that I have known (including doctors, lawyers, and PhDs, along with waitresses and busboys and gardeners) who have had a genuine satori—or a Waking Up to what is claimed to be ultimate Truth—I would say that at least 90 percent of all of them feel that their satori disclosed a genuinely ultimate Truth, or certainly the closest thing that they had ever experienced that could be called an "absolute" or "ultimate" reality. Their satori or Waking Up experience is variously said to be "the most certain experience I've ever had," "the most real experience," "the most undeniable," "the most meaningful," "the most timeless and changeless," and on and on. We'll see what you think of it as we go forward, but remember that later on we'll be giving some real exercises that directly lead to a Waking Up experience, so you can decide on its reality ("ultimate" or otherwise) for yourself. But remember that, to the extent that we accept a real Waking Up in our tool kit of Big Wholeness, we are indeed dealing with the only major practice in world history that has been unanimously claimed to disclose a truly ultimate Truth.

What's more, this experience is said to be a oneness with everything, and it's felt or experienced as exactly that, a oneness with the entire universe. In other words, the Wholeness that Waking Up provides is about the largest Wholeness you can think of—it's almost as big as "big" can get—short of a truly Big Wholeness. Waking Up does provide a large part of the wholeness of a Big Wholeness (but not all of it, which would require the other four types of Wholeness). After all, it claims to be a unity of everything both infinite and finite, and that's *really* big.

EVIDENCE OF WAKING UP

There are many different references that I could give pointing to the genuine reality of these states of Waking Up, starting with the genius William James's book *The Varieties of Religious Experience* (by which James also means, in our terminology, the variety of "spiritual experience"), or the renowned MIT scholar Huston Smith's wonderful book *Forgotten Truth* (a title which means that there is indeed universal agreement among virtually all the major Paths of Liberation about what constitutes ultimate Truth, but this is a truth largely forgotten in modern times). But I'll give just one major reference, mostly because I don't want to get in a fight this early in the book. I'll use the clinical psychologist Jordan Peterson, professor emeritus at the University of Toronto, who is a very well-known online superstar. As a respected clinical psychologist, Peterson has spent tens of thousands of hours treating clients with mental disorders, and so presumably he can recognize the difference between delusions and reality, so at least we know he's not crazy and likely won't be giving his support to some sort of truly weird religious belief. People tend to be very divided on what they think of Dr. Peterson—it's a "love him or leave him" kind of thing—but most people agree that Peterson usually backs his ideas with very solid experimental and scientific research. So we can assume that his opinions will be backed by considerable evidence.

And about this topic, all that Peterson does is tell the bloody truth: "There is an overwhelming amount of evidence that those two kinds of consciousness exist, one being your consciousness, of you as a localized and specified being [your individual ego], and the other being this capacity to experience oceanic dissolution and the sense of the cosmos being one [or ultimate Wholeness]."[2] Peterson also says, "The fact that those different states of consciousnesses exist is not disputable." And he also says, "So the case that the transcendent experience is not real, is wrong." He adds, almost under his breath, "It actually challenges, to some degree, our concepts of what constitutes real."[3]

Boy, I'll say. This Waking Up experience has always been taken to be a waking up to an ultimate Truth or absolute reality—a Ground of All Being—a reality that exists in contrast to our ordinary more-or-less sleepwalking reality, which is by comparison seen to be more of a dream that we ignorantly call "reality." It is in comparison to that dream state that this absolute consciousness is known as "Waking Up." And that is very much what a genuine satori feels like: Just as you can wake up from a nightmare and say something like, "Thank God that dream wasn't real!" likewise with satori you wake up and see that the entire ordinary world is just a dream—or, in any event, that's exactly how it feels. That's why this experience has indeed been known as "Awakening" or "Enlightenment"—or "Waking Up." So I'll simply take it, with Peterson, that the evidence for the reality of this Waking Up "absolute consciousness," as he calls it, is so overwhelming that it is indeed "not disputable."

5 MAJOR STATE-STAGES OF A COMPLETE WAKING UP

The various meditative or contemplative traditions around the world present a path of meditative training that leads directly to this ultimate Unity consciousness. There are, of course, many different ways that the various stages of this Waking Up transformation are presented in the Great Wisdom Traditions. If we put all the major paths of Waking Up on the table (there are several dozen major ones) and carefully compare and contrast them all, we find that this transformation involves a common spectrum of states of consciousness that stretch from the constricted egoic self-contraction to the expansive, all-inclusive spaciousness of Enlightenment. These evolutionary *states*, as they historically unfolded, were actually incorporated—as meditative *stages*—in the various contemplative paths (with some paths covering more of these stages and thus being more complete, and a few of them covering all of the known major stages).

The paths that are considered by the traditions themselves to be their very highest offerings—such as Mahamudra and Dzogchen in Tibetan Buddhism, Advaita Vedanta in Hinduism, contemplative

Taoism, Neoplatonism, Jewish Kabbalah, contemplative Christianity, and Islamic Sufism—generally include all these major states and stages of Waking Up. There is no need whatsoever to remember these stages—later we will go over everything you need to know, and we'll especially focus on exercises that will help you to directly experience the two very highest states (Witness and One Taste). But just to show what's involved, I'll give a quick example of the major state-stages of a complete process of Waking Up transformation based on recent research in this area, using Daniel P. Brown's and Integral Metatheory's terminology.[4]

There are 5 basic stages of a meditation path, according to a meta-analysis of the Traditions. The first stage, where most people start, is that of gross thinking and the ego, the so-called monkey mind, or incessant, internal, mental chattering. Many traditions just call this "the waking state," which means the ordinary, conventional, or "illusory" state of waking awareness (which Integral calls the "gross state"). Almost all of the major meditative traditions maintain that this egoic state is the direct cause of the pain and suffering inherent in the human condition (certainly in its fallen, ignorant, or unenlightened state). One of the first things they want to do is help human beings move beyond this narrow, nasty, vicious monkey mind (Hobbes's classic definition of the natural condition of humanity perfectly describes this state: "solitary, poor, nasty, brutish, and short").

The transcendence of this pitiless state starts to happen with stage 2, which Brown calls "Awareness," because this state starts to move beyond gross thinking to a thought-free Awareness, where the ego is dropped and there is instead what Brown calls a very "subtle personality." Integral calls this stage the "subtle state," which is marked by the luminosity of the subtle personality, which Integral identifies as being not the ego but the soul. The self-sense is beginning to expand from the cramped, narrow, skin-encapsulated ego on its way to the Supreme Identity of the ultimate state, which Suzuki Roshi calls "Big Mind."

Brown calls stage 3 "Awareness Itself," because this is a pure Awareness that sheds all gross and subtle phenomena and is plugged into the core, background, spacetime matrix of the entire universe. Integral calls this the "archetypal" and "causal state." The causal state is often intuited in the pure formless Silence between thoughts. The Traditions also maintain that everybody experiences the causal state each night in deep dreamless sleep, a totally formless state where we are plugged directly into pure Awareness itself with no objects, thoughts, or ideas—which is why sleep is deeply refreshing.

Brown calls stage 4 "Boundless Changeless Awareness"—and just by its name you can tell that this is truly a significant step. This stage is a pure Consciousness without an object, which Integral, following Advaita Vedanta, also calls *turiya*, which is a Sanskrit term that literally means "the fourth." It is named that because it is the fourth major state of consciousness after the first three of gross, subtle, and causal. Stage 4 is a pure, timeless Witness, the sense of pure I Amness, an ever-present Awareness and not any content of Awareness. Later on, we will see what this ever-present state really means and why it embodies the actual meaning of "eternity." "Eternity" does not mean a really, really long time; it means a point without time, a timeless Now, and this is not something hard to attain but impossible to avoid. This Witness awareness is one of the highest states in the meditative traditions, and, as indicated, it's one that we will soon be exploring in several exercises, so you'll have a chance to check this out for yourself.

Brown calls stage 5, the highest state, "Nondual Awakened Awareness," which Integral, following Advaita Vedanta, calls *turiyatita*, which literally means "beyond turiya." It's pure nondual Suchness or Thusness, ultimate Unity consciousness, or One Taste—an ultimate Oneness or Nonduality. The direct realization of this radical state is known as Enlightenment, Awakening, Metamorphosis, Fana, Moksha, Satori, the Great Liberation, the Supreme Identity.

This state really does make me one with everything—a pure Unity or nondual Oneness, where *nondual* means "not-two." This One Taste is indeed the absolute consciousness whose existence, based on a staggering amount of evidence, is indeed "not disputable."

We will also be doing exercises to realize this ultimate state, so you can definitely check this out for yourself (as well as whether or not you think this state represents any sort of "Ultimate" Truth). And notice what that claim implies—that is, the claim that you and I will be doing exercises to directly realize this ultimate state. It means that many of the essentials of these 5 major states of consciousness can be peak experienced right now. Even though these states of consciousness are arranged in an ascending order (from gross to One Taste), and even though those states tend to unfold in those specific stages during a complete meditation practice, nonetheless because they are indeed states, they are ever-present (even a baby wakes, dreams, and sleeps—gross, subtle, and causal) and thus they can indeed be peak experienced at almost any stage of Growing Up, which means that they can be experienced right now. So hang on for those Waking Up exercises!

In the meantime, you don't have to remember those "state-stages"—as I said, we'll go over everything you need to know later. But do notice that we find variations of these major states of consciousness given in the meditation stages found throughout the Great Traditions. Although the number of stages vary, if you look closely, you can see similarities in all of them: Saint Teresa's seven interior mansions, Yogachara's eight levels of consciousness, Saint John of the Cross's stages of contemplation, Kabbalah's ten sefirot, Patanjali's state-stages in the *Yoga Sutras*, Zen Buddhism's ten ox-herding stages, the five major stages of the Sufis, and Evelyn Underhill's five major stages of mystical development. As with all developmental models—in both Waking Up and Growing Up—some models of Waking Up have a few more stages, some have a few less, but in all of them you can see variations on the same 5 major state-stages: gross, subtle, causal, the Witness, and One Taste.

Besides the direct realizations of each of these, all of them are said to also manifest themselves in ordinary states of consciousness. For example, according to both Vedanta (Hinduism) and Vajrayana (Tibetan Buddhism), the gross state appears in ordinary waking consciousness, the subtle state appears in dream consciousness, the causal state appears in deep dreamless sleep, turiya or the ever-present Witness is fully present in the everyday mind, and the ultimate Nondual is the Ground of them all—thus we have waking, dreaming, deep sleep, Witnessing, and One Taste—the major natural states of consciousness.

These major *states* of consciousness become the major *stages* of meditation, because a person's central identity starts out confined to the typical ego-dominated waking state, and with increasing meditation, it ends up traversing all of those state-stages in consciousness, resulting in a pure Awakening of ultimate Unity consciousness. I refer to this sequence of state-stages, in whole or part, as Waking Up.

ETERNITY AND INFINITY

As I said, we will be looking at the two highest states of Waking Up—that is, the pure Witness and One Taste—and exercises that will give you a direct experience of both a bit later (see chapter 16). But right now, I want to explain two ideas that almost all religions or spiritual systems talk about at some point but which most everybody totally misunderstands in truly outrageous ways: eternity and infinity. Since Waking Up is often (unfortunately) discussed in religious terms (because it was first discovered by the mythic-religious stages of human consciousness), you will often hear the terms "infinity" and "eternity" used, and I want to make sure that you are not as confused as most people are who use those terms. "Eternity" does not mean a really long time, and "infinity" does not mean a really big space—in fact, that's pretty much exactly what they are not.

Start with eternity. Most people take eternity to be a really, really long stretch of time, often an everlasting amount of time, going on forever and forever endlessly. But if that were the meaning of *eternity*, how could anybody ever have an experience of an eternal spiritual reality? In order to do that, you would have to live forever and ever, which is definitely not going to happen. So if a Waking Up experience is claimed to be the experience of an eternal reality, and *eternity* means everlasting time, then we would never be able to have a Waking Up experience. Something is definitely off kilter here.

The solution to this tricky problem is actually very simple. *Eternity* does not mean everlasting time; it means a point without time, timelessness. Because *eternity* means "timelessness"—a point without time—then *all* of eternity can fully and completely fit into every moment of time. And because eternity is timelessness, there is no conflict or tension between eternity and time—all of timeless eternity is fully present at every moment of time. That means that eternity is *ever-present.* Since eternity is timeless, 100 percent of eternity is fully and completely present at every point of time. Right now, in your own present experience, you have access to 100 percent of eternity—not 95 percent, not 99 percent, but all of it—100 percent, right now. This is often called the "timeless Now" or the "pure Present." Precisely because eternity is indeed timeless, all of eternity is totally present in each and every moment—each timeless Now. And that means that you have full access to eternal life, right now—all of it.

So experiencing eternity definitely does not mean that you have to live forever. It does not mean that you must accept some unwavering belief in various magic myths such as Elijah going straight to heaven in a chariot, or Lot's wife being turned into a pillar of salt, or your living endlessly forever in some sort of heaven after death. I don't want Waking Up to be associated with anything like that, and I don't want you to worry that it is. As witness to the utterly hardheaded reality of eternity, I call on, arguably, the most hardheaded philosopher in the West, Ludwig Wittgenstein. Wittgenstein in his youth was as hardheaded as they come; in fact, with his work *Tractatus Logico-Philosophicus*, he almost singlehandedly invented the field of logical positivism, which is as hardheaded as they come and definitely does not accept any pie-in-the-sky religious silliness. So notice that, in the *Tractatus*, Wittgenstein gives an absolutely perfect definition of eternity, while also endorsing its reality—and please, read this carefully; it's the solution to the entire problem: "If we take eternity to mean, not everlasting temporal duration, but a point without time, then eternal life belongs to those who live in the present."[5]

Exactly. And this means that eternal life is fully available to you, right now—in fact, it's available to you at no other time except right now (hence "timeless Now"). Falling into the timeless Now is what happens with an authentic Waking Up—which therefore does indeed include a discovery of eternal life—*your* eternal life.

So what about this "timeless Now"? If it's basically the same as an ever-present eternity, then is this timeless Now really available right now? Is it really *ever-present*—fully and totally present at every point in the stream of time? Yes, definitely. Alan Watts, in his wonderful *The Wisdom of Insecurity*, gives a perfect explanation of why this is so. I've repeated versions of this explanation many times, and I'm going to do so again in just a moment, because it's so simple and obvious.

The problem is that we are clearly living in a stream of time, and yet somehow in every moment of this temporal duration, there is supposed to be an ever-present eternity, a "timeless Now" that is not hard to attain but impossible to avoid. And somehow, becoming aware of this timeless Now is finding eternity, and finding eternity means finding a genuine Waking Up. Thus, if the timeless Now is fully ever-present, then a genuine Waking Up is also fully present, all of it, right now. And that is totally correct. Notice that virtually all of the Paths of Liberation maintain that the Enlightened Mind is absolutely impossible to achieve or attain. The Christian mystics claim that in reality you don't have to do a single thing to reach complete salvation—by the grace of God, you are already fully saved. Zen says that "everyday mind, just that is the Tao"—which means that the everyday state of consciousness that you have right now is indeed the Enlightened Mind, just as it is. The *Prajnaparamita Sutras*—the core of virtually all of Mahayana Buddhism—make one point over and over again: "If you could just realize that the Enlightened Mind is not attainable, you would be Enlightened." The Enlightened Mind is not attainable because you already have it, all of it. You can no more attain Enlightenment than you can attain your kidneys or acquire your feet. And that's the simple paradox: you are always already enlightened, but you still have to recognize that fact.

The exercises that I will be presenting in a later chapter will help you to directly recognize your own ever-present Awakened Mind. But this ever-present nature also applies to the "timeless Now." It, too, is ever present and only needs to be recognized. This is indeed the discovery of eternity and a direct understanding of why eternity is indeed ever present, fully present at every moment of time, including the present moment, so that "eternal life belongs to those who live in the present."

You are already living fully in the present, in the timeless Now, but you probably don't recognize this. Correlated to this lack of recognition of the timeless Now is the belief that time itself is real. We seem not to live in the Present because we take the past and the future to be real, and thoughts about those realities keep us so absorbed and distracted that we miss the timeless Present and the Enlightened Mind. And according to the Paths of Liberation, the stream of time is no more than an illusion—it's not really there—it's just part of the "dream world" that we are supposed to awaken from, even though, in reality, we actually don't have to do anything but recognize the ever-present, timeless, eternal Now that is always already the case.

So is this stream of time running through your mind really real, or is it actually illusory? Let's check it. Go ahead and think of something from your past, something that seems especially real. Get a really good sense of that past reality; see it as clearly as you can. This is the past that you think is real. As you are seeing this past event very clearly, simply notice that, in reality, all you are truly aware of is a memory of that event, and that memory itself is arising only in *this* Now-moment. Further, when that event actually occurred, it was in a present Now-moment. Thus, in your own direct awareness, you can never see an actual past event; you are aware only of a fully present Now-moment.

Likewise, think of some future event. It's fairly clear that the same thing is operating: you are not seeing any truly real future; you are seeing only a present image, or thought of the future, and that image exists nowhere but in this present Now-moment. And when and if what you are thinking of actually happens in the future, it will be occurring in the Now-moment.

It's pretty inescapable: all you are ever actually aware of is a timeless, ever-present Now-moment, an ever-present Present. This Now-moment doesn't move through time; time moves through it. And *ever-present* does mean EVER-PRESENT. As Erwin Schrödinger, the cofounder of modern quantum mechanics, put it, "The present is the only thing that has no end."[6] The present (the timeless Now) indeed has no end, and it has no beginning, either. Beginnings and endings have to do with time, not timelessness. Because eternity is timeless, it does not enter the stream of time—it is ever-present, or always present, not because it's in the stream of time for a really long duration but because it doesn't enter the stream of time to begin with.

Many of the Paths of Liberation therefore refer to the Enlightened Mind as "the Unborn"—it's unborn because it never enters time; it is never born in the temporal stream. And this means that, in your direct awareness right now, your own Enlightened Mind is Unborn. You can never give birth to it because it is already fully present in its entirety and thus is indeed unattainable—just like the timeless Now.

But notice that the Paths of Liberation also call the Enlightened Mind "the Undying." It never dies because, having never entered the stream of time (it's Unborn), it never leaves the stream of time. In other words, it never dies. This is why your own True Self or Big Mind is never born and why it never dies—it is Unborn and Undying—in short, it is truly eternal and right Now. As we saw with the timeless Now, this is indeed an ever-present reality, and this is also why—to give just one example—most people intuit that they will never die. Oh, they know their superficial, conventional self and body will die. But there is something in them—the deepest, truest part—that they know will *never* die. You yourself almost certainly know this—or basically intuit this—which is why you directly cannot be aware of your own death, or your own ceasing to be. (You can't do it because your True Self is Unborn and Undying, and hence you cannot actually picture your own awareness either being born or truly dying.)

Again, intuiting that the deepest part of you will never die (or is Undying) does not mean that you will live in time forever; it means that your True Self plugs straight into an eternal and infinite Ground of Being, a Ground so deep—and so timeless and eternal—that its core is totally untouched by the stream of time. When people even vaguely intuit that Ground, or their True Self, they are actually intuiting the Unborn and Undying. And in their deepest awareness, they know that *they are that*, and they cannot truthfully imagine otherwise.

This is sometimes called "the paradox of instruction." When it comes to Waking Up, there is not a single thing that you can do to bring this Awakened state into existence. Just like the timeless Now, the Enlightened Mind is always already fully present and fully functioning in your awareness right now. AND—the paradoxical part—you still have to recognize that this is so. It short, it takes a satori to realize that you don't need satori. (That's why we'll return to exercises that are "pointing-out" instructions that will help you do exactly that.)

How serious are the great Paths of Liberation about this timeless Now or a timeless and totally ever-present True Self? I usually give examples from Zen not because I am Asian-centric but because of all of the major Traditions, East and West, Zen places the most emphasis on actually having a satori, a direct recognition of the ever-present reality of their True Self—a genuine Enlightenment. So Zen says, "Show me your Original Face"—"Original Face" means your ever-present True Self. "Show me your Original Face, the face you had before your parents were born." *Before your parents were born?* Does this mean that your True Self is something that existed before your parents were born? That's symbolic or metaphoric, right? No, actually, it's literal and very straightforward; there's absolutely nothing symbolic about it. But it does *not* mean that your parents existed in the stream of time, and that your True Self existed in that same stream of time but at a point before your parents were born. Rather, it means that your Original Face, your True Self, exists prior to the stream of time itself; it is truly timeless, ever-present, eternal—*literally*. Your True Self exists prior to your parents' birth, prior to the birth of this earth, prior to the birth of this solar system, prior to the birth of this galaxy because it exists prior to the stream of time, period.

This means that you are not living in the narrow, passing present, which is brutally squished in between a huge past and a seemingly endless future. You are not crammed and wedged into a temporal sequence running from the past to the passing present to the future. Rather, you are living in the limitless Spaciousness of an all-embracing timeless Now, through which all past, present, and future events arise within the vast openness of this boundless, borderless Presence. You are not in the entire past-present-future sequence, but it is within you. You embrace it all; you are open to it all, and this awareness really does "make room for everything." This is the staggeringly colossal Wholeness that Waking Up delivers to all who engage it in the paradox of instruction.

Those are some of the basic points about eternity that needed to be made clear. They directly address the inescapable fact that virtually everybody who has a genuine Waking Up experience feels that they are directly and profoundly connected to an eternal, absolute, all-pervading, all-inclusive Reality, which is felt not only as a Waking Up to Reality but also as a "Coming Home," since this is where they truly belong and always have belonged. This Reality is a supreme Identity that is always already the case, timeless, ever-present, eternal. This fact hits them smack in their Original Face—and they know it.

The simplest *explanation* for this direct *experience* is not that your brain has had a physiological meltdown and that you are deeply confused and delusional. It's that in the timeless Now-moment of Waking Up, you have directly and immediately experienced the fundamental, all-pervading, groundless Ground of All Being—which is timeless, which means ever-present, which means eternal. I honestly don't care if you take that as metaphoric or symbolic or just a (possibly confused) philosophical explanation—the experience itself is what counts—and the experience itself is "not disputable."

Having discussed some simple explanations of eternity (and the timeless Reality that people experience upon Waking Up), we can now briefly address infinity, because the basic points are the same, only applied now to space instead of time.

Similar to eternity, many people misunderstand *infinity* to mean "a really, really big space." Again, that's pretty much the opposite of infinity. If *infinity* meant "a gigantically humongous space," then if anybody had a spiritual awakening that seemed to disclose a reality that is infinite, wouldn't that mean their soul had physically and literally stretched beyond even the Milky Way? If that were the case, it doesn't look like many people are going to have any infinity-disclosing satoris. Except, of course, *infinity* does not mean "a really, really big space," it means "a point without space." It doesn't mean "a whole bunch of space," it means "spaceless." And just as eternity, being timeless, means that all of eternity is fully present at every point of time, so infinity, being spaceless, means that all of infinity is fully present at every point of space. In other words, 100 percent of infinity is totally and fully present right HERE. The other side of the planet does not have a different infinity than this side, and Jupiter doesn't have a different infinity than the earth does, and so on. Put somewhat crudely, the overall number of infinities (and eternities) is just one—which is why people feel such a shocking Oneness across the board with a genuine Waking Up: they are plugging into a single, nondual, infinite, and eternal Ground of All Being that is the source, condition, and nature of all beings (and that is the absolute consciousness that is the "not-disputable" part of this experience). If you discover a real infinity right here, then you have discovered it everywhere.

This is indeed why people who have a profound Waking Up experience will often feel that they are one with even the most remote galaxies anywhere. They truly are one with everything; they are not consciously one with all relative truth (most of which, like the structure of quarks or the existence of various multiverses, they actually know little about), but rather they are one with ultimate Truth itself (which is their own true Nature and ever-present Condition and is the same single Ground of everything else in existence, the Nature of all natures and the Condition of all conditions).

This simple understanding of infinity and eternity is exactly where the cliché "Be Here Now" comes from. The manifest universe exists in space and time—usually conceived as a single spacetime continuum.

But be fully "here" and you are directly in touch with spaceless infinity everywhere (since infinity is fully present at every point of space), and live directly "now" and you are in touch with timeless eternity (since eternity is fully present at every point of time). So "be here now" and you are directly in touch with the infinite and eternal Ground of All Being—right here, right now. This infinite, eternal Ground of Being is not hard to achieve; indeed it's impossible to avoid: it is literally unattainable. There is no way that you can move from a point where it is not to a point where it is, because there is no point where it is not—it's the Suchness of every single point of spacetime anywhere in existence. *And you are That.*

Of course, while it is definitely true that you are perfectly one with the Ground of All Being just as you are, right now, you still need to recognize that fact. This is the paradox of instruction: it takes a satori to see that you don't need a satori. That's what Waking Up is all about, and it's a process that Integral takes very seriously. It is the doorway to an ultimate Truth, a One Taste, whose realization opens you to an ultimate Wholeness that can be found anywhere and everywhere.

And yet, oddly enough, this is just the beginning of the Wholeness that is available to you. Big Wholeness, after all, includes 5 types of major Wholeness, and Waking Up is just one of them. We'll be returning to Waking Up later in this book and will pursue it in depth; but first there are four other major types of equally exciting Wholeness that I want to cover.

Shall we get started?

2

Why Do We Need Growing Up?

As we begin to explore the other major types of Wholeness that are available to us in a truly Big Wholeness, it's worth spending some time discussing why Waking Up itself does not cover all of the important bases. Waking Up can give us an infinite and eternal Wholeness, but this is, strangely enough, not the Big Wholeness (or not the "biggest" Wholeness) that is available to us. But the belief that Waking Up is a realization of the biggest Wholeness is very common among those who have had a profound Waking Up (and it's very common among Zen students)—namely, that Waking Up is so utterly One with everything that nothing else is needed. If everybody could just become Awakened or Enlightened, humanity itself would flourish, wars would end, peace would reign, and all would be well. And certainly for the preceding several millennia, that assumption, in one form or another, was very common, and formed the core of most forms of religious belief.

Then, starting just a few hundred years ago, the modern sciences emerged, rational modes of cognition supplanted more magic and mythic modes, and the traditional mythic world of Zeus and Jehovah gave way to the modern world of Copernicus, Darwin, and Freud. And along with these changes, culturally sanctioned modes of Waking Up tended to decline. This was not because there was any inherent lack in the experience of Waking Up itself but because, in many cases, it was deeply confused with the previous, traditional, mythic worldview, which had indeed largely been supplanted by the rationality of a modern science. We'll explore just what this confusion involves and how it came about a little bit later (see chapter 14). To put it simply, a direct Waking Up experience was confused with relatively primitive types of magic and mythic explanations of it, and so unfortunately, a huge baby was tossed out with the bathwater.

The criticisms that modern science leveled against all forms of Waking Up do not bear serious scrutiny, and we'll see why as we proceed. But Waking Up does have some significant limitations, and I want to briefly outline them, because otherwise we might miss why there are other forms of Wholeness in addition to Waking Up that are available to us and that are extremely important.

I'll first explain these limitations abstractly, but then I'll give some very simple examples. The Waking Up experience presents itself as a direct experience of the unity of an ultimate Ground of All Being—or an ultimate Emptiness one with the entire universe of manifest Form—but it gives no specific information about that relative universe of Form. You are indeed one with everything—a massively important absolute realization—but that doesn't actually tell you anything specific about anything in particular.

This limitation has been central to many of the problems of how religion has unfolded in our history; and it's also pivotal for individuals today who have had this direct Waking-Up experience or satori and who often think that this experience is all that is needed for humanity's future well-being. The idea here is that because this satori discloses a genuine Ground of Being, all the world needs is this experience of Waking Up—nothing else is really required. These dear souls, who have had a profound satori and experienced its expansive version of Wholeness, simply cannot believe that anything else fundamental can be added to the realization of Waking Up.

Here's the problem. These profound Waking Up experiences go back at least several thousand years (and in their early shamanic forms, perhaps tens of thousands of years). So imagine a person, say two thousand years ago, having an ultimate Waking Up experience. The person is walking through the woods; they see the sun glaring; they feel the earth under their feet; they see the trees going by. At that time in history, people believed that the sun circled the earth and that the earth itself was flat—and they experienced themselves as separate and different from all those forms. So this person is walking through the woods, and then all of a sudden, they have a major satori: they go through an oceanic dissolution (as ego) and awaken in a pure Oneness with everything (their True Self). They are one with the sun, one with the earth, one with all the trees in the woods. They awaken to the awesome, all-inclusive Ground of pure Being, and they *are* that. That's an ultimate Truth. But notice, they get no information, knowledge, or truth about any specific thing or relative event in the universe. They feel one with the earth, but they still think that the earth is flat! They are one with the sun, but they still think that the sun circles the earth! And they are one with all the trees in the woods, but that experience of oneness gives them no information at all about the atoms, molecules, and cells that make up those trees. Precisely because this Ground is one with absolutely everything—the same infinity is everywhere—it actually gives no specific information about any individual thing at all.

In a certain sense, this is deeply shocking. No wonder that all the Great Religions, even though they had deep experiences of ultimate Waking Up at their core, did not move forward very much in the relative world. They did not produce any major rational sciences; or free their slaves; or give women the equivalent of getting the vote; or know about the neurotransmitters whose release correlated with their satoris; or understand anything about the atoms, molecules, and cells making up that brain; or know about Growing Up, Cleaning Up, or Opening Up.

This occurs precisely because all those advances (including science) occur in the relative or finite realm. For example, take the things that we learn as we continue to grow and develop through the various stages of Growing Up. Growing Up does not involve the Real Self or ultimate Truth; it unfolds in the relative world of space and time and growth and development—in other words, it *evolves*. We learn relative truths from the evolutionary realm of space and time. But the ultimate and infinite Truth does not itself evolve; it is spaceless or infinite; timeless or eternal, and thus, boundless and unchanging; and it has no parts and thus nothing to evolve. In other words, the relative world is engaged in an ongoing process of Growing Up, a developmental or evolutionary process that continuously creates greater and greater complexity, unity, and consciousness, constantly replacing specific lacks with greater wholeness. But ultimate Truth lacks nothing, and so Waking Up gives a sense of utter and absolute completeness. And, as we'll see, these two processes—Waking Up and Growing Up—are two quite independent processes. While the Traditions were often quite highly attuned to Waking Up, virtually none of them were very developed in Growing Up because humanity had not yet evolved very much along that particular pathway; it was largely still at magic or mythic stages. Nor were they clearly aware of Cleaning Up, Showing Up, or Opening Up (all relative truths).

Thus, all of those new areas of Wholeness that the Integral approach has added to a wonderful Big Wholeness essentially have to do with *relative truth*. This relative truth is something that no amount of Waking Up to ultimate Truth will show you. The single, infinite, and eternal Ground of Being in a tree, a frog, and a human body is the same Ground, and thus discovering that Ground will tell you nothing specific about any of them. It shows you the Ground of All Being itself—or Beingness—but it shows you nothing about any particular being at all.

Notice that at least three of the major types of Wholeness—Growing Up, Opening Up, and Cleaning Up—were discovered only within the last one hundred years or so. And anything discovered that recently wouldn't be included in any of the Great Religious Traditions. Nor are these new types of Wholeness to be found in virtually any of today's self-enhancement or self-transformation courses.

So even when you experience ultimate or infinite Truth in a profound Waking Up, it will reveal very little about finite Growing Up, Opening Up, Showing Up, or Cleaning Up (all of which occur in the relative world). That is a serious lack, which also had a profound impact on history. What makes the Integral model so revolutionary is that it includes all these areas of Wholeness.

It's nonetheless still quite true that Waking Up to a genuine ultimate Truth or "absolute consciousness" is stunningly, staggeringly important (in addition to being "not disputable"). Of all of the 5 types of Wholeness, Waking Up is clearly the most profound—and it is the only truth in the world that has been cross-culturally claimed to be a genuine "ultimate Truth" by serious investigators. (And, as I keep promising, we will be investigating that absolute consciousness and going into specific ways to immediately awaken that awareness in your own case, so you can make up your own mind.)

Next, I want to explore the process of Growing Up. Understanding this process is important because the stage you are at in Growing Up determines how you interpret and make sense of any experience that you have—*and that includes any Waking Up experience (or any spiritual experience)*. This changes everything. The Great Wisdom Traditions were, as we mentioned, almost completely unaware of this Growing Up process. But clearly, any genuinely Big Wholeness should include both Waking Up and Growing Up (not to mention Opening Up, Cleaning Up, and Showing Up). And the stage of Growing Up that you are at will determine how you interpret or explain all of them.

So let's look at this almost unknown process of Growing Up. We will explore the very specific type of Wholeness that Growing Up offers, see why it is so unrecognized, and make it very clear what this new Wholeness is like, which you can have in your own life—if you Grow Up.

WHAT IS GROWING UP?

I've been discussing the importance of Growing Up, how it supplements Waking Up, and why it is so crucial to include the Wholeness that Growing Up offers in any sort of genuine Big Wholeness. But I haven't really explained what Growing Up is, let alone outlined any of its major stages. You might be scratching your head by now. So let me provide a very brief overview of what this process involves, and I suspect things will become much clearer. And I think it will become obvious why I believe that this process (and the type of Wholeness that it offers) is so incredibly important.

Start by taking any human discipline—it could be medicine, law, mathematics, or psychotherapy. Could a six-month-old child be accomplished in any of these? No, of course not. A five-year-old? No. A twelve-year-old? Not likely. A twenty-five-year-old? Well, maybe, if they're really good.

Why is that? Because human beings grow and develop. And that means a human being's capacities—all of them—grow and develop. Not only do their bones, skin, and muscles develop, but also their thoughts, emotions, language capacity, mental capabilities, and their moral intelligence. They all grow and develop. We are not born with any of our capacities fully functioning. All of them have to go through some form of Growing Up.

As for the capacities that do develop or Grow Up: we have learned fairly recently that humans don't have only one kind of intelligence. It used to be thought that we possessed just one major intelligence, cognitive intelligence, which was measured by the all-important IQ test. But recently we have discovered that humans actually have multiple intelligences, perhaps up to a dozen different kinds of intelligences."[1] In addition to cognitive intelligence, we have emotional intelligence, moral intelligence, musical intelligence, intrapersonal intelligence, mathematical intelligence, verbal intelligence, aesthetic intelligence, and something called "spiritual intelligence." As we'll explore in a moment, spiritual intelligence is a type of intelligence that is important to develop in Growing Up, and it's very different from a spiritual experience in Waking Up, so please don't confuse these two. Working on accessing all of our multiple intelligences or lines of development is a process I call "Opening Up." Opening Up carries its own particular kind of Wholeness, a Wholeness that accessing all of our multiple intelligences can bring to us (more on that later).

Notice that a person's multiple intelligences can be very unevenly developed. A person can be very high in one intelligence (such as cognitive), medium in another intelligence (such as emotional), and very low in yet others (such as moral)—think of Nazi doctors: very high in cognitive intelligence, very low in moral intelligence. All these intelligences are virtually at zero when we are born, and yet all of them grow and develop to higher and higher levels as we ourselves grow and develop.

A second thing we have learned about these intelligences is extremely important and relates directly to the topic of Growing Up. Although these intelligences, which are often called "lines of development," are all quite different from each other, they grow and unfold through the same basic *levels* of development. Different lines, same levels. You can be high or medium or low in any of those intelligences, but the scale, with its levels of high, medium, and low, is the same for all of them.

We call this general, vertical scale—this basic measure of the levels or stages of development—an "altitude" of Growing Up, because it represents how high any particular intelligence or line of development has progressed. An altitude is different from an aptitude, which refers to how well you can do a skill at any particular level. Changing the altitude of an intelligence is switching its level entirely. Most people have lines of development that are at different levels or altitudes of Growing Up. You might be low in some lines, but virtually everybody has some intelligences at a high level. You might be low in cognitive development and a genius in emotional development. But no matter what altitude you might be at in any intelligence, you don't have to feel bad about that, because you can always increase that altitude. There are things you can do to increase the altitude of virtually every one of these intelligences—including spiritual intelligence. So keep all of that in mind as we go forward.

The process of increasing the altitude of lines of development—the process of Growing Up—brings its own type of Wholeness as well. And, as we just saw, increasing access to our different lines of development is Opening Up. Since the levels of development in Growing Up are the same across all intelligences, the same levels of Growing Up apply to the different lines in Opening Up. Each increase in a level of Growing Up is indeed marked by its own increasing Wholeness—a greater degree of complexity, greater unity, and more consciousness in any intelligence in which Growing Up occurs. Thus, any time that we talk about Growing Up, it means the increase in altitude in any of our dozen or so intelligences.

There are now some two dozen major models of Growing Up that attempt to describe those various levels of development. If you put them all next to each other, you'll notice that there are around 6-to-8 major levels or stages of development that keep showing up in almost all the models. Some models have fewer levels, some have more, but you can see the same basic 6-to-8 major levels showing up again and again. In my book *Integral Psychology*, I looked at over one hundred developmental models, in order to help create an Integral Metatheory using all of them (there are charts of all one hundred models in the back of the book)—and you can see these same basic levels repeatedly showing up in all of them.

The discovery of the process of Growing Up, with its 6-to-8 stages of development, is one of the most important advances in psychology of the last several centuries—it changes our understanding of almost everything, as will increasingly become obvious. Growing Up is so important that we will spend several subsequent chapters going through each of its major 6-to-8 levels. But in just a moment, I will give a very simplified overview of Growing Up that includes just 4 major stages, so we can easily see what it involves and how it functions.

Recall that the process of Growing Up was discovered only around one hundred years ago. That is indeed a very recent discovery. Given humanity's several hundreds of thousands of years on this planet, why did it take so long to figure this out, especially given its importance? There are several reasons, but the simplest is that you cannot see any of these stages of Growing Up simply by looking within or introspecting (or meditating). This is because Growing Up consists of 3rd-person *structures* of consciousness, whereas Waking Up consists of 1st-person experiences or *states* of consciousness. Let me explain what this means. Because structures are harder to understand, we'll spend a fair amount of time in this chapter going over *structures* of consciousness. (*States* of consciousness are easier to understand; they are simply your everyday, immediate, and direct 1st-person experiences—nothing hard about those to understand. We'll come back to those in the next chapter.) After all, these structures of Growing Up are so hard to see and understand that they were not discovered until around one hundred years ago. Why was that?

The structures of consciousness in Growing Up are very much like the rules of grammar. Everybody brought up in a particular culture ends up speaking that culture's language quite accurately. They put subjects and verbs together correctly, they use adjectives and adverbs correctly, and in general they follow the rules of grammar of that language quite accurately. But if you ask someone to write down all of those rules of grammar, virtually nobody can do it. You and I right now can follow the rules of English grammar, but I doubt we can write them down. We can't do this because we cannot see these structures simply by looking within.

The same is true for the structure-stages of Growing Up. (I often call them "structure-stages" to differentiate them from "state-stages," which are the stages that various *states* of consciousness go though in practices such as meditation—that is, from stage-1 egoic to stage-5 turiyatita.) Because these structure-stages are like rules of grammar, which cannot be seen by simply introspecting or looking within, we had no idea that they existed until quite recently (which is why none of the world's Great Traditions were aware of them, either).

Notice that structure-stages are not the same as the various stages of biological growth or maturation (infancy, childhood, latency, adolescence, young adulthood, elderhood). Those stages can be seen fairly clearly. But that's not what the structure-stages or vertical levels of Growing Up are like. These structure-stages are indeed much more like grammar, and no amount of simply looking within will disclose them or their stages. And this is why, for the three hundred thousand years that humanity (*Homo sapiens*) has been on earth, it was only one hundred years ago that we spotted these particular stages. Exactly what that means will becomes clearer as we proceed and you begin to see exactly what these structure-stages look like. The type of Wholeness that Growing Up offers will, I believe, surprise you—but you'll immediately see how important this type of Wholeness really is. Let's start with a simplified, 4-stage model: (1) egocentric, (2) ethnocentric, (3) worldcentric, and (4) integrated.

A SIMPLIFIED, 4-STAGE MODEL OF GROWING UP

When a child is born, it does not easily distinguish between its own internal world "in here" and the external world "out there." The child cannot tell where its body stops and the chair begins. It's in a state that is often called an *adual* "undifferentiated fusion state"—where *adual* means that there is no difference or duality between the self and the other. Now this is definitely not a *nondual* spiritual oneness with everything, which will be subsequently lost to produce an "alienated ego," and then regained in awareness to achieve an "ultimate unity consciousness," as many retro-Romantic thinkers would have you believe. The newborn is not, in any way, totally one with everything—that is, this structure-stage is not totally one with matter, body, mind, soul, and spirit. Rather, it's mostly just one with matter, or its immediate material world—the lowest level in the Great Chain of Being, which it confuses with its self. So *adual* means the self is confused with the lowest stage—matter—whereas *nondual* means a real unity with all the stages—from matter to body to mind to soul to spirit. Each one of those stages will sequentially emerge with higher structure-stages of Growing Up, until, at the very highest stage—that of spirit itself—a pure Nonduality or total Unity will finally emerge.

So that's the initial, adual fusion structure-stage; it's the first of a series of early stages where the self is narcissistic, self-centered, and egocentric. Although the young child will develop likes and dislikes of other people and aspects of the world, it will always fall back to treating others as narcissistic (undifferentiated) extensions of its own self. The feminist Carol Gilligan presents a simple 4-stage model of

Growing Up (which matches our simplified 4 stages), and she calls this first structure-stage (her level 1) "selfish," and Integral often calls it "egocentric."

The next structure-stage (Gilligan's stage 2) is called "ethnocentric." To demonstrate both how incredibly important this structure-stage is and why it's not usually spotted, I like to describe the two-colored ball experiment. Take a ball colored red on one side and green on the other. Place it directly between you and a young child who is still at the early egocentric structure-stage, two to three years old. Turn the ball several times so the child can see it's colored differently on each side. Then place the red side toward the child and the green side toward yourself. Ask the child, "What color are *you* seeing?" The child will correctly say, "Red." Then ask the child, "What color am *I* seeing?" And the child will say, "Red."

In other words, at this early stage 1, the child has no idea that you are seeing the world from a different perspective than it does. It cannot, as we say, put itself in your shoes and walk a mile in them; psychologists say it cannot yet "take the role of other." Its view, at this early stage 1, is still limited to its own perspective—its own selfish, narcissistic, egocentric viewpoint. And notice that its Wholeness, when it comes to self-identity, is limited to that very narrow view as well—it's egocentric.

But when the child reaches ethnocentric stage 2 (starting around four to five years, and often lasting long into life), all that changes. If you now ask the child, "What color am *I* seeing?" it will correctly say, "Green." The child's viewpoint has expanded from its own limited egocentric stance, where it saw only its own view, to an ethnocentric stance, where it can actually take the role of other. It switches from an ego-centered self-sense to an essentially group-centered self-sense (or a 2nd-person-aware self-sense). It starts to understand deeply that other people see the world differently, that there are perspectives contrary to its own, and that it needs to start taking those into account. (Younger infants can understand that different people see the world differently, but they cannot actually take any of those perspectives.)

The major battle at this structure-stage thus shifts from how the ego can get along with the body and its impulses (especially sex, aggression, and power—where the main battle is egocentric) to how the ego can get along with other egos and all the different roles they inhabit. Here, by far the most common way to handle these conflicts is by strongly conforming to what others say. So ethnocentric stage 2 is often given descriptors such as "conformist," "conventional," "my country, right or wrong," "nice boy, good girl," "mythic-membership," "patriotic," and so on. It's also described as absolutistic not because it discloses some sort of ultimate Reality but because it treats its own views as if they were absolute, unchallengeable, and infallibly true. Most fundamentalist and extremist groups have a strong foothold here, as do stringent zealots and fundamentalists on virtually any topic (fundamentalist scienticians, fundamentalist Marxists, fundamentalist feminists, fundamentalist postmodernists, the list goes on). Structure-stage 2 is often called "ethnocentric" because people at this stage have expanded their identity from their own self (egocentric) to an entire group of people. In terms of Wholeness, since here one's overall identity has switched from egocentric to ethnocentric, one's sense of Wholeness likewise expands from self-centered to group-centered.

This vertical movement toward ethnocentric is good in that it expands the Wholeness of the self's identity from being limited to its own organism (a selfish stage where it cares only for itself) to an entire group of organisms (where it expands its care to an entire community). But it cannot yet expand its identity to include all groups, all people, all humans—a degree of Wholeness that occurs at stage 3 (which is called "worldcentric").

The emergence of care for an entire group is why Gilligan calls this stage the "care" stage. Here, at least, real care can emerge and be developed for other people, and this is a stunningly important development. But it is indeed very much an "us-versus-them" mentality, caring for those in one's own special group but deeply suspicious of all outsiders (or unbelievers, apostates, heretics, or, in general, the "Other"). Still, at this care stage, the care extended to the in-group is very genuine (Nazis truly loved their families and their country).

That snide Nazi comment has two senses: (1) Their love was genuine; I don't doubt that the Nazis loved their own families very deeply. But (2) Nazis were extremely ethnocentric. And the term *ethnocentric* has a negative connotation—namely, somebody is said to be ethnocentric if they promote or privilege a special group and are deeply suspicious of—or bigoted and prejudiced toward—any outside "Other." They will often see such an Other with outright bias and bigotry (from soft prejudice to outright aggressive hatred). That's how most people think of a Nazi—somebody who is wildly prejudiced and thinks, for example, that their own privileged group is superhuman and some other group is subhuman" (for example, Jews). That's the second sense of that comment—namely, that most of the truly nasty prejudice, bias, and bigotry that we encounter in this world has at least a foothold in this ethnocentric stage of Growing Up, with its overpowering "us-versus-them" mentality, its absolutism, and its inability to genuinely rise beyond an ethnocentric to a truly higher worldcentric morality and its greater Wholeness.

That next structure-stage, the worldcentric stage 3—which moves from ethnocentric (care for a privileged group) to worldcentric (care for all groups)—is a major, staggeringly important development. This stage extends moral care not just to a chosen group but to all groups, to all humans, without exception. This is why Gilligan calls her third stage not "care" but "universal care" and Integral calls it "worldcentric." I really cannot overemphasize the general importance of this broad stage. It attempts to treat all people fairly, regardless of race, color, sex, gender, ethnicity, or creed. This structure-stage sees all humans as part of a genuine Wholeness, a genuinely new and higher type of Wholeness. This is clearly a universal Wholeness that all of us need to acknowledge and at least behave as if we were aware of. This worldcentric morality and awareness—this new and universal Wholeness—is the direct result of a genuine Growing Up and really can't be found elsewhere.

You might think that this kind of worldcentric morality, where we treat all people fairly, is a common and typical view, so much so that it hardly needs pointing out. But that is a truly mistaken view. The simplest way to understand this is to look at something like slavery (or at how any minority group has been historically treated by society). Most countries outlawed slavery less than two hundred years ago, although human societies have been engaging in it for some three hundred thousand years. And this is where you can really see a difference between the different types of Wholeness that Growing Up and Waking Up offer. All the cultures that first introduced major forms of Waking Up nonetheless embraced slavery. Most early religions did. St. Paul tells slaves to "obey your master and love Jesus Christ." Even American Indians had slaves—they even took their slaves with them on the Trail of Tears.

Many of these cultures that embraced slavery (including the religious ones) had profound practices of Waking Up; yet in all of them, their cultural center of gravity was at the ethnocentric structure-stage of Growing Up, which has no major objections to slavery (as long as it's "them" not "us" that are enslaved). Some advanced individuals in those ethnocentric cultures had moved to higher worldcentric stages—Aristotle, is an obvious example—but not the culture itself. In fact, it was only with the Western Enlightenment of the eighteenth century, when the cultural center of gravity moved from ethnocentric to worldcentric, that slavery was found morally intolerable on a large scale. (The "us" in "us-*versus*-them" had moved to an "us that *includes* all of them," so all human beings were understood to have the same universal rights, at which point slavery became detestable.) Think about that—it was only around two hundred years ago—out of a three-hundred-thousand-year history—that human beings finally realized that one person owning another was truly an immoral act. You can see how deeply embedded an ethnocentric view of the world is, and how rare (and recent) a truly worldcentric view is.

The highest structure-stage in this simplified, 4-stage model of Growing Up is generally referred to as "integrated," "systemic," or "integral," since it integrates the perspectives of all of the previous stages. Gilligan, for example, calls her stage 4 "integrated" because it integrates masculine and feminine modes to give a full human awareness. I think of it as integrating all the previous stages—but the idea either way is there is yet a further increase in Growing Up Wholeness.

We have now seen that in the process of Growing Up, we have ever-increasing structures of Wholeness, in the relative realm, that go from egocentric to ethnocentric to worldcentric to integrated. From "me," to "us," to "all of us," to "integrated." Notice that all of those structure-stages are holons—that is, the whole of each stage becomes a part of the whole of the next, which is why Wholeness just increases and increases.

And this is, generally speaking, a type of Wholeness that is not obvious. It's not obvious because it can't be seen "out there"—and it can't be seen "in here" either. If we have, say, a room of one hundred people, not all of them will be at an integrated stage of development. In fact, research suggests that less than 7 percent will be at that integral stage. Very roughly, around 20 to 30 percent will be at egocentric, 60 to 70 percent will be at ethnocentric, 10 to 20 will be at worldcentric, and 5 to 10 percent at integral. But this isn't something that you can see by simply looking at everybody in the room—these stages are "interior" realities, not "exterior," so just staring at people or watching their behavior won't tell you anything. And, moreover, you can't see these structure-stages by looking within or introspecting, any more than you can see the rules of grammar by looking within (even though they do exist within you, somewhere in your brain-mind, just like these structures of Growing Up do).

Notice that as we introduced each of the 4 structure-stages, very likely you did not see any of those stages coming or the new type of Wholeness that each would bring. Once you were introduced to the sequence—from egocentric to ethnocentric to worldcentric to integrated—they all probably made sense. No wonder nobody figured this out until around one hundred years ago!

Researchers discovered the emerging structures of Growing Up only when they started studying how people acted in ways that were egocentric, ethnocentric, worldcentric, or fully integrated and then inferred the type of interior maps or structures that could cause those behaviors. They tested these theories with different groups, and if they got the same results, they concluded that a common set of interior maps or structures were responsible. They then followed these maps as they changed over time in different individuals, and they found that these structures always unfolded in one direction only. For example, if somebody with an ethnocentric structure changed their view, it always changed from ethnocentric to worldcentric; it never went from ethnocentric to egocentric. In other words, those maps or structures were not just different *responses* in general, they were different *stages* (in this case, structure-stages). Growing Up had been discovered. Hence, after spending 299,900 years of our 300,000 years on this planet in complete ignorance about this, we finally figured out there was a process of Growing Up.

I think you can clearly see the importance of this reality. Even quite sophisticated measurements indicate that around 60 to 70 percent of the world's population are still at ethnocentric (or lower) stages, which is a number that is truly alarming. We're used to looking at the cause of human conflict, hatred, and warfare as being due to economic, political, or religious causes, and no doubt they all play a part. But with some 60 to 70 percent of the world population at stages of development that are ethnocentric or Other-distrusting, do we really have to look much further? Yet this is a factor that virtually all leaders—and people in general—remain ignorant of.

Perhaps you are starting to see why the Wholeness offered by Growing Up is indeed so stunningly important. It offers the Wholeness of humanity itself—a profound unity of all people, regardless of their race, color, sex, gender, ethnicity, creed, or belief. The fact that slavery was outlawed only a few hundred years ago shows just how recent—and rare—this Wholeness is. This Wholeness does not come with the natural territory of being a human. It has to be culturally fostered and fought for; it must be cherished and renewed with each generation, or it will disappear into that same black hole where it existed for 99 percent of our history. And in your own life, your own being and awareness, this is a path of growth and development that you must commit yourself to in order to bring it forth fully—it's far from a done deal. Robert Kegan's research, for instance, found that three out of five people living in the United States do NOT make it to worldcentric levels of growth (that is, some 60 percent remain at ethnocentric levels).[2] For those at ethnocentric levels, this lack of worldcentric Wholeness is suffered in their being as if it were a vicious gash in the head, a gaping hole in their awareness that lets this profound Wholeness leak out and get lost, diminishing them most of all.

We will not forget this Wholeness. It took humanity as long to discover this Wholeness as it took to discover quarks, the Big Bang, and DNA. It is an indelible part of the Big Wholeness that, in this book, we will be carrying forward with us, uplifting each of us when we do so.

MAGIC AND MYTHIC STRUCTURE-STAGES

We just saw that the worldcentric structure-stages of development emerged only around two to three hundred years ago. And the highest of those stages, Integral, with 5–10 percent of the population, is starting to emerge only in the first quarter of the twenty-first century. For around ten thousand years before that, human civilization's cultural center of gravity was mostly at one or another of the ethnocentric-mythic stages of development, and before that, going back perhaps fifty thousand years, mostly at one or another of the egocentric-magic stages.

As we'll see, developmentalists have often given those structure-stages of Growing Up different names, depending on which aspect of development or which intelligence they are studying. One of the most famous set of names for these 6-to-8 Growing Up structure-stages was given by the developmental genius Jean Gebser. As we saw, he called these stages "archaic," "magic," "mythic," "rational," "pluralistic," and "integral." Those stages correspond with our simplified, 4-stage model as follows: archaic and magic = egocentric; mythic = ethnocentric; rational and pluralistic = worldcentric; integral = integrated. We'll soon see exactly what those names mean; but for the moment, notice the "magic" and "mythic," which are two of the earliest and lowest levels of Growing Up. These were the names that Gebser gave to the major egocentric and ethnocentric structure-stages of development. They represent very important observations, because most of the "great civilizations" emerged during the magic-mythic stages, whereas the "modern civilizations" were largely born with the emergence of the worldcentric-rational stage—"The Age of Reason," which occurred only a few hundred years ago with the Enlightenment. These modern worldcentric stages marked the end of slavery, as we just saw, along with the emergence of modern rational sciences—chemistry, physics, astronomy, biology, and so on.

But the great Mythic Era (10,000 B.C.E.–1500 C.E.) saw the rise of most of the world's great religions as well. This is significant, because it means that their religious texts were written from the magic or mythic structure-stage of human development. And this means, among other things, that these texts were written without any understanding of modern rational science. And thus, with the rise of the Western Enlightenment, and the rise of modern science, virtually all religions were tossed out, because not only did they contain little science but they also were full of magic and mythic stories about magical miracles and mythic supernatural beings, which were looked upon the way today's world usually looks at such beings as Zeus, Aphrodite, Santa Claus, and the tooth fairy.

This was unfortunate, because among other catastrophes, this meant that when the modern world tossed out religion in general, it tossed out both the Growing Up and the Waking Up versions. In other words, it tossed out not only the magic and mythic stories and beliefs found at the ethnocentric stages of Growing Up but also all Waking Up experiences of a real Enlightenment. Religion was gone—"God is dead"—but so was spirituality. And the West was left with a colossal battle between science (all good) and religion (all bad). Why did this happen? The structures of a person's Growing Up determines how they will interpret any experience they have. This means that they will interpret any spiritual experiences of Waking Up that they have according to whatever stage of Growing Up they are at, and if they are at prerational stages—such as magic or mythic—then they will interpret even their spiritual experiences in those magic and mythic terms. Thus these experiences will likely be thrown out (by others who are at rational stages) as not being rational. And this is exactly what happened in the West. The major background philosophy of the modern West soon became—and remains to this day—a rational *scientific materialism.*

This was indeed a catastrophe. But it is completely understandable. Everybody interprets their experience according to the structure-stage of Growing Up that they are at. If you are at a magic or mythic stage, you will tend to interpret your world in magic and mythic terms. The volcano explodes because it is mad at you; you become ill if your major God figure is upset with you; if your crops need water, and you pray correctly to the great earth Goddess, then it will rain. These are the types of thoughts that are naturally produced by the magic and mythic structures of Growing Up (just as when you were at one of those early stages, you believed in Santa Claus and the tooth fairy). The more you move into rational stages of Growing Up, the less tolerable those magical mythical stories become, which is indeed what happened to the West as it moved into the Age of Reason.

This is important not only because each of us needs to learn how to tell the difference between Growing Up and Waking Up. It's also important because you can have a genuine Waking Up at any level of Growing Up—not only at its magic-mythic stages but also at its rational and integral stages. But if these various stages are not differentiated, then you will tend to confuse all Waking Up with some sort of prerational stage, such as magic or mythic, and then repeat the mistake that the Enlightenment made, which was to toss out all Waking Up spirituality with all Growing Up magical and mythic tales, religious superstitions, and miracles. This would repeat the so-called crime of the Enlightenment and move us toward nothing but more scientific materialism. Science is a wonderfully important activity, but reducing everything to science is indeed a disaster, and is certainly not something that we want to include in any sort of a genuine Big Wholeness.

So, let's have a closer look at this process of Growing Up and how it comes about that our structure-stage of Growing Up interprets all of our experience. This is necessary if we want to genuinely understand the role that a truly Big Wholeness might play in our lives. It will also help us to understand the important difference between Waking Up and Growing Up, which is a central part of awakening to the reality of a Big Wholeness. And, of course, this will help you to understand your own being and awareness with much more consciousness, clarity, completeness, and care.

3

Growing Up Interprets Waking Up

The structure-stage of Growing Up that a person is at will tend to determine how they think and feel about everything else. This gives Growing Up a place of staggering significance. You can think of Growing Up as the major process used to *interpret* our world. As you can infer from the names that Gebser gave to each of these structure-stages (archaic, magic, mythic, rational, pluralistic, integral), each one will interpret our world quite differently.

This happens because human beings do not passively perceive a world lying around them that is the same for everybody. It's true that external material objects—a rock, a tree, a mountain—are often perceived similarly by most people. But the bulk of the "things" that we "see" (or are aware of) are not simple physical objects. They are instead things such as love, mutual understanding, concern, hatred, mercy, kindness, compassion, jealousy, envy, anger, and care—things that are not simply lying around waiting for all and sundry to see them, and that are the same unchanging phenomena for everybody.

The world is not just a perception; it is in part a conception. And that means we don't just see the world, we interpret it.

Although our capacity to see simple physical objects (a rock, a tree, a mountain) emerges during the first two years of life (with what Jean Piaget called "sensorimotor intelligence"), our capacity for interpretation and explanation continues to grow and evolve across the entire spectrum of the stages of Growing Up. And each one of the 6-to-8 major stages of Growing Up experiences the world very differently. Each stage will thus interpret the world differently (for example, it will interpret the world in archaic, magic, mythic, rational, pluralistic, or integral terms).

We've briefly seen that the 6-to-8 major stages or *levels* of development apply to around a dozen different *lines* of development (or intelligences). But this means that every intelligence that we use will unfold and develop through these major Growing Up stages. Whether it's cognitive intelligence, emotional intelligence, moral intelligence, aesthetic intelligence, or spiritual intelligence, each of them will move through these same basic 6-to-8 stages. As we noted, different lines, same levels. And since all interpretations or explanations are products of our intelligences, all of our explanations of our experience will go through those stages. That means that all of our experiences—including our spiritual experiences of Waking Up—will be interpreted or explained by the structure-stage of Growing Up that we are at, which profoundly changes our entire view of spirituality itself.

Now you can see why I say that Growing Up interprets and explains Waking Up. This is a fact that virtually no religion or spiritual system anywhere in the world has yet realized (mostly because Growing Up was discovered only one hundred years ago). Before we move on, I want to make sure that this idea is very clear, because it is so important in understanding the relationship between the Wholenesses offered by both Waking Up and Growing Up. And if it's a truly "big" Big Wholeness that we want, this topic is crucial.

In order to see exactly what's involved here, I'm going to use our simplified, 4-stage model of Growing Up and show how each of those structure-stages will differently interpret and explain an experience of Waking Up. Although they always interact with each other in complex ways, Growing Up and Waking Up are relatively independent. This means that you can be highly developed in one and very poorly developed in the other—or vice versa, and in virtually any combination. If any of the major spiritual systems had been aware of Growing Up (and how it affects Waking Up), they would have carefully worked out all the profound consequences, because it massively changes what "salvation," "liberation," or "enlightenment" means. But none of them were aware of the major stages of Growing Up, and thus, no matter how advanced they were in Waking Up, they missed this extraordinary interaction.

So let's briefly walk through how each of the 4 structure-stages of our simplified model of Growing Up will very differently interpret a similar experience of Waking Up (or an ultimate Unity consciousness). Of course, if you want to avoid anything that looks like spirituality (whether religious or not), then instead of Waking Up you can think of any other item you like—a building, a conversation, a grade of education—and simply notice how differently each of the Growing Up stages will interpret it. No human being is born with a fully functioning language, a socialized sense of reality, a developed moral sense, or even the capacity to take the role of other. All of those capacities, and all of our multiple intelligences, have to grow and develop over time, a difficult and often painful process. And most importantly, the world itself looks quite different at each and every one of those structure-stages (and it looks different at each stage because it *is* different at each stage). This is the shocking realization that the discovery of Growing Up introduced to humanity.

So let's start. It might initially sound fairly odd, but you can be at an egocentric stage 1 of Growing Up and nevertheless have a real

Waking Up experience. For example, if you are Christian, you might realize that your Real Self is a genuine Christ consciousness (using "Christ consciousness" in its very cleanest, nondual, unifying sense), but if you are at an egocentric stage of Growing Up, you will tend to believe that you, and only you, are actually Jesus Christ. Sadly, our institutions are full of such unfortunate souls (often called "schizophrenic"). I've often repeated the story that Ram Dass used to tell of his brother, who was institutionalized for just that reason. Ram Dass said that as soon as you met his brother in person, you could immediately see that he had indeed had a very genuine and very deep Enlightenment. Ram Dass was just back from India, where he had met several major teachers who had had this experience of Waking Up Oneness, and he said that it was completely obvious and unmistakable in his brother. Due to his cultural Christian background, his brother interpreted this realization, acceptably enough, as a pure Christ consciousness, but he could not acknowledge the possibility that other people could have this realization—including Ram Dass, who spent a great deal of time trying to convince his brother otherwise, to no avail. So this is a straightforward example of someone who had a genuine Waking Up experience—the person directly felt a true Oneness with the entire world and realized their own Christ consciousness—but who interpreted this experience through a very primitive, egocentric level of Growing Up—only they can have this experience. They instantly *interpreted* this Oneness as an extension of their egoic self (just like they do with everything else). The experience was real; the explanation was primitive. The awareness was of a selfless Self; the interpretation was by a selfish ego. It was an authentic state of Waking Up; but it was an archaic stage of Growing Up.

It was an authentic Self because, according to the mystics, the Real Self enters the fetus at some point between conception and birth; some Christian mystics have put this at around four months. In any case, by the time a human being is born, they already have a true Witness, although they will not become aware of this Real Self until they have a genuine Waking Up experience. And because Waking Up and Growing Up are indeed relatively independent, and because the Real Self is a changeless, boundless, ever-present awareness, a real Waking Up can occur at virtually any stage of Growing Up, including the egocentric stage—where, despite their limited capacity to take other people's perspectives, someone can still awaken to their own ever-present Real Self and feel that they are one with everything.

As a person continues to grow and develop, by the time they have reached the ethnocentric stage 2, they have learned to take the role of other; they have learned to see the world through another person's eyes. We saw this with the two-colored ball experiment, where the person's identity expands from egocentric (or self-centered) to ethnocentric (or group-centered). There is a shift from concern with just myself to concern for a whole group (for example, one's family, clan, tribe, nation, or religious affiliation, and so on)—in short, a shift from me to us, from egocentric to ethnocentric.

A person at this structure-stage can indeed have a genuine Waking Up. But if they are, for example, a fundamentalist Protestant (and *fundamentalist* means "ethnocentric," no matter what belief, religion, or philosophy), then they will think that only those who have accepted Jesus as their personal savior can have this Waking Up experience of being "reborn." Other people might think that they have had this experience, but they really haven't—in fact, it is very likely that their experience is demonic in its source—it's not the real thing, whatever it is. And remember the historical examples of this: some cultures that codified Waking Up (Hindu and Buddhist monasteries) had slaves, because that was acceptable when interpreted by ethnocentric structure-stages (even for those with a Waking Up experience).

Recall that Waking Up is a direct, 1st-person experience of being one with everything, but it tells you little about the relative truths of anything. It will definitely tell you that you are one with all beings, but it won't tell you what the perspective of any of those beings is (whether it is egocentric, ethnocentric, worldcentric, integral)—and thus those perspectives will not enter into any of the person's considerations, which, historically, is exactly what happened. In all of these examples, we see a genuine Waking Up, but it was interpreted, for instance, through an ethnocentric stage. Thus, a Christian mystic of the Middle Ages might have a profound Waking Up and realize their own Christ consciousness and their Oneness with everything yet still firmly believe that all unbaptized children will burn in hell forever (or, at best, be sent to limbo). That's an example of an authentic Waking Up but a crude and limited ethnocentric-stage interpretation. (And yes, many ethnocentric Nazis were extremely interested in paths of Waking Up, including really nasty Nazis like Himmler, who plugged straight into a Deity mysticism with a bunch of Aryan gods, and could do so precisely because Waking Up and Growing Up are relatively independent.)

If the person keeps growing, they will move from ethnocentric to worldcentric, from care to universal care, from an ethnocentric "us" to a worldcentric "all of us." Because of this, when their Growing Up mind looks, for example, at those human beings who are being treated as property—namely, slaves—they are collectively outraged by it. A person at this Growing Up stage may—or may not—have a Waking Up experience. But in any event, they will—to stay with the Christian example—begin to interpret Jesus Christ not as the one and only son of the one and only (ethnocentric) God and the savior of the world but instead as just one (worldcentric) World Teacher among many other World Teachers, all of whom have something important to teach us. Even if this person has a genuine Waking Up experience, they nonetheless will often say that they are Christian because, when they use their spiritual intelligence to interpret their Waking Up experience, it interprets reality according to its own structure, which in this case is worldcentric. And in this case, that intelligence is most comfortable with the Christian explanatory scheme, and so they use that scheme—as it is worldcentrically interpreted—for their narrative content (although they will also be completely open to incorporating aspects from other World Teachers, such as perhaps adopting a Buddhist mindfulness practice). This can be a real Waking Up, but it is interpreted through a high level of Growing Up—that of a worldcentric stage that includes all of humanity.

Notice that during Vatican II, the Church admitted (I'm paraphrasing) that comparable religious salvation to that offered by Christianity can be had by other religions. This is a staggering leap in growth from their nearly two-millennia-old ethnocentric claim that their religion is the one and only true religion to an acknowledgment that Spirit is universal, worldcentric, and open to all humans regardless of race, color, sex, or religious creed. (One can't help but think of Voltaire's scream "Remember the cruelties!"—the cruelties inflicted by the Church on millions of people when it was in its ethnocentric stages, from the Spanish Inquisition, to witch hunts killing tens of thousands of women, to the Crusades. Voltaire's lament became the heartfelt battle cry of the Enlightenment, which was the first major worldcentric social movement in human history—which is indeed why it ended slavery.)

Now you can clearly see the difference between Waking Up and Growing Up and that the stage of Growing Up you are at is incredibly important because it will interpret your Waking Up experience. It's true that an experience of a total Wholeness, which includes "all of us," is the core nature of the Waking Up experience at any of these major stages. That is, each stage of Growing Up has an experience of Waking Up in which it feels that it is "one with its world"—but "its world" keeps expanding in each stage of Growing Up. It grows from just "me" that can have this realization of Oneness (egocentric), to just "us" that can have this realization (ethnocentric), to "all of us" (regardless of race, color, sex, gender, or religious creed—worldcentric). So a profound sense of Oneness and Wholeness is indeed present in a Waking Up experience at each and every stage of Growing Up, but Growing Up does indeed grow, unfold, and evolve through 6-to-8 major structure-stages—moving from "me" to "us" to "all of us" to "integrated."

We'll get to the integral stage in a moment. For now, just let me point out that what makes this entire concept so difficult is that you can't tell that the relative world is expanding just by tracking Waking Up because (1) Waking Up tells you virtually nothing about the relative world of Growing Up, and (2) Waking Up always gives that totalistic "one with everything" feeling that is constant and doesn't change. Oneness is oneness—it is everywhere said to be a "boundless, changeless" awareness, which represents the timeless "Oneness" or the eternal "Unity" in "ultimate Unity consciousness," but the way that it is interpreted grows and changes with Growing Up. Recall Spong's distinction between spiritual *experience* and the *explanation* of that experience: the experience is timeless and eternal, but the explanation exists in the world of time and evolution, where it can unfold and develop, changing significantly as it does so.

This discovery is of stunning importance. It provides a new perspective on what we know about spirituality and religion. It certainly explains an enormous amount of history—for example, why Waking Up cultures still had slavery, were often harshly patriarchal, and rarely developed rigorous sciences. That is, the cultures that originally discovered Waking Up were also at relatively mediocre stages of Growing Up (usually mythic, ethnocentric) when they did so—and clearly these are two relatively separate processes.

When religious experience is interpreted from a low level of Growing Up (for example, egocentric or ethnocentric), we get some of the meanest and most malicious forms of religion imaginable.

Such religions are ready to engage in things like the Spanish Inquisition, which brutally tortured unbelievers (they're not one of "us," after all, they're "Other"), or the Crusades, which gladly killed infidels (our ethnocentric version of religion is clearly the one and only true religion possessing the one and only true God), and many of those who supported such practices were genuinely awakened mystics. When religion is interpreted from an ethnocentric stage, it is indeed the largest source of hatred, torture, and warfare in humankind's history; while when it is interpreted from the higher stages (worldcentric or integral), it is one of the greatest sources of love, charity, and compassion. That is how this brutal "paradox of religion" came into existence (the paradox is that religion has been the source of *both* the greatest amount of hatred, torture, and warfare, and also the greatest amount of love, compassion, and care). That paradox is still with us: no matter how much Waking Up a spiritual system might have, it is still totally ignorant of Growing Up, and thus its students can be at any of those developmental stages of Growing Up, no matter how primitive.

Finally, if individuals move on from the third stage to a genuinely integrated or Integral structure of Growing Up, their interpretive capacity for all experiences—including Waking Up experiences—will likewise move to that larger, more expansive, Integral stage. This means, among other things, that they will "transcend and include" the perspectives of all their previous stages. Hence at this stage, they are dramatically more inclusive, synthesizing, and integrating. Reaching this Integral stage also means a person will begin to dramatically expand the areas, ideas, fields, and disciplines that they consider true, real, or important. If they are diehard scientific materialists, they might start considering the utter contradictions in such views and be more open to transcendent realities; if they are religious fundamentalists, they will start to find invaluable truths in other spiritual systems; if they are hardheaded nationalists, they'll be more open to globalist views and see their understandable patriotism in the larger context of a community of other welcomed nations and an integrated humanity.

Finally, if individuals at this Integral Growing Up structure have a real Waking Up experience, they will—finally!—give this ultimate nondual Unity experience the full, whole, and deeply integrated interpretation that such an experience calls for. In offering the greatest embrace in the realm of relative reality, it offers the fullest amount of nonduality uniting the relative realm with the ultimate. In other words, in offering the most amount of Form, it provides the greatest nonduality of that Form with Emptiness; in embracing the most amount of samsara, it gives the fullest unity of samsara and nirvana; in providing the most amount of Earth, it discloses the greatest unity of Heaven and Earth.

The most evolved minds of yesterday—for example, Plotinus, Longchenpa, Shankara, Maimonides, and Schelling—have always been pushing into not only the furthest reaches of Waking Up but also the highest stages of Growing Up (although in ways that they did not fully understand, since Growing Up itself was not yet discovered and thus not consciously understood). As individuals, they were haphazardly pushing their way into the Integral stages of development, thus offering the greatest interpretation (in Growing Up) of the ultimate experience (of Waking Up).

However much that higher Growing Up did (or did not) occur in the past, the good news is that today each of us have an opportunity to start reaching this greatest consciousness that is now available. We have this extraordinary opportunity precisely because our cultural center of gravity in Growing Up has, in the past two hundred years, moved into modern, worldcentric stages, and thus, each of us, growing up in such a culture, very likely has been exposed to these worldcentric stages and therefore stands on the brink of the next higher, Integral stages. We also have, via the Internet, for the first time in history, basic access to every culture in the world, including all of the cultures of Waking Up that have previously emerged, and there are communities right now all over the world that are plumbing the depths of these Waking Up practices and making them fully available to anyone interested.

Nonetheless, we have already seen that, being at the leading edge of evolution and development, these higher Integral stages are, in today's world, relatively rare, with only around 5 percent of the population located at an Integral stage. Still, these structure-stages are available to any individual that wants to make the effort to reach them. (We will discuss what this effort involves when we discuss each of the major levels of Growing Up, starting in chapter 5.)

All that is now required, in my opinion, is to bring together both of these pathways—Growing Up and Waking Up—into a truly Integral approach, capital *I* Integral, which means not just a particular Integral structure-stage of development (although that stage is happily included) but an approach that fully embraces both Growing Up and Waking Up—along with Opening Up, Cleaning Up, and Showing Up. This would provide us with the most complete Big Wholeness that has ever been offered in our history.

Why not take advantage of that? Why not set your goals and aspirations for that all-inclusive Big Wholeness that exists right now? Stated negatively, given the fragmented, partial, and broken nature of so much of our present world—and ourselves—what have we got to lose? Stated more positively, just how much happiness can we endure?

Well, let's find out . . .

4

Spiritual Intelligence versus Spiritual Experience

Before we look more carefully at some of the details of Big Wholeness, including practices for directly Waking Up and an Integral sexual Tantra, it would be useful to explore some of the differences between the type of spiritual engagement that occurs with Waking Up, which involves *states* of consciousness, and the type of spiritual engagement that is involved with Growing Up, which involves *structures* of consciousness. This is the difference between direct spiritual experience (in Waking Up) and the indirect spiritual engagement known as spiritual intelligence (one of the multiple intelligences found in Growing Up). This is indeed another way of talking about direct 1st-person *experience* (of *states* of Waking Up) versus 3rd-person *explanation* (via *structures* of Growing Up). These two very different types of spiritual engagement are rarely distinguished, and confusing them generates an enormous amount of misunderstanding and muddleheadedness, not to mention a staggering number of historical atrocities.

Spiritual intelligence is indeed one of the multiple intelligences or lines of development in Growing Up, and the Wholeness it offers is dramatically different from the Wholeness found in Waking Up (although, of course, both are included in Big Wholeness, which embraces both Growing Up and Waking Up). If you're interested in spirituality in general (or Wholeness in particular), I think you'll very much want to be aware of the difference between spiritual experience and spiritual intelligence.

Spiritual intelligence is an *intelligence*, it's how we *think* about Spirit or ultimate Reality. Anytime we think about Spirit, or form spiritual ideas, or use words and concepts to describe Spirit, we are using our spiritual intelligence (as opposed to a *direct experience* of Spirit, which is what Waking Up involves).[1] Anytime we think about any sort of ultimate reality or infinity or unlimited being as, for example, a mathematician or philosopher might, we are using our spiritual intelligence. And since spiritual intelligence is a line of development, it can go through the same 6-to-8 major levels of growth and development that any line of development can.

Hence, "spiritual" in the spiritual intelligence of Growing Up is how we *think* about Spirit (or any ultimate Reality), whereas "spiritual" in Waking Up is a *direct experience* of Spirit. The direct experience of Awakening or Enlightenment is what spirituality looks like in the Waking Up pathway. If we then *think* about that direct spiritual experience, give it ideas and labels, or fit it into some sort of theology, philosophy, or metaphysics, we are using our spiritual *intelligence* in Growing Up. In other words, Waking Up involves a spiritual knowledge by *acquaintance*; Growing Up involves a spiritual knowledge by *description*: direct spiritual *experience* in Waking Up versus spiritual *thinking about* in Growing Up.[2]

The ways that spiritual intelligence functions in people's lives—including in *your* life—are not generally understood very well, if at all. If you're basically normal, you are using this spiritual intelligence all the time, but you probably don't realize it. We will be examining the 6-to-8 major structure-stages that this spiritual intelligence (along with all other intelligences) can undergo in your own lifetime. You might want to be aware of how spiritual intelligence is manifesting itself in your awareness right now, whether or not you explicitly believe in anything called "spirit." (And in just a moment, I'll give some clear evidence that you are using spiritual intelligence right now, whether or not you are aware of it, and whether you are atheistic, agnostic, a true believer, or anything else.)

We saw that spiritual intelligence is one of around a dozen or so intelligences—or lines of development—that all human beings possess. These lines include cognitive intelligence, emotional intelligence, moral intelligence, aesthetic intelligence, spiritual intelligence, and so on. The crucial evolutionary point is that each of these intelligences addresses a fundamental question that life throws at us, and over the hundreds of thousands of years that humanity has evolved, these intelligences evolved to address these central questions and issues. For example, moral intelligence addresses the question "What is the right thing to do?" Emotional intelligence addresses the question "What do I feel about that?" Cognitive intelligence addresses "What exactly am I aware of right now?" Aesthetic intelligence addresses the question "What looks the most attractive or most beautiful to me?" And spiritual intelligence? Spiritual intelligence addresses the central question "What is it that is of *ultimate concern* (or *ultimate reality*) for me?"

The phrase "ultimate concern" was often used by Paul Tillich, the modern genius and systematic theologian. (He also used the important phrase "the Ground of Being," which he borrowed from Plotinus, another genius and integral thinker.) And then, just recently, James Fowler, yet another brilliant pioneer, *directly measured the developmental stages that people go through when they think about their ultimate concern—that is, the structure-stages that a person's spiritual intelligence goes through.* And small surprise, Fowler discovered that thinking about what is of ultimate concern goes through the same 6-to-8 structure-stages of Growing Up that all the other multiple lines go through (Fowler found 7 stages; we'll return to his work very shortly). And to state the obvious, for both these theorists, "what is of ultimate concern" is essentially synonymous with "spirit." They found the term so useful because almost all the typical terms—such as "God," "Jehovah," or "Allah"—have so much bloody baggage (literally) or so many mythic meanings attached to them that they are virtually worthless (and unbelievable) today. In contrast, the phrase "ultimate concern" points directly to a dimension in your own life that is spiritual (but not necessarily religious) or to something that you consider to be ultimately real or of ultimate importance, even if you think you aren't spiritual. I said that I would show you that you are using spiritual intelligence in your life, even if you think you aren't. Here goes: Make a list of all the truly and deeply important things in your life—the most important of the most important things—and at the top of that list is your ultimate concern. That's *your* God. You do have one. That was easy.

The point of this example is to help you start to think about "spiritual" in new ways, which I hope will continue to happen. The shocking point, which we will continue to pursue, is that most of what we today call "religion" or "God" is indeed an interpretation made by Growing Up, but in almost all cases—especially if we think in specifically religious terms—the stage of Growing Up that is represented is a very early and fairly primitive stage (usually magic or mythic). Although everybody still has to go through that early stage—because in Growing Up everybody starts at square one and moves up from there through all of the various stages—nonetheless this early mythic-religious stage is an extremely limited place to stop your development. Many modern people recognize this and intuitively avoid anything that even vaguely looks or sounds "religious." (Remember the title of Spong's book, *Unbelievable*.)

SPIRITUAL BUT NOT RELIGIOUS

Once we realize that our religious explanations and interpretations often come from an earlier stage of Growing Up that we were once at, then we are perfectly free to release our spiritual intelligence from its confines in those earlier, magic-mythic stages and allow it to expand into much more modern, postmodern, and integral forms (rational, pluralistic, or integral), including ones that are quite comfortable with science and rationality. This opens us to forms of "spiritual but not religious" that are staggeringly novel and exhilarating. Not only does it open us to new ways to integrate science and spirituality but it also opens us to genuine forms of a truly Big Wholeness, and this almost certainly will have a profound impact on our life—how we look at reality, how we feel about it, how we act toward it. It's a new world, and in this world, there is room for everything.

To return to "ultimate concern": interestingly, and slightly strangely, one's concern could be almost anything. For an addict, it might be heroin. For a six-month-old child, it's probably breast milk. For somebody deeply in love, it could be their mate. For a super-wealthy person, perhaps their money. For a Christian fundamentalist, it's very likely Jesus. For a teenager, maybe their brand-new car. For a Marine, it might be love of country. For a postmodernist, it might be planetary survival and climate change. Spiritual intelligence itself doesn't necessarily give us answers that look typically religious. Rather, the emphasis is on what is *ultimate*. You use spiritual intelligence whenever you are engaged in seriously thinking about the most important of the most important things in your life, or the most real of the most real realities.

Whenever you think about some sort of ultimate reality, you automatically switch into a type of thinking that connects to the most absolute of your concerns—something you might even lay down your life for. But, in any event, it is of profound importance for you—in other words, of *ultimate* concern—and your thinking about it is spiritual intelligence. As we noted earlier, human beings have been assessing things that were of utmost importance or reality for them almost from the start, and spiritual intelligence is the intelligence that evolved to deal with such issues. And why wouldn't it? The existence of spiritual intelligence is really no more surprising than that of cognitive intelligence or emotional intelligence or moral intelligence. Did we think about what we're aware of (cognitive intelligence) and what we're feeling (emotional intelligence) and what we should ethically do (moral intelligence) and yet never think once about what was the *most important* of those things in our lives?

No, we have been thinking about what is of ultimate concern virtually from day one. Using Gebser's terms for the major stages of development, at the beginning we have the archaic stage of what is of ultimate concern; then we moved into the magic stage; then the mythic-literal; and then with modernity, we moved into rational, then pluralistic, and now integral stages of development of our ultimate concern. Throughout the same spiritual intelligence was evolving and responding, moving through ever higher, ever more complex, and ever more conscious levels of Growing Up. You and I are still doing this—still using our spiritual intelligence—because we still have things that are very important in our lives and others that are not so important, and we assess where things lie on this scale of importance. Our spiritual intelligence, even when we are adults, can come from any one of those 6-to-8 structure-stages, because today a human being has all of those stages available. So even if we don't explicitly believe in spirit or anything religious, every day that we get up we will be pursuing our God.

That's our spiritual intelligence. And notice, spiritual intelligence is NOT spiritual experience. It's thinking about an ultimate Ground; it's not directly experiencing that Ground. It exists in the stream of relative Growing Up (as one of several intelligences, or a *structure* of consciousness) and not in the stream of Waking Up (as an altered *state* of consciousness or a direct 1st-person experience). As we saw, the evidence for the existence of that radical Waking Up experience is truly overwhelming, or "not disputable." But such a direct and radical experience is not the same as spiritual intelligence, and that difference is what we're dealing with right now.

Among other things, notice that there are around 6-to-8 *structure*-stages of Growing Up (archaic, magic, mythic, rational, pluralistic, integral) and 5 major *state*-stages of Waking Up (gross, subtle, causal, turiya, turiyatita). We have not yet discussed all of the stages of Growing Up; we will start to do so in chapter 5. But we have already briefly discussed the 5 states of Waking Up, when we discussed the 5 major state-stages of a complete meditation and the 5 major states of natural consciousness: gross waking, subtle dreaming, causal dreamless, turiya or Witnessing, and turiyatita or One Taste. All the 5 state-stages of Waking Up are indeed direct and immediate state experiences, unlike the Growing Up stages, which are all indirect interpretations or structures of a Growing Up development. When I talk about Waking Up experience in the singular, I mean specifically the *ultimate* states of Waking Up—which are said to be turiya and turiyatita—which are indeed quite different from any of the Growing Up stages, since they are immediate and direct 1st-person experiences (knowledge by acquaintance), unlike the Growing Up structures, which are merely 3rd-person knowledge by description, or interpretation.

One of the reasons that I'm bringing this up and making such a fuss about it is that, in today's world, both religion and spirituality are almost always taken to mean a belief system coming from Growing Up. And worse, religion and spirituality are usually identified with a belief system that has been taken from one of the *earlier* stages of Growing Up and not from any of the later and more evolved stages. Honestly, somewhere over 90 percent of the meanings of those "religious" words are tied to those early magic-mythic structure-stages. This makes it virtually impossible to give an acceptable explanation of what spiritual intelligence has to say when it comes from any of the higher structures of Growing Up (rational, pluralistic, or integral) not to mention coming from any sort of genuine Waking Up, which is itself a "boundless, changeless" state that is altogether different from any structure of Growing Up.

If you were trying to advertise for a genuinely spiritual viewpoint coming from any of those higher stages of Growing Up, and you were using any of the traditional words like "God" or "religion," you would have to start the advertisement with some sort of denial of those traditional meanings (as I am doing here). The advertisement would have to be something like "This is not your father's religion" or "This isn't the God you think you know."

So let it be said now that when I use the term "spiritual," I mean it in the "spiritual but not religious" sense—that is, a sense of a spiritual intelligence that comes from any and all stages of Growing Up. This includes the standard religious structure-stages of magic and mythic, but it also includes any of the higher structure-stages of modern rational, postmodern pluralistic, or systemic integral. In short, some sort of spiritual intelligence exists at each stage of Growing Up, as do all the other intelligences.

It is often said that interest in religion has steadily declined in today's world. That's true enough for mythic-literal religion. The "mythic" and "mythic-literal" stages of development are aspects of ethnocentric stages. In chapter 6, we'll see what those terms mean in more detail. For now, I note that they refer to stage 3 in a typical 8-stage model of Growing Up. The mythic-literal stage of spiritual intelligence really believes that everything it says is empirically and historically true—that the myths are all true—for example, that Moses actually did part the Red Sea and Christ really was born from a biological virgin. Many of the world's great mythic religions began at this stage, although today it is a fairly low level. As for the decline in mythic-literal religion, in Europe those with interest in traditional mythic Christianity is now down to less than 15 percent of the population in virtually all countries, from Germany to Britain to France. Not only is the mythic God dead, mythic Christianity is nearly dead.

Yet that decline refers to only one of the stages of spiritual intelligence, the mythic-literal stage. The use of spiritual intelligence has not itself gone down, it has simply changed its content, changed its objects, changed its items of ultimate concern, changed its stage of Growing Up, often quite dramatically—since now it's coming from the rational, pluralistic, or integral stages. But an ultimate concern is still there at every stage of development, and spiritual intelligence is still very much being engaged. For example, you might think about whether there is ultimate reality or an ultimate Wholeness or an ultimate Spirit, and you might decide there isn't one and that you're an atheist. Well, that's your form of spiritual intelligence—you're still thinking about ultimate realities, so you're still using spiritual intelligence, even if you think there isn't an ultimate reality. Or you might think you're just not sure—you're agnostic. That's also the use of spiritual intelligence. Looked at this way, you can see that pretty much everybody uses their spiritual intelligence, at least every now and then.

As another example of how spiritual intelligence functions differently at different stages of Growing Up, I want to go over two widespread versions of spiritual intelligence: (1) the fundamentalist Christian version of Jesus (which springs from stage 3 in a typical 8-stage Growing Up model), and (2) a postmodern version of ecological sustainability or Gaia (which comes from stage 6 in an 8-stage model). You might be surprised by their differences—and their similarities.

JESUS VERSUS GAIA

We have seen that the narratives, stories, or ideas that we create when we use our spiritual intelligence don't have to look typically religious. But obviously they can, and often do. If a person is a fundamentalist Christian, for example, then the narrative created by their spiritual intelligence might be something like this: "I accept, as my personal savior, Jesus Christ, the Son of God, who was born of the Virgin Mary, was dead and resurrected in three days, physically ascended into Heaven and now sits on the right hand of God the Father. If I truly accept Jesus into my life, then I am absolved from original sin and I will live in Heaven next to Jesus and God for everlasting time. I know this is true, because it says so in the Bible, and the Bible is the word of God." That story is indeed generally backed up by a (mythic-literal) belief in the Bible as the divine, unerring, and literal word of God. So the ultimate concern for this person is their relationship with Jesus Christ as God.

Because this kind of spirituality includes stories, it is often called a *narrative form* of spirituality. Many of the products of spiritual intelligence include some sort of story or narrative that is built around one's ultimate concern—in this case, Jesus Christ as personal savior.

A more recent, postmodern, worldcentric form of narrative spirituality might go like this: "If we look at all of the recent breakthroughs in modern natural science, we see the emergence of a new paradigm. This new paradigm tells us that all the things and events in the universe are totally interwoven with all the other things and events, so that the entire universe is a single, great, interwoven Web of Life. The more I see myself as being merely one of the strands in this great Web, the more I see clearly what my true place in the world is. Quantum mechanics shows us that everything in the universe is deeply entangled with everything else, and the more we realize this—the more that we realize that each of us is simply one part of the Whole—the more we will live in accord with Nature and stop the utterly suicidal resource depletion and global warming that we are now causing, which will soon destroy the biosphere and all human life with it."

For this sort of person, their ultimate concern is Gaia and its ecological balance, and so that's what their spiritual or ultimate-concern narrative is focused on. They might think of this as being a spiritual story, or they might not; they might think of it as being the product of truly leading-edge science, a genuinely new paradigm, and believe that it points to the same interconnectedness of the universe that the great mystics have announced, except this version is truly scientific. Either way, this narrative involves their ultimate concern, and so they are using their spiritual intelligence when they think about it.

As different as the content of those two belief systems are—Jesus and Gaia—they both share the narrative form of spirituality produced by spiritual intelligence (in Growing Up). That is, each of them is taken to be a real, 3rd-person, objective description of reality (whether Jesus or Gaia); they both take it to be the most true and most important reality that there is; they both believe that if their own ultimate concern is not taken seriously, then all of humanity itself will suffer enormously and likely even die; they both believe that people can deviate from this ultimate concern or they can obediently follow it and thus prevent disaster, and that this reality is the source of their ultimate concern. Thus, when they use their spiritual intelligence, this belief system is what comes out as the most important of the most important things in their life. They both express this belief in a narrative that they maintain is an objective and descriptive truth—spiritual intelligence is, after all, a 3rd-person knowledge by description—and this narrative (Jesus or Gaia) describes the nature of what is of ultimate concern, why it's important to them, why they believe it's ultimately true, and so on. In short, both are products of a spiritual intelligence that is found in the Growing Up path. In a moment, we'll see that they come from different levels of Growing Up (stage 3 amber versus stage 6 green).

However, that their spiritual intelligence has produced a narrative doesn't carry any implication about whether they have had a Waking Up experience. It might very well be that neither one has had a genuine, direct Waking Up experience. If so, then their spiritual engagement is not with the path of Waking Up and its direct spiritual experience but rather is with the path of Growing Up and its indirect spiritual intelligence. They do not have spiritual knowledge by acquaintance but rather knowledge by narrative description. There is absolutely nothing wrong with this; in fact, it's extremely common. It's common because everybody is using some stage of spiritual intelligence almost all the time, whether or not they've had a Waking Up experience. If, however, someone has a Waking Up experience, then for the Christian (especially if fundamentalist), it will likely be something along the lines of what St. Paul counseled: "Let this consciousness be in you that was in Christ Jesus, that we all may be one." They have that type of ultimate Unity consciousness experience—a genuine Waking Up experience—and then use their spiritual intelligence to think about it, to elaborate it, to explain it. Often, in this fundamentalist Christian context, this Waking Up will be described and interpreted as an experience of being "reborn" in Christ consciousness ("Not I but Christ lives in me"). This experience, at least at its authentic peak, can indeed be a direct experience of a timeless, ever-present Ground of All Being; in other words, it's an authentic spiritual experience, as William James himself observed about Christian mystics. But notice that, in this example of a fundamentalist Christian, the stage of Growing Up at work is amber mythic-literal, the mythic stage from which most forms of literal fundamentalism spring. At this stage of Growing Up, people will very likely take the myths of the Bible to be literally and historically true, even if they've had a genuine Waking Up (hence, "mythic-literal"). We can see that is true by the sheer number of people who call themselves "reborn Christians"; they have very believable accounts of their own "rebirth" as a genuine Waking Up experience, and yet still believe every word in the Bible.

We've already introduced the notion that all experiences—including Waking Up experiences—are interpreted by the person's structure of Growing Up. In this example, the mythic-literal stage takes the Biblical myths as true, literally. Recall that even a profound Waking Up satori cannot correct the belief that the earth is flat, and if the person's spiritual intelligence is at the mythic-literal stage, it cannot correct any myths, no matter how silly, that may be found in the Bible either.

Let me briefly expand on the notion that Growing Up interprets or explains Waking Up. Now it's true that some profound Waking Up experiences are themselves without words, labels, concepts, or ideas—they are very close to a pure experience or pure wordless awareness. But as soon as the person comes out of that nonconceptual state—and at some point they will—they begin to think about the experience, interpret it, ask what it means, why it occurred; they might even place it in a very elaborate philosophy or metaphysics. In other words, they are using their mind and its words and concepts; that is, they are using some sort of intelligence—in this case, spiritual intelligence (probably combined with cognitive intelligence, but they can also use any other intelligence they want to help explain this—emotional intelligence, moral intelligence, aesthetic intelligence, and so on). In these cases, they will engage whatever level of development that particular line of development is at, which means that their interpretations and explanations will spring from that Growing Up stage, whatever it might be. This really is unavoidable. And this is why Waking Up is always interpreted by Growing Up, itself coming from a particular level of development (in whatever line).

Thus, for the reborn Christian fundamentalist at this ethnocentric, mythic-literal stage of Growing Up, even if they've had a genuine Waking Up, they will very likely still think of Jesus as the one and only Son of the one and only God, born of a biological Virgin, and think that Jesus literally died for their sins (all ethnocentric and mythic beliefs). Further—and this is the real problem—they often will think that the experience of being reborn (that is, their genuine Waking Up experience) proves to them beyond all doubt that these beliefs are absolutely true, and now they know that Christianity is the only real and true religion. The mythic-literal stage is part of the broad ethnocentric stages of development, and thus its beliefs are often ethnocentric and prejudiced, even for a person with a Waking Up. This is a perfect example of the stage of Growing Up (no matter how primitive or "low") interpreting the experience of Waking Up (no matter how authentic or "high").

We can see the same thing with the believer in Gaia or the great Web of Life as an ultimate Reality deserving of ultimate concern. This person might also have a direct Waking Up experience. As they step out of that direct, wordless, nonconceptual experience of radical and unqualifiable Oneness, their spiritual intelligence (at its particular stage of Growing Up—in this case, green, postmodern pluralistic) begins to think about the experience, giving it words and meaning and spinning concepts and theories about it. Given this person's strong Great Web or Gaia belief system, they will likely see this experience as being a oneness not with Christ but with all of Nature. In other words, a direct experience of Nature mysticism.

Notice that these people are not actually thinking that when they are having the experience. That is, during that nonconceptual experience of Waking Up, they are not thinking, "This is an experience of Nature mysticism." They are not thinking, "There is a great Web of Life, with trillions and trillions of strands, and I'm totally one with all of these living strands, therefore I have to live my life in order to be in balance with the whole thing." Rather, they are experiencing only a direct, nonconceptual oneness with all their reality, a oneness with all of Nature. It's only when they come out of that experience and begin to engage their mind (at whatever stage of Growing Up their particular intelligence is at) that they start to think something like, "There is a great Web of Life with trillions of living biological strands. I'm one with all of it, and as such, I need to live my life so that I am completely in balance with all the other strands—my life, my work, my diet, my profession, all of it must be brought into accord with this great unified Web. The belief in an atomistic world is not only wrong, it's killing all of humanity and must be stopped. Global warming is a good example of this, and I must fight it every way that I can." It's not that such a statement isn't relatively true; it is true for this person at the rational pluralistic level. But the idea itself is a product of spiritual intelligence, not direct spiritual experience.

So, if someone has experienced a direct Waking Up, they will use their spiritual Growing Up (spiritual intelligence) to give that experience an explanation, to flesh it out, to give it all sorts of details and descriptions. In this example, they see reality as a Great Web of Life. The green stage is egalitarian, because it wants to see everything and everybody as completely equal. Thus a person at that stage of Growing Up will often interpret their Waking Up in those terms—their ultimate concern is this great egalitarian Web of Life.

Further, because green is a relatively high stage of development and has already passed through the rational, universal, worldcentric stage, unlike amber mythic, it will tend to want its beliefs to be scientific. Despite green's stated belief that all viewpoints are equally valid, it definitely does not believe that Christian mythic-literal values are to be embraced. By the time the green, pluralistic stage emerges (which is two or three stages after the mythic-literal stage), the mythic God is long dead, and you will find very little that looks like traditional religion coming specifically from this green level (although, of course, this level still has its own spiritual intelligence, which is producing the notion of a great egalitarian Web of Life). Spiritual intelligence at this structure-stage will often try to demonstrate that modern science itself is offering proof of the ultimate unity experience of total interconnectedness that the Great Web claims to offer. This will frequently include systems theory, ecological interwovenness, chaos and complexity theories, and especially references to quantum mechanics and quantum entanglement.[3]

Thus, at this green stage—whether or not they have had a direct Waking Up—they will tend to arrive at the belief in a New Paradigm in Science (with capital letters), which is what is worthy of their ultimate concern. I say "whether or not they have had a Waking Up," because the structures of Growing Up offer the tools used to interpret and explain *any* experience a person has—*including* spiritual experiences but also ordinary experiences as well. We saw in the previous example that a fundamentalist, amber mythic-stage Christian will likely believe that Jesus was born from a biological virgin, whether or not they have had a Waking Up experience. Likewise, in this example, someone at green pluralistic who is interested in spiritual concerns will often adopt this New Paradigm, with or without a Waking Up. In either case, the New Paradigm is the product of their green, egalitarian Growing Up stage; it expresses what is "really really real" for them. It's an ultimate concern of their green spiritual intelligence.

Indeed most believers in this New Paradigm in Science have not had a Waking Up realization; they are simply thinking about this oneness using their spiritual intelligence—and that's totally fine; it's just not Waking Up. We've spent so much time talking about the differences between Waking Up and Growing Up in order to help us recognize one point: simply learning systems theory, or learning about quantum entanglement, or learning a supposed New Paradigm will do nothing to produce a Waking Up in you. That conceptual kind of knowledge is only a knowledge by description; it's not a knowledge by acquaintance. It will not help you Wake Up but will only advance your capacity to think narratively and conceptually using the spiritual intelligence in Growing Up. It's learning horizontally, not transforming vertically.

And again—and I mean this: there's nothing wrong with doing that; just be aware of what you are actually doing. Do you want to engage Growing Up spiritual intelligence or Waking Up spiritual experience? Be aware of what you truly want, and learn to distinguish between these two profoundly different types of spiritual engagement. Engaging only in theoretical concerns—for example, thinking about a New Paradigm using your spiritual intelligence—is not engaging in a practice of Waking Up. That requires an entirely different approach (which we will explore later). But because most people don't understand or recognize the many differences between Growing Up and Waking Up, they don't realize when they are practicing only one of them, and thus they are liable to confuse merely thinking about an ultimate Reality with the direct realization of it. And worst of all, when they engage in that New Paradigm, they might stop seeking a real Waking Up, imagining that they have all the bases covered—and thus their spiritual intelligence ironically prevents their spiritual Waking Up.

Let's finish this chapter by very briefly looking at a point that I earlier introduced rather sketchily (with a promise to return to it)—namely, James Fowler's research on the structure-stages of spiritual intelligence. This is fitting because in the next chapter we will begin examining, in some detail, around 6 of the 6-to-8 basic stages of Growing Up. Fowler's research gives a detailed description of the 6 major stages we've only briefly mentioned so far—namely, archaic, magic, mythic, rational, pluralistic, and integral—but Fowler's details on each of them are incredibly telling, and they add enormously to our understanding of the profoundly differing ways that human beings view their world. So we can naturally ask, with reference to Fowler's work, will spiritual intelligence also move through those 6 levels of Growing Up?

The answer is a definite "Yes." Fowler is a brilliant and pioneering developmental researcher and theorist. In his empirical studies, Fowler examined thousands of people and asked them about their spirituality—what it meant to them, what was important about it, how they described it, what they were supposed to do to keep it, how it changed their lives, and so on. This research was about how people think about spirituality or ultimate reality, or about what Fowler explicitly called "ultimate concern." His research showed that thinking about some sort of ultimate reality—spiritual intelligence—went through 6 or 7 major stages of development. (Fowler numbers his major stages from 1 to 6. But he also includes a stage 0, which is the original infantile fusion stage. So depending on whether or not you count that stage, you get 6 or 7 stages.) He was careful to separate these stages of ultimate concern from any sort of actual Waking Up—he was *not* investigating mystical experiences or direct awakenings; he was investigating how people *think about* spirit, or about what was of ultimate concern in their lives. In short, he was investigating spiritual intelligence, which is a spiritual Growing Up, not a spiritual Waking Up.

He found that almost invariably people's understanding of their spirituality unfolded through 6 or 7 major stages of development, and their spiritual viewpoints were profoundly different at each stage. These were essentially the 6-to-8 major levels of development that all the various lines of development go through in the process of Growing Up. *Moreover, people went through these major structure-stages of Growing Up whether or not they had ever had a Waking Up experience.* Clearly, how people think about Spirit (Growing Up) and how they directly experience Spirit (Waking Up) are two very different things. When we examine these stages closely in the next chapter, you will be able to see exactly how they apply in your own life, as well as what stage you are at yourself.

I'm not suggesting that using these structure-stages of spiritual intelligence is something that we *should* do. I'm not suggesting that we *should* look at our spirituality (or anything else, for that matter) through these 6-to-8 stages. I am saying we *are already* doing this. It's already happening to us—whether we know it or not. Every one of us is going through these stages of Growing Up in each of our multiple intelligences. We can be at a low altitude (archaic, magic), a medium altitude (mythic, rational), or a high altitude (pluralistic, integral) in any of them. But exist these stages do, and they are influencing, even governing, how we interpret, experience, and explain our reality, moment to moment. (But no matter what stage a given intelligence is at, remember that we can always continue our growth, development, and evolution—and that's an important notion we'll come back to.)

STRUCTURES VERSUS STATES

One last, quick technical point. In the last chapter, I carefully explained structures of consciousness, and I promised to come back to states of consciousness and give them a decent explanation. So, let me do so now. We've seen that Growing Up consists of *structures* of consciousness and Waking Up consists of *states* of consciousness. Structures are not at all the same as states, and this is the real reason that these two realities are indeed so starkly different.

A *state* of consciousness—which is involved in any Waking Up—is a direct, 1st-person, immediate experience. "Small" states constitute your ongoing experience: states that are happy, sad, joyous, anxious, excited, dejected, elated, expectant, depressed, fearful, and so forth. "Big" states are waking (gross state), dreaming (subtle state), deep sleep (causal state), hypnogogic (twilight awareness), turiya (pure

Awareness), turiyatita (One Taste)—and those big states include all 5 major states of consciousness in a full Waking Up pathway (gross, subtle, causal, turiya, and turiyatita). In this book, when I talk about states, I mean big states (unless otherwise indicated).

But the especially important thing about states, big or small, is that when you have one, you know it. When you experience a state, including any Waking Up experience, you definitely know it. If you have a satori experience of radical Oneness and feel that you are one with the entire universe in bliss and love, you are clearly and definitely aware of it. In other words, because these states are all 1st-person, direct experiences, when you have one, you are always fully aware of it.

The exact opposite is true of *structures* of consciousness, which comprise the stages of Growing Up. When you are at a particular stage of Growing Up—and the structure of that stage is determining how you see your world—you don't necessarily know that it is happening. In other words, while you are almost always aware of states, you are almost never aware of structures. States are 1st-person, direct experiences; structures are 3rd-person, objective realities.[4]

Notice that since *structures* nearly always emerge in *stages* of development (as they do with Growing Up), we often call them "structure-stages," and this is to distinguish them from "state-stages," which refers to *states* that often emerge in *stages*, like the stages of meditation states. We've already seen that a comprehensive Waking Up meditation path generally unfolds in 5 major stages (that is, state-stages). It's true that many people don't think of Waking Up as having stages, and that's because the majority of people who have a Waking Up usually have just one major awakening, not a sequence of them. They have a profound state of Oneness experience that occurs once and then never again (which is why I often use the term "Waking Up" in a singular fashion, as if it were a single state instead of covering 5 natural states), although once is enough to change their lives irrevocably and forever. But as a one-time occurrence, it is fairly common. In fact, polls consistently show that around 60 percent of the population have had a significant Waking Up experience, an experience that lasts anywhere from a few minutes to a few hours, and then eventually fades. It's only if they take up an effective, ongoing, meditative awakening practice that those experiences will continue to unfold through a series of state-stages (in general, 5 of them).

But no matter how many Waking Up experiences individuals might have, when they have a state experience, they will definitely know it; it is indeed a direct experience that clearly enters their 1st-person awareness. In contrast, the structure-stages of Growing Up are much more like the rules of grammar, which we all use without knowing that we are using them. When individuals are at a particular stage of Growing Up, they (usually) have no idea that a particular structure-stage is governing how they interpret and experience their world. You can see states of Waking Up by looking within or introspecting, but you can look within, introspect, meditate, or contemplate all you want and you will never see a structure of Growing Up—just as you can look within right now and never see the rules of grammar that you are otherwise following so accurately.

Thus, when a person is at a particular structure-stage of Growing Up, that structure will largely govern their worldview, values, morals, and interests in the relative, manifest realm (because each one of their multiple intelligences is at one of those 6-to-8 levels of structure-stages). And yet the person is (usually) completely unaware that this is happening. This is the primary reason that these structures were discovered only about one hundred years ago. They were not discovered by any of the great meditation systems or spiritual practices precisely because they cannot be seen by looking within, meditating, or contemplating. Thus all the Great Religions are completely bereft of knowledge of the numerous stages in the process of Growing Up.

And turnabout is fair play: the modern schools of developmental psychology—which indeed discovered the major structure-stages of Growing Up around one hundred years ago—had virtually no knowledge of Waking Up or any of its practices and state-stages because they were primarily studying structure-stages of Growing Up. This means that throughout human history, if you wanted to grow or improve yourself or discover your own highest potential, you had to choose either Waking Up or Growing Up—there was no system anywhere in the world that included both of them. In other words, throughout its entire history, humanity has been practicing to be broken.

It is because states and structures are so fundamentally different that the paths of Waking Up and Growing Up are indeed so relatively independent. You can have a profound Waking Up experience (in a *state* of consciousness) at virtually any one of the stages of Growing Up (in a *structure* of consciousness). They're two radically different things, two very different types of transformation, with very different types of Wholeness. This is important, because (as we will explore later) you can be very high in Waking Up and quite low in Growing Up. And vice versa: you can be highly advanced in Growing Up without having had a single satori or Waking Up experience. Or you can have any mixture of the two. This is quite important.

As for the difference in the types of Wholeness offered by Waking Up states and Growing Up structures, we've already seen that Waking Up offers an ultimate Truth (and an infinite Wholeness) and Growing Up offers a relative truth (and a finite Wholeness). Waking Up puts us directly in touch with an infinite Reality or a Ground of All Being, which gives us a sense of "being one with everything"—what Jordan Peterson called an "absolute consciousness" that is "not disputable." But this ultimate Truth will tell us little about the realm of relative truth—the manifest, finite world of everyday life (except that we are "one with all of it"). We've already seen several times that a Waking Up will not even tell you that the earth isn't flat or that it actually circles the sun.

This is where Growing Up enters the picture, since it deals with the relative truths found in the finite realm. And one of things that it tells us is that our everyday, finite self grows, develops, and evolves to higher and higher stages of Wholeness in the finite realm, and it does so through a given number of structure-stages of development (around 6-to-8 or so). Each of these stages brings an increasing number of perspectives (from 1st person to 2nd person to 3rd person and higher), and each of them brings a greater and larger sense of self-identity (from "me" to "us" to "all of us" to "all perspectives combined and integrated"), which means a greater and greater sense of Wholeness in the finite realm.

And further, since it is the same infinite Ground of All Being that is equally present at every point in the finite realm, a person can be at any structure of Growing Up and have an authentic experience of the infinite state of Waking Up—and that infinite state of Waking Up will then be interpreted by the person's structure of Growing Up. And that's because, when it comes to states and structures, Growing Up interprets Waking Up. In other words, structures interpret states. This is especially true because the pure Waking Up experience itself is often a state of consciousness or awareness that is beyond words, symbols, and concepts; it is an ecstatically free, unqualifiable, direct, nonverbal and nonconceptual experience of a Ground of All Being, by whatever name. Because of this "nonverbal" condition, it is often called a "mindless" state (a "cloud of unknowing," Zen's "no-mind" awareness, "consciousness without an object," "divine ignorance," pure "Emptiness," "infinite abyss," and such). But, eventually, the person will come out of that direct experience—their "mind returns"—and that means that one or more of their many intelligences will begin to operate again, in order to explain the experience, give it some sort of meaning and framework, and perhaps even elaborate it into a full theology, philosophy, or metaphysics. But this requires using some sort of mind or intelligence, and that means using one or more of the dozen types of intelligences. And every one of those intelligences grows and develops through the 6-to-8 major structure-stages of Growing Up. Hence any Waking Up will be explained by Growing Up. When an individual interprets one of these peak experiences, they can use only the tools that they already have, the tools that they have already developed—and those tools have gone through some of the major 6-to-8 structure-stages of Growing Up. Thus, whatever Waking Up experience they may have, it will be interpreted by the stage of Growing Up that they are at. So one of the things that this unified Integral approach discovers is that Growing Up interprets Waking Up.

Starting with the next chapter, I will explain the 6 major structure-stages of Growing Up, with an emphasis on how they appear in the line of spiritual intelligence. Keep in mind that every person alive is going through these structure-stages of development in their own lives. And this includes the development of their own spiritual intelligence, even if they are atheist or nonbelievers or "new paradigm" advocates, since, as we saw, the products of spiritual intelligence don't have to look or sound spiritual or religious. They only have to deal with a person's ultimate concern or what they take to be an ultimate reality, the most important of the most important things in their life.

5

The Early Stages of Growing Up

As we begin this chapter, let's be clear about exactly what we are attempting to understand here. We are looking at the type of Wholeness that is involved with the pathway of Growing Up. Growing Up itself is a developmental pathway, laid down in its various stages during a million years of human evolution and still evolving today. Growing Up consists of many relatively independent lines of development—multiple intelligences—and there are thought to be around twelve of them, such as cognitive intelligence, emotional intelligence, moral intelligence, aesthetic intelligence, interpersonal intelligence, spiritual intelligence, and so on. And as different as those *lines* of development are, they all move, grow, and unfold through the same basic *levels* of development. In this chapter, we will be investigating these basic levels of Growing Up—as well as the type of Wholeness each level offers.

Although these 6 levels of Growing Up are basically similar in all the various lines of development, the way that a given level of Growing Up appears depends in many ways on the line in which it is occurring. As you can imagine, the same level will show up looking somewhat different in the cognitive line, the emotional line, the moral line, the spiritual line, and so on. Likewise, these levels will usually be given different names depending on which line is involved. Thus, for example, the same ethnocentric stage of development will be named "concrete operational" in the cognitive line (Piaget), "conventional" in the moral line (Kohlberg), "conformist" in the ego-development line (Loevinger), and "belongingness" in the needs line (Maslow). They all refer to the same level of the Growing Up process (you can see this in the similarity of the terms used).

Thus, coming up with just one name for each level of Growing Up that works for all the various lines is very difficult. This is why Integral often uses colors for each of the levels of Growing Up, especially when they are discussed in terms of their common characteristics and not just as they appear in a given line. Thus, we can say "orange cognition," "orange morals," "orange self-identity," and "orange aesthetics," where "orange" indicates the same level of altitude in all of those lines. (See figures 5.1 and 5.2 for examples.) Likewise, sometimes extremely broad terms are used—for example, "egocentric," "ethnocentric," "worldcentric," and "integrated" (and occasionally Gebser's "magic," "mythic," "rational," "pluralistic," and "integral"). These terms are generally okay, too, although the way they appear in each line does vary. So, basically, we stick with colors and a handful of general terms.

Figures 5.1 and 5.2 depict developmental lines in the columns and levels of Growing Up in the rows. Each line has its own terms for the levels of Growing Up, but these levels are standardized using Integral's color terms, at the far-left of each diagram. We call this type of diagram an "Integral psychograph," and you can represent as many different vertical lines or multiple intelligences as you wish. You can also represent your own Growing Up and indicate where you are developmentally in each line (more about that later).

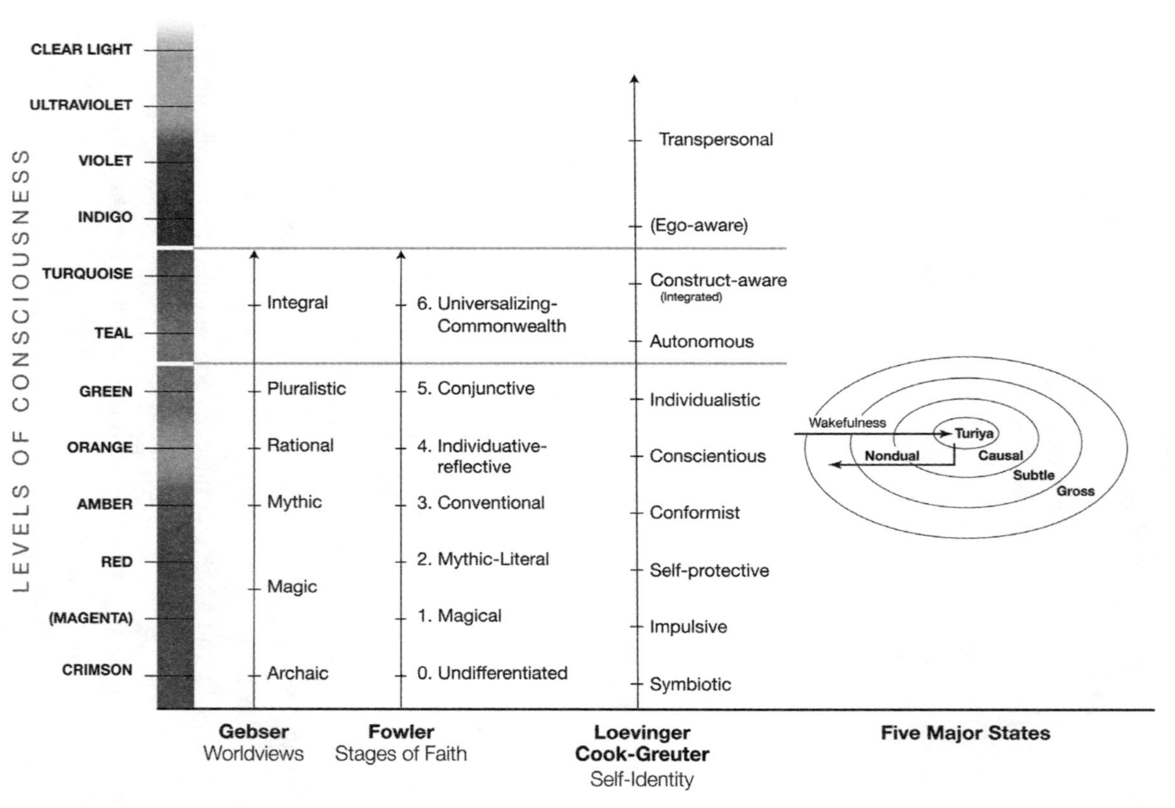

FIGURE 5.1. Structure-stages and state-stages in development.

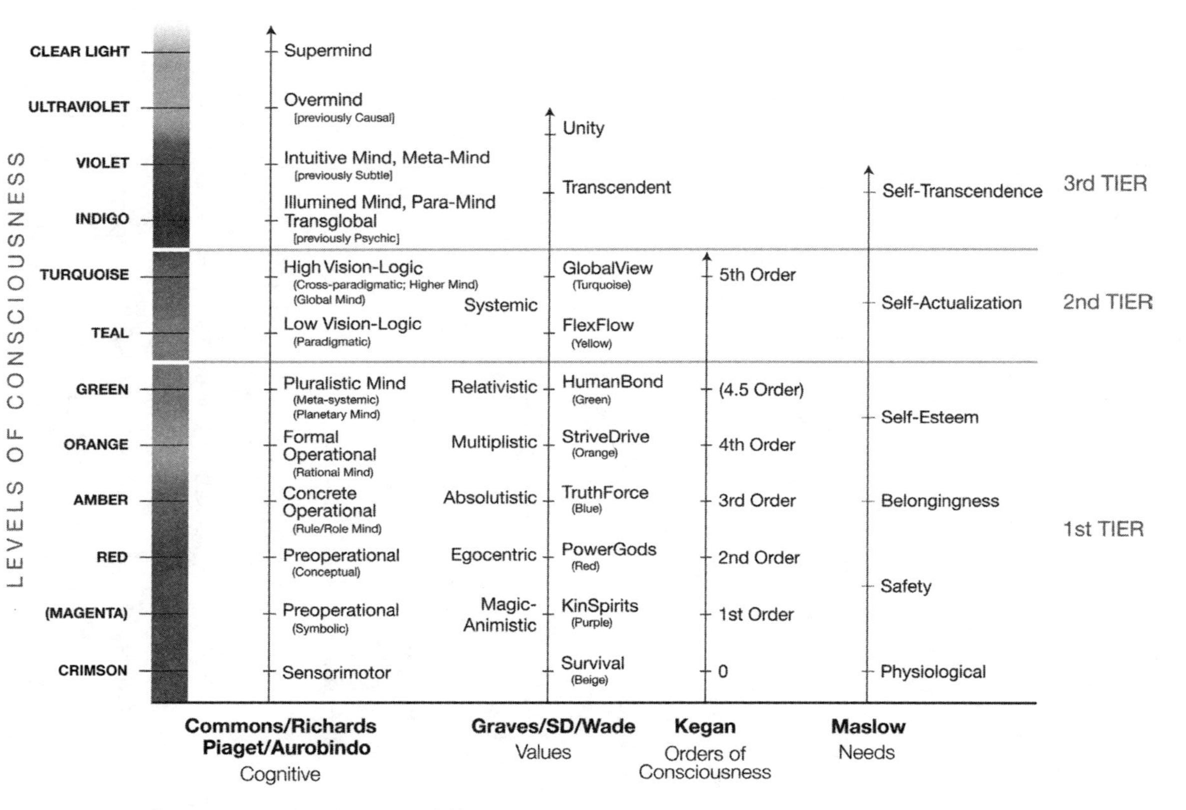

FIGURE 5.2. Some major developmental lines.

Notice that on figure 5.1, Waking Up is shown as a series of concentric circles (each circle representing a different *state*-stage of Waking Up). This is not a part of Growing Up but represents a fundamentally different pathway, Waking Up, which develops or unfolds in a relatively independent fashion (so that any circle can appear at any level or color—that is, any state of Waking Up can occur at any structure of Growing Up).

In this chapter, and continuing through chapters 6–9, I will describe in general terms 6 of the major and most common levels of development (crimson, red, amber, orange, green, and turquoise).[1] This means we will be discussing mostly the levels themselves, what these levels have in common as they appear in each line—for example, the amber level in general and not just as it appears in moral or aesthetic or needs development. We will be discussing mostly levels, not so much lines.

However, because we have been focusing on spiritual intelligence, and since we need to use some specific terms if we want to discuss any level in detail, I will be framing the discussion with an emphasis on how the various levels show up in spiritual intelligence. So, for example, we'll discuss amber in general, and then how amber shows up in spiritual intelligence.

Further, since Christianity is now the most popular religion on the planet (with over 2 billion of the world's 7.5 billion people embracing it), I am also going to present the ways that spiritual intelligence appears in Christianity at each of the 6 levels and will title each level according to the way that Jesus Christ is interpreted by that level. This does not include the various types of direct spiritual experience or Waking Up that a Christian might encounter—that's a different parameter entirely—rather these are the ways that a Christian will interpret their ultimate concern, whether or not they've had a Waking Up realization (for example, the magic level is named "Jesus as Magic Superhero," and the rational level is named "Jesus as Rational

World Teacher"). Because Christianity has, throughout its long history, touched so many people all over the planet, and because almost everybody knows at least some basic facts about Christianity, it will be instructive to see how the interpretation of Christianity varies so dramatically from level to level. Yet the fundamental aim is, like that of this book itself, to help open you to a deeper, wider, and higher understanding of your own being and awareness.

Although I will be using Christianity as an example of how these levels of Growing Up appear, keep in mind that these are stages not of a particular religion but of spiritual intelligence itself. These stages of spiritual intelligence will appear no matter the religion or object of ultimate concern: atheistic, agnostic, Hindu, theistic, Buddhist, Jewish, new paradigm, the New Atheists, nihilists, and so on.

And, one last final point: to give a sample of the extraordinary number of developmental models that have found compelling evidence for each of these stages, for each level, I have provided a table listing some of the major researchers and their names for that level (see table 1).

THE ARCHAIC-FUSION (OR CRIMSON) STAGE

TABLE 1. Equivalents to the crimson archaic-fusion stage

Researcher/system	Growing Up stage
Integral	crimson archaic-fusion
Fowler	stage 0
Freud	oceanic state
Gebser	archaic
Kegan	order 0
Kohlberg	stage 0
Loevinger	symbiotic
Maslow	physiological needs
Piaget	early sensorimotor intelligence

This is the earliest general stage of human development. Phylogenetically, it marked the evolutionary transition from the great apes to human beings proper (about a million years ago) and is basically just a bundle of physiological needs. It shows up in an infant largely as a fusion state, an almost total lack of differentiation (or lack of separation) between the infant and its immediate physical surroundings during the first six months or so after birth. The self-system—which will differentiate the self from its environment and others—has not yet formed, not to any significant degree. The infant can't tell where its body stops and the chair begins. This indeed represented a transition from apes' needs and perceptions to those of humans—so it's marked by survival needs such as hunger and thirst, sensations of pleasure/pain and warmth and cold, and early sensorimotor intelligence. It's as if this fusion state says, "You humans think you're so great, but you are actually just an animal, and you're not really any different—there's no separation—from the entire material world."

This state is sometimes called "adualism"—no dualism, no twoness, no separation—but this should be clearly differentiated from "nondualism." The difference is that adualism and nondualism are at opposite ends of the spectrum of human consciousness. The adual fusion state occurs when an organic body first starts to differentiate itself from its material environment, and at first it's not able to separate itself from those surroundings. To use the Christian form of the Great Chain of Being (matter, body, mind, soul, and spirit), it is a oneness with the lowest of those levels. The nondual state of Waking Up, on the other hand, can embrace all of those levels (it can be totally one with matter, body, mind, soul, and spirit)—it's really night and day. But there is no end to the imagination of retro-Romantic theorists who want to see this fusion or indissociation with the material realm as being a total union with Spirit and all of its manifestations. Their battle cry is "Back to the Origin!" But they confuse origin with the lowest and beginning state of evolution (that is, matter at the Big Bang), instead of the highest and beginning state of involution (that is, Spirit, all-inclusive and prior to time itself, or eternal). They confuse the lowest state of union with the highest state of union, simply because both are a type of union. And the one thing you don't want to do with spirituality is confuse the entire Chain of Being with its very lowest link.

Most of the earliest schools of psychoanalysis and psychotherapy realized that, at birth, not much of a self has yet been formed, so if things go wrong at this point, serious problems ensue—usually something like psychosis, which is the worst form of mental illness. (In psychosis, there is often a confusion or fusion of self and other, so it was natural to see psychoses as originating in disturbances at this very young age.) We now know that psychosis is mostly a neurophysiological problem, often genetic. But in any event, this early fusion stage is definitely not the origin of neuroses. Neuroses, unlike a psychoses, are caused when the self—after largely being formed—represses or denies some internal thought or impulse. Thus, a neurosis requires an active and fully formed self-system (to repress something), and the neurotic person is still in touch with reality, although they misinterpret it. With psychosis, on the other hand, the psychotic person is largely out of touch with reality (they can't tell the difference between their own body and the surrounding environment, they frequently hallucinate or fully imagine various realities, and so on).

In between these two dysfunctions (psychosis and neurosis), in terms of seriousness, are the appropriately named "borderline" (and "narcissistic") disorders, so named because these conditions are on the border between psychosis and neurosis. In psychosis, the self is not yet formed; in neurosis, the self, now largely formed and actively functioning, can turn on itself and repress aspects of its own being. In the borderline conditions, the self has not correctly or fully formed. It is having problems getting out of the fusion state. Therapists treating a client with a borderline condition consider it a real advance if the client can develop the capacity to repress material and actually produce a neurosis! These psychological problems reflect the very primitive nature of this early adual fusion state and the difficulties that humans have in getting out of it.

This state dominates the first six months of life. It can show some of its remnants in conditions like borderline disorders, but it's rarely found alone in adults, unless there is some sort of severe brain damage, dementia, advanced Alzheimer's, and so on.

In a sense, this stage is not a single stage but a culmination—namely, the culmination of the hundreds of transformations that evolution had created up to the point where the human body itself emerged. At this juncture—going back some million years or so—the human body fully embraced and contained in itself all the major emergent realities (or holons) that had ever been created since the Big Bang itself. The emerging human body fully contained quarks, atoms, molecules, cells, and higher-level systems (for example, muscular, nervous, digestive, skeletal), and transcended and included the essentials of all of the previous evolutionary stages—plant, fish, amphibian, reptile, mammal, and primate. All of those realities were still alive and very active, and their essentials were all present and contained within the emerging human body—all of which are referred to as the crimson stage, archaic stage, or Maslow's stage of physiological needs. So again, this isn't so much one stage as it is dozens of minor stages, all enfolded and encapsulated in this most basic and primitive level. (Piaget himself included six sublevels in this sensorimotor intelligence; a cat reaches sublevel 4.)

In other words, this stage represents the result of evolution and all the ways the human organism has had to adapt to thousands of variables in order to stay alive—its oxygen requirements, carefully calibrated; its food and nutrient needs, driven by a powerful hunger; its vast numbers of sensors, adjusting each moment to pleasure and pain and altering the organism accordingly; its need for water, hooked to a powerful thirst drive; the beginning of its fight, flight, or freeze mechanisms, hardwired into a reptilian brain stem; its rudimentary emotional states, wired into the mammalian limbic system. All of these (and more) are gifts from the past and represent the many prehuman realities, needs, and drives still found in today's humans, courtesy of yesterday's evolution—and all of them are the "archaic" needs that each human body still must meet on a day-to-day basis.

Thus, when a human infant first drinks milk from a mother's breast, what it is drinking is the result of 14 billion years of evolution, enfolded and presented to it. All of those factors—which were created and emerged and evolved over those 14 billion years—are summarized in this simple archaic stage with its physiological needs and its beginning sensorimotor intelligence. This stage represents everything poetically depicted in *Genesis* up to the creation of Adam and Eve.

These archaic stages represent an evolution inherited from a prehuman past, but starting at the very next stage (magic), we see the beginning of all the human realities that started to evolve as human beings themselves began to emerge, with *Homo sapiens* itself starting to show up as early as three hundred thousand years ago.

Nicholas Wade (general science editor of the *New York Times*), in his superb book *A Troublesome Inheritance*, points out that for liberal theorists (especially what I will call "Leftist humanities professors," which today means pretty much all of the humanities in academia), evolution itself was believed to fully operate in human organisms up until around fifty thousand years ago, *and then it completely stopped operating in humans and has not operated since*. At the time that this conclusion was reached (around six decades ago), no major structural brain changes could be detected in human beings after 50,000 B.C.E., and therefore evolution of human beings was thought to have ceased by that point. (In my view, the attractiveness of the belief that human evolution had stopped by 50,000 B.C.E. was dramatically increased by the emergence of the egalitarian, pluralistic, postmodern stage in development—stages 5–6—which wanted to see all humans as fully and completely equal, with none higher, more advanced, or more evolved than any other.) This has been a dogma of the Left for around five or six decades now (not that the Right does any better, but, in my view, academia is largely the province of the Left).

But the real reason that human evolution was denied by liberal theorists, Wade points out, is that the early theories of evolution applied the idea to human beings in ways that were often thoroughly inappropriate, inaccurate, and often highly bigoted and repugnant—social Darwinism being a typical example, or misuses of Nietzsche's "superman" by the Nazis. Thus all caring, decent people today do not even mention "cultural evolution" because this might imply that some cultures are more highly evolved than others. Therefore, according to these liberal theorists, we should stop applying evolution to human beings entirely—the very attempt to do so is said to be horribly prejudiced, and—as Wade points out—the very mention of "(recent) evolution in human beings" to this day might likely get you summarily fired from any Ivy League or top-notch university in the United States.

Of course, this is all deeply mistaken. It was with all good intentions, Wade notes, that evolution was so hurriedly tossed in the garbage bin when it came to humans. But the massive amount of recent research done during just the last few decades—especially in genomics and nucleic acid reproduction—makes it absolutely certain that not only did evolution continue beyond fifty thousand years ago but it is still active and operating today. (As we shall see in chapter 11, "Showing Up," evolution is occurring right now in all 4 dimensions of reality, which I call "quadrants.") It takes a courageous genius like Jürgen Habermas to write a book entitled *Communication and the Evolution of Society*, because the "evolution of society" is exactly what the Left has denied and condemned for half a century now, and on pain of having your entire career ruined, it is something that you had better deny as well.

Unless, of course, you're concerned with truth, which I take it that you are. So we'll simply notice that, starting around fifty thousand years ago (with the magic stage of Growing Up)—when evolution was supposed to have stopped entirely in human beings—evolution was actually just getting started in its deeply and profoundly and incredibly important human forms. This wasn't the point that evolution stopped in humans; it was the point that it literally exploded. It was nothing less than a Cambrian explosion in the individual and collective interiors of human beings. This was exactly when the stunningly original and brilliant forms of magic, then mythic, then rational, then pluralistic, then integral and beyond, would soon start to evolve and be laid down as products of a psychological and cultural evolution staggering in its "creative advance into novelty."[2] Evolution, in fact, was about to evolve past the early archaic stage of proto-human existence and begin to evolve and enact the truly human forms of development and evolution (magic, mythic, rational, pluralistic, integral). These were laid down, one after another, as perpetually available structures of consciousness for human beings from each emergent point forward so that every human being alive today has all of these major structure-stages of evolutionary Growing Up fully available to them. Once a stage is laid down, it remains in existence, just as the forms of atoms, molecules, and cells remain in existence once they have emerged. That same evolution—some view it as "Spirit-in-action"—is still alive and active right now, and it is this "evolutionary Love" that will continue to evolve and take us into the future, showing us eventually and quite remarkably the religion of tomorrow, as the Face of Spirit continues to unfold, producing more and more structures in time of that which is timeless, simply because "eternity is in love with the productions of time."[3]

When human beings first emerged out of this archaic ground floor, they emerged unmistakably as magicians.

THE MAGIC-POWER (OR RED) STAGE

As the self begins to emerge and form out of the archaic, crimson, adual fusion stage, it goes through several initial and still very primitive stages, on the way to the first truly civilized stage, the amber mythic or the mythic-literal stage. Two stages of these primitive stages I call "magic" (or impulsive) and "magic-mythic" (or egocentric power). The magic stage is magic proper, where human beings themselves are believed to possess magic powers—for example, they can make something real by thinking of it, or they can change something by altering a symbol of it. In the next stage—the red magic-mythic, or power stage—humans realize that they themselves cannot actually perform magical activities but various mythic figures such as Zeus, Jehovah, Apollo, or Venus can, and those mythic figures are taken to be literally real (hence the name "mythic-literal"). If human beings approach those mythic figures correctly—with, for example, a worshipful prayer—then they can get those god figures to magically do what they want on their behalf. Because of this power that humans have, this is often called "the power stage," and because this stage involves mythic beings with magic power, I also often call it the "magic-mythic" stage.

Because both of these early stages still involve a good deal of magic belief and power, I've combined them here into a "magic-power stage." In table 2, you'll see that, of the researchers who have studied these stages, over half of them give two stages, and the others give one stage (as I am doing here).

Note the prevalence of such terms as "egocentric," "impulsive," "animistic," and "magical" and the presence of a magic stage, which I am combining with the next major substage—power.[4]

TABLE 2. Equivalents to the magenta impulsive-magic and red magic-mythic power stages

Researcher/system	Growing Up stage
Integral	magenta impulsive-magic and red magic-mythic power
Commons and Richards	nominal actions
Fischer	single representational set
Fowler	magical (magic) and projective (power)
Gebser	magic
Graves	magical-animistic (magic) and egocentric (power)
Kegan	impulsive (magic) and imperial (power)
Kohlberg	naïve hedonism
Loevinger	impulsive (magic) and self-protective (power)
Maslow	safety
Selman	egocentric
Spiral Dynamics	KinSpirits (magic) and PowerGods (power)
Torbert	impulsive (magic) and opportunistic (power)
Wade	reactive (magic) and egocentric (power)

Here, at one of the very earliest recognizable stages of human evolution, the magic-power stage, the self is just starting to differentiate itself from its surrounding environment. Because self and other, mind and world, are still largely fused and confused, the self thinks that if it manipulates its own mental images and symbols, that will magically change the world as well. This is not a real paranormal capacity; it's simple "word magic," where the self believes that if it acts on the word for a thing or the image of it, that will magically alter the real thing that the word or image represents. This is the essence of all human magic, and it springs from this evolutionary stage where the young organism is learning to differentiate itself from its surroundings. It's not a real capacity; it's just the incapacity to tell these things apart, so it thinks that to manipulate one is to manipulate the other. Hence, magic!

For the most part, at this stage, the world is still a very dangerous place, and the search for power and safety in a dog-eat-dog world is paramount. Impulsive magic and egocentric power dominate this level. (These are often treated as two different stages simply because they often emerge in this order.) As I've already indicated, I have, for this introductory presentation, combined these two basic stages and treated them as one. I'll be doing this in a few places in this presentation, but only when there is a great deal of similarity between the combined stages, and treating them together greatly simplifies things. So combining them gives us a magic-power stage, similar to the stage Spiral Dynamics calls "PowerGods," a nice term since it focuses on the (magic) power of supernatural beings (mythic gods), which is an idea that is very common to this stage.

Needless to say, this plays out directly in the religious sphere. At this early red magic-power stage, there is a strong emphasis on miracles, the supernatural, and magic in general. Almost every world religion has some central elements that reflect this magical realism. This goes back tens of thousands of years, where some shamanic feats perhaps reflected real paranormal powers but many were simply magic tricks to gain power. In Christianity, Jesus can raise the dead, cure the sick, turn water into wine, heal the lame, read other people's minds, fly through the sky, walk on water. Wow! That's a truly powerful supernatural being with lots of magic power.

Children at this early magic stage of development love Saturday-morning cartoon shows, because the superhero can magically do anything—zap people with x-ray vision, walk through walls, fly through the air, and so on. That type of magical power is what is so appealing about religion to somebody at this stage—and they want those miracles to happen to them. In what is known as the "prosperity gospel" in Christianity, for example, if a person believes correctly and has enough faith, they will get that new job, get the girl, get the new car, become rich, and so on—all magically through the power of faith in Jesus Christ.

Because, at this early stage, humans are just beginning to learn how to differentiate themselves from their environment, there is still a great deal of fusion between subject and object, between self and other, and thus those realities are often fused and confused, with subjective human traits ascribed to objects—so-called animism. (Note Graves's term for this general stage: "magical-animistic.") Animism is not simply seeing nature as alive everywhere; it's seeing nature as alive everywhere with specifically human traits—the volcano explodes because it's mad at you; the sun keeps shining because of its ongoing benevolent care for you; it rains for your crops because nature is favorably responding to your sacrifices. Animism is a very humancentric, anthropomorphic view of the world.[5]

We are, in this chapter, particularly focusing on the stages of Growing Up, with an emphasis on how these levels appear in the line of spiritual intelligence, which all humans—including atheists, even the "New Atheists"—fully possess and often use. But in the next several sections, we will briefly look at the historical evolution of the major types of Waking Up, or actual spiritual experiences, which are much more rare; some individuals go through life and never have a spiritual experience of Waking Up at all. Waking Up, nonetheless, concerns ultimate truth and is profoundly important, and in these following sections we will look at the most common form of Waking Up at each of the stages of Growing Up, starting here with the red magic stage.

We have seen that any spiritual belief—or what we'll call "spiritual awareness"—is the product of the stage of Growing Up that holds the belief (that is, the *structure-stage* of spiritual intelligence) and any *state-stage* of Waking Up that might be present. In short:

Spiritual Awareness = Spiritual Intelligence × Spiritual Experience

Or in more general terms:

Spiritual Awareness = Growing Up × Waking Up

Of course, all of these are set in an overall AQAL Matrix, which is needed for a full Kosmic Address.[6] And if there isn't a Waking Up experience, then the spiritual awareness of a person is determined primarily by the Growing Up stage itself—that is, by spiritual intelligence alone (which is most commonly what happens).

In this chapter, we are primarily tracking the deep ways that the Growing Up component—magic, mythic, rational, pluralistic, or integral—contributes profoundly to spiritual awareness, because that is the component that is always present but almost never included or understood when it comes to spiritual consciousness. (Mostly it's not included because you can't see these stages by introspecting or looking within. You have to read a book like this, or a developmental studies text, to know anything about these stages of Growing Up.)

During each of the major epochs of human history, as each new Growing Up stage successively emerged and generically defined its particular epoch—paleolithic magic, Middle Ages mythic, the modern Age of Reason, postmodern pluralism, the coming Integral Age, and so on, through around 6-to-8 stages of overall growth—a few individuals at each of those stages were also having Waking Up experiences. But, as I pointed out, I will, in the midst of the discussion of each major epoch and its defining stage of Growing Up, make a few summary comments on the general types of Waking Up experiences that were the most commonly available during that particular epoch (which could be any one of the 5 major state-stages of Waking Up: gross, subtle, causal, turiya, or nondual).

In order to discuss the types of Waking Up experiences that were common, we need some sort of theory or metatheory about Waking Up experiences. As it turns out, I happen to have one. I've already introduced 5 major natural states of consciousness—namely, gross, subtle, causal, turiya or pure awareness, and turiyatita or nondual One Taste. My metatheory maintains that if a person's proximate self (or central self) has an intensified peak experience of any of those 5 major states, it results in a different type of mystical spirituality, and these types in fact match the most common types of mysticism that are found worldwide. In other words, when any of those 5 states are experienced in a conscious, immediate, direct, and intensified fashion (across a spectrum of intensity that ranges from communion to union to identity), the result is a type of mystical experience, and this spiritual experience differs according to the particular state of consciousness that is being called forth in the spiritual experience itself.

THE MAJOR TYPES OF MYSTICAL EXPERIENCE

If there is a peak experience of a direct unity (ranging from communion to union to identity) with the entire gross realm (the entire physical or natural realm), the result is a feeling of oneness with all Nature, a *Nature mysticism* (for example, a feeling of a pure interwoven unity or pure oneness with a Great Web of Life or Gaia).

The subtle state of consciousness includes states like dreaming, and in the dream state, there is no nature, no Gaia, no physical or natural realm, just a "trans-physical" or "super-natural" or "metaphysical" realm of images, fiery forms, symbols, impulses, cascading ideas, images of gods and goddesses, and various mythic forms. If there is an experience of a direct unity with this dreamlike, transcendental, subtle, supernatural Deity form, the result is a subtle *Deity mysticism*, often marked by a vast illumination or intense luminosity and feelings of oneness, love, compassion, and redemption. Because all humans are born with all 5 types of natural consciousness available to them (gross waking, subtle dreaming, causal dreamless, turiya, and turiyatita) but are originally aware of only one of them (the gross waking state), when they have a peak experience of any of the other states, those mystical experiences usually seem to have some degree of otherworldliness about them.

The next higher state, the causal state, has two major dimensions, formal and formless. It is said to be the home of the very first and the very subtlest Forms in manifestation, which the Greeks called the "archetypes" and the East calls "vasanas." Moment to moment, as Spirit gives rise to the entire universe, the very first Forms that emerge are the archetypes, and these Forms are said to be the forms on which all the other forms in the universe are based. The direct experience of these Forms results in a general *Archetypal mysticism*. For example, Jung said, "Mysticism is the experience of archetypes."[7] It's very common in Platonic and Pythagorean mysticism and in kataphatic or *saguna* (with qualities) class of mysticism. At the highest point of this causal state, the archetypal Forms themselves shade entirely into a formless, imageless, unmanifest realm said to be experienced by everybody in deep, dreamless sleep. If there is a direct, conscious experience of this dreamless, formless realm, the result is a *Formless mysticism* (or infinite Abyss mysticism). This formless realm is often called the "God beyond God," and it's actually quite common; the Cloud of Unknowing is of this type.

The 4th state or turiya (pure Awareness or I AMness) is a pure Knowing or Witnessing awareness, which itself is said to be wholly unqualifiable, beyond all categorization (including that one), radically empty or open. If the Witness (or I AMness) aspect is especially realized, the result is a pure *Consciousness-only mysticism* or *I-AMness mysticism*—also known as Unique Self, Mind-only, Absolute Consciousness without an object, Absolute Subjectivity, or True-Self mysticism. If the unqualifiable or empty or open aspect of turiya is more emphasized, the result is a pure *Emptiness mysticism*, which often combines with the previous Formless mysticism—these both are variations on the *neti, neti* (not this, not that), *apophatic, nirguna* (without qualities), *via negativa* class of mysticism.

If the 5th state or ultimate nondual state (of turiyatita) is awakened, the result is a *Nondual mysticism*—a pure Suchness, Thusness, One Taste, or ultimate Unity consciousness.

These are some of the most typical types of spiritual or mystical experiences that are elicited at each of the 5 major states of consciousness—and, as noted above, they happen to match the major types of mysticism that researchers have claimed it is possible to experience. Sophisticated researchers around the world have been aware of these major types of mysticism (although they have not seen how these Waking Up experiences are interpreted by Growing Up stages).

Take, for example, Evelyn Underhill, probably the greatest scholar-practitioner of Western mysticism. She presents four or five major state-stages of mystical development, and they correlate well with the types I have delineated. Thus, she maintains, a complete mystical development starts with *Nature mysticism* (or gross-state mysticism)—so named because a person who is at the gross waking state of consciousness expands that consciousness to include a union with all other phenomena in the gross state. This is a real union with all of Nature, but it leaves out the subtle, causal, turiya, and turiyatita states, hence there is not much "vertical" development here, just a "lateral expansion of consciousness." Still, these experiences are, as I said, a genuine union—not a Big Wholeness but a real Wholeness (a Wholeness with the entire gross realm)—and thus even one of these experiences of Nature mysticism can change a person's life profoundly and indefinitely.

Beyond a union with the gross, obvious, physical realm, there are states that are considerably higher and more inclusive. Beyond Nature mysticism, the next stage is, in Underhill's research, what she calls *metaphysical mysticism*. This includes states of archetypal recollection, contemplation and divine love, and especially a radical illumination (in the subtle states), which then deepens (in the causal) into what Underhill calls a *divine ignorance* and even "cessation," which is an indication, as I would put it, of a moving into a causal Formless mysticism or even into turiya or pure Awareness. (Turiya is a divine ignorance because turiya or the Witness is that which knows all objects but cannot itself be known—it is the Knower, not anything known; it's the Seer, not anything seen; and the Knower itself is radically unqualifiable, unnameable, and unknowable, and is thus itself experienced as divine ignorance, which is Zen's "don't know mind," pure unspeakable Emptiness or Openness.)

Finally, for Underhill, spiritual development moves into forms of *divine mysticism*. She also notes that this stage commonly begins with the "dark night of the soul," a concept introduced by the extraordinary St. John of the Cross (St. Teresa's mentor). Many people think that the "dark night" means a period of painful searching before a person finds God and true spiritual liberation, and the term can be used that way. But for St. John, it means almost the opposite: it's the state that occurs *after* you have had a profound Spirit experience in which you directly know radical Freedom. When that God passes or fades (as it initially will), the lack of that state of radical love and bliss can leave you in what amounts to a state of real hell—and *that* is the real dark night. It's one thing to have never found God; it's quite another to have lost a God once found. Having the experience of an authentic metaphysical mysticism, a person is indeed plunged into genuinely divine states of love and bliss and radical freedom; but in order to progress to a state of permanent union, that previous state has to be let go of, and the pain of that can be the darkest of the dark nights imaginable.

The pain of the dark night is the pain of looking for a truly timeless and eternal reality in states that are only of temporal and finite being, no matter how glorified—as one mystic put it, "Fussing about in the world of time looking for the timeless." This is overcome by a direct realization of the truly infinite and eternal, ever-present Ground of All Being, or Underhill's final state of *ultimate Unity consciousness*, which is not earned by diligent practice or work, but, according to most Western mystical schools, is simply given to all by Grace—it is fully *given* to you, right here and right now, and not something earned, found, or discovered. The Eastern traditions would simply say it is *sahaja*, a totally spontaneous, uncaused, ever-present reality. Either way, *tat tvam asi*—"Thou art That." Or as the universal children's game says, "You're it!" And you are, indeed, It—radically one with the infinite and eternal Ground of All Being, and hence one with everything, something the Sufis call the "Supreme Identity." As one Zen master put it, "A human being's real body is the entire universe." And that turiyatita is what you finally, fully, and truly are.

THE WILBER-COMBS LATTICE

These major types of mysticism, as I noted, have been recognized by sophisticated theorists all over the world, East and West. A study of a complete course of contemplative development (from Underhill to Daniel P. Brown to Dustin DiPerna) shows us that these are not just five types of mysticism, but they are also five stages (or state-stages) in a full course of mystical or meditative unfolding. Further, these states are not dogmatic beliefs, mythic claims, theological constructs, or some conceptual hunches but rather direct, immediate, 1st-person experiences, so that individuals can check out the reality of these states directly for themselves—they are a knowledge by acquaintance, not mere knowledge by description. (Later on, you'll be able to judge this directly in your own case, when we go through various exercises that will allow you to directly experience some of the very highest of these states yourself—especially the two highest or ultimate states, turiya (the Witness) and turiyatita (One Taste).

Now—to finish this brief mystical metatheory—since the average individual today has potential access to all 6 major stages of Growing Up that have emerged thus far in evolution, a person at any one of those 6 stages can experience any one of the 5 major Waking Up states. That is, any stage of Growing Up can experience any state of Waking Up. This fact is now generally understood and accepted and is represented by the Wilber-Combs Lattice (see figure 5.3).

Horizontally, across the top of the diagram, are labels for the 5 major states of consciousness, which also represent the major realms of Waking Up experience and thus the 5 major types of mysticism: Nature mysticism, Deity mysticism, Formless mysticism, I-AMness mysticism, and Nondual Unity mysticism. Vertically, along the left side are labels for the 7 major stages of Growing Up, which govern how a person's world is interpreted and experienced (including their

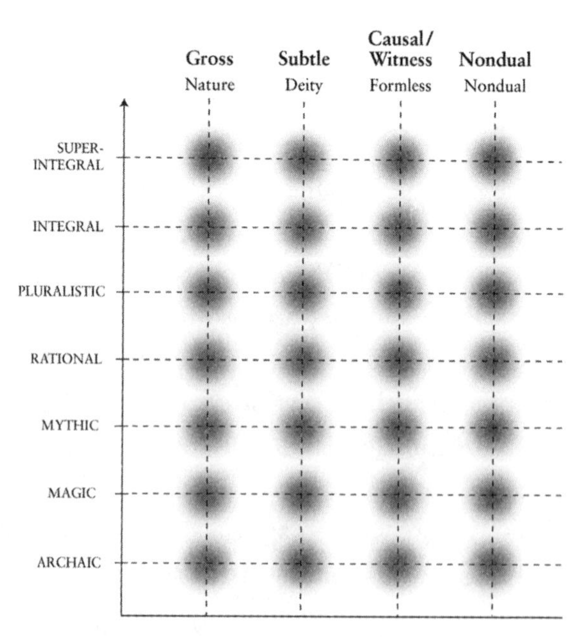

FIGURE 5.3. The Wilber-Combs Lattice.

spiritual world or Waking Up realization). Thus, across the top run the states of Waking Up, and up the side run the structures of Growing Up.[8]

Now, in this metatheory section, this is the most important point for you: In today's world, most people have potential access to every one of the cells in figure 5.3, since evolution has unfolded that far at this time.[9] This means that the aim of a life well lived is, starting in the cell at the lower left, where you are located at birth (namely, the adual, archaic structure in the gross, physical, waking state), to move, grow, and develop from there to the cell in the upper right (namely—the One Taste state-stage experienced by the Integral structure-stage). That growth would give you access to the most complete and fulfilled life that you could possibly experience. It would be, in short, the map of a life well lived. (The fact that people today have potential access to all the cells in the Wilber-Combs Lattice doesn't mean that everything is sweetness and light, because something can go wrong at every stage or level—thus the more levels, the more things that can go wrong. We'll address this when we get to Cleaning Up.)

So, for now, we note that the average human being today has potential access to all 7 major stages of Growing Up and at least 5 major states of Waking Up, however functional or dysfunctional they may be. Given the fact that few people at archaic will have peak or plateau experiences, this means that there are 6 major structures of Growing Up (magic, mythic, rational, pluralistic, integral, super-integral), each of which can experience any of the 5 major states of Waking Up, giving a total of thirty types of structure/state experiences, or thirty types of spiritual awareness (which, as explained above, is defined as Growing Up × Waking Up). We have significant evidence that every one of those thirty types of spiritual awareness are fully available today. But we'll be focusing on experiencing only the highest one or two of them in both of those pathways, so there's not nearly so many to worry about.

So that—the Wilber-Combs Lattice—is the metatheory put in a brief form.

Let me mention that the reason why I am not promoting all 5 major types of spiritual experience is that, in the latter part of this book, I will be carefully and directly addressing the two highest states—turiya and turiyatita—and I will be working to give you an immediate experience of both. In other words, although we will not be dwelling on all 5 types of direct spiritual experience, we will be spending a fair amount of time working to experience the two highest or ultimate states of Waking Up itself—the very heart of Waking Up—and that's what is most crucial for this particular presentation.

But none of that will give you an understanding of the stages of Growing Up, which is why, in this chapter and chapters 6–9, we will be walking through each of those Growing Up stages carefully, giving you exactly that understanding.

As we scan our evolutionary past, we find that when human beings (*Homo sapiens*) first began their evolutionary development on this planet some three hundred thousand years ago, none of the higher stages of Growing Up were yet available—humans were at the archaic stage, with the magic stage just beginning. In the following years, the major stages of Growing Up emerged, evolved, and became a permanent acquisition of the human condition, so that every human being that followed had the possibility of developing through each of the major structure-stages of Growing Up that had evolved by that point in time and to do so in the same order that they were originally laid down. Each time a new structure-stage was laid down, human beings had yet another level through which they could enact and experience their world—including their spiritual world.

As for the various states of Waking Up, access to each of them (during a particular era) tended to depend upon the degree of evolution through the states that had occurred in a given culture by that time. Most of the states of consciousness are indeed just that—states of consciousness. But humans are not born with an easy, conscious access to all of them. They are born with conscious access only to the waking state; and thus all the higher states are not directly realized in consciousness (a typical person dreams, for example, but doesn't lucid dream). In order for such realization to occur, a person has to voluntarily undertake various practices and exercises (and receive pointing-out instructions), and these were almost always obtained from one of the Great Traditions (or Paths of Liberation) that were present in their culture.

If we track these Great Traditions over evolutionary time, we find that conscious access to each of these Waking Up states tended to unfold historically in the order that those states are usually listed: that is, access to these 5 states evolved from gross to subtle to causal to turiya to turiyatita—giving rise, in order, from shamans to yogis to saints to sages to siddhas, anchored respectively in Nature mysticism, Deity mysticism, Formless mysticism, I-AMness mysticism, and nondual Unity mysticism. So what the Wilber-Combs Lattice shows is that, as evolution proceeded in the Growing Up path, it started at the archaic structure-stage, and then new and higher levels of consciousness (magic to mythic to rational to pluralistic to integral) successively evolved through which humans could approach and enact their world. And simultaneously, access to the various states of consciousness started with the gross waking state, and then proceeded to grow and evolve through access to successively higher states (subtle to causal to turiya to turiyatita).

THE MAGICAL NATURE MYSTICISM OF SHAMANISM

We have seen that, using the Wilber-Combs Lattice as our framework, human beings began their history at the lowest (archaic stage) and leftmost (gross state) position possible (that is, the lowest cell on the left)—none of the other cells were consciously available then. So the earliest type of spirituality that we tend to see in human evolution is shamanism—a type of Nature mysticism interpreted largely through the magic stage.

The shamanic view often saw reality as divided into three major realms: the lower world, the middle world (this world), and the upper world—and the shaman understood the secret unity of these worlds and could travel to all three of them. (This unity of the three worlds is a direct result of the Nature-mysticism type of spiritual experience, carried out—according to the intensity scale from communion to union to identity—mostly at the communion degree. That's why you don't hear, in the shamanic literature, of any state resembling a strong identity degree of the *unio mystica* type.) The core of shamanism included the shamanic journey or "soul flight," in which, because of initial forays into the subtle realms, the awareness of the shaman could "fly" or "travel" to any of these three worlds due to shamans' unique understanding of their interwoven nature—not to mention the adoption of a "subtle body" that could do the flying. You could think of these journeys as similar to lucid dreams, since that's essentially what they were (that is, a waking-state access to a subtle, dream-state realm).

Remember, these were the very first voyages to higher, alternate states and realms that had ever been undertaken by human beings. This means that, as far as we can tell, this was the first time in 14 billion years that any holon anywhere in the Kosmos managed to break through the common sensorimotor world and began to explore the further reaches of higher states in the spectrum of consciousness. So we can see these ventures as being somewhat crude and a bit wobbly, as all first starts are; but we should also recognize that they were, above all else, breathtakingly pioneering and deeply heroic. And thus, for all the "childish" characteristics that we might ascribe to this stage—after all, as humankind's very first venture in this realm, it is by definition "immature"—we should never forget that we are standing here, truly, in the presence of greatness.

The benefits of shamanic journeying included having subtle-state visions (engaged specifically by vision quests), discovering one's power animal and subtle spirit-guide, and—especially when done by the shaman or medicine person—retrieving various types of medicine said to possess curative or healing capacities for many types of illnesses (ayahuasca is still a great favorite of Westerners). Shamanic journeys also included various experiences of luminosity or spiritual light (luminosity is a typical characteristic of the subtle state).

However, there is very little evidence that shamans accessed the causal, turiya, or turiyatita states, as Roger Walsh, in his superb *The World of Shamanism*, makes very clear, using exactly that terminology.[10] Shamanism is best understood as a communion with the subtler aspects of the gross realm and a beginning entry into the subtle states themselves (which yogis would soon bring to an intense peak)—and these subtler states were interpreted through magic stage of evolution, which had recently emerged. In short, it was a type of magic Nature mysticism (just as much shamanism came from the magic structure as from Nature mysticism). The heavy influence of the magic stage on shamanism can be seen in the widely acknowledged existence of trickery and magic deceptions practiced by many shamans. But in most cases, these "tricks" were not immoral or even intentionally deceptive; the shaman simply saw the world as magical in nature, and thus acted as if that were actually the case, helping it along if necessary with apparent "trickery."

SUMMARY

We pick up the story of the evolution of the stages of Growing Up with a continuation of the discussion of the red magic structure itself, because when humans first emerged from their archaic-stage fusion with nature, they indeed first emerged as magicians.

We noted that, during the red magic epoch, the typical spiritual belief, which was contributed mostly by the magic stage itself, involved a type of animism present in shamanism. It sees Nature as alive and full of intentionality and agency. Nature is indeed all of that, but the traits ascribed to Nature were not the Nature-centric versions of those traits; they were human-centric, anthropomorphic, and egocentric (in keeping with the typical characteristic of this magic-egocentric stage). Although, in some sense, there is a type of unity that is given with this worldview, it results more from magic indissociation and undifferentiation than from a genuine holistic, integrated, or truly unified worldview.

We especially noted that, at this stage of Growing Up, because the subject and object are in many ways still fused (or poorly differentiated), people believe that altering the subject will alter the object, hence they believe that the subject and object are magically connected (which is why this stage is often termed "magic"). At this stage, the world is seen as superstitious and miraculous, drenched in magic and miracles—an enchanted world, even if dangerous and threatening. As in the practice of Voodoo or Santería, if you make a doll representing a real person and stick a pin in the doll, the real person will be magically hurt. Or if you do a rain dance, nature will be forced to rain. Change the subject, and you will change the object (change the mental image of a thing, and you directly change the thing). This magic is indeed very animistic and egocentric. The magic worldview is present-moment focused, impulsive (another common name for this stage), and often power driven (as a realistic response to a very dangerous world). It looks for miracles (or magic) in many situations and employs special rituals, ceremonies, and spells to directly bring about those miracles. This is what we mean when we say that when human beings first emerged, they emerged as magicians.

For a Christian at this stage, Jesus Christ is the premier magician and magic superhero. He can perform miracles whenever he wants—including walking on water, raising the dead, turning water into wine, healing the sick, curing the lame, teleporting and flying through the air, raising himself from the dead, seeing the past and the future, reading minds. If I believe in Jesus with sufficient faith, I will magically get the items that I ask Jesus for—a job, a new car, more money, or success in general. Prayer is magically capable of bringing about anything that is prayed for, if the prayer is performed with sufficient faith. This stage is usually very "consequentialist," in that the amount of success that a person experiences in this life (economic, romantic, work, financial) is a direct consequence of the degree of faith in magic Jesus Christ.

A surprisingly common version of this magical Christianity is seen in snake-charmer sects. The idea comes from passages in the Bible that indicate that a poisonous snake would not, indeed could not, bite or harm a person of true faith. So these sects actually practice handling rattlesnakes as a way to evidence their real faith. In fact, the fairly young leader of a large U.S. branch of these practitioners was killed in recent history—by a rattlesnake.

This is not to say that there are no such things as miracles or that no real paranormal events exist. In fact, several meta-analyses of tests of paranormal capacities (ESP, clairvoyance, precognition) have concluded that the existence of these paranormal events is "virtually certain." I totally agree. The point is not that real magic doesn't exist; the point is that most of the time when human beings think that it exists, it really doesn't—and that belief can indeed kill you. But all of us, deep down, have some bit of us that does believe in magic; and we do so because every one of us began this life believing that magic existed—and that we ourselves could perform it—and we continued to believe that until it became genuinely clear that we could not. We finally let go of that false belief, but that doesn't mean that we don't believe that there are at least some amazing beings somewhere that still possess that magic capacity.

Jesus Christ, for example.

6

The Mythic-Literal (or Amber) Stage

There are an enormous number of researchers who have found evidence for the existence of the extremely common mythic stage (see table 3). Note in particular the terms *mythic*, *conformist*, *absolutistic*, *ethnocentric*, and *traditional*.

Since the mind has now developed the ability to take the role of an other, how one socially fits in and conforms with one's fellow human beings comes to the fore in this mythic-membership world.

As magic starts to die down, it doesn't completely disappear at first but is transferred to a host of mythic and supernatural figures—gods and goddesses and elemental spirits—and although you yourself can no longer perform magic, these god-figures can. And further, they will perform magic on your behalf if you know how to approach them correctly (for example, with a special type of prayer; or animal sacrifice, which was and still is quite common; or even human sacrifice and cannibalism, which historically was not unheard of—we have empirical proof of cannibalism with some native tribes in the southwest United States, for example).

TABLE 3. Equivalents to the amber ethnocentric mythic-membership stage

Researcher/system	Growing Up stage
Integral	amber ethnocentric mythic-membership
Commons and Richards	primary actions and concrete operations
Fischer	representational mapping and system
Fowler	mythic-literal and conventional
Gebser	mythic
Graves	absolutistic/saintly
Kegan	interpersonal/traditional
Kohlberg	law and order
Loevinger	conformist
Maslow	belongingness
Selman	reflective roles
Torbert	diplomatic
Wade	conformist

Cognition becomes more complex at this stage, moving from simple magic (which tends to operate mostly in the present, desires immediate gratification, and is basically focused through a 1st-person/egocentric perspective) to much more sophisticated mythic forms, which tend to involve complex narratives, stories, and belief systems, and is essentially focused through a 2nd-person/ethnocentric perspective (hence Gebser's magic stages are followed by mythic ones).

Human beings at this stage believe their myths to be literally true. Zeus really exists. Moses really parted the Red Sea. Lao Tzu really was nine hundred years old when he was born. Lot's wife really was changed into a pillar of salt. This is why James Fowler calls this stage of spiritual intelligence the “mythic-literal” stage (which has its roots in the previous “PowerGods” stage and develops into this stage of a conventional, conformist, absolutistic belief in those realities).

THE LITERAL MEANING OF ORIGINAL MYTHS

Unlike the way many modern Western thinkers want to see them, myths are not profound metaphors or analogies with deep meanings—they are simply, literally, exactly what they say they are—accounts of historical events: God really did rain locusts down on the Egyptians; Christ really was born of a biological virgin; Elijah really did go straight to heaven in his chariot at death; Lot’s wife really was turned into a pillar of salt; and so on: there is nothing deeply metaphoric about any of that, it’s simply mythic literal.

Religions that take the myths to be absolutely and literally true are often called “fundamentalist,” and virtually all fundamentalist religions have roots in this amber mythic stage. The fundamentalist myths are taken as the core of the *absolute* truth, as seen from this stage. And *absolute* here does not mean some sort of ultimate Truth; it means that the truth presented here is taken to be absolutistically true, empirically real, and unerring. This is why pioneering genius Clare Graves called this stage “absolutistic.” Questioning or doubting the absolute inerrancy of the religion is regarded as pure blasphemy or heresy by virtually all spirituality at this level. This is one of the things that makes moving beyond this stage so difficult—to give up the mythic beliefs is literally to lose one’s soul and burn forever in hell. This stance, needless to say, does not support a self-questioning and critical attitude, and so when the next stage—which involves the emergence of rational science—comes into being, a ferocious battle between mythic religion and rational science is primed to occur (although, of course, it does not have to be that way; but given the absolutistic nature of this stage, it usually is).

The worst aspect of this "science versus religion" battle is that it identifies science with rationality and religion with just this fundamentalist-mythic stage of Growing Up, ignoring entirely Waking Up, which is never discussed in the argument (and ignoring as well the fact that the rational stage itself has its own form of spiritual intelligence, which you can see in any of the many "New Paradigms"). If we want to identify religion as dealing with the mythic-literal aspects of spirituality, then placing it primarily at this stage is fine, more or less. But if by *religion* we mean "spiritual intelligence" in general, then it is a developmental line (one of the multiple intelligences) that is present at every level of Growing Up—including the rational level, where science deals with empirical, objective truth and its spiritual intelligence deals with any ultimate concern or ultimate reality, both of which are definitely present at the orange rational level. The typical form of this argument—"It's just a higher (orange) rational science versus that idiotic childish (amber) mythic religion"—is idiotic in almost every conceivable way.[1]

We've seen that absolutistic beliefs usually come from this mythic stage, which is, relatively speaking, a fairly low stage of Growing Up. This can happen in one of two ways: (1) you can evolve and arrive at this absolutistic stage in your own growth, or (2) you can regress to it from a higher stage. (Your being at this stage means that all, or at least a significant portion, of your proximate or central self is identified with this stage.) As for (2), whenever your belief system—whatever its nature and from whatever higher stage—is held in a fanatical and zealous fashion, and with such an absolutistic faith that it becomes virtually unquestionable, then you indeed tend to regress to this absolutistic stage. After all, with that ferociously absolutistic attitude, you feel really at home. When science becomes scientism, when Marxism becomes a fundamentalist religion, and the same with feminism, racism, or sexism—beliefs become endowed with a mythic-literal absolutism. The belief that they have the one and only

Truth is indeed just a myth—but it is taken very seriously, very literally, as it were. There is a premium on conformity with this absolutely believed truth—in fact, many psychological models call this stage the "conformist" stage. "Mythic membership" is also a good description of this stage, as are "absolutistic" and "ethnocentric" (your tribe, and only your tribe, has the ultimate truth).

A mythically interpreted subtle God itself tends to be full of magic power, and the major role of human creatures—at this mythic stage—is figuring out how to act toward this God so as to fulfill its commandments and covenants, or how to please this God so as to receive some of its magic boons. In its most intense forms, a chosen people (a deeply ethnocentric notion, which is in keeping with this level) is handed the one and only absolute Truth from the one and only God, and their deeply ethnocentric attitude to the rest of the world is some form of jihad—which means to convert, coerce, torture, or kill infidels until they accept the one and only true God. The intensity of jihad runs from the gentlest version (missionary conversion) to more forceful forms (attempted coercion) to the most brutal versions (torture and death for all unbelievers). It is astonishing that, in all of these cases, their jihad is backed by the belief that this group of people—and only this group—is a chosen people who have the absolute sanction of nothing less than the ultimate God of the universe. (This profoundly *ethnocentric* belief structure comes almost entirely from the amber mythic stage of Growing Up, no matter what state of Waking Up, if any, a person might be experiencing.)

If any Waking Up elements are present, they are often an awakening to a broad range of subtle dreamlike states (in a Deity mysticism). Since the subtle state is also said to be the source of dreams, consciously awakening to that state is very like what we today would call a "lucid dream." And lucid dreams change everything.

First, let me say something about the Growing Up structure that would have interpreted that subtle Waking Up state, because these "relative" states of Waking Up (that is, gross, subtle, and causal) especially need to be seen in light of what is interpreting them. Evolution at this stage had indeed, in a leading-edge way, transformed upwardly from egocentric-magic to ethnocentric-mythic. Whether that transformation was good or bad depends largely upon the direction from which you look at it. From the egocentric level, the ethnocentric level is a major step up and a truly significant advance. It introduces the extensive capacity to take the role of an other (a truly 2nd-person perspective), thus expanding human identity from small egocentric clans and tribes to megatribes and much larger ethnocentric societies, and increasing the degree of care and love that one group of humans can extend to others (remember that, according to Carol Gilligan, this ethnocentric stage is named not "selfish" but "care"). For this reason, this stage should always be included (or more technically, "transcended and included") in any healthy development in today's world.

But looked at from the higher view of orange worldcentric rationality (the next major stage), this amber ethnocentric stage is something of a nightmare. Humanity is in the slow and painful process of being able to join together, into social collectives, one human being after another human being after another—from extremely small clans (forty people at most), to bigger tribes (a hundred people), to small villages (thousands of people), to larger towns (tens of thousands), to major cities (hundreds of thousands), to massive empires (millions of people), and eventually to a staggeringly huge global village (of some 7–8 billion people). Humanity was not born loving its neighbor (or more than a small clan of them); it had to grow and evolve into that capacity for care and a social structure that would hold it, and from all indicators this was a very long and difficult road. At amber ethnocentric, humanity was, so to speak, right in the middle of that growth—it had hooked together many tribes into early city-states on the way to extremely large empires and finally to a worldcentric global village. At this mythic stage, it had gone from "me" to "us"—but it still hadn't gone from "us" to "all of us"—it had not yet gone from ethnocentric to worldcentric. It still divided the world into "us versus them," and "them" (the "Other") was inherently the enemy—they are not to be trusted; they are to be hated; they are infidels, apostates, and unbelievers; and they must either be converted or erased.

Thus, in the great spectrum of Growing Up, this is the great in-between realm—the ethnocentric "us" in between egocentric "me" and worldcentric "all of us"—that would generate the greatest source of hatred, murder, slavery, warfare, and all-around brutality than any other period in all humankind's history. Wherever and whenever it appears, this mythic stage absolutistically divides the world into "us versus them" and then often attempts to wreak havoc on "them." This occurred, not just during the historical period that we are now looking at, but throughout all subsequent history, because everybody is born at square one and has to develop through all the levels of Growing Up that have emerged thus far, and from that time in history forward, an amber ethnocentric level was available to all. Thus, even in the twentieth century, it was Hitler's ethnocentric racism that led to the murders of some thirteen million people (including six million Jews as "Other"); believable estimates put the number of Stalin's Gulag murders at 1.7 million and the number murdered during Mao Tse-tung's "cultural revolution" at close to 1.5 million—all of them driven by an ethnocentric chosen people who had absolute truth.

Since the vast number of the Great Religions were born in this amber ethnocentric "in-between" period, religion itself often carried forward this brutality. Even in the modern and postmodern eras of worldcentric rationality and pluralism, the movements that engaged in truly barbaric and murderous actions were those that, if they had not started at this amber stage, regressed to it, treating their own ideas as a fundamentalist and absolutistic religion, with all unbelievers and apostates deserving anything from disregard to intense violence. At this ethnocentric mythic stage, humanity had reached the point where it could expand its social boundaries from an egocentric "me" to an ethnocentric group or "us." The boundaries expanded enough to include dozens or even hundreds of other tribes but not enough that it could worldcentrically include all tribes and reach a universal level of inclusion, and thus desire to treat *all* humans fairly, "regardless of race, color, sex, gender, ethnicity, or religious creed." And thus, throughout this great "in-between" period, there might be a degree of love within the megatribes, and vicious brutality between them.

Yet year by year, humanity demonstrated less and less violence—and this corresponded *precisely* with the ever-increasing growth of humanity's social boundaries to include more and more human beings, until virtually the entire human race was worldcentrically included, and then it became a widely valued ideal to treat *all* humans with care and respect, regardless of the color of their skin, their sex, or their ethnicity. (Remember that Gilligan called this worldcentric stage not "care" but "universal care.")

Yet, as we just noted, once a stage has emerged, it remains in existence, and thus the amber ethnocentric level—once activated—would eventually, in the modern world, drive everything from the Holocaust to the Gulag to worldwide terrorism. So, at this point in the narrative, we are still in this great "in-between" period, and the "in-between" is often hell.

A MYTHIC SUBTLE STATE

At this time in the Growing Up pathway, the majority (or at least a plurality) of people had moved to the amber mythic stage, while around one-third or so remained at the magic stage, and a very small number pushed ahead into an orange rational-modern stage. And from any of those Growing Up stages, an individual could have a variety of Waking Up experiences—experiences of a gross-state Nature mysticism (access to which had already emerged during the previous magic era), or a subtle-state Deity mysticism (access to which fully emerges during this mythic era), or for a few at the leading edge, a higher causal-state Formless mysticism (access to which would fully emerge at the next major era, or orange)—with the most common and most sanctioned form of advanced spirituality being a mythic-stage interpretation of a subtle-state Deity, or simply a mythic Deity religion. The subtle-state elements (from the Waking Up dimension) make this Spirit a subtle-state Spirit indeed, a Spirit often felt to be composed of subtle, transcendental, dreamlike, otherworldly, supernatural, metaphysical qualities. The mythic elements (from the Growing Up dimension) interpret this subtle-state (Waking Up) Spirit as being the possession of a chosen people, ethnocentric, mythic literal, conformist, and absolutistic. That's the subtle-dream state interpreted by mythic.

But then there is lucid dreaming, and that really does change everything. Even if many of the specifics of a mythic-Deity religion were first delivered by individuals who were indeed awakened to the subtle state—essentially just like a lucid dream—for those who have had lucid dreams, reality has shifted dramatically. First of all, note that the typical dream is a largely unconscious process. The person dreaming has no idea they are dreaming; everything that happens in the dream is outside of their control—they are simply bashed and buffeted by often strange if intensely vibrant elements. But with a lucid dream, the person knows that they are dreaming; they are fully aware of that fact. Moreover, in the dream, if they want something, all they have to do is think of it. Want to fly? Just think that thought, and you are automatically flying. Want a huge buffet? Just think that, and a luscious banquet is all yours. Sex? Give it a thought, it's available. Want to see God? Be careful what you wish for. . . .

People who lucid dream are seeing a very different reality, and they know it. It's a reality that is true in the subtle, dream state but not true in the gross, waking state. Thus they can become hugely visionary, because they can see their thoughts materialize in the subtle realm but not in the waking, gross realm. So they can start yelling and pushing at the gross realm to get with the picture and help to bring this dreamed vision about. In other words, they can advocate for changes in the gross realm that will finally match the changes they have seen in the subtle. They can become prophets, seers, visionaries—those through whom higher realities speak. If, in their waking state, they perform some religious practice or have intuited some sort of Divine reality and they wish for that reality to be present while in the subtle dream, they will eventually experience some version of it (at this mythic stage of Growing Up, it's usually a Deity mysticism of subtle-stage Waking Up). But they will come down from that mountain and tell people what they have seen, and what the people themselves can see, too, if they but believe. And all of this, at that time, was usually interpreted through a mythic structure.

At the mythic era in human evolution, the subject had evolved from the red magic stage to the amber mythic stage in the Growing Up dimension, and the most common state of Waking Up that was consciously experienced at that time had evolved from the gross realm (of Nature mysticism) to the subtle realm (of Deity mysticism)—in short, a mythically interpreted Deity mysticism. Those who did not have a significant Waking Up experience itself—that is, most people—had only their spiritual intelligence (in Growing Up) with which they formed a mythic-literal conception of Deity without any direct experience of such.

And keep in mind that every human being alive today will automatically grow and evolve through the major stages of Growing Up that are available (crimson, red, amber, orange, green, turquoise), but whether or not a person has a direct, conscious, awakened, spiritual peak experience of a particular state of Waking Up (gross, subtle, causal, turiya, turiyatita) is, to a large degree, a matter of voluntary choice and practice. Individuals don't choose to Grow Up; all they have to do is keep living and they will generally keep Growing. But individuals do have to choose to Wake Up. Unlike Growing Up, Waking Up is not automatically given to humans but for the most part is the result of voluntary and often strenuous practices and exercises. These practices are usually ones that the Great Traditions have discovered to be especially effective in awakening a particular higher state of being and awareness—that is, a particular state of Waking Up (an expanded peak access to the gross, subtle, causal, turiya, or turiyatita).

Thus, although the major states of consciousness are present from birth—all humans wake, dream, sleep, have an implicit Witnessing awareness, and have an ultimate Ground of Being—nonetheless, no human is automatically given full conscious access to all of those states. Humans are originally given a full consciousness only of the gross, waking state—which is where their state-identity begins at birth. Apart from that, human beings have to take up a deliberate path of spiritual awakening (and undertake specific voluntary practices and yogic exercises and receive pointing-out instructions) in order to move consciousness from an identity with the gross realm to an identity with any of the higher states (subtle, causal, witnessing, nondual)—which gives rise to a Nature mysticism, a Deity mysticism, a Formless mysticism, an I AMness mysticism, or a Nondual Unity mysticism—all of which are varieties of Waking Up (or Wholeness) spirituality. And, no matter which variety of Waking Up spiritual experience arises, it will be interpreted according to the stage of Growing Up that has the experience (crimson-archaic to turquoise-integral). And while everybody will automatically advance to some degree through the available stages of Growing Up, only a relatively small number will undertake the voluntary practices that will move them into a genuinely conscious experience and awakening of any of the higher states of Waking Up.

We should note that this mythic-ethnocentric stage of development is, in general, the most common stage of Growing Up found today. Robert Kegan's research has shown that, as he puts it, "some 3 out 5 people do not make it beyond this stage." In other words, some 60 percent of the world's population are at the mythic-ethnocentric stage (or lower). (A person is said to be at the mythic-ethnocentric stage if the average altitude of all their multiple intelligences—their "center of gravity"—is at amber or amber/orange.)

This fact signals perhaps the most grievous, threatening, and deleterious state of affairs that humanity faces today. With a majority of the world's population still at an ethnocentric "us versus them" altitude, the chance for genuine human solidarity and authentic world peace and harmony is close to zero. In our interiors, most of us are still a collection of megatribes, and thus most of us are intensively associated with different and conflicting identities, value systems, general ideals, and ethical drives—much like hundreds of Hatfields and McCoys—split and fragmented and utterly unable to reach a unified harmony and caring agreement with each other.

A CONVEYOR BELT

For the most part, religion is not helping with this issue. In fact, with many religions still operating from this ethnocentric, mythic-literal level, they simply exacerbate the problem. The only cure for this, as far as I can see, would be to implement what could be called a "conveyor belt" of spirituality, where the major religions present how their religion and its basic tenets would look from each of the major stages of Growing Up (as I am doing in this book with Christianity). *People are going through these stages in any event*, whether they know it or not, *so we might as well tell them about it in the first place*. And with a plan clearly laid out for the religious seeker to take up a full path of Growing Up—using the levels of their own refurbished religion as a guidebook—the world's religions would become a source of authentic and genuine social transformation (magic to mythic to rational to pluralistic to integral) instead of what they mostly are today, which is a source of arrested development at some of the lowest and most primitive levels of growth and development (magic and mythic). Bless them each and every one, but there it is.

If a conveyor belt were in place, and you went to see a priest or minister or pastor about becoming a Christian, for instance, you would be given a pamphlet that outlines the six or so major levels of Christian understanding—for example, magic Christianity, mythic Christianity, rational Christianity, pluralistic Christianity, and integral Christianity. Spiritual education would proceed in the same way that public school education, and virtually any education, already does, through a series of grades. You start at first grade and proceed through at least sixth grade and then beyond to higher grades. We have no problem understanding and accepting a grade-oriented approach in education—since we already use it—and I see no reason why we would have any problem if this approach were equally applied to spiritual education. And in this view, it does not reflect negatively on someone to be at any of the "lower" levels of faith, because one's real salvation still rests with Waking Up, and a person can experience a profound Waking Up at almost any stage of Growing Up. (Although it is true that the better interpretations come from the higher stages of growth.)

If someone has chosen to pursue a path of Waking Up, that is their choice—some people will wish to do so and some will not. But if they do choose to do so, then they would take up contemplation or meditation practices to address their own Waking Up, and they would start, in any event, at the appropriate stage of Growing Up for them, which would be the stage of the religion that matches their own stage of growth at that time, and they would interpret their experiences from that level. Then when it is appropriate (that is, when they have moved to the next stage of their own Growing Up), they would move to the next grade of their religion (while they also continue, if they want, to progress in their Waking Up development).

This system would act as a conveyor belt because it would help people see and understand their own major stages of Growing Up—which they are moving through in any event—and thus their religion would act as a *transformation pacer* for them, helping them move to higher and higher stages of Growing Up (while they can also, if they choose, expand their contemplative Waking Up). In contrast, most religions today often act not as a pacer or catalyst of Growing Up but as a cause of arrested development and fixation at some of the lowest stages of Growing Up. What they are doing to the majority of the population on this planet is something of a disaster, a cultural catastrophe of enormous proportions. It's easy to understand why the New Atheists (Richard Dawkins, Christopher Hitchens, Sam Harris, Daniel Dennett) claim that all religion is a nightmare. They're half right.

To conclude, how does this amber stage understand Christianity? It firmly believes that Jesus Christ is the one and only Son of the one and only true God, the embodiment of absolute Truth, and the sole doorway to a true salvation. All other religions are mistaken and incorrect and will not lead to genuine salvation; their followers are unfortunately destined for eternal damnation and hellfire. Only by accepting Jesus Christ as my personal savior can I find eternal life with God. And notice that all of the (mythic) beliefs found in such documents as the Nicene Creed and the Apostle's Creed have strongly mythic-literal and ethnocentric cores: a literal belief in the Father, Son, and Holy Ghost; the Virgin Mary; Jesus who was dead for three days and then resurrected and is the one and only Son of the one and only Creator God, and so on. These beliefs are absolutely and literally true, and my being an authentically saved Christian depends upon my acceptance of those statements. God has a plan for each of us, and faith in God through Jesus Christ assures me that I will fulfill that plan. The Bible is the literal word of God, and all of it is historically, empirically, and literally true, and is not open to criticism or questioning. Especially for Christian groups like Pentecostals and Evangelicals, a real salvation means a direct spiritual experience of "rebirth" (or being a "reborn Christian"), which sometimes involves a direct, subtle-state, religious peak experience of direct Deity mysticism (in a degree of intensity that includes the entire spectrum, from communion to union to identity with Christ). Experiences of higher states—all the way to nondual oneness—although relatively rare, are not completely unheard of in Christianity; although if any of them occur at this stage of Growing Up, they will tend to be interpreted mythically and absolutistically.

Technically, today any level of Growing Up can have the spiritual experience of subtle-state Waking Up, but for most Christian traditions, this Waking Up experience will be interpreted officially and dogmatically from the mythic-literal level (since this is where it originated). Part of this interpretation is that one was given this extraordinary experience of subtle Waking Up solely through one's genuine acceptance of Jesus Christ as one's personal savior.

The spiritual intelligence of this amber stage operates with other religious belief systems in similar ways, although, of course, with different contents. The most common factors are absolutism, ethnocentrism, and fundamentalism. In its absolutism, the spiritual intelligence of this level firmly believes that it possesses the one and only true approach, and everybody must conform, ethnocentrically, to this accepted reality. Your belief system can come from this stage in two ways: (1) if you are passing through it for the first time in your development, or (2) if you regress to it from a higher stage. Most likely, you are regressing to it if you start to hold any of your beliefs in a zealous, frenetically absolutistic fashion, because then this amber absolutistic level of awareness is where you will feel most comfortable. If you do regress, you will likely also become retribalized (ethnocentric) and highly polarized, and you will start to hold your beliefs in a fundamentalist-religious fashion, seeing heretics everywhere—as when science becomes scientism; Marxism becomes a religion; and social justice activists (in the culture wars) go from healthy green to broken green, holding their beliefs so fanatically that they maintain that they don't even have to talk to those who disagree with them, since all those "others" are "Nazis." This claim has indeed become quite common on the far Left in the culture wars. Social commentators have noted that this broken green has become a "secular religion or fundamentalism." It has developed its own myths, and it has often been called the "regressive Left," which illustrates what I'm saying—the extreme far Left has indeed become a regressive, fundamentalist, mythic religion, rife with absolutism and heretics.

What's so fascinating about all the stages that I have described so far (archaic fusion, egocentric magic, ethnocentric mythic, and any of their substages) is that, for 99 percent of the time human beings have been on this planet, they have been in those stages. The first higher, rational, worldcentric stages emerged in a widespread fashion only around two hundred to three hundred years ago. The development of these worldcentric stages was a stunning tear in the fabric of history, and they did indeed change everything. The expansion of the type of Wholeness that Growing Up offers inexorably continued its increase to greater and greater levels. We now turn to those higher, worldcentric stages. We can embrace immediately the type of Wholeness they provide—if, indeed, we know where to look.

7

The Modern-Rational (or Orange) Stage

We move now to one of the most important stages of Growing Up that has emerged thus far. It is not the most important stage that has emerged—that would be the Integral stage—but of all the stages that we have discussed, it is by far the most compelling, the most holistic, and the most historically significant. It's the rational stage. For a listing of the terms various researchers have used for this stage, see table 4. Note the emphasis on such terms as *rational*, *formal*, *modern*, *achievement*, and *individual*.

This stage involves a continuing cognitive growth and hence the emergence beyond the 2nd-person capacity of ethnocentric mythic (with its "us versus them" mentality) to a 3rd-person capacity of universal rational (which embraces not just "us" but "all of us" in a single, global humanity). This indeed means a more universal viewpoint, or what we call a *worldcentric* stance, which profoundly moves beyond the previous *ethnocentric* stance. So here, for the first time, it becomes a major social value to treat *all* people fairly, regardless of race, color, sex, ethnicity, gender, or creed (which means, regardless

TABLE 4. Equivalents to the orange modern-rational egoic stage

Researcher/system	Growing Up stage
Integral	orange modern rational egoic
Commons and Richards	formal and systemic
Fischer	abstract set and mapping
Fowler	individual reflective
Gebser	mental rational
Graves	rational multiplistic
Kegan	formal institutional/modern
Kohlberg	prior rights
Loevinger	rational conscientious
Maslow	self-esteem
Selman	individual role
Torbert	achiever
Wade	achievement/affiliative

of religious or ethnocentric belief). And this capacity for 3rd-person, worldcentric, universal, and rational (and not just mythic) thinking brought with it the quite sudden emergence of all the pioneering modern sciences—modern physics, modern astronomy, modern biology, modern chemistry, and so forth, all starting around three to four hundred years ago. At the same time, the sense of self shifted from an ethnocentric-conformist role to an individualistic-egoic role, with an emphasis on universal individual rights, liberty, and freedom.

Historically, this is a fairly recent stage, only a few hundred years old, starting with the Renaissance and the Enlightenment (although rationality had several precursors in the Greek culture of Plato and Aristotle). And because this stage, for the first time in history, believed in the universal rights of all humans—that is, it moved from ethnocentric to worldcentric—it became the first stage that finally outlawed slavery. During a one-hundred-year period, from around 1770 to 1870, slavery was outlawed in every rational industrial society on the face of the planet, the first time anything like that had ever occurred. This had not happened even during the great Axial period—roughly, the first millennium B.C.E. (the period when virtually every major religion was first created). The societies of that period did not ban slavery, because they still existed in a great mythic-ethnocentric era, which accepted slavery, or at least didn't object to it. In Athens, vaunted home of democracy, one-third of the population were slaves. This happened in almost every major culture, even ones that possessed a Great Religion. Human beings have been on this planet for up to one million years, but it was only two hundred years ago that a significant number of them finally agreed that one human being owning another was actually a bad thing. (If you ponder anything in history, ponder that.)

RATIONALITY AS DEMYTHOLOGIZING (OR *THE JEFFERSON BIBLE*)

This orange stage is often given names that have to do with reason or rationality, since cognition here moves from a more concrete mythic-literal thinking to more rational, universal modes of awareness. But here *rational* does not mean arid, dry, and analytically abstract. It means capable of self-reflection and standing back and taking a more universal, worldcentric, 3rd-person, global perspective. So at orange we do indeed find the first emergence of the modern, rational, universal sciences—modern physics, modern chemistry, modern astronomy, modern biology, and so on—not Hindu chemistry versus Protestant chemistry, just chemistry, universal in its reach. For the same reason, spiritual intelligence becomes much more rational or universally inclusive, and there is a very widespread move, often called "demythologizing," where the mythic-literal elements of the culture's religion are downplayed or even fully rejected in favor of more rational, moral, universal beliefs.

Thomas Jefferson is a perfect example. There's an apocryphal story of Jefferson sitting on the steps of the White House, with the Bible in one hand and a pair of scissors in the other, furiously cutting out all the mythic and supernatural elements of the Bible, leaving only its rational and moral aspects. Jefferson did create a text by removing some sections from the New Testament and cutting and arranging others, and it was published posthumously as *The Jefferson Bible*: supernatural myths and magic miracles are out, rational and moral ethics are in. Welcome to orange-stage religion. And remember, this stage can function with or without a Waking Up—and whether you have a Waking Up or not, if you are at this stage, you will interpret them according to the rules and principles of this orange worldcentric-rational stage.

At orange, one begins to question and examine one's previously unshakable and absolutistic beliefs; demythologizing occurs as mythic-literal elements are downplayed or even denied entirely. Jesus is not seen as the sole biological son of the one and only true God, since, at this stage, God appears in many different, equally valid forms around the world. Instead Jesus is seen as a very important World Teacher—that is, a worldcentric World Teacher—who still has many important lessons to teach us today; he exemplifies a profound moral authenticity that should be the primary example for our own rational behavior.

Since the basic elements of the religion have been demythologized and are now more rational in content at this stage, Jesus Christ can start to represent being a "God-man" not in a mythic fairy tale way but in a very humanistic manner—namely, Jesus of Nazareth was a full-fledged human being but one who had a profound and extraordinarily deep Waking Up experience. He truly realized that "I and the Father are one"—except now this is understood in a fully demythologized form. That is, he awakened to the fact that his own deepest Self or I AMness was fully one with universal Spirit. He realized that his own True Nature was literally God—he realized, in short, his Supreme Identity. He was indeed a "God-man," not by special status or birth but by *metamorphosis* (transformation)—which is the Greek word actually used, and used quite often, in the New Testament—that is, a real Awakening, Enlightenment, Moksha, Recognition, Great Liberation. When Jesus stated the core of his realization—which was that "before Abraham was, I AM"—this was a genuine realization of causal Formlessness as it connected to a veritable I AMness mysticism. It was at this point that Jesus of Nazareth became Jesus the Christ.

Christ is not a name, it's a title. It means "anointed," which means "one who discovered and expressed their divinity";[1] it thus means Waking Up. Christ's I AMness was indeed awakened to his Oneness with Spirit. Importantly, he interpreted his realization from the orange universal-worldcentric stage not the amber mythic-ethnocentric stage, which is why Jesus the Christ clearly wanted his realization to be given to all the gentiles as well as the Jews. Not only was it a true I AMness recognition, he wanted it taught worldcentrically not just ethnocentrically. He himself insisted that he was most fundamentally "the son of Man," which meant the "son of all humans," not just the son of one people. This was a true, universal, I AMness awareness—"Before Abraham was, I AM"—and, in Hebrew, the syllables for "I AM" are the same syllables that the Hebrews used for "God" or "Spirit" ("I AM that I AM"). Thus, everybody's True Nature is Christ consciousness, and Jesus of Nazareth had that realization in a particularly strong fashion, transforming him, indeed, to Jesus the Christ.

Christ had moved beyond a mythic-ethnocentric realization to a universal-worldcentric realization beyond ordinary words. It was a causal Formlessness as it moved into a genuine turiya or I AMness realization. And the fact that his I AMness is one with Spirit is actually the claim that got Christ crucified. "Why do you stone me?" he asks at one point. "Is it for good works?" And the crowd responds, "No, it is because you, being a man, make yourself out God." And that is exactly what he was—a "God-man"—and that got him crucified.

Once one has realized a universal-worldcentric truth and opened at least the causal Formless domain, generally, one can open oneself to virtually any of the higher Waking Up stages, particularly turiya Emptiness or I-AMness mysticism but also the highest turiyatita or One Taste domain. If one uses worldcentric rationality to move beyond a mythic domain and open oneself to a universal causal Formless realm, this then clears consciousness of all the Forms in awareness, thus allowing higher states to emerge (states that transcend Form altogether, such as turiya and turiyatita). We'll see later that Gautama Buddha interpreted his entire realization according to rationality itself (and the Formless causal), and because of that, he opened himself to the Emptiness or Nirvanic realm. Like *Christ*, the word *Buddha* is not a name but a title. What does it mean? When Gautama Siddhartha became Enlightened (and thus went from Gautama Siddhartha to Gautama the Buddha), he was asked if he were a god. He replied "No." "Then what are you?" he was asked. He replied, "Awake."

Opening to the causal Formless does not guarantee that one will open to turiya or turiyatita, but it will allow it. It puts a person beyond the mythic-literal ethnocentric domain, opening them at least to a rational, universal interpretation. This certainly happened in the case of Buddha, and it very much looks like a similar opening occurred with Jesus Christ, when he opened to a turiya I AMness that was one with Spirit itself.

In any event, this metamorphosis makes him not the sole biological son of the sole mythic-literal Deity but rather one of the great universal Realizers—individuals such as Gautama Buddha, Shankara,

Padmasambhava, Lady Tsogyal, Meister Eckhart, Bodhidharma, the Baal Shem Tov, and Lao Tzu. In this worldcentric sense, he offered to anybody who wished to follow him not some sort of everlasting life in a mythic heaven but an Awakening to their own Divine consciousness, right now on this very earth—a Waking Up to a genuine Kingdom of Heaven, their own eternal Christ consciousness. (Since, as we saw, *eternal* means a moment without time, a timeless Now, this ever-present, timeless Now is the real Kingdom of Heaven.) There is nothing mythic about this; it's simply an extraordinary perception into an ever-present but rarely recognized Reality—and it is this Reality, realized in authentic Waking Up to a true I AMness, that the God-men and God-women throughout history have come to remind us of. From this viewpoint, Jesus was just another human being who had a profound Waking Up to his own turiya True Self, one so profound that it left a wake of influence in the stream of time that still lives to this day—but there's nothing mythic about it.

With this view, suddenly all the mythic-literal accoutrements of Christianity come crashing down—none of them are needed, not for this stage, anyway. They would remain in existence, however, as part of the religious view at the earlier magic and mythic stages of an implicit conveyor belt. But starting at orange rational, they could be largely set aside—or "transcended and included"—and they were indeed set aside and transcended by the greatest of the Christian mystics.

The myths could, however, now be used in deeply symbolic and metaphoric ways—if we are very, very, *very* careful.

THE NATURE OF MYTHS

Myths are often taken to be transrational or translogical, meaning that they are believed to offer deeper or higher meanings than mere rationality can—and myths are often highly valued for this transrational wisdom. There are literally thousands of books on the market right now that extol the wisdom of myth over reason.

But notice that Joseph Campbell—perhaps the premier mythologist of the past century—maintained that any myth that was taken *literally* was a "perversion" of the myth (his term). Only myths that are held in an "as if" fashion (exactly as described by Immanuel Kant, says Campbell)—are real and authentic. In other words, the true mythic version of the idea that, for example, Jesus Christ was born of a virgin would actually say something like "Christ was so pure that it was *as if* Christ were born of a virgin." Campbell maintained that the vast majority of myths around the world are taken literally and are thus *perversions*.

So much for the thousands of books that extol the wisdom of myth over reason—most of them, according to Campbell, extol perversions. But Campbell doesn't know the half of it. Every myth produced by the amber mythic-literal stage is taken literally, as its name implies. This stage is by far the largest source of myths—and they are all taken literally. Hence, Campbell would maintain, they are all perversions.

However, Campbell (and apparently many others) failed to realize that "as if" phrases emerge at—and can be understood only by—the formal, operational cognition stages (that is, orange rationality). In other words, "as if" (and "what if") are themselves the products of rationality, as has been demonstrated by Piaget and many other developmental psychologists. That means, as Campbell himself maintains, that only myths *held in the space of reason* can be authentic. And with that, gone is the notion that myths offer some sort of transrational wisdom. Only myths held by reason are authentic.

What exactly does that mean for spiritual or religious symbols? The early Christian theologians—Clement, Origen—who were often at orange rational (or higher) stages of development, were faced with the very embarrassing reality of so many mythic-literal images and stories in the Bible, and, to put it bluntly, they needed a way out. The Bible was supposed to be the word of God, but these myths are ridiculously unbelievable—so how could they acknowledge them but also effectively get rid of them?

Very cleverly (and, I believe, quite correctly), they maintained that the myths themselves could be read at three levels. Level 1, the lowest level, was literal. At level 1, Moses parting the Red Sea meant, well, exactly that—Moses really did part the Red Sea (at least in terms of this level's reading). Level 2 was metaphoric or symbolic—the myths were symbols of something deeper or higher. (This is where the myths would have to be held, à la Campbell, in a rational "as if" fashion; so from this view, it was *as if* Moses parted the Red Sea, although something else deeper than that—something symbolic—was usually meant at level 2.) Here, Moses parting the Red Sea really means that, for instance (I'm just making this up as an example of a level-2 interpretation), the Israelites badly needed to pull all their tribes together and create their own country, their own nation, and the Red Sea represented all the obstacles that they faced on the way to creating that country and that strong identity as a people. So Moses parting the Red Sea "really" means that he led his people through a series of very difficult obstacles toward their own sovereign nationhood. That would be an example of a level-2 interpretation, reading some sort of deep meaning into the myth (which the myth itself plainly does not say or in any way display). So Moses overcame so many impossible obstacles that it was *as if* he had parted the Red Sea itself. Or, Lot's wife did something so bad it was *as if* she were turned into a pillar of salt. Or Jesus Christ himself was so pure it was *as if* he were born from a biological virgin. And thus in one stroke, there go all those ridiculously silly meanings of the literal myths, and so you can be a good Christian without endless embarrassment. And note, that "as-if" interpretation is not beyond rationality; that interpretation demands rationality and rests within its "as-if" structure.

Level 3 was mystical (or transcendental). Here the myths mean realities that are related to an actual mystical experience or Waking Up reality. For example, the Red Sea represents a barrier or constriction in awareness—the self-contraction of the limited ego—and that has to be passed through if one's deepest and truest Reality is to be found. This would be, not a prerational but a transrational Reality, and thus rationality would again be needed (if transcended) in level 3.

So starting with rationality itself—starting with this orange stage—myths are open to being interpreted in symbolic ("as if") or mystical (transcendental) ways, and as long as that is done with full awareness, that is perfectly fine. Thus, for example, Christ's death and resurrection on the cross does not mean that he actually died and then physically arose and ascended to live in a mythic heaven forever—which is what the myth itself plainly says—but rather that, as is required for all genuine Awakening or Metamorphosis experiences, he had to die to his separate-self sense ("Jesus of Nazareth"), and once he did that ("It is finished"), his awareness was resurrected as his own I AMness, his deepest and truest Christ consciousness ("Jesus the Christ"). The Ascension meant not moving to a mythic, physical heaven "up there" forever (where exactly was this "up in the sky" heaven located—around the moon somewhere, or around Mars, or perhaps outside of the Milky Way?) but rather the Ascension of his own awareness to its highest Christ consciousness (or formless True Self) in the eternity of a timeless Now, a real Kingdom of Heaven. Thus, Christ's physical death and physical Ascension to an actual heaven could be read in a deeply "as-if" fashion. Christ had so transcended his illusory ego that it was *as if* he had physically died to it and had been resurrected and transported to heaven as his own True Self, thus realizing his own Supreme Identity. "Christ died for my sins" thus means that if I am truly to follow Christ's example, that's what I must also do—fully die to my own ego and thus resurrect my True Self, so that "Not I but Christ [consciousness] lives in me."

It's crucially important to realize that the literal myths produced by the amber mythic-literal stage are not "perversions" of true myths. They have, if anything, the real nature of myth itself—they have the original and natural form of myth, which is created by every healthy person in the world at the amber stage of their Growing Up. Myth in its literal form is exactly how the world looks from that mythic-literal stage of development. When it was first written that "Moses parted the Red Sea," the author most certainly did *not* mean that metaphorically or symbolically (let alone mystically). The author did *not* think, "Let's see, it's important that all these Israelite tribes really get their act together and create a real nation. So we're standing here in front of the Red Sea, so I've got it—I'll just say that Moses actually parted this Red Sea, and that will represent us Israelites finally overcoming all our obstacles to creating a nation." And are we supposed to think that, having that in mind, the author then simply wrote, "Moses parted the Red Sea," and that was that. That makes no sense whatsoever. (And virtually nobody would understand what it was supposed to really mean anyway. How on earth would anybody know that "Moses parted the Red Sea" *really* meant all of those other deeper and symbolic meanings?) *Almost no myths are originally metaphoric or symbolic.* They are just what they say they are—they are literal; there is no hidden meaning. "Lot's wife was turned into a pillar of salt" means exactly what it says it means—she was literally turned into a pillar of salt. Likewise "Moses parted the Red Sea" is exactly how that event was remembered by the mythic-literal mind, as are virtually all the myths in the Bible and other religious treatises. (There are so many myths in the Bible because it was written almost entirely during the mythic-literal stage of humanity's own evolution.)

It is only when a rational (or higher-stage) mind looks at one of these literal myths and tries to figure out what the hell it could possibly mean (because many of them, since they are all *pre*-rational, just don't make much reasonable sense at all) that it is begun to be read in various metaphoric or deeply symbolic ways. So interpret myths however you wish; just don't pretend you're reading something into them that was originally put into them. In effect, you're just making it all up when you try to say what a myth "really means" (if it's anything other than what the myth itself plainly says it means).

Thus, myths start in a simple and literal form, meaning exactly what they say, however silly that might sometimes seem. This is a level-1 approach, which is actually the myth's *real and original meaning*. If this meaning often looks childish, it's because this stage of development itself is a childish stage of humankind's growth and evolution. Then if rationality emerges and looks at one of these myths, it can read them in an "as if" fashion, and thus invent and create much deeper and more sensible meanings, which it then claims are what the myth "really means" or is its "authentic meaning"—whereas it is just a rationally invented "as if" meaning—which is a level-2 approach. (Notice that many of today's Bible scholars—from Jordan Peterson to Dennis Prager—give long and detailed lectures devoted to a "rational reading of the Bible"—which is fine, it's just a level-2 invented meaning.)[2] And if a person has a Waking Up experience, they can give any myth they want a level-3 reading and find something deeply mystic and transcendental in it.

Most theologians have spent their entire lifetimes taking the Bible's level-1 myths and working hard to give them level-2 or even level-3 meanings. But now is the time to simply drop the mythic-literal approach (except for those on the conveyor belt who are at the amber mythic stage themselves) and move to a higher level of spiritual intelligence (orange, green, or turquoise)—as any Religion of Tomorrow will almost certainly do. In other words, go ahead and use the level-1 myths (since you can't really avoid them) but realize that their original meanings came from the stage that originally produced them (which will usually be the magic or mythic stage). And then, with that in mind, go ahead and give them a higher stage-2 or stage-3 interpretation, realizing that none of those interpretations will get at the original meaning of the myth. But that's okay—you have access to its *literal* meaning, which is its *original* meaning, but you can't help reinterpret that from a higher stage (for example, rational, pluralistic, or integral). Just realize that those reinterpretations of the level-1 myth will never be their original meanings, and simply keep that in mind, even as you necessarily make use of those higher reinterpretations.

From this demythologized view (orange rational or higher), Jesus of Nazareth was an ordinary human being, just like anybody else, and he had a stunningly profound experience of Waking Up to his own Divine Self—his own Supreme Identity—just like anybody else can have (not often as profound but still perfectly possible). And as such, he discovered his own truest and deepest Self—his own turiya Christ consciousness—at which point he went from being Jesus of Nazareth to being Jesus the Christ, where, as we have already seen, "Christ" is a title, not a name, and refers to an anointment by one's highest and truest Self (turiya), which is one with Spirit itself (turiyatita). Indeed, Jesus had several Waking Up experiences: he had his first Metamorphosis in the River Jordan at the hands of John the Baptist, then the Transfiguration, then final ego-death on the cross, and then his Ascension to Unity or Supreme Identity (essentially gross, subtle, causal/turiya, nondual.)

This is also very much like Prince Siddhartha, who for six years sought his own truest reality and finally realized it with Enlightenment, whereupon he was known as the "Buddha," which, like "Christ," is not a name but a title. What does the title mean? As we previously have seen, when Buddha was asked, "Are you a God? Are you a divine Being?" Buddha replied, "No." "Then what are you?" he was asked. And he simply replied, "Awake."

Altered states such as peak experiences, flow states, plateau experiences, spiritual experiences, and Waking Up in general are very common and natural events—as we noted, polls consistently show around 60 percent of people have had major "unity consciousness" experiences. Therefore, understanding the event that defined Jesus Christ as a straightforward (if profound) Waking Up experience takes Christ (and spirituality in general) out of the realm of the surreal, mythic-literal, once-upon-a-time fairy-tale land, and puts it smack in the middle of *this* presently existing reality. There's nothing Santa Claus about what made Jesus into the Christ (whereas most mythic-literal religions are almost nothing but fairy tales, no more real—for any stage higher than amber—than are Zeus, Apollo, Aphrodite, or the tooth fairy). The reality of what the great Adepts and Realizers like Christ and Buddha are all about will then focus not on some sort of mythic story or fairy tale (which have already been fully discredited by both the modern and the postmodern mind) but instead on the reality that altered states themselves actually reveal.

Abundant research makes it very clear that, in many instances, altered states reveal *genuine realities*—real realities that are dimensions of this world, just rarely seen or felt. For example, baseball players regularly report that when they are at bat, they can count the number of stitches on the baseball as it speeds toward them. They are in an altered state. We don't doubt the reality of the baseball or that it actually has a certain number of stitches—those are genuine realities. But very few people can count the stitches of a baseball while it is speeding 100 miles per hour at their face. As we'll see later in this book, when we go through some practices that will allow us to experience some of the highest spiritual states, counting the stitches on the baseball is just like seeing realities in the highest spiritual states. These realities are something that are always present, but very few people can see them, even though they are as real as the stitches on a baseball. There's nothing mythic or fairy-tale about them. As the mystics have maintained from day one, mystical realities are direct experiences open to anyone who wants to sincerely look. This is certainly true of the 5 major states of Waking Up. The stories of the great Realizers, the great God-men and God-women of the past and present, are not stories of magic or mythic superheroes; they are not born gods and goddesses but are ordinary men and women who have awakened to their own deepest and truest Reality—exactly as Jesus the Christ and Gautama the Buddha did over two thousand years ago, and exactly as you can do today, right here and now.

To state what is probably very obvious, the viewpoint of Jesus Christ (as defined primarily by a profound Waking Up realization and not by a merely magic-mythic fairy tale) is not necessarily a view maintained by all those who reach the orange rational stage of their spiritual intelligence. But it is a view that becomes possible at this stage, given this stage's postmythic nature. In other words, when the myths are gone, one begins to look elsewhere for an explanation of the staggering influence of these Realizers (many of whom founded entire religions or influential branches of religions), and the most obvious one is the profound depth of a genuine Waking Up realization, which leaves a morphic field of major dimensions in its wake, which often has a profound impact on those who follow it.

Accepting this notion depends primarily on the person's Waking Up experience, which, as we've seen, is unlike Growing Up in that the recognition (and certainly the practice) of Waking Up is often purely voluntary. People can Grow Up all the way to turquoise integral and never have a single Waking Up experience, or even suspect its existence. If they do have a Waking Up realization, they will almost certainly recognize this understanding when it appears in Realizers such as Jesus Christ or Gautama Buddha, and they will understand that they themselves can do what St. Paul recommended and "Let this consciousness be in you which was in Christ Jesus, that we all may be one" (be in true Unity consciousness). And if not—if Waking Up is not known to exist or is denied—then at this rational stage of a person's spiritual intelligence, if they do not become straightforwardly atheistic or agnostic, then they will often go the route of Thomas Jefferson and see religion as a primary source of universal moral principles and rational guidelines and totally ditch all the magic and mythic images.

THE RATIONAL ATHEIST

Now we come to a very common form of this orange stage's spiritual intelligence, which is that it will often rationally decide that it is atheistic—or, at the very least, agnostic. These decisions are still decisions made by spiritual intelligence, because they are made only when considering what might be an ultimate reality, an ultimate concern—what is really, really real. This is what spiritual intelligence does; it doesn't matter what it finally decides—the decision could be theistic, atheistic, agnostic, materialistic, nihilistic, or some other version of what ultimate reality is thought to be. The New Atheists think about those issues more than anybody I know, and in concluding that there is no spirit, they use spiritual intelligence more than anybody else on the planet. They often write entire books about it (for example, *The God Delusion*, *God Is Not Great*, *Letter to a Christian Nation*, *Waking Up*).

I'm not going to say a great deal about their viewpoint, except that it's about as simplistic an orange-versus-amber argument as can be imagined. All orange (science) is good, and all amber (religion) is bad—and this is indeed about as nonintegral a stance as is possible. It doesn't even acknowledge developmental realities (for example, red to amber to orange—or magic to mythic to rational), so it doesn't have a decent explanation of where mythic-religion or rational science comes from in the first place. Therefore it claims that everybody who just happens, out of the blue, to end up using rationality is right on the mark, and everybody who engages in an amber religion—

some 60–70 percent of the world's population—happens to be a congenital idiot.

In any case, starting with this orange rational stage, spiritual intelligence can begin an extensive and aggressive questioning of, and often an attack on, all religion, which it sees as nothing but mythic-literal childishness. (But if rationality began attacking a narrowly conceived religion, it could also begin rationally embracing a more expanded religion.) As a result, rational science versus mythic religion became the premier cultural battle of modernity, no matter how idiotic its central assumptions are. This orange stage is the first stage that can claim (and often does claim) that "God is dead." That claim—made famous first by Nietzsche—was loudly pronounced across Europe during the Enlightenment as this orange stage continued to emerge—and this meant that *the mythic-God was dead*—and that it certainly was.

THE CAUSAL FORMLESS STATE

The mythic-God was dead, and it was indeed dead for orange and all higher Growing Up levels but still lives on, vividly, at lower magic and mythic levels. Since everybody is born at square one—that is, at crimson archaic—and then develops through magic and then mythic on the way to orange rational and higher, most people, even atheists, go through a magic-mythic religious period, even if it's just believing in Santa Claus and the tooth fairy. But during the orange rational era, we see in some people, in the Waking Up dimension, an advance from a subtle-state Deity mysticism to a causal-state Formless mysticism. And whereas Deity mysticism is often interpreted by mythic, Formless mysticism is often interpreted by reason.

But here there is usually some confusion about exactly what the causal state means, because most Traditions themselves present several different meanings, many of which seem to be contradictory. For those who are familiar with world religions, the causal is a bit of a nightmare, and I'm going to try and shed a little light on it. (What follows is a bit of a technical sidebar. If you're not interested, feel free to breeze through it, and we'll pick up the story with a look at Buddhism as a "rational" religion with the goal of Waking Up.)

The causal indicates the very first of the manifest dimensions of existence. That is, as Spirit creates and manifests this universe moment to moment—or as the entire manifest universe emerges from the Ground of All Being, moment to moment—the very first forms that are created or emerge are said to be the "causal Forms"—the Greeks called them "archetypes" (primordial forms). Some Traditions (such as Vedanta) call this state "causal" because it is the cause of all the lesser forms and dimensions of existence; other Traditions (such as Tibetan Buddhism) call it the "very subtle" (beyond the "subtle") because it is the subtlest of all manifest dimensions. These highest and most subtle Forms, upon which all lesser forms depend, are found in such notions as Plato's ideal Forms, Whitehead's eternal objects (things you have to have in order to have a manifest universe at all, such as colors), Yogachara Buddhism's vasanas (collective memory Forms), the eternal Forms in the akashic record, and so on.

Several Traditions maintain that you can directly experience the archetypes, and the result is a type of archetypal, spiritual, mystical experience. This was certainly true for the Platonic Forms, the collective vasanas, and the Forms in the akashic record; even Jung said that "mysticism is the experience of archetypes."[3] When this archetypal, causal state is indicated, I usually call it "archetypal" and its direct experience "archetypal mysticism" (as with all spiritual experience, it will be interpreted according to the Growing Up stage the person is at, and at orange, that's the universal-rational, so these Forms are almost always claimed to be universal).

Most Traditions divide the causal state into two major dimensions: (1) the archetypes themselves, and, at the highest point of the causal, (2) a pure, Formless emptiness, which is said to be seen in states such as deep dreamless sleep and formless states of meditation. For this reason, the exact definition of the causal can become confusing—it's either the highest and most subtle Forms in all of existence (archetypes), or it's a pure, infinite, formless, unmanifest realm (Formless). Most Traditions maintain it contains both, so we have to be very careful when we talk about the causal, and if one of those meanings is specifically intended, I'll definitely say so.

There's one other slight confusion that is common: as the causal shades into the pure, Formless, unmanifest realm, it is often combined with the turiya state itself. Turiya, recall, is the 4th state of consciousness (which is the next state beyond the causal, which itself is the 3rd state, because it is after the gross and the subtle). It is the pure, empty, formless Witness; pure, content-free Awareness; Consciousness without an object; it's also known as the True Self, I AMness, Absolute Subjectivity, one's Original Face, and so on. In itself, turiya is radically unqualifiable and free of all characteristics whatsoever (including that one).[4] In essence, the Witness is radically free of all manifestation: "I have sensations, but I am not those sensations. I have feelings, but I am not those feelings. I have thoughts, but I am not those thoughts. I am the pure Seer, not anything that can be seen; the true Witness, not anything witnessed; the pure Knower, not anything known." And thus turiya is sometimes referred to as a pure Emptiness or pure Formlessness (with capital letters), but it's also the cognizing or knowing aspect of pure Awareness—a pure, Empty, unqualifiable Witness. (This turiya state is one of the main states we will be exploring and experiencing later on.)

When turiya is combined with the causal, which is often done, what is always meant is the pure, Formless aspect of both states, so this drives a pure, Formless mysticism or a radical Emptiness mysticism (while the pure knowing aspect of turiya drives a Consciousness-only, or True-Self, or I-AMness mysticism).

The "causal" state can thus mean either or both of those two central meanings—the highest of all Forms (archetypes) or a pure Formlessness beyond all forms (as when the causal is said to be present in deep dreamless sleep—which is a purely Formless state). When evolution began to push into the causal state, making it available to awareness, we tend to find both of those aspects come to the fore. On the one hand, we find, around the world, the discovery of archetypes—whether Plato's Forms, the akashic record of the East, the vasanas of the *Lankavatara Sutra*, or Pythagorean geometries (these seem to be the primordial dimensions that modern-day string theory finds it necessary to postulate, strings being the primordial dimensions that generate all other dimensions). And following close on that discovery was the direct realization not only of those highest Forms but also of the Formless (causal/turiya): the truly unmanifest, infinite, formless realm of pure cessation, a One beyond the Many, an Emptiness beyond all Form, and, most notably, *a nirvana beyond all samsara*. This pure turiya state is literally the state of nirvana or *nirodh* (pure cessation), and to discover nirvana is to be totally free of all samsara and hence to discover a pure, infinite Freedom. This Freedom is not a theoretical postulate but a direct experience of a pure and unqualifiable I AMness. Because this pure, formless Emptiness clears all forms from consciousness, it also opens consciousness to virtually all of the higher states of Waking Up (from turiya itself to turiyatita).

To conclude this section, note that during the period when, in the Growing Up line, evolution moved from amber mythic to orange rational, in the Waking Up line evolution often pressed into the causal state—where "causal" has a range of meanings: It could be marked by a type of Archetypal mysticism (Platonic and Pythagorean being the most typical). Or it could be marked by a strong sense of the pure Emptiness or pure unmanifest Formlessness of the high causal (deep dreamless sleep). When that happened, then commonly the turiya state itself (the Witness or formless I AMness) was also being engaged (a Formless nirvana free of all Forms of samara, as in original Buddhism).

ORIGINAL BUDDHISM

The infinite, empty Ground of Being (causal/turiya) is a state that—like virtually all states—can be experienced and interpreted from any major stage of Growing Up (provided that stage had already emerged in evolution). One of the spiritual approaches that prominently uses the orange rational stage is that of Gautama Buddha. The aim of Buddha's original system was to awaken from the realm of samsara (the entire manifest universe of form) and discover instead a purely formless, empty, unmanifest state known as "nirvana" (which itself was a radically empty turiya "no-ego" state). This meant a complete cessation or extinction of all manifest forms in awareness, so that one becomes completely free of the suffering, sin, illusion, and fallenness of the entire manifest world (samsara). This was a pure Waking Up experience of a radical turiya state, but what made Buddha's approach so significant is that he explained it in a completely rational fashion. Buddha does not refer to gods or goddesses or nature spirits or anything like that—nothing magic or mythic at all. Rather, he gives very clear, straightforward explanations that are completely rational. He explains that his aim is the realization of a state of pure extinction or cessation (nirvana or nirodh), which especially is an extinction of all suffering (samsara). But the Awakened or Enlightened state cannot itself be captured by rationality or by any thought process whatsoever. Rather, Buddha explains, to attain that Waking Up experience, one must instead take up meditation and work to awaken a purely empty state of complete cessation and extinction—a state Buddha specifically called "nirvana" (and is technically known as "nirodh," or the total cessation of all mental forms). All of this is delivered in an utterly rational fashion, including the instructions for the practices of meditation that alone can lead one to a transrational Enlightenment. Buddha is interpreting this causal Formless/turiya state of Waking Up from a purely orange rational stage of Growing Up.

Nirvana is a Sanskrit word, which, like many Sanskrit words used in connection with spirituality, has the prefix *nir*, which means "without," "not," or "none." Nirvana is a state "without grasping or desire." Some other terms with *nir* as a prefix became common, including *nirvikalpa* (without thought forms), *nirguna* (without qualities, totally unqualifiable), and *nirodh* (pure extinction or total cessation), since they all pointed to variations on this completely Empty, Formless, Unqualifiable Reality that had just been evolutionarily accessed for the first time, and to a radical Freedom from all of the torments, tortures, sin, suffering, and illusions that the entire manifest universe had been charged with. This is a very, very real state of turiya Waking Up—as is its radical Freedom—and it was experienced at this time in history because evolution itself had moved beyond mythic forms into the beginning orange rational realms, which because of their own transcendental capacity to move beyond myths, also opened up the transcendental possibility of a turiya Awakening in the process of Waking Up.

Original Buddhism is one of the very few world religions that originated at the orange rational level of Growing Up (although it aimed for the pure empty turiya state of Waking Up). Scholars have perennially scratched their heads about why Buddhism seems so different from the other major religions—and whether it even should be included as a religion at all. Different it indeed is. Its difference is not found in its ultimate aim—the pure Emptiness of Waking Up—because that goal could be found in many other religions that had accessed the orange rational level (including the nothingness of the Cloud of Unknowing, Judaism's Ayin, and Gnosticism's formless Godhead beyond God). Rather, its difference from other world religions is that virtually all the other world religions have significant magic-mythic backgrounds as their interpretive base, while Buddhism has almost none. This lack of magic-mythic elements led many scholars—who identified religion primarily with these elements—to claim that Buddhism wasn't really a religion at all—it was more like a pure psychology. In my view, although the pure cessation of infinite Emptiness that was the goal of Buddhist practice was not particularly new or different from that of many other religions, its interpretive grid, or the level of Growing Up from which it interpreted its Waking Up, was indeed quite different. It was not magic or mythic but orange rational—and this was definitely quite new and, at the time, profoundly different from virtually any other major religion.[5]

As for the aim or goal of Buddhism, we see other examples, at this time, of a turiya state described as pure Oneness, infinite Emptiness, Godhead beyond God, or a nirvana beyond all samsara. We see it also in Parmenides's One; Samkhya's Purusha (Pure Self) versus Prakriti (a manifest Many); and in the paradoxes of Zeno and similar thought experiments, which explicitly used a precocious and newly emergent orange reason to show that the entire manifest world itself was inherently contradictory, fallen, even unreal. The Samkhya's dualistic doctrine of a pure Purusha versus a manifest Prakriti turned out to be the foundational spiritual approach of almost all the great religions of India (the mother ship of spiritual and religious traditions). It separated reality into a real component (Purusha, the Witness, I AMness, the True Self, Consciousness without an object, or pure empty Awareness) and a totally manifest component (Prakriti, the entire manifest material world), with the goal of gaining total Liberation, the discovery of the radical Freedom of empty Consciousness versus the inherent suffering of identifying with an objective, material, manifest world (that world—after all, was *completely* fallen, illusory, and suffering laden). And that indeed became the enduring goal of numerous subsequent Indian religious systems, although later variations—which we will explore—moved from dualistic versions, such as the original Samkhya, to nondual versions, such as Vedanta and Vajrayana, and they did so precisely when the access to higher states of consciousness evolved from a pure empty Consciousness of turiya—which is inherently dualistic (a world split into a nirvana versus samsara)—to the ultimate Unity Awareness of turiyatita—which is profoundly nondual (a nirvana united with samsara).

At this point in our narrative, we are talking about the dualistic versions—causal/turiya—which are versions that separated the infinite Formless realm from the finite world of Form—nirvana from samsara—and counseled a pure identity with the Formless One and a complete rejection of the manifest Many.

THE DEATH OF THE MYTHIC GOD

When the death of the mythic God occurred in the West, it was a horrendously painful and wrenching transition. People really thought that, without their traditional God, anything would be allowed, there would be no morals left anywhere, sin would run rampant, the world would collapse. But the world did not collapse, and in one of the most staggeringly huge transformations in all of humanity's evolution, a mythic God was replaced by rational science as the most trusted source of true knowledge. The mythic God was pronounced dead.

With this transition, in your own case, you are still allowed to believe that your religion (if you have one) is the very best religion in the world *for you*—but it's no longer automatically the best for everybody else.

Everybody interprets their religion based primarily not on what the religion itself says but on what Growing Up stage they are at. With respect to Christianity, especially since the Enlightenment, there have been sincere, faithful, intelligent people interpreting

Christianity in essentially rational (and demythologized) terms—starting with Deism, the first major, mostly rational approach to Christianity that reached a large following (many of the most influential founders of the United States were Deists). This has continued to this day. One of the better-known examples of such a rational Christian is, as I've pointed out, Bishop Shelby Spong. He states flat-out that he doesn't believe any of the major myths or miracles of Christianity (including truly central myths like the virgin birth, the one and only true biological son of God, and the physical resurrection), and further, he says, he doesn't know any modern theologians who do. (Well, if he doesn't, I do—lots of them. But the point is taken.) As we've already seen, the title of his recent book *Unbelievable* says it all: every one of the central myths in Christianity is utterly unbelievable in today's world. But he also clearly says that despite his rejection of these myths, he still considers himself a true, fully faithful, and genuinely authentic Christian—and I couldn't agree more!

Thus, more rational forms of spirituality do become very common at this orange structure-stage (as well as at the next major worldcentric stage, the green pluralistic stage). As one's stage of Growing Up moves beyond the mythic, then all higher stages will be postmythic or rationally accepting. As spiritual intelligence begins moving away from more traditional forms of mythic religion, often rational sciences like systems theory start to be used to explain spirit as a great Web of Life; or quantum mechanics is used to offer proof of the interconnectedness of all life (an admittedly pantheistic view).[6] One may or may not have a direct Waking Up experience at these orange or green stages; but if one does, it will be interpreted according to the terms of that stage itself. If orange, the spiritual intelligence of this stage is usually rational, science compatible, universal, worldcentric, and evidence based, often dipping into leading-edge sciences like systems theory, quantum mechanics, or complexity theory, with Spirit itself commonly interpreted as the total interwovenness of the entire manifest universe (or a pantheistic Great Web of Life).

If one's spiritual system at this rational stage is based on an authentic mysticism (that is, if it's based on practices that help a person to directly experience Waking Up to a higher state of consciousness—such as causal or turiya), then one can interpret and explain that ultimate Spirit in rational terms, much like Gautama Buddha did. But if one's spiritual system at this orange rational stage does not involve a Waking Up or a change of state of consciousness, then one will have only the spiritual intelligence itself (of Growing Up) to create a spiritual awareness, and therefore often the "scientific" explanations and theories—using everything from quantum mechanics to systems theory—will themselves start to take on an aura of theology. That is, simply knowing these scientific descriptions of reality will be mistaken for a direct Waking Up experience of an ultimate Reality. These systems of knowledge by description will be thoroughly confused with a genuine knowledge by acquaintance—the fingers pointing to the moon will be confused with the moon itself.

We want to remember, as we start to "get rational" about Spirit, that holding any of these opinions about a New Paradigm in science is obviously not the same as a direct Waking Up experience itself, and this really should be remembered or we will never even try to Wake Up. If you spend your time reviewing and studying a New Paradigm in science, then you are exercising your spiritual intelligence in Growing Up. That is totally fine! But such Growing Up efforts do not contribute in any direct way to your own Waking Up. Most people confuse Waking Up and Growing Up, and so they imagine that the time they put into thinking about some new science paradigm is advancing their Waking Up. But it isn't—in fact, it often hurts it. When Waking Up and Growing Up are confused, then you will think that the work you are doing in Growing Up is the same as Waking Up, and thus you won't really do any Waking Up work at all, and thus . . . , well . . . , you simply won't Wake Up. So particularly beginning at orange, where rationality starts offering a huge number of alternatives in the spiritual market, you want to keep that warning in mind and remember both the important differences between Waking Up and Growing Up and the extraordinary importance of fully including and integrating both.

EVOLUTION—THE "WHAT" AND THE "WHY"

At this orange rational stage, the notion of evolution itself often becomes reinterpreted by spiritual intelligence as something like "Spirit-in-action." The entirety of conventional Darwinian evolution is not necessarily embraced at this stage, but, at the very least, it is no longer thought that evolution itself is incompatible with a legitimate spirituality. But this is almost always done with a very specific understanding of evolution. To wit: there are at least two quite different aspects of modern evolutionary theory—there is the chronological *what* of evolution, and there is the theoretical *why* of evolution. The "what" is almost always accepted by a smart orange rationality, the "why" almost never.

The chronological "what" is a simple description of the many stages of evolution as it actually unfolded and as it continuously produced new and emergent holons, with an overall trend toward more and more complex, unified, and conscious entities—from quarks to atoms to molecules to cells to organisms, and with organisms, a whole Tree of Life of ever-greater and more complex wholes, from plants to fish to amphibians to reptiles to mammals to primates to humans—and with humans, a continuing drive of ever-greater wholeness, from egocentric to ethnocentric to worldcentric to integral. That is the "what" of evolution—the empirical record of what actually occurred—and it is generally accepted by the spiritual intelligence of this stage (and the core of this "what" is likewise accepted by virtually all schools of modern evolutionary theory).

As for the "why" of evolution, this is where it gets tricky, and even orthodox scientists have serious arguments and disagreements about this. There seem to be several factors involved. Whitehead called the unmistakable drive of evolution in a particular and inherent direction "the creative advance into novelty,"[7] which he saw as an "ultimate" that is required to get any universe in operation. Erich Jantsch called it "self-organization through self-transcendence"; Ilya Prigogine's Nobel-prize-winning work called it "order out of chaos"; Francisco Varela called it "autopoiesis" and "enactment"; some philosophers often call it simply "Eros"; and probably the most-often used name at this time in science itself is simply "self-organization." The inherent drive of the universe to self-organize has set evolution in motion and then pushed it from within to ever-greater and ever more unified wholes (or holons), with the result of 14 billion years of this self-organization through self-transcendence being nothing less than this unbelievably beautiful world that we find ourselves in. This is an *inherent* drive—an actual force—present in the universe itself. It's as real a force as gravity, electromagnetism, and the strong and weak nuclear forces.

This Eros or self-organization also pushes our own growth and development and opens us to higher and higher stages of evolutionary unfolding. The force that produced galaxies from the Big Bang, gorillas from dirt, and global worldcentric concern from egocentric narcissism is the same force that will drive us to higher and higher stages of our own growth, development, and evolution. And if you see evolution as being driven by "Spirit-in-action"—which is one possible view that emerges at this orange stage—then the very drive of this Eros or self-organizing activity can be seen as the creative drive of Spirit itself, creating something from nothing in every moment of existence, as the creative Ground of Being of everything that is.

Regarding the "what" aspect of evolutionary theory, which traces the many temporal stages of this evolutionary unfolding—very few rational thinkers doubt that part of the theory. When scientists say that evolution is not doubtable, that's the part of evolution that they mean—and they're right. Atoms really did come before molecules, which really did come before cells, and fish really did come before amphibians, which really did come before mammals, and so on. This "creative advance into novelty" is simply unavoidable and undeniable if you really look at the actual history of the Kosmos.

But *why* this happens is a different story, and fewer and fewer evolutionary biologists themselves agree about this anymore. The neo-Darwinian explanation is that it is all caused by chance mutations triggering chance variations, and then those chance variations that just happen to be favorable to survival and sexual reproduction are preferentially selected—so-called natural selection. But few scientists today believe that anymore, not as a complete theory. Thus, leading-edge evolutionary theorists such as David Sloan Wilson speak of things like psychological and cultural evolution, which don't even involve sexual reproduction. It is extremely unlikely that mere chance variation could give rise to the massive diversity and constantly increasing complexity and unification of form that we see unrelentingly operating in evolution. (As only one example, the probability of correctly producing a single protein chain containing 150 amino acids in the correct order—by chance—versus incorrectly doing this is 1/1077; that is, several times greater than the total number of organisms on the planet.) In other words, there has to be, built into the universe itself, a drive to greater order, wholeness, and self-organization—exactly what Whitehead called the "creative advance into novelty," and without some version of that creative novelty, the universe would not have gone one nanosecond beyond the Big Bang.

In short, within the universe itself, there has to be some sort of inherent push to greater order, some sort of probability-increasing machine, as it were. At the very least, we need something like Prigogine's intrinsic drive to produce "order out of chaos" (for example, even dead matter itself, when pushed far from equilibrium, escapes that tension by jumping to a higher level with more order, as when water chaotically splashing down the drain suddenly jumps into a perfectly formed whirlpool). This drive to create "order out of chaos," according to Prigogine's Nobel Prize–winning work, is an inherent drive of the material universe itself, which started with the Big Bang. Stuart Kauffman, of the famed Santa Fe Institute, says that the complexity in the universe is "some sort of mixture of self-organization and natural selection"—with self-organization being that inherent drive to greater novelty, complexity, and order.

You can find variations of this view in any number of really bright theorists. Bruce Damer is a highly respected pioneer in abiogenesis, scientific research into the very origins of life. (I've spent a fair amount of time with him, and he's as close as anybody I know to this breakthrough.) And right at the beginning of his explanatory scheme is something without which the entire system won't move forward at all: *a probability-increasing machine* (which is where I got that phrase). In other words, in order for life itself to originate, there has to be something that drives the creative emergence of higher-ordered entities and actively works against randomness (and against the second law of thermodynamics). The universe is not winding down; evolution occurs because there is a drive for the universe to wind up—that is, it's a probability-increasing machine.

Or take Charles Peirce—widely agreed to be one of the greatest philosophical geniuses of the United States.[8] Peirce maintained that evolution was driven by four forces: the first two were standard chance and necessity—which in standard Darwinism are what drive mutation and natural selection (which together are usually what is called "evolution," which is the third force). But Peirce maintained that those three forces couldn't give you anything even vaguely resembling evolution. For that, he said, you need a fourth force beyond chance, necessity, and evolution—a force Peirce called "creative evolution" or "Evolutionary Love" (his term and his caps; Peirce added, quoting John, "God is Love"). In other words, you need Eros, the inherent drive of the Kosmos to create order out of chaos and consciousness out of rocks. (Given that evolution is ultimately driven by Eros or Evolutionary Love—and given that God is Love—this is exactly why anybody as brilliant as Peirce could easily see evolution as being Spirit-in-action.)

So that inherent drive to greater complexity, order, and wholeness can indeed be legitimately pictured either as just an inherent drive of the universe or as the creative drive of Spirit itself, a creative drive or Spirit-in-action that brings something out of nothing moment to moment to moment. Spiritual intelligence, grappling with these issues, can see this inherent drive that creates order out of chaos as being an intrinsic feature of the universe itself or as a primary form of Spirit's own creativity. One of these two versions—secular or spiritual (both of which embrace self-organization)—is the most common explanation of the *why* of evolution, starting at orange. But gone is the insanity of there being nothing but chance mutation and natural selection driving evolution—a notion so utterly idiotic that it reminds one of Arthur Lovejoy's comment that "there is no human stupidity that has not found its champion."

But this view of inherent order cannot legitimately believe that a mythic Jehovah (or any other mythic god or goddess) is necessary in order to provide the "why" of evolution. That conclusion, which is common with Intelligent Design theories, is not a rational conclusion. It is the result of the working of spiritual intelligence, for sure, but one that is still operating in many ways at the previous, mythic level. Intelligent Design theories aggressively attack the major inadequacies of the natural-selection explanation of the "why" of evolution, and their often-correct criticisms make them interesting theories.

But they then sneak their own mythic explanation of the "why" into the equation (usually in the form of the God of the Bible), and not only is that completely unwarranted but it doesn't work anyway. The real problem with Intelligent Design is the "intelligent" part. Evolution, as Michael Murphy puts it, meanders more than it progresses. There are simply too many aspects of evolution that although surely driven by an inherent drive to create higher order, nonetheless are often fairly happenstance; not every itty-bitty item of evolution is clearly and carefully intelligently designed (some things still happen by chance, for one thing). Eros, or self-organization, is a general push, a broad tendency, a rough directive, a generalized morphogenetic field not a precise and detailed blueprint. The only way a truly Intelligent Designer actually created something as loopy as a duck-billed platypus is if it got drunk that week.

So at this stage, the "why" of evolution is often seen as the way that Spirit itself actually creates this world, the way that it spontaneously introduces new elements, novel emergents, increases in consciousness, the whole creative drive of Spirit-in-action—a "creative advance into novelty." In reference to Christianity, scientifically oriented evolution often replaces mythically oriented Genesis at this stage. The work of Michael Dowd is a good example of the many Christians who have started taking this orange (or higher) approach and see evolution itself as the primary evidence and product of Spirit's own creativity—the glorious evidence of a truly abundant creative drive. And further, from this point of view, Jesus Christ himself becomes a beacon of humanity's own future evolution.

8

The Postmodern-Pluralistic (or Green) Stage

The green postmodern stage—also known as the pluralistic or relativistic stage—is a good example of the ways in which evolution has continued to unfold in our world. In 1959, only 3 percent of the American population were at a green stage of development; today, around 23 percent are. Evolution continues!!! This brought many new changes to the United States—perhaps the most important is the postmodern, which included, among many other things, a nasty series of culture wars, still quite rampant. For a listing of the terms various researchers have used for this stage, see table 5. Note the emphasis on such terms as *pluralistic*, *relativistic*, *postmodern*, *multicultural*, and *egalitarian*.

This green stage adds a 4th-person perspective to the previous stage's 3rd-person perspective, so there is a very strong emphasis on multiple perspectives, all of which are seen as having equal importance (a view known as "egalitarianism"); hence this stage's embrace of equity, diversity, and multiculturalism. Because of its 4th-person metasystemic capacity to reflect on the systems created by the previ-

TABLE 5. Equivalents to the green pluralistic-postmodern stage

Researcher/system	Growing Up stage
Integral	green pluralistic-postmodern (multicultural egalitarian)
Commons and Richards	metasystemic
Fischer	systems
Fowler	conjunctive
Gebser	pluralistic
Graves	relativistic
Kegan	postformal/postmodern
Kohlberg	social contract
Loevinger	individualistic
Maslow	beginning self-actualization
Selman	symbolic interaction
Torbert	existential
Wade	affiliative

ous 3rd-person rational stage, it is often highly critical of those systems, claiming that they are created by "tyrannical power" and need to be "deconstructed," especially if they are seen as creating inequalities between groups that should be treated equally.

Thus, there is a strong emphasis on the complete equality of all humans and a tendency of spiritual intelligence at this level to embrace as an ultimate concern a notion of *social justice*. It fights anything seen as discrimination, marginalization, or oppression; and it is extremely sensitive to what happens to the environment—some version of an ecological Gaia as ultimate Spirit (or as part of its ultimate concern) is especially prevalent. In other words, both engaging in social justice and ecological activism are seen as aspects of the same ultimate concern. The Web of Life for orange modern rational is often a scientific fact; for green postmodern pluralistic, it is a moral imperative.

At green, if one is a Christian, Christ is seen as one among many authentic, multicultural World Teachers. Other religions are not just to be tolerated (as they are with orange) but are also possible supplements to be incorporated into one's own practice (for example, taking up the Buddhist practice of mindfulness); all of this is acceptable to a pluralistic Christianity.

FREEDOM VERSUS EQUALITY

Both orange and green are worldcentric, so they both desire to treat all people fairly, regardless of race, color, sex, gender, ethnicity, or creed. But although both of them believe in worldcentric fairness, what each of them means by *fairness* is quite different.

Fairness, for freedom-oriented orange, is that all people should be given *equal opportunity*. This means, for example, in the Olympic 100-meter dash, absolutely everybody who is qualified gets to run in the race—no member of any group (race, color, ethnicity, creed) is excluded just because they belong to that group. Then whoever finishes first gets a gold medal, second silver, and third bronze. It is very much merit based, and "may the best person win"—as long as *everybody* gets a fair shot and none are excluded.

But for egalitarian green, fairness means *equal outcome*, sometimes referred to as "equity." Green doesn't just want everybody to start the race at the same time, it wants everybody to finish the race at the same time. If any group consistently finishes behind any other group, that is because the winners—or at least some other malevolent powers—are discriminating against them, holding them back, oppressing them. They are not losers but victims. The orange distinction of winners and losers is replaced by the green distinction of oppressors and victims. (Clearly, both distinctions exist in the real world. The trick, Integral maintains, is how to integrate them, since neither orange nor green wants to do this.)

Both orange and green, being worldcentric, tend to say that they are in favor of both freedom and equality for everybody. But there are some significant differences in how they use those terms, which are related to the differences between equal opportunity (orange's *freedom*) and equal outcome (green's *equity*). For example, there is equal opportunity when everybody who is qualified to perform a particular job is able to apply for it and will be considered solely on their merits. Nobody is rejected just because they are gay, black, female, or a member of some minority. That is embracing *freedom*—orange wants to make sure everybody who is qualified has the freedom to apply. If everybody who applies has equal opportunity, and the best person for the job is chosen on their merits, then orange is not so concerned with which group or minority the person hired belongs to, even if it appears that people from some groups are usually not being hired. For example, if the belief is "May the best man win," and if the word *man* means "person," but a lot more males get the job than females, then as long as the hiring decisions are genuinely merit based, that's fine with orange. Freedom is freedom.

But that is radically not fine with green. Equality is equality, and that orange result might be freedom but it is *not* equality or equity. (If males and females have the equal opportunity to apply for the job, but twice as many males actually end up being hired, then they all have an equal amount of freedom, but twice as many males as females have equality.) In other words, there is a big difference between freedom and equality. And if green has to step on a few freedoms to get more equality, fine with green. If we need to do something like introduce quotas that limit the freedom of males to apply and we deliberately select more females, that's okay with green.

Freedom and equality do not get along very well. In fact, they're opposites. It was Thorstein Veblen who first pointed out that, paraphrasing, "Human beings are born with many differences. Therefore, you can have either freedom or equality, but you can't have both."

For example, in the early 1960s, around 61 percent of all college degrees were being given to males, and only 39 percent to females. This was not because females were being discriminated against when they applied to college. By that time, it was, in fact, illegal to discriminate against women in this fashion—there were laws against denying women equal opportunity in almost every area, and if you did, you could be fined or sent to jail. No, this was a lack of equal outcome—it was an inequality in the number of female versus male graduates. Women did not lack freedom; they lacked equality. Although men and women were equally free to apply to college, they were not graduating in anywhere near equal numbers.

Here we have to be extremely careful. Green will tend to look at *any* deviations from equal outcome as being due *solely* to discrimination and oppression. Healthy green will not tend to do this as much, but a dysfunctional green—a "broken green"—will see any and all deviations from equal outcome as being due solely to discrimination or oppression. If the ratio of men to women in a society is 1:1, then any profession should have 50 percent men and 50 percent women, and, as broken green sees it, any deviation from that number is due solely to oppression (which creates nothing but victims).

But this is categorically false. As only one example, in Scandinavian countries—which are universally acknowledged to be the most *gender egalitarian* countries in the world—the ratio of men to women in engineering is nowhere close to 1:1, as one would expect if men and women were indeed treated equally. Rather the ratio of male to female engineers is a staggering 20:1. Since this is occurring in gender-egalitarian countries, what is causing it? The same thing is true if we choose professions that are stereotypically female oriented, such as nursing, where the ratio of women to men is an equally startling 19:1. So again, what on earth is causing this?

These huge differences are *not* due to a difference in intellectual capacity, they're due to a difference in *interests*. Women can do just as well as men in engineering (and many do), it's just that most women are not that interested in engineering (and so they don't do it). Men are more interested in engineering, and thus more of them enter the field. Moreover, this difference in interests has been tested in numerous cultures all over the world, and the *more egalitarian the culture is, the greater those differences become*—which tends to indicate that the more equally men and women are treated, the more their own natural interests are allowed to come to the fore. The *London Times* has reported on at least three research projects testing that theme (namely, the more egalitarian the culture, the greater the differences in interests), and it calls their unanimous conclusion "the sturdiest finding of modern sociological science."

Human beings are indeed born and develop with a vast number of differences—with different talents, gifts, handicaps, skills, preferences, desires, goals, and interests. Whenever human beings engage in areas that involve any of those items, it is ridiculous to suppose that they will all cross the finish line at the same time, and green's unyielding demand that everybody be given absolute "equality" is simply unworkable. The very real—and often extremely important—differences in human beings (including their different interests) need to be taken into account whenever we see anything other than a strict equal outcome (as we see with female engineers and male nurses in Scandinavia). This is not because of a difference in capacity but a difference in interest (it's not that men cannot be as good at nursing as women, it's that they don't have anywhere near the same amount of interest in it).

But this doesn't mean that achieving an equal outcome has no importance at all. It's true, for example, that in some cases—especially in the past—there have been groups that the ruling powers (personal or impersonal) have indeed discriminated against and oppressed. These groups often had no equal outcome because they were denied equal opportunity in the first place—they didn't finish the race because they weren't allowed to run in it to begin with. But there are also cases where, even after the freedom of equal opportunity was made fully available, a particular group did not do as well as they could, and in many cases that was because, over the years, they had adapted to not running in the race at all, and so, even when allowed to do so, they did not participate. (In many ways, this was true of women in higher education.) But in looking to redress that imbalance, we want to be careful not to focus on just equality and overlook freedom. That is not the way to integrate orange and green; that is to be caught in broken green, absolutistic green.

In the culture wars, people almost always side with green equality *or* orange freedom—but clearly we need both. The number of women graduating college in the 1960s is a clear example of a huge difference in outcome—a difference not in freedom but in equality (61 percent of the degrees going to men and only 39 percent to women). Advocates of orange equal opportunity were not that concerned with this result because, after all, women had been given an equal opportunity to apply to college, and so any unequal outcome was thought to be the product of merit (in other words, it was thought that men were more interested than women in attending college, and thus more were admitted and eventually graduated). But this difference in outcome is well worth looking into. It turns out that, historically, higher education was not often an option for women, but due to the changing roles of females in society, those options opened. By the 1960s, orange equal opportunity had made it illegal to deny giving women those opportunities. But women's roles, in too many cases, did not include higher education. So beginning in the mid-1960s, U.S. society (led by the Boomers, the first generation in history to have a leading edge of green values) began to adopt practices that helped young girls and women orient themselves to achieving a higher education. These efforts were wildly successful. In fact, by

2015, the percentages of men and women receiving college degrees had completely reversed: 61 percent of all college degrees were being given to women and only 39 percent to men.

Some critics say that this was the result of policies that had gone too far, that they had extended to an all-out attack on males in education and in many other areas (for example, see books with titles such as *The War against Boys* and *The Boy Crisis*). Harvard, for example, has been sued by a group of Asian students who claim that they have been discriminated against in favor of black students when it comes to admissions. Because Asians as a group routinely scored higher than blacks (as well as all other races) on SAT scores, and Harvard wanted to create a racially diverse student body, Harvard (and other colleges) added hundreds of points to the SAT scores of blacks, and then compared the adjusted score to the nonadjusted score of Asians, and selected those with the higher score for admission. This, of course, limited the *freedom* of Asians to enter Harvard in the name of more *equality* in the number of accepted blacks—it limited the Asians' opportunity in order to achieve a more equal outcome. Clearly, merit on its own is a value that favors freedom and limits equality.

Integral points out that because these two value systems represent real stages of development through which everybody grows, they need to be integrated and not simply pitted against each other, as they are in today's culture wars. To a large degree, the culture wars—amber against orange against green (the traditional values of ethnocentrism versus the modern values of freedom versus the postmodern values of equality)—are the result of the developmental unfolding of Growing Up. Until that fact is taken into account, there seems to be no end in sight for the ever-increasing polarization of society. The only antipolarizing force on the cultural horizon seems to be the slow but steady increase in the emergence of the Integral stages.

THE PROGRESSIVE LEFT AND THE CONSERVATIVE RIGHT

Let me quickly draw out a few more points with regard to these culture wars, since they will help us understand the green postmodern stage and its values. Recall that Graves labeled the amber, orange, and green stages, respectively, "absolutistic," "multiplistic," and "relativistic." Notice the progression—from an ethnocentric group *absolutistically* having the one and only truth (which is a myth), to a *multiplistic* rationality that recognizes that anything can be looked at from many different perspectives (including that of modern science, whose rationality is believed to give a much more accurate truth than myth), to a *relativistic* postmodernism, whose increased complexity cuts truth loose from any anchoring and makes it deeply relative (and since in this "posttruth" world, all truths are relative, they all have the same value; hence this stage's emphasis on egalitarianism, multiculturalism, and equal outcomes). If either the multiplistic view (orange) or the relativistic view (green) is held in a truly fanatical, zealous, and absolutistic fashion—as often happens in the culture wars—then the person can actually regress to absolutistic amber, which, along with all other amber beliefs, is deeply ethnocentric and quite convinced that it has the one and only truth.

Unfortunately, since its emergence in the 1960s, green has in many cases become more and more dysfunctional, zealous, fanatic, and absolutistic—green has too often become "broken green," and this is a very large player in the culture wars. Broken green dominates the liberal arts fields in academia—and is increasingly invading the STEM fields as well, as Jordan Peterson reports—entertainment, and the media. It drives political correctness, identity politics, and far-Left politics. Identity politics starts out wanting more of an equal outcome for all minorities, but it is, by definition, *ethnocentric* identity politics. That you deliberately choose to belong to one identity rather than another means that you are deliberately choosing to be ethnocentric. The more zealously and absolutistically a person holds those identities, the more likely they are to regress to amber ethnocentric. Thus they inadvertently become living examples of the types of ethnocentric racism or sexism they are protesting against so aggressively. This is why the far Left are sometimes called "the regressive Left"—they are indeed regressing from green to amber. So regressively ethnocentric do they become, they imagine that it is not even necessary for them to talk to their opponents, who are often simply shouted down. In other words, they have become a new fundamentalist religion, with their own dogma and heretics and blasphemers. (This has also been noted by various social commentators, who refer to the far Left as "America's new religion.")

The central problem with broken green is that it believes that all differences between groups are solely the result of discrimination and oppression. If everybody does not finish the race of life at the same time, this not because there are winners and losers, or differences in interests or desires—there are only oppressors and victims. And that is the only choice a person has: to be a victim or an oppressor. These otherwise idealistic and often good-hearted folks tend to regress to amber absolutistic, which is indeed ethnocentric, and this is why they think that they don't even have to talk with anybody who disagrees with them (no truly worldcentric stage would ever say anything like that).

At this amber absolutistic level, they join the truly ethnocentric groups that are already there—real neo-Nazis, members of the KKK, white supremacists, and so on. This is a primary cause of the powerful retribalization, polarization, and increasingly nasty culture wars that grip the United States, as ethnocentric identity tribes fight other ethnocentric tribes with no end in sight, each of them acting, in effect, as a *fundamentalist religion*.

Politically, this has produced something of a nightmare. The rise of modernity, which included events such as the French and

American revolutions, involved the emergence of the orange rational-worldcentric stage of development (which the historian Will Durant called "the Age of Reason and Revolution"). The rational-worldcentric view of freedom held by modernity was in sharp contrast to the conventional, traditional, mythic-oriented sense of ethnocentric values, which a political conservatism did indeed want to conserve. This new orange worldcentric orientation desperately wanted progressive social change, an increasing freedom for all, and this was such a novel value that a new term had to be invented for its political stance. The term chosen was *liberal*, taken from *liberty*, which reflected orange's strong embrace of individual freedom and liberty as its central values.

It just so happened that, in the French assembly, the old conservatives sat to the right of the king, and these new-fangled liberals sat to the left—and the terms *Right* and *Left* stuck and continue to be used today for the names of these two major political orientations—the conservative/traditional Right and the liberal/progressive Left.

For a few hundred years, the amber conservative Right and the orange liberal Left were the two dominant orientations in Western politics. They faithfully represented the central values of the two stages that gave birth to them. The conservative Right, driven largely by ethnocentric amber, was very traditional, fully embraced the conventional mythic religion, was devoted to a mythic God and country and family, and was often ethnocentric in unpleasant ways (perhaps unavoidable at that stage): they were often racist, sexist, homophobic, xenophobic, militaristic, and assigned rights to special group. They embraced all of this as something close to absolute truth.

The new liberal Left, on the other hand, was indeed mostly orange: deeply worldcentric and rational instead of ethnocentric and mythic, they believed in science instead of mythic religion (hence they would, for example, almost immediately accept the theory of evolution, unlike the Right, which abhorred it). They were often known as "progressive," and they especially believed in liberty as individual freedom (equal opportunity) and that these freedoms were the universal rights of all.

Liberal philosophers began writing treatises with names like *The Declaration of the Rights of Man and of the Citizen.* The notion of universal rights was indeed radically new, since the only rights in existence at that time were ethnocentric rights, the rights of a privileged group. When you die, for example, if you are a Christian, then you go to heaven and live with God forever. But if you are a Hindu, or a Jew, or a Buddhist, you have no rights; you burn in hell forever. Liberal philosophers were shocked at this. They believed that a person had individual rights universally or worldcentrically, simply in virtue of being born a human being.

It turns out that titles like "the Universal Rights of Man"—where "man" refers only to "males"—were accurate. Even these original, orange philosophers were almost entirely white, European, able-bodied, property-owning, cisgendered, heteronormative males. Not exactly universal. But the liberal principles of freedom that they introduced were indeed universal, so these orange principles of freedom (as equal opportunity) inexorably began to expand beyond white European males. Historically, they expanded first to include black males, then women, then gays, and are now moving to include all transpersons and any other minority whatsoever, because *worldcentric* means worldcentric.

The ever-more inclusive scope of these rights was enormously helped by green postmodernism. It, too, was worldcentric, so both modern orange and postmodern green wanted to treat all people fairly, regardless of race, color, sex, or creed—but what orange and green meant by "treating fairly" was quite different. As we've seen, fairness for orange means that everybody has equal opportunity (or freedom), whereas fairness for green means everybody has an equal outcome (or equity). Historically, the original Right (amber) and

Left (orange) dominated the political landscape for several hundred years. However, in the 1960s, a third major player—the relativistic, multicultural, egalitarian, postmodern green stage—began to emerge. And since "two's company, three's a crowd," the addition of this third player threw U.S. society into the culture wars.

This was particularly confusing for liberals. For centuries, the Left had represented orange values of individual freedom and liberty (as universal equal opportunity). But precisely because they were "progressives," as the new green stage began to emerge, a large number of liberals progressed to this postmodern stage. Those who did were often surprised to find that the values generated at this green stage were quite different from those of the classic, orange liberal stage. Where a classic, orange liberal—call them the "old Left"—believed in freedom (as equal opportunity), the green "new Left" believed in strict equality (as equal outcome). Orange old Left believed in individual rights, green new Left believed in social rights; old Left believed in democracy, new Left believed in socialism; old Left believed in individual justice, new Left believed in social justice. As usual, freedom and equality, being opposites, did not get along very well. (And, as usual, Integral claims both of these should be integrated. Sophisticated political thinkers know this, since many of them are actually coming from Integral stages of development.)

For the Left itself, the words *liberal* and *Left* no longer meant the same thing. Being liberal now meant being a classic liberal, an old Left liberal, representing orange values of freedom as equal opportunity, which were opposite to the values of equality that the new Left believed in. Thus the Left itself came to mean just the "new Left."

This has caused enormous confusion in politics, because while everybody recognizes the difference between freedom and equality, almost nobody sees their real source, the development from orange to green. Many classic orange liberals—who could not embrace these new green values—would lament, "I didn't leave the Democrats, the

Democrats left me." It became common to say, in so many words, "These new Democrats have lost their collective mind." It's certainly true that the new Left (postmodern green) largely replaced the old Left (classic orange) in voicing the now-accepted values of its political party (the Democrats).

In many ways, liberal and Left went their separate ways. This split between liberal (classic orange) and Left (postmodern green) is one of the things you hear most lamented in political discussions on YouTube —such as any PragerU video—although nobody seems to understand the reason for its existence. The difference between liberals and the new Left is widely noted by both groups, and new-Left Democrats are often viewed by many people as being "crazy" (because broken green is indeed rather crazy).

Interestingly, the party that did start embracing classic liberal values was the conservative "new Right." That is, as evolution continued forward, just as a portion of the original Left had jumped up a stage from orange to green, so a portion of the original Right also jumped up a stage from amber to orange. After all, since the new leading edge of culture was green, one of the older, now more traditional values worth "conserving" was orange! People aligned with the orange new Right were often called "Wall Street Republicans," since they embraced the orange values of modern Wall Street. The new Right openly embraced the worldcentric values of the original orange or classic liberal. Thus, for example, the new Left often opposed free speech if it hurt minorities—it maintained that "hate speech is not free speech," although the Supreme Court had already ruled that hate speech is fully protected by the Constitution (hate speech is exactly what is protected by free speech). But now the new Right—coming from an orange worldcentric stage—vigorously supported this originally orange liberal value of free speech, and almost alone vocally championed it. The old Right, of course, was the original Right—still coming mostly from an ethnocentric amber—and it stayed where it had always been—amber, ethnocentric, sometimes racist, sexist, homophobic, fundamentalist. But the new Right, having moved into orange values, fully supported the modern worldcentric liberal values of individual liberty and freedom.

The new Left, on the other hand, especially when it operates from a broken green, tends to see anybody who disagrees with them as being a Nazi (it literally makes these charges daily). Of course, any sane society should oppose real fascism (generated at ethnocentric amber) wherever it shows up. But without understanding the developmental realities that are usually involved in these value systems, green has no way to estimate the real threat of amber fascism, and thus almost always vastly overestimates it. (For example, green is always pointing to members of the KKK as being the real fascists that we desperately need to watch out for. But the KKK in the 1920s had close to 4 million members; whereas today, according to the Southern Poverty Law Center, it has a mere six thousand—not even enough to fill one football stadium. A major reason for this huge decrease is that the social center of gravity of the United States has continued to evolve to higher levels of worldcentric and thus there are fewer numbers at ethnocentric—something that is only obvious if you are aware of those stages to begin with.)

Fascism (of the amber type) is at least two major developmental stages behind leading-edge green, and hence there is no realistic chance of amber fascism taking over the influential centers of this society. The universities are dominated by green, the media are dominated by green, entertainment is dominated by green. There is no university anywhere in this country where you can take a course on "how to be a good neo-Nazi." Of course, you want to do what you can to reduce any real amber fascism that is present, but what is much more troublesome about the culture wars is that the leading-edge of cultural evolution is green—which is still a fragmented 1st-tier stage, not an integral 2nd-tier stage—and therefore green can do little to help unify or integrate the world. Even worse, it is often a broken green, which puts a regressive pull on cultural progress (the "regressive Left"), and this regressive embrace of absolutism is not helping things at all.

Most of the moves toward strict equality and equity (whether they are truly justified or not) stem from the egalitarian, multicultural, relativistic perspective of this green stage. It differentiates the unity of the world's different cultures and populations, the unity of systems that strongly characterize orange rational, and therefore it emphasizes the resulting *diversity* (which is a primary value of green). But it can't yet fully integrate this diversity or truly unify it on a higher level, and thus it inadvertently contributes to a fragmented, relativistic, retribalized, and segmented world, which tends toward violence and extreme polarization. It's only at the next stage (the Integral) that this genuine unification or integration can truly occur.

THE VIRTUES OF GREEN

I'd like to devote a little space to extolling the virtues of green and its pluralism. I tend to focus on the negatives, because in today's culture, much of green is broken green, which is indeed a massive problem, given that green is today's leading edge of cultural evolution (which is the major reason that the media, academia, and entertainment tend to be dominated by green—and that also means that they are also more open to a broken green). But healthy green has many virtues, which I summarize as (1) *contextualism* (all meaning is context dependent), (2) *constructivism* (all realities are constructed, in the sense of possessing development, as stage after stage is constructed), and (3) *aperspectivism* (there is no dominant and exclusively correct perspective). All of those terrific ideas were contributed by green pluralistic.

In terms of the discussion that we have been having about the culture wars, what green contributed becomes obvious (here we have to be careful to try and separate healthy green from broken green, since broken green is what you often see in the culture wars). Green itself, being worldcentric, agreed with orange that all people should be treated fairly, regardless of race, color, sex, gender, or creed. Orange had spent some two hundred years attempting to apply freedom (as equal opportunity) to all people. As we mentioned, this expanded over time from white men to all black men to all women to all gays to all transgender people to all minorities everywhere. And in a stunning number of ways, this was wildly successful.

For instance, in 1871, a woman in Illinois finished law school, applied for her law license, and was told that it was illegal for a woman to practice law. She took it to the Illinois Supreme Court, and they agreed: it was illegal. So she took it to the United States Supreme Court, and in an 8-to-1 decision, the highest court in the land ruled that it's illegal for a woman to practice law. But by 1920, women had gained the vote, and today, female lawyers are everywhere. Today the United States has gone from being a country where slavery was legal, there were laws against women practicing law, Jews were horribly discriminated against, and homosexual activity was morally and legally prohibited to a country where there are *laws against* every one of those things. Orange equal opportunity has, by law, been extended to virtually every minority. This is why most people in today's criminal justice system strongly maintain that *all* our laws are written so that they apply fairly to all minorities and no group is excluded or marginalized by law—so, for example, in this sense, there is no legal systemic racism, sexism, or marginalization in general.

Now technically that is true. There are no laws that say, for example, "If you are a bank, give women fewer loans," or "You must create hotels for whites and hotels for blacks, and they have to be separate." There used to be laws like that, but today if a bank does that, it can be severely fined and the perpetrators even sent to jail. In the objective, material world, where the laws are written and are part of institutions—the objective world that orange rationality largely created—there is very little legal, systemic racism or sexism. It used to be everywhere in that world, but you can hardly find any of it now. Most laws themselves are indeed worldcentric, applying equally to everybody (thanks to orange freedom). But there are still plenty of ways that our institutions are not equitable.

In the subjective, interior world, where the people who make decisions about how to apply those nondiscrimination laws grow and develop from egocentric to ethnocentric to worldcentric to integral, there are still ethnocentric prejudices to a fairly large degree. Being ethnocentric is not a law but a level of development through which every person, without exception, passes; and we already saw that, according to Robert Kegan's research, three out of five people remain stuck at an ethnocentric stage. So if 60 percent of our population is at an ethnocentric stage, they are going to apply worldcentric laws in ethnocentric and discriminatory ways. And, obviously, here in the interior world, you cannot make a law against being ethnocentric. If somebody is at an ethnocentric stage of development and they happen to be in charge of applying the objective laws (which are technically worldcentric), the decisions that they make will often—no surprise—themselves be ethnocentric. There is no law that says, for example, "Traffic police should stop black people at a higher rate than white people," but that nonetheless still happens. In today's world, most of the really pernicious racism, sexism, and bigotry are found not in systemic, objective institutions or laws but in subjective, interior decisions and applications of those laws.

Unfortunately, the elements necessary to understand this problem—namely, the existence of interior stages of development—are almost totally unknown in the culture at large. There is no cure for a disease whose cause you do not know.

Here is where green has focused its attention, even if it doesn't understand the causative factors very well (and where broken green badly distorts and amplifies them). Even though the laws themselves in the criminal justice system are almost entirely worldcentric, they are not always being applied worldcentrically. The people who are applying them are not mostly worldcentric (orange or green) but are variously egocentric (red) or ethnocentric (amber), and so naturally some of these real people are applying the laws in much less than a worldcentric fashion. Green has mostly focused on that kind of discrimination. Even if the major problem now is getting the culture at large to understand where these ethnocentric values come from, green has done a great deal to attack and limit the personal embrace of those values, and that has been perhaps its greatest contribution to Western society at this point. This has been the focus of much of green's social activism, and in that regard, green has performed a major social service.

Just listen to this list of things that social justice activists point to—but I think that what they really mean in each case is not that the objective institutional laws themselves need to be changed but that the subjective human attitudes that go into making decisions that apply these laws need to be addressed (even if these activists still have no understanding of the stages of development that are involved). Here's the list: discrimination in the educational system (such as who gets admitted to leading universities), the medical system, the legal system, the financial system, the economic system, family systems, and political systems (members of the Right are constantly blamed for being anti-women, anti-black or racist—and if they are indeed members of the amber ethnocentric old Right, they might actually be racist, sexist, or otherwise ethnocentric—that's rather the whole point here).

I want to emphasize this one point again: there are no written laws that mandate any of these types of discrimination. There is not a single law that says, "You must give minorities the death penalty more often than everybody else"—and yet that is often exactly what happens, and it especially happens when the people who apply the laws are themselves at lower than worldcentric stages of development (and this includes broken green who have absolutistically regressed from green to ethnocentric amber—the "regressive Left"). So again, this is not because of the law itself but because those who apply the law are at ethnocentric levels of development. And whereas we can make ethnocentric laws illegal, we cannot make ethnocentric stages of development illegal, unless we want to arrest every person in the country at some point in their lives.

This is where the culture wars go completely insane. Both of the worldcentric stages (orange and green) want everybody to be treated fairly, regardless of race, color, sex, ethnicity, or creed. But, as we've seen, for orange fairness means the freedom of equal opportunity, but for green it means the equality of equal outcome. Thus, for orange, blacks are being treated fairly if they have equal access to all society's goods and a nondiscriminatory equal opportunity to obtain any of its jobs—and orange believes this has largely been achieved. But for green, fairness means equal outcome, and because blacks make up 13 percent of the population, blacks should hold at least 13 percent of all professions and major positions—otherwise they are being discriminated against, they are still being oppressed, they are victims. Hence, orange maintains that "there has never been a place that treats blacks, women, and minorities better than the United States does at this time—things have never been better!" But green—seeing that there are less than 13 percent of blacks and less than 50 percent of women in various jobs—sees oppression and discrimination everywhere—responds, "Things have never been worse!" And here the culture wars explode into wildly polarized stances. (Amber, of course, doesn't like either one of them and contributes its own fundamentalist religious values to the war.)

All of these views are true but partial, but their partial truths can be seen only in a larger context, the genuine Wholeness of a complete Growing Up. In other words, as we'll see, the only real cure for this warfare is the emergence, as a new leading edge, of the Integral stages. All these combatants—amber, orange, and green—are 1st tier, which means that they are focusing on a reality that is indeed true but partial. None of them are capable of fully including the others. A 1st-tier stage thinks that its truth and values are the only important truth and values in existence, whereas a 2nd-tier (or Integral) stage begins to integrate them all and pull them into a genuine Wholeness, and thus it can wind down the massive conflicts—and culture wars. Everybody is still born at the beginning at square 1, and we will always have individuals moving through those less than Integral stages, but when an Integral stage becomes the leading edge of cultural development, the entire tenor of a society changes. The leading-edge question becomes not "Which of these values is right and how can we get rid of the others?" but "How can we bring them all together? How can we transcend and include them all?" In short, the only real cure for the culture wars is the emergence of 2nd-tier Integral as the leading edge of cultural evolution.

GROWTH HIERARCHIES VERSUS DOMINATOR HIERARCHIES

I'll return to that topic when I discuss turquoise Integral, but since I am especially focusing on green now, let me point out a particularly egregious confusion that has been part of the leading edge for several decades, a confusion that almost defines green (especially broken green): green usually confuses *growth hierarchies* with *dominator hierarchies*. Precisely because of its egalitarian stance (its desire for equal outcomes), if everybody is not finishing the race at the same time, the only possible cause is discrimination and oppression—that is, the sole cause of any variation in outcome between groups is that there is a dominator hierarchy structured by tyrannical power.

Dominator hierarchies are all the nasty things that green says they are. In dominator hierarchies such as a caste system, the Cosa Nostra and organized crime, oppressive social systems, master-slave relationships, and autocratic governments, the higher you are on the rungs of the hierarchy, the more people you can oppress, exclude, dominate, and marginalize. The higher the level, the more dominance there is; the lower the level, the more oppression there is. To the extent that green saw all hierarchies as dominator hierarchies, they naturally viewed them as being utterly horrid and deeply immoral. Under those circumstances, "Flatten all hierarchies" understandably became the only advice they offered.

But, as we've noted, there are many reasons why a particular person or a group might have a different outcome than other people or groups. These reasons certainly can include their being oppressed or marginalized, and those need to be seriously examined. But if that is all that we look at, we are massively stuck at green. There can be completely legitimate reasons from all over the spectrum of development for there to be some sort of unequal outcome—for example, different interests, skills, preferences, desires, and goals. And yes, people can also be born with different genetic inheritances (including aspects of IQ)—these come with the territory of the human being.

As we've seen countless times, there are fundamental stances—egocentric, ethnocentric, worldcentric, and integral—which are stages in a very real *growth hierarchy* (Growing Up), where each stage gets more and more inclusive. You are not born with green values of diversity and multiculturalism. The only way you get to those values is through 5 or 6 major stages of Growing Up, which are stages of a growth hierarchy. But green hates all hierarchies; it sees all hierarchies as dominator hierarchies in which the upper levels exercise power to oppress and victimize those on the lower levels. And thus green actively denies and fights the very path to its own goals and values—that is, growth toward the next level of Growing Up.

Green, in order to be genuinely healthy, needs to relax its zealous and absolutistic embrace of equal outcomes as the sole aim of social justice. There are an enormous number of legitimate reasons why there are differences between people in this culture, from interests to biological factors to cultural specialization; not all of the differences in outcomes are due to people being oppressed or victimized. Foremost among these factors are the stages of Growing Up, which constitute a genuine growth hierarchy headed toward some of the very values of green itself.

The vast number of hierarchies in nature are not dominator hierarchies but growth hierarchies. The hierarchy of quarks, atoms, molecules, cells, organisms is not a dominator hierarchy but an evolutionary or growth hierarchy. Molecules do not hate and dominate atoms; they include and embrace them. If anything, they love them. Further, it's only the lower levels of Growing Up (egocentric and ethnocentric) that want to create and use dominator hierarchies in the first place. The higher levels of Growing Up (worldcentric and, especially, Integral) not only don't create dominator hierarchies but they actively fight them. They grow and expand beyond the narrow and limited identities that want to control and dominate people, and instead disclose more global, inclusive, diverse, and worldcentric identities that treat all people fairly, regardless of race, color, sex, or creed. In short, the only way that you can cure dominator hierarchies is by moving to a higher level in a growth hierarchy.

Green gets into this mess not because it is stupid but because it is so smart. Remember that green is actually a higher stage than orange—and orange gave us everything from the abolition of slavery to modern physics to landing a person on the moon. It is precisely because green can reflect on the universal products of orange—and criticize them—that it suspects all hierarchies are problematic. It's smart enough to see the problem, but not smart enough to solve it.

The good news is that all people are thus open to a genuine tolerance, fairness, and care. The bad news is that, in denying all hierarchies, green multiculturalism does not itself distinguish, in any understandable fashion, between cultures that are egocentric, ones that are ethnocentric, and ones that are truly worldcentric, or even integral. According to the unyielding tenet of egalitarianism, they must all be treated the same way ("flatten all hierarchies!")—and thus, theoretically, we must invite to the multicultural table, and treat completely equally, Nazis, the KKK, racists, and sexists of all varieties. Of course, this is not what multiculturalism really wants; but it has no way to get out of this mess because it has already stated that the one fundamental tenet that cannot be denied is that all cultures and all values must be treated as radically equal (and thus all deserve an equal outcome). Because this stage has no idea how to integrate these many differentiations, it is not until the next stage, the Integral stage, that this problem can be solved. In the meantime, green is a politically correct Spirit seeking social justice, and this Spirit is usually taken as being some sort of ecologically interwoven, systems-theory Gaia, with numerous multiple and different cultural interpretations, all of them equally valid (although many of them are rejected for emotional reasons, starting with the interpretations made by white males).

GREEN RELIGION

Religion at this green stage, emphasizing equality, is often used as a primary justification for the activist pursuit of social justice. A large number of Buddhist schools in the West, for example, are actually called "socially engaged Buddhism," and before that there was Christian liberation theology. This occurs because this stage, in introducing a 4th-person perspective, can actively reflect on the 3rd-person universal systems that orange created. As it reflects on these monolithic, universal systems, which are everywhere the same (there is not Hindu chemistry versus Protestant chemistry; there is just chemistry), it sees instead a relativity of numerous differences in all the various cultures and social values that fluctuate, diverge, and alter considerably around the world. So green can effectively differentiate these grand systems—hence, multiculturalism. But because it cannot yet integrate these many differentiations, it simply, by default, maintains that you must treat all of them equally—hence, its primary belief in egalitarianism, its drive to equality, and its embrace of multiculturalism (and its confused denial of all hierarchies).

This green-stage approach to spirituality is probably the most prevalent one among middle-class, educated, leading-edge, social-media savvy people in the United States—40 percent of millennials say they favor socialism. This approach is definitely the most prevalent in anything calling itself "New Age." And we already saw the wide reach of "socially engaged Buddhism." In Christianity, it's a bit rarer. When you do find a green Christianity (with or without a Waking Up), it's usually a Christianity championing social justice, feminism, charity, love, Leftist politics, a stewardship ecology, open-border immigration, LGBTQ rights, and anti-Islamophobia—in other words, the green level itself is a primary determinant of its beliefs.

Note that the higher the altitude of Growing Up that a particular spirituality embraces, the further it moves from any of the original amber myths that might have become dogmatic for that religion and that first arose during that religion's own mythic-literal stage—and thus the more delicate an individual has to be in terms of how to use their spiritual intelligence to interpret any of the basic myths and mythic tenets of their religion. This becomes especially obvious with the green pluralistic-postmodern stage, where the green multicultural values in many cases directly contradict many of the core mythic-ethnocentric beliefs of the religion. In Christianity, these beliefs include its patriarchal bias, a pervasive misogyny, a weak ecological stance, a slavery-embracing attitude, and a significant anti-homosexual prejudice—all of which the green stage finds totally unacceptable—and therefore they are, at this stage of spiritual intelligence, often firmly rejected.

These types of clashes challenge religions like Christianity to find higher-level interpretive frameworks that truly bring forth what is most crucial to them. The central question that religions all over the world face today is the following: *If you give up the myths, what is actually left of your religion?* Think about that. Whatever the answer, it is going to be much more relevant than things like "Moses parted the Red Sea," "Lot's wife was turned into a pillar of salt," and "Lao Tzu was nine hundred years old when he was born." And, with any luck, it will certainly include things like a real Waking Up. "Let this consciousness be in you that was in Christ Jesus, that we all may be one" is not a myth; it is a direct pointing to a real state of unity in Waking Up, and this experience is at the core of whatever else it may be that you can find in an authentic religion. Christianity is particularly open to subtle Deity mysticism ("I and the Father are One") and causal Formless mysticism (the gnostic "God beyond God" and the Christian Cloud of Unknowing), and it can push into a genuine turiya I-AMness mysticism (Christ's statement that "Before Abraham was, I AM" is a perfect turiya intuition, which is often called "Christ consciousness") and occasionally Nondual mysticism (at its highest, "the Word made flesh" is a nondual intuition, and Christianity at its best is an "incarnational mysticism," or a Spirit/flesh nonduality).

As we've already seen, the fact that one has reached a causal Formless mysticism means that one is open to almost any of the higher-stage mystical experiences, and that is certainly true here. Although Christ definitely brought a subtle-stage Deity mysticism ("I and the Father are One"), he also stepped into a causal, Formless mysticism, which opened him to a direct turiya I-AMness experience ("Before Abraham was, I AM"). This statement of "I AMness" is the central element of Christ's message to humanity.

There are some individuals at green who are drawn to Christianity, and they are tending toward a green postmodern Christianity. (I'm not saying that we *should* look at religion through these stages but that some human beings are *already* looking at religion through these stages, and thus we should make it consciously official.) Some of the better-known writers at this stage are Bishop Shelby Spong and Marcus Borg (being authentic green, both writers "transcend and include" orange rationality). Liberation theology was one of the earliest forms of a green approach to spirituality. Originating in Central and South America, it emphasized that, given Christ's stress on caring for the poor and disadvantaged, Christianity itself should focus on social justice for the disadvantaged of this world and not just a promise of the redemption of souls in a wholly other world. Real love should be manifest now, not be some pie-in-the-sky promise. (Liberation theology should have added that although this-worldly justice is an important aspect of any comprehensive spirituality, you also need to include real Liberation in liberation theology—that is, you need a real Waking Up to go along with a green, postmodern Growing Up value system.)

For a Christian at green, Christ is seen primarily as a force of social deconstruction ("I bring not peace but a sword" and "Woe unto you who are rich, who are well fed, who laugh, whom everyone speaks well of"—in other words, everything thought to be good is totally deconstructed), and this involves inverting hierarchies ("The meek shall inherit the earth, the poor in spirit will gain the Kingdom of Heaven," and so on). That is, by inverting hierarchies—which green believes are the major forms of oppression—Christ brings love as social justice to *this* world. Because systems are also held together by love, Christ is an ecologist at heart and wants to bring a loving care to all beings on the planet, emphasizing their fundamental equality (*bioequality*—all living beings are equal strands in the Great Web of Life). In reaching out to the gentiles, Christ demonstrated his profound commitment to diversity and inclusion (the primary values of green). One religious scholar has summarized Christ's teaching as being a "radical egalitarianism," which pretty much sums it up.

Likewise, if one is a Buddhist at this green stage, one will tend toward a "socially engaged Buddhism"—a Buddhism that is anchored in social justice, Leftist politics, feminism, LGBTQ rights, ecology, open-border immigration, and so on, through a fairly standard list of green values.

Focusing specifically on green's spiritual intelligence, how can we best summarize what green brings to the picture (quite apart from whatever Waking Up experience may or may not be present)? The core of the green spiritual worldview could be called a type of *multicultural pantheism*. The totality of the interwoven manifest universe (Gaia or the Great Web of Life) is ultimately Spirit (identifying Spirit with the totality of the created universe is why it's pantheism), but Spirit appears differently to the various cultures around the world, each of them equally valid (that's the *multicultural* part). However, because green doesn't know how to integrate these multiple cultural systems, it defaults to claiming that all of them are fully equal, and thus its primary concern is a social justice that ensures not equal opportunity but equal outcomes for all people.

This stage will go down in history as the preparatory ground for that "cataclysmic" and "monumental leap of meaning"[1] that the Integral stage will bring as it leaps beyond green (and 1st tier altogether) into a genuine 2nd tier, which is the first truly holistic and integrated stage in human history. Let's take a careful look at this and at the profound type of Wholeness that it brings, and at how you can incorporate this Wholeness into your own life right now, shall we?

9

The Inclusive-Integral (or Turquoise) Stage

The Integral stage has an enormous amount of evidence supporting it. For a listing of the terms various researchers have used for this stage, see table 6.

TABLE 6. Equivalents to the teal holistic and turquoise integral stages

Researcher/system	Growing Up stage
Integral	teal holistic and turquoise integral
Commons and Richards	paradigmatic and cross-paradigmatic
Fischer	systems of systems
Fowler	universalizing
Gebser	integral
Graves	systemic/integrated
Kegan	integrated interindividual
Kohlberg	universal ethical
Loevinger	autonomous and integrated
Maslow	advanced self-actualization
Torbert	ironist
Wade	authentic

Note the emphasis on the terms *integrated*, *systemic*, *holistic*, and *cross-paradigmatic*.

THE NATURE OF THE INTEGRAL STAGES

All previous stages—archaic fusion, red magic, amber mythic, orange rational, and green postmodern—are often combined into what is called "1st tier," because they all have one thing in common: each 1st-tier stage thinks that its truth and values are the only important truth and values in existence; all the others are childish, confused, goofy, or just plain wrong. But starting at the Inclusive-Integral stage, with what is called "2nd tier," the idea is that all the previous stages are deeply significant—if nothing else, each of them is a stage in human growth and development, and so none of them can be deleted or skipped. This makes Integral 2nd tier the first truly holistic and inclusive stage in existence and a stunningly profound leap in evolution—Clare Graves called it "cataclysmic" and a "monumental leap in meaning." Although it is just beginning to emerge, it promises to profoundly change human nature as we know it.

As I did earlier with magenta and red (magic and magic-mythic), I am here combining two major stages into one. The two stages are teal Holistic and turquoise Integral. Whenever I mean just one of them, I'll use the separate names/colors, but for the most part, I'm here combining them into turquoise Inclusive-Integral because they both are 2nd tier, both are very rare, and together they represent the very best of the Wholeness that is offered by Growing Up. Depending on which developmental model you use, the percentage of the population at teal Holistic is 5–7 percent and at turquoise Integral 0.5–2 percent, so we could say that the percentage of the population at the combined stage of turquoise Inclusive-Integral is around 6–8 percent. In any case, 2nd tier is clearly the leading edge of evolution at this time, and it will almost certainly be the main stage from which any truly genuine Religion of Tomorrow will spring.[1] (People at even higher stages of 3rd tier, or super-integral stages, are extremely rare today, making up less than 1 percent of the population, so they have very little impact on world events—but they will become increasingly significant in the future. So for now, we put almost all of our interest in 2nd tier.) When I use the term *Integral*, I mean both this 2nd-tier stage of development (turquoise Inclusive-Integral) and also Integral Metatheory itself, which includes the entire AQAL Kosmic Address.

The developmental model of Harvard's Michael Commons is typical of the sophisticated models that include both these integral stages. One of his followers, Hanzi Freinacht, describes Commons's paradigmatic level (in my terminology, teal Holistic) as follows: "Can deal with several very abstract metasystems to create new ways of thinking of the world, new paradigms, new sciences or branches within sciences."[2] Commons calls the second level, his highest level, "cross-paradigmatic" (in my terminology, turquoise Integral) because it takes (teal) paradigms and cross-synthesizes them with other paradigms to create even greater Wholes. Freinacht describes this cross-paradigmatic level as follows: "Can deal with several paradigms to create new fields. Examples are Newton's reformulation of physics, Darwin's theory of evolution, Einstein's theory of relativity, the invention of quantum physics, the invention of chaos mathematics and complexity, the invention of computing, the invention of the holistic 'integral theory' of Ken Wilber, the invention of string theory."[3]

You can see that both of these Integral levels, whatever their subtle differences, involve an extraordinary amount of detailed complexity brought together into incredibly new Wholes. And these wholes—at least according to "the holistic 'integral theory' of Ken Wilber"—include Waking Up, Growing Up, Opening Up, Cleaning Up, and Showing Up—which, when thus brought together in a cross-paradigmatic fashion, form a genuine Big Wholeness. Yes, turquoise Inclusive-Integral does involve the capacity to do that. And just as important, turquoise involves ways to look for entirely new *types* of Wholes. For example, Plotinus was a beautiful genius who was also as integral as a thinker of his time could be. He dealt mostly with Showing Up (which includes all of the fundamental dimensions of reality) and Waking Up (how to directly experience the One), but there was no specific understanding of Growing Up, Opening Up, or Cleaning Up when he was alive, and so those forms of Wholeness were not included. But for any of today's approaches, those forms of Wholeness are crucial.

TURQUOISE INCLUSIVE-INTEGRAL AND ONE TASTE

It should be clear from Freinacht's examples of cross-synthesis that any contemporary Integral approach would include mainstream sciences, and Integral Metatheory certainly does. But in this book, I am focusing especially on spirituality and spiritual intelligence, so in this section allow me to continue to focus on that topic.

When turiyatita or One Taste first came into significant existence in Waking Up, it was primarily accompanied by the Inclusive-Integral stage of Growing Up. Of course, with the emergence of rational, causal Formlessness, the existence of all higher states of mystical experience became at least possible, because consciousness itself had been cleared of all forms. But when turiyatita One Taste came into existence, it was almost always accompanied by the Inclusive-Integral stage of development, which made the interpretation of One Taste so incredibly inclusive. Although the stages of Waking Up and Growing Up are relatively independent, when the turquoise Integral stage of Growing Up first became available, by its very nature it tended to push the highest stage of Waking Up into a turiyatita realization. It was the combination of these two (turiyatita One Taste interpreted by the Inclusive-Integral stage) that gave rise to such holistically inclusive and integrative approaches as Tibetan Buddhism, Tantra, Vedanta, and Vajrayana in general.

If one were a Christian, since all stages of Growing Up are important and none can be skipped, at this turquoise Integral stage, Christ's teaching would be seen clearly as something that should be interpreted as it appears at each developmental stage. Thus it would be able to speak effectively to every stage of Growing Up and would not make one stage the dogmatic and only correct stage (which would free Christianity from its typical "mythic-literal" dogma). Further, educating its followers on how the Christian message is interpreted at each of the major stages of Growing Up makes Christianity function as a *pacer of transformation*—an instigator of an authentic Growing Up, in addition to any Waking Up that it might provide. I refer to any system that helps with this Growing Up transformation as a "conveyor belt," and Christianity as conveyor belt reflects this Integral understanding.

Because of its truly comprehensive nature—which is open to embracing a genuinely Big Wholeness—turquoise Integral can potentially include Growing Up and Waking Up (as well as Cleaning Up, Opening Up, and Showing Up), and these would all be embraced together for the first time in our history in what is indeed a Big Wholeness. This Integral approach will occur whether or not religion gets on board; but if it does, we will have a genuine and authentic Religion of Tomorrow, coming at us from a future and higher stage of evolution, not from a past and considerably lower stage of evolution. We have all come up from Eden on our way back to Heaven.

This will change our deepest notions about human nature itself—what it is, and what it can become. And religion will become not what it is now—which is too often the recipient of mocking and reviling ridicule from the modern and postmodern mind—but instead a primary pacer of social transformation itself, helping humanity not only Wake Up but also Grow Up, thus genuinely demonstrating that it is indeed an authentic Religion of Tomorrow acting as a true conveyor belt of genuine social transformation. Given the truly holistic nature of this Integral stage, if its spiritual intelligence directly acknowledges the reality of spiritual states of consciousness in Waking Up, it will usually be open to all 5 types of mysticism, with an emphasis on turiya and turiyatita. It will also recognize that although turiyatita is indeed the ultimate state of Waking Up that has been realized to date, all the other major spiritual states can also be included—and each of them can and will be interpreted from one of the 6-to-8 major stages of Growing Up (in this case, the Integral stage).

In other words, a truly comprehensive spirituality (or any sort of Integral Life Practice) launched from the turquoise Integral stage will be open to the full recognition of each and every cell in the Wilber-Combs Lattice (see figure 5.3). The Wilber-Combs Lattice is perhaps the most compact summary of the totality of potentials available to human beings at this point in evolution. There are other important potentials (Cleaning Up, Showing Up, and Opening Up), but Waking Up and Growing Up are central to the growth potentials. As we saw, across the top of the lattice are the 5 major states of Waking Up, and up the side of the lattice are the 6-to-8 major stages of Growing Up. Thus, the lattice gives a cogent summary of the some of the highest human potentials discovered during the entire premodern-to-modern-to-postmodern-to-integral sweep of human evolution. To actualize all the cells in the lattice is thus to realize the very best and brightest of a million years of human evolution. And since that represents a version of the good life, from now on, anything less will be deeply unsatisfying.

Of course, reaching the Integral stage itself does not automatically include a Waking Up experience, since Growing Up and Waking Up are indeed relatively independent. At the same time, because the most adequate, inclusive, and thus "best" stage from which to experience and interpret a Waking Up awareness is indeed the turquoise Integral stage (because it's the most comprehensive), the ideal aim of somebody at the Integral stage, when it comes to spiritual engagement itself, is to undertake practices and exercises that will help them directly experience a genuine Waking Up. This would include, if one were aiming for both of the ultimate states of Enlightenment, a direct realization of turiya and turiyatita. (And since turiyatita is predisposed to the Integral stage and turiyatita fully "transcends and includes" turiya, both states are generally taken care of in an Enlightenment that occurs with the turquoise Integral stage.) Besides, if one takes up a comprehensive form of meditation—that is, one that includes all 5 states of consciousness as state-stages—then one will automatically include all the possible stages of Waking Up, including the two highest or ultimate states. And having the highest states of Waking Up interpreted by the highest stages of Growing Up (that is, turiyatita One Taste interpreted by turquoise Integral) is indeed an ideal situation, since it would "transcend and include" all the cells in the Wilber-Combs Lattice.

Although this is technically a separate issue, I have already suggested that it seems very likely that the spiritual schools that were created in relation to the experience of One Taste were founded by teachers who also had access to an Inclusive-Integral stage of development, or at least to a type of proto-Integral cognition (for example, Nagarjuna and Plotinus). Although Waking Up and Growing Up are relatively independent, Nondual approaches to Waking Up represented such a radical and revolutionary approach to spirituality, those who had already undergone the radical shift from 1st tier to 2nd tier (thus moving into stages such as turquoise cross-paradigmatic, with its enormous capacity for Wholeness) would be more ready to accept them.

Keep in mind that, at any time in our history, there were some people who were at every stage of the entire spectrum of Growing Up (Habermas even estimated that there were a few people in tribal times that were at formal operational—that is, orange in the Integral system). As for the other end of the developmental spectrum, some people have estimated that the percentage of people who are today fully at any stage in 3rd tier (super-integral) is less than 0.01 percent, but that still means that some 33,000 people in the United States are at one of those very high stages. So it's possible that the founders of any breakthrough discipline were often wildly advanced or evolved (at least to 2nd tier, some to 3rd), even if their many followers rarely were.

Thus it would not surprise me if the founders of any or all of the Nondual schools of Waking Up spirituality were at 2nd-tier Integral or proto-Integral stages of Growing Up (such as cross-paradigmatic, with its staggeringly huge holistic capacity, made to order for accurately interpreting a One Taste consciousness). But what is certain is that, like Nagarjuna, they pushed from turiya to turiyatita in Waking Up, from a formless Emptiness to an "Emptiness that is not other than Form," from an Absolute Subjectivity (or Consciousness without an object) to a nondual One Taste that totally transcended (and included) subject and object, from a nirvana totally separate from samsara to a nondual Ground that included them both in a larger Wholeness. And this wasn't simply the unity of a Nature mysticism, where there is no realization of infinite Emptiness and there is just a pantheistic spirit seen as the sum total of Form or the totality of the finite manifest universe—what Underhill called a "horizontal expansion of consciousness" not a "vertical transformation of consciousness." This, rather, was a genuine Ground of All Being, which fully included Emptiness and Form, nirvana and samsara—not a Heaven divorced from Earth but a real Heaven on Earth, a genuinely vertical transformation of consciousness.

Perhaps the most brilliant harbinger of this evolutionary revolution was the Buddhist genius Nagarjuna. So let me very briefly go over the role of Nagarjuna and his revolutionary discoveries from an explicitly Integral perspective so we can see exactly what was involved.

Nagarjuna had grown up in an atmosphere saturated with early Buddhism, with its roots in a causal/turiya realization and a belief that samsara itself—the manifest, finite, relative world—was inherently and totally awash in *dukkha* (suffering), grasping, and illusion, and that the only way to escape that illusion was to achieve a perfect extinction of all phenomena in awareness, an extinction known as "nirvana" (a nirvana that was totally separate from samsara, which was rendered completely extinct).

This causal/turiya realization was in fact deeply dualistic. Nirvana is separate and different from samsara; Emptiness is separate and different from Form; the One is separate and different from the Many. This was, at best, the world of empty, Formless turiya, fully accessed in a pure nirvana (extinction) and total *nirodh* (cessation)—a state that didn't integrate samsara but completely deleted it.

Nonetheless, this state of nirvana is not a myth. It is a very real, very attainable state of Waking Up consciousness (namely, 4th-state turiya). We saw shocking examples of it during the Vietnam war, where monks protesting various things (from being prohibited from displaying the Buddhist flag to the war itself) sat in meditation, got into a nirvana/nirodh state of pure cessation, had their bodies doused in gasoline, and then set themselves on fire. And right there on live TV, in front of millions of viewers, they burned to the ground, and not one of them flinched once. Nirvana is a very, very real state, and it does provide a type of genuine freedom and liberation from the entire manifest universe.

Nagarjuna doesn't question the existence of this state of nirvana; he questions whether it is the highest state available. And he answers that "No," it is not. Beyond nirvana is the newly accessed nonduality (the 5th state)—and this is a profoundly deeper and higher realization that unifies and makes whole the lesser reality of nirvana alone that is sought in early Buddhism. That is, instead of a nirvana totally separate from samsara and an Emptiness totally divorced from all Form, Nagarjuna points to a Nondual Reality that seamlessly unites nirvana and samsara, that completely joins Emptiness and Form, that renders whole the One and the Many. Those dualisms were discovered to be, at the deepest level, two different aspects of an underlying nondual and holistic Reality, much as the north and south pole of a magnet are two different aspects of a single underlying reality (they are "not two" or "nondual"). The *Heart Sutra* would soon put it in this way: "That which is Emptiness is not other than Form, that which is Form is not other than Emptiness," which means that which is nirvana is not other than samsara, that which is samsara is not other than nirvana. And that insight would change the entire world of spirituality. For example, instead of seeing sex as a hindrance to spiritual realization, sex and Spirit were now seen as not-two, and thus sex became not a sin against Spirit but a direct road to Spirit—as we'll see in chapters 17–19, when we explore Integral sexual Tantra.

Nagarjuna refers to this new and whole Reality by the term *Shunyata*, which technically means "Emptiness." But clearly this Emptiness is quite unlike an Emptiness that is different from Form. That is, it is not "Formless"; rather, this Emptiness "is not other than Form," which means that this Emptiness actually includes all Form—it is a Nondual unity that fully includes regular Emptiness *and* all Form (they are actually "not two"). In short, it's not a dualistic fragmentation but a nondual Wholeness; it's not an Emptiness split from Form but an Emptiness one with Form—and that new Wholeness is the *real* Emptiness (Shunyata or true Spirit).

But Nagarjuna's point is even deeper than that. Because the question is, How can you truly know or directly realize this Nondual Emptiness, this ultimate and absolute Reality? And Nagarjuna's point is that you *cannot* simply understand a verbal and conceptual explanation of Emptiness. That will give you only a knowledge by description. Rather, in order to be truly known and fully realized, any ultimate Reality (true Emptiness or Spirit) has to be directly and immediately experienced, or somehow enter direct awareness—it's a knowledge by acquaintance, not merely a knowledge by description.

So imagine, as an example, someone at the orange stage of Growing Up. They get a book about the turquoise-Integral stage—two stages higher than their own—and they read it several times, memorize all the characteristics of the Integral stage, take a written test about it, and answer 100 percent of the questions accurately, so they get an A+. Does this mean that they know the Integral stage directly? No, they're still at orange; they are nowhere near directly knowing the Integral stage by acquaintance or actual awareness. All they know are labels and descriptions, not real experiences. It would be like taking a vacation to Bermuda by looking through a book of maps—that's not a real knowledge of Bermuda at all. Likewise, for Nagarjuna, you have to directly experience Shunyata (in other words, ultimate Unity consciousness, pure Nonduality)—because otherwise, no matter how "accurately" you can describe that state, you still don't really know it—you're just looking at maps, not the real Bermuda.

Nagarjuna formalizes this central point by saying that no matter what quality or characteristic you choose for ultimate Reality—call it *x* (which can stand for Spirit, God, Consciousness, the One, Nonduality, Love, Light, the Good, the True, the Beautiful, or anything else)—Reality is neither x nor not-x, nor both x and not-x, nor neither x nor not-x. So much for words, right? You might say that ultimate Reality is pure Truth—but Nagarjuna would say that Reality is neither Truth nor not-Truth, nor both, nor neither. No words whatsoever are adequate, because none of them will give you a direct experience of that Truth. In the terms of semiotics, if you don't actually know the real referent, no signifier whatsoever will substitute for it. You can say the word *orgasm* again and again, but if you've never had an orgasm, the word is nowhere near close to the real thing . . . and never will be.

When it comes to truly knowing any ultimate Reality, any and all words and concepts will fail us (yes, including those). Virtually all of our words make sense only in contrast to their opposites—pleasure versus pain, good versus bad, infinite versus finite, life versus death, and so on—but ultimate Reality has no opposite, because it is totally and radically all-inclusive (but even that word won't work, because it also makes sense only in terms of its opposite, *all-exclusive*—get it?).

But we *can* know this ultimate Truth—not by using relative words and concepts but by changing our awareness to an ultimate state of consciousness—such as an ultimate Unity consciousness or ultimate Nondual awareness or One Taste. In that state of consciousness, we are directly aware of that ultimate Reality itself, and the activation of that state is the only correct answer to the question about what is ultimate Reality or Spirit. If we haven't had a genuine Waking Up, then any idea we have about it will be based on opposites, and that's not it (and what I just said won't work either—it's all based on opposites). If we want the real territory and not just another map of it, then we must awaken to that Reality directly—a real Waking Up, a genuine vertical transformation of consciousness.

To summarize: the first thing about "real Emptiness," "Nonduality," "ultimate Reality," or "Spirit" is that it is beyond any and all words and concepts (including those). It's an actual state, a real Reality, but in order to truly know it, it has to be a knowledge by acquaintance (or immediate Awareness) and not merely by description (or words and concepts). And for that to occur, you need a direct and immediate experience of the state itself. Prior to that experience or direct realization, *no words whatsoever will work*; after that realization, any words will work. (This can be easily seen in Zen koans or stories, which make no rational sense whatsoever; they're based entirely on direct experience or satori, which, if you've never had, will make no sense to you at all.) So you can be at any stage of Growing Up and say anything you want to describe the ultimate Reality of Waking Up, but none of those words will automatically give you a real Waking Up experience—only the experience itself will show you the true Reality.

Words and concepts are fine for relative reality, for relative truth. We can say, for example, "Water is made of two hydrogen atoms and one oxygen atom," and that's fine, that works well. But when it comes to ultimate Reality, we might be tempted to say, for example, "In relative truth, water is made of oxygen and hydrogen, but in ultimate Truth, water is made of Spirit." Although that statement sounds like it makes sense, it doesn't really work; it is hollow—it actually has no real meaning, because just saying "Spirit" isn't at all the same as truly knowing Spirit, and the only way that statement really can be understood is if you yourself directly and fully experience Spirit itself. And for that to happen, no words at all will substitute. For that to happen, you don't need a Growing Up statement, you need a Waking Up experience. Prior to that direct Waking Up, no words or labels or concepts whatsoever will be genuinely true. We can say that, at best, these statements are metaphoric, not descriptive. So my statements here are all metaphoric, which means that you can interpret them however you like, but to understand exactly what I mean by a Waking Up experience, you will need a Waking Up.

So Nagarjuna tells us that mere Growing Up statements (or ideas of spiritual intelligence) won't get you anywhere near ultimate Truth. You have to have what Zen calls a "satori," which is a direct Waking Up realization, a pure nondual experience. And thus when it comes to questions like "What is Spirit?" or "Does God exist?" the only correct answer that can be put into words is "Get satori and find out." You literally cannot say, for example, "Yes, God or ultimate Spirit truly exists"—that's nothing but a statement whose meaning depends on opposites. You must get satori or have a genuine Waking

Up experience, and hence directly see this ultimate, absolute, all-embracing Reality for yourself.[4]

THE DUALISM INHERENT IN THE NEW PARADIGM IN SCIENCE

We have to be especially careful when some "New Paradigm" in science purports to show that the unity it has discovered is the same Unity that the mystics have always pointed to. It's common to say, for example, with David Bohm, that the "new physics" demonstrates that there is an "implicate order" of ultimate unity underlying the "explicate order" of separate things and events and that this "implicate unity" is the same ultimate Unity that has been seen by the world's mystics. But one thing is certain: even if you learn every detail about some "New Paradigm" in science, you're nowhere near having a real Waking Up experience that would actually show you that Reality. You're just looking at more maps, and Bermuda itself is nowhere in sight.

Worse, these maps themselves are deeply dualistic, and the unity they refer to makes sense only in terms of its opposite. Bohm's "implicate order" makes sense only in terms of an "explicate order" that is separate and different from it (and that's what Bohm himself maintained). This is just the same ole nirvana versus samsara, Emptiness versus Form, One versus Many, that Nagarjuna savagely criticized for its dualistic fragmentation. I mentioned this problem to Bohm once, and in subsequent work, he introduced a "super-implicate" order, which was said to underlie both the implicate and explicate orders and unify and integrate them both. But that's just more dualistic words—"super-implicate" makes sense only in contrast to "super-explicate." All that this will end up giving you—as Nagarjuna demonstrated—is an infinite regress of silliness. The correct answer here is a Waking Up realization—a direct experience of Bermuda itself—not more Growing Up maps being confused with the real territory of Waking Up.

We see the same problem with quantum mechanics. The very common New Age (and New Paradigm) view about quantum mechanics is that it directly shows us that reality is a single, interwoven, entangled Unity, a real Oneness underlying any separateness—in other words, it shows us an "ultimate Unity" that is the same as that which is directly experienced in the ultimate Unity consciousness of turiyatita (in the same way that, for example, Fritjof Capra's *The Tao of Physics* claimed that modern physics shows us the same reality that a person practicing Zen perceives when they have a real satori).

The intractable problem with that belief is that professional physicists themselves never have anything like a real satori just by understanding modern physics and the vast majority of professional physicists deny this line of thinking entirely (they reject completely the idea that studying modern physics will give you a mystical-unity experience of Waking Up). If it were true that modern physics shows us an ultimate-Unity reality, then to master modern physics would necessarily be to have a Waking Up experience and directly know this ultimate Unity—however, in fact, that pretty much never happens. It is indeed possible to have an ultimate Unity consciousness, but that almost never happens by merely studying modern physics. Just how similar can they be?

So, when a "New Paradigm" in science claims to show the ultimate oneness of the world (the same unity that the spiritual mystics discover with satori), be very, very careful of what you're buying. It might give you some sort of conceptual overview of things like systems theory and quantum mechanics (and conceptually hook it to something like the akashic record of the East). However, you can rest assured that whatever else this paradigm might be doing, one thing it is not doing is giving you a real Waking Up to the real territory. The Paths of Liberation would say that all you've done is switch from iron chains to gold chains (but you're still in chains). For that genuine Reality, you need a real satori (or Waking Up) of some sort. And there is *no accurate way* to describe what it is that you will see with satori; you can only get satori and directly see for yourself.

Be very careful not to confuse a conceptual system of spiritual intelligence in Growing Up with a direct experience of spiritual Reality in Waking Up. Don't confuse the finger pointing to the moon with the moon itself—the stakes are simply too high.

THE MEANING OF TANTRA

Tantra is a form of spirituality best known, if not entirely correctly, as being deeply connected with sex. What it does connect with is life force or prana (which does include sex), and it does so in a very nondual way. Almost all the earlier, pre-nondual (and pre-turiyatita) schools of spirituality, East and West, had made some sort of sharp distinction between the present state that we find ourselves in (this-worldly samsara) and the new state that we want to get into (otherworldly nirvana). Those states were usually seen as being quite different (the former, all bad, and the latter, all good), and the essential point was to get out of sin, suffering, and samsara, and get into a blissful liberation, salvation, and nirvana. In many of these schools, the body itself was demonized, and anything that fed the flesh was seen as a severe impediment to a realization of spirit. At the top of that list was sex. There were few schools of Deity, Formless, or True Self mysticism that didn't recommend celibacy.

This is where we see the revolutionary impact of Tantra. Precisely because, at its best, Tantra was deeply Nondualistic, it did not see Spirit and sex as radically separate, or even opposed, but rather as two aspects of an underlying Whole. And thus, sex was no longer an impediment to Spirit; sex could actually be a direct path to Spirit. Hence, wherever Tantra emerged (it developed in India from the eighth to the eleventh centuries C.E.), spiritual initiation ceremonies often included sexual elements. In fact, in India, tantric initiation often included what were called the "five *M*'s," which were five things whose Sanskrit names all happened to start with the letter *m* that had been prohibited in most of the religions of the time—for example, sex, alcohol, and red meat. These were instead fully embraced in tantric initiations and practices as symbolic of the fact that, ultimately, there is only Spirit wherever you look—absolutely nothing is excluded. This was a kind of spiritual Wholeness, the likes of which had rarely been seen before. Humanity's virtually inherent recoil at existence itself as being deeply wretched, fallen, and alienated—marked by original sin, intrinsic dukkha, or existential angst—was finally seen through and let go of, and the metaphorically ever-present, all-inclusive Great Perfection of this and every moment was deeply realized. Again, we will be exploring an Integral sexual Tantra in chapters 17–19, as part of the realization of a genuine Big Wholeness.

As for this nondual Waking Up, the experience itself is that of feeling oneself to literally expand to being one with the entire universe, and this oneness is felt to be present in every state of consciousness that you may have. You literally no longer see the sun—you *are* the sun. You no longer feel the earth—you *are* the earth. You no longer see the stars—you *are* the stars, all of them. What's more, you directly feel that. In other words, your awareness expands to include the entire world, and you directly feel that you are one with all of that world. Your sense of being a separate-self sense simply disappears. Your ego no longer *has* an experience—your ego becomes every experience it has. That is, your sense of self expands to enfold every single experience that it is having—it reaches out and embraces the entire world, and you are all of that. This is why this experience is often given names like "cosmic consciousness"—your consciousness has become one with the entire cosmos, directly and immediately.

And remember, this state is *not disputable*.

In Indian philosophy, it is called *satchitananda*, which means "Being/Consciousness/Bliss." Your Consciousness has become one with all Being, which generates very blissful feelings because you are no longer identified with any pain or suffering that might come from being just your separate-self sense. You have completely let go of the ego and instead discover a profound Unity or pure Oneness with the entire universe. That is exactly what this turiyatita state feels like—like you have become one with everything. Everything in the world is arising within you, and you are indeed literally one with all of it. This is the true meaning of nonduality—the subject and the object, your self and its entire environment, the seer and everything seen, you and the entire world, are fully "not two," a state of Wholeness that is truly all-inclusive, a genuinely perfect Oneness.

SUMMARY: THE NECESSITY OF INCLUDING BOTH GROWING UP AND WAKING UP

In looking at all of these structure-stages of Growing Up and the various state-stages of Waking Up, one thing stands out: we desperately need both of these pathways, or at least as much of both as we can get. Both Growing Up and Waking Up disclose profoundly important, but very different, types of Wholeness. And neither of these kinds of Wholeness is simply lying around, waiting for all and sundry to see. You really do have to know where to look and what exactly to do, in order to see and realize their ever-increasing benefits. What's more, understanding one of these types of Wholeness will not show you the other type. Even if you do not agree with my version of Growing Up or my version of Waking Up, I do hope that you can see how stunningly important they are, in whatever version of them that you might find acceptable. That is, do you at least accept that human beings go through some sort of process of maturation and development (Growing Up), and that they also have access to some kinds of extraordinary Waking Up peak experiences? Both of these are indeed profound realms of meaning and wholeness on the way to a genuinely Big Wholeness.

Although we have been focusing the Integral framework on religion and spirituality, it is applicable across an extraordinary number of fields. In fact, the Integral framework has been fully applied to over 60 different disciplines to create more integral and comprehensive versions of all of them (Integral Business, Integral Medicine, Integral Education, Integral Politics, Integral Marketing, Integral Art, Integral Spirituality, and so on in over more than 60 different fields). So I trust that, even as we have been focusing on religion and spirituality, you could translate these Integral ideas into any other area or field that you find interesting.

With regard to spirituality and Growing Up, we have seen that all individuals, precisely because they grow and mature through around 6 major developmental stages, at each stage have a significantly different understanding of any religion or spirituality that they are involved with (because they have a different understanding of essentially everything). Religion—and I don't mean to insult the entire field, but this is true—is one of the very few areas where its students, and even its teachers, as adults, can be at almost any stage of Growing Up. For example, there are adult human preachers, ministers, and pastors who are at red magic or amber mythic in their spiritual intelligence, and they believe *literally* in every single magic-mythic word of what they are saying. There are also those at orange, and occasionally green and turquoise—in other words, the entire spectrum of the stages of Growing Up. You rarely find this in other disciplines, at least not when it comes to their official teachings. In science, for example, you don't find science professors teaching red magic animism or amber astrology—rather, they teach orange astronomy; and they don't teach amber alchemy—rather, they teach orange chemistry; and so on. Nor do their teachings span stages. It is not that the first year of medical school teaches magic leeches and bloodletting, the second year teaches mythic phrenology, and then finally the third year teaches rational antibiotics and surgery. No, they are rational from the start. But there are versions of religion whose teachers speak from each of these levels. There are some spiritual teachers whose self-sense and teachings are red, some are amber, some orange, some green, and some even turquoise integral.

The fact that religions pass through all of these levels means that it is tailor-made to be a *conveyor belt* of Growing Up. Religion is already (unconsciously) coming from virtually the entire spectrum of development—why not do that consciously? This is quite idealistic and even utopian, I admit, but can you imagine?

All human beings are going through these Growing Up stages in any event, whether they belong to a formal religion or not. But if they do belong to a religion, and that religion becomes Integral and makes these stages known to its followers, then that religion could indeed act as a conveyor belt—it would provide an actual map of, and a genuine guide to, personal transformation in Growing Up. Whether the person has experienced a Waking Up or not, *they will still be progressing through all 6 or so of the major levels of Growing Up*, as we saw with James Fowler's work; and these levels will also apply to how their religion itself appears to them (as it is interpreted from each of those stages). And if the religion does make these stages clear, available, and conscious, it will actively enhance an individual's actual growth and development—it will be acting as a conveyor belt of genuine transformation in Growing Up.

As a person begins the study of a conveyor-belt religion, they would pick up the religious beliefs and practices as they appear in whatever stage they themselves are at. They could be at the magic or mythic or rational or pluralistic or integral stage, and they would pick up their religion as it is explained and presented for that particular stage. *They are going to be doing this from their own stage in any event*—it's unavoidable—so why not make the process conscious?

As the person continues their own growth and development, they would adopt the successively higher stages of their religion, all the way into the fully matured turquoise-Integral stages of Growing Up, which involve the most whole, most complex and unified, and most conscious stages available at this time in our evolution—a type of Wholeness offered only by the process of Growing Up. Religions that do this would immediately cease their growth-preventing fixation on the lower magic and mythic stages of growth, which makes them subject to ridicule by most modern and postmodern educated individuals. They would instead become a conveyor belt of transformation, helping people move to higher and higher stages in their own growth and development and becoming a genuine pacer of transformation. Individuals would then, under guidance from their own religion, simply follow the developmental sequence forward, growing and developing in a fully conscious and aware fashion as they move through successively higher stages of Growing Up. If they belong to a particular church, there might be weekly gatherings for members of each stage—stage-2 groups would meet on Tuesday, stage-3 groups Wednesday, stage-5 groups Friday, and so on.

And at any one of those stages of Growing Up, a person could still pursue a Waking Up practice and experience, thus directly realizing the ultimate Ground of Being in their own case—which is the ultimate goal of genuine spirituality itself. Waking Up is still possible and very desirable—it's just that the Waking Up experience, with the ascent to higher stages of Growing Up, will become more and more adequately and fully interpreted.

As it is right now, these stages of Growing Up are virtually unknown to pretty much every person alive. The evidence for them is overwhelming—some of the models of Growing Up have been tested in over forty different cultures, and no major exceptions have been found to the general stages and sequences. If religions around the world were to become conveyor belts, then these stages would indeed become much better known, and individual growth and development would be profoundly accelerated. Studies have shown that if people learn the stages of a legitimate developmental model, they develop through those stages more quickly. Further, we would free religions from being stuck at mythic-literal or ethnocentric stages of development. Making all of these stages of Growing Up known and available to all would be perhaps the single greatest change that any genuine Religion of Tomorrow could bring about.

And best of all, we can make this change right now, for ourselves, in our own understanding and awareness. And that is exactly what we're attempting to do in this book, on the way to understanding a truly Big Wholeness.

Remember that in Waking Up, the claim (metaphorically) is that we are directly realizing a Oneness with ultimate Reality itself—a direct experience of being one with the Divine, one with Spirit, one with our own highest and deepest Ground of Being, one with the Great Perfection. Waking Up directly increases the territory of your self by moving you through various dimensions of increasing wholeness until you reach a radical Oneness with the entire universe. But in Growing Up, you are increasing the number of other perspectives with which you can identify in each of those dimensions. If Waking Up goes from gross to subtle to causal to turiya to nondual, Growing Up goes from egocentric to ethnocentric to worldcentric to integral. They clearly are not the same, and you definitely should want both.

The Growing Up sequence is crucial, especially since every major religion in the world leaves it out, not to mention virtually all other disciplines as well. And if a religion is at, for example, an ethnocentric stage of development, then it will tend to think that its group, and only its group, has the one true religion and the one true God. It will be stuck at that absolutistic stage of development. And almost all the world's great religions came into their basic form when they were at this amber ethnocentric stage of growth, so they originally thought that they, and they alone, had the one true path and the one true God. As we saw, it wasn't until Vatican II that the Catholic Church itself finally admitted that salvation could be had by other religions. This is why so many of the world's religions remain, to this day, the premier source of human conflict, discord, and suffering, not human solidarity, unity, and love—although they claim they are. And they yet could be!

I noted earlier that almost every major terrorist act in the past half-century has come from a (fundamentalist) religious group at the amber mythic-ethnocentric stage of development. In fact, fundamentalist religion at this ethnocentric stage is the single greatest source of terrorist activity in the world today—and, of course, it's all done in the name of the love of God. Whether they are Southern Baptists blowing up abortion clinics in the South, or Catholics and Protestants at each other's throats in Northern Ireland, or Hamas and Hezbollah in Palestine, or Pakistani Muslims and Indian Hindus in border warfare in north India, or al-Qaeda and Isis Islamic extremists, or white supremacists in Charlottesville, or Antifa in Berkeley—they are, in effect, *ethnocentric fundamentalist religious groups* convinced that they, and they alone, have the one true pipeline to God (or an absolute Truth or ultimate concern).

Humanity will never reach a harmonious worldwide peace and solidarity unless and until our religious organizations move up at least to the worldcentric (orange or higher) stages of their own spiritual development and make that understanding clearly available to all their followers. This conveyor belt would almost certainly be the single greatest change in world religions since their conception. And best of all, this is a change we can introduce in our own lives, right here, right now, thus making a Religion of Tomorrow something that we can begin practicing immediately today.

However, although such a Religion of Tomorrow would give us an access to both Waking Up and Growing Up, there is one area of a Big Wholeness that it would not be able to give us. I call this "Cleaning Up," an approach that put us in touch with the broken, fragmented, or repressed areas of our own mind and being, and that therefore gives us access to the Wholeness of our own healed and reunified mind. As we keep seeing, when it comes to all 5 areas of a Big Wholeness, knowing any one area will tell us little to nothing about any of the other areas. We've already seen that this is true of Waking Up and Growing Up—learning about one tells us nothing about the other. Nonetheless, each of them can still be accessed quite easily and fully—if we know where to look. The same is true of Cleaning Up. This is a therapeutic approach to a form of Wholeness that we can easily practice and access today, right here and right now, if we but know where to look.

Shall we give it a try?

10

Cleaning Up and Shadow Therapy

Let me remind you that we are in search of a Big Wholeness. This Big Wholeness includes a series of very real, if smaller, types of Wholeness: Waking Up, Growing Up, Opening Up, Cleaning Up, and Showing Up. I think that you've seen enough to know that these smaller areas do indeed represent very real types of Wholeness and that the Wholeness of one area won't give you the Wholeness of another; therefore we need to consciously include all of these areas if we want anything like a truly holistic Big Wholeness.

In this chapter, I want to focus on the process of Cleaning Up and how it can genuinely help you to integrate and include your shadow material (that is, unconscious and split-off elements of yourself), thus providing you with a true Wholeness with your own real and total individual being.

Start by taking one of the most historically profound and significant discoveries about human nature that has been made during the modern era—during just the past few hundred years: the nature of the psychodynamic unconscious, the nature of repression, the nature of the shadow, and the various therapies to address, and even heal, those dysfunctions (the sum total of which we call "Cleaning Up"). This healing itself genuinely helps us to discover a new type of Wholeness—the wholeness that results when the reduced, fragmented, and repressed mind is returned to its normal, larger, and more healthy state.

It's generally acknowledged that Sigmund Freud and his colleagues dramatically and profoundly changed the way that we look at human nature itself. It's said that along with Darwin's notion of evolution and Copernicus's idea of the heliocentric view, Freud's ideas are one of the three most profound changes that have ever occurred in how we view human nature.

Freud's ideas refer to a process that we call neither Waking Up nor Growing Up but Cleaning Up. Freud's view of psychoanalysis (his version of Cleaning Up) is based on the idea that when individuals repress or seal off various emotions and mental impulses, this repression causes various types of mental illness. Psychoanalysis aims to reunite the mind with this repressed shadow material and produce a Whole and healthy psyche.

We're not talking just about negative or defiled emotions. Almost all of the Great Religions have teachings on defiled emotions—that is, emotions that are harmful to human beings and that contribute to suffering and fragmentation—and ways to replace those defiled emotions with healthier, more wholesome, more joyous emotional states. But with Cleaning Up, we are talking about emotions that are actually *repressed*, emotions (or any mental qualities) that are deliberately denied, pathologically dissociated, disowned, and defensively sealed off and split off from the rest of the psyche (which fragments the true wholeness of the mind, a wholeness that the process of Cleaning Up was created in order to help restore). The *active repression of emotions*—which then creates, in their unconscious forms, painful neuroses and even psychoses—was, indeed, a relatively recent discovery, associated particularly, of course, with Sigmund Freud and his original inner circle, all of whom were truly geniuses—Carl Jung, Alfred Adler, Otto Rank, and Sándor Ferenczi. This discovery subsequently exploded into the work of thousands of researchers around the world, a discovery that would change, as we said, the most basic way that we view human nature itself.

Freud is credited with introducing (although there were several forerunners) the fundamental idea that the human mind, because of its evolutionary past, has an extensive area that itself is quite primitive but still active. We humans (as a conscious "ego") can seal off and repress various conscious elements and hence push them into this primitive unconscious region (the "id"—which is Latin for "it," or 3rd-person realities or "its" in general). These "shadow" elements can then create various disturbing emotional and mental illnesses (neuroses and psychoses), and psychoanalysis aims to bring these unconscious "id" elements back into a healed state of oneness with "ego" consciousness. When Freud was asked to summarize what his new technique of psychoanalysis did, he famously said, "Where id was, there ego shall be." That's a perfect summary.

However, Freud never actually said that. Most people don't know that Freud never once used the words *ego* or *id*. His official translator, James Strachey, added those words, which are Latin, because he thought they made Freud sound more scientific. The "ego" was the mostly conscious sense of self that we have (or our "I"), and the "id" was this mostly unconscious primitive material that was causing all the problems (an "it"). But Freud really never used those Latin terms. He used the German pronouns that are more accurately translated into English as "the I" and "the it." So Freud would not say, "Derivatives of the id can negatively impact the ego," although that is how Strachey would have translated it. A more accurate translation of something he said would be "Derivatives of the it can negatively impact the I." He wrote and spoke just like that (in German).

And that's what he was actually doing. He was looking at how we take material that belongs to the self or the "I"—some feeling or emotion, some thought or impulse, some trait or quality—and we deny that it's ours; we push it out of our awareness, we disavow and disown it. When we do that, we convert it from a quality that is part of the "I," part of my conscious self, and instead make it appear like it is not mine, like it is other, like it is an "it." So instead of being responsible for my own anger, my greed, or my jealousy, I disown it and say, "The anger, 'it' just overcame me," or "This greed, I don't know where 'it' came from," or "I don't know how to control 'it,' this jealousy." To fix this, we have to take that "it" back and make it part of the "I," part of the self. So what Freud actually said was not "Where id was, there ego shall be." He said, "Where it was, there I shall become." That was truly brilliant; that really summarized psychoanalysis.

Freud gave a really wonderful analysis of disowning or repressing some trait. The "ego" and the "id" are just some weird Latin names and are really abstract; but the "I" and the "it" are immediate and very real realities—we all have some sense of an "I" as well as many areas of the mind that are uncontrollable and just appear as an "it." We create shadow material by taking some "I" elements and disowning them as an alien "it." We deny it, we disavow it, we disown it, we split it off from our conscious self, and then it appears as if it belongs not to my own 1st person or "I" but to some 3rd person—him, her, or it. But it's actually mine.

A perfect example of this, which I often use, is a real research project, where zealous antihomosexual crusaders—men who had spent much of their lives actively fighting against laws that protect gay people—were shown images of homosexual pornography (that is, actual gay sexual erotica), and these antigay crusaders demonstrated much more sexual arousal than the average straight male did. In other words, these crusaders themselves had homosexual desires, but they repressed those desires as shadow elements, projected that shadow material onto gay men, and then they tried to get rid of their own shadows by getting rid of gay men. This is classic shadow projection—and the shadow-boxing that results.

In order to cure the problem, we have to take that "it" back and re-own it, reintegrate it, return it to the self, to the "I," and thus restore the psychological wholeness that we lost when we repressed this shadow material. "Where it was, there I shall become." And every time we do this, we are creating a greater mental Wholeness, which expands our self-sense from a narrow persona that is split from our shadows to a more complete, accurate, and whole psyche. Welcome to the Wholeness of Cleaning Up!

You can see why this is important, even from the research with antihomosexuals. Most homophobia is generated by shadow projections. Men who have not come to some sort of peace and acceptance about their own homosexual impulses will often project those impulses as shadow material and then hate gay men the way they originally hated their own shadows. If the Great Religions had been aware of the existence of repressed shadow material and the enormous amount of hatred, anger, and jealousy that it created, they would have had much more love and compassion than they did. In general, simply having ways to recognize and heal our own shadows gives us a profoundly important tool for increasing our own understanding, growth, and Wholeness.

All of us have shadows—and this includes our spiritual teachers. And further, if severe, our shadow issues can completely derail both Growing Up and Waking Up. Therefore, the understanding and techniques of Cleaning Up will almost certainly be included in any genuine and legitimate Religion of Tomorrow—not to mention any of today's other growth processes.

Healing emotional dysfunctions—the process of Cleaning Up—is very different from both Waking Up and Growing Up. For one thing, all three of these processes are relatively independent of each other. You can be highly advanced in one and lagging behind in the other two, and in any combination. Solving problems in one area won't necessarily solve any problems in the others. That is why you can have somebody who is highly enlightened—with a profound Waking Up—yet very emotionally and socially immature (low in Growing Up) and also strongly riddled with major neuroses and shadow elements (poor in Cleaning Up). And meditation itself will not necessarily clear up shadow elements, just like it won't necessarily help with Growing Up; in fact, in some cases it can make them worse.

Thus, any genuine Big Wholeness will almost certainly include not only Waking Up but also Growing Up and Cleaning Up (and, as we'll see, also Opening Up and Showing Up). And this is very likely something that you would want to include in your own Integral Spirituality or your own Integral Life Practice. I will explain exactly how to do this as we go forward, using a process of Cleaning Up that I refer to as the "3-2-1 process." This 3-2-1 process is a tool you can use to attain the Wholeness of your own healthy psyche. And you will get a very good idea of some major areas of your life that need to be taken into account for your own life journey, especially if you value anything like "holistic."

Just as human beings have been Growing Up to some degree since day one—even though they didn't consciously understand the details of that process—so individuals have been suffering shadow issues from day one—even if they didn't understand its details well. And this goes for the Great Religions too. As we said, most of them have some sort of understanding of "defiled" emotions, or "unhealthy" emotions, or "sinful" emotions, and how to deal with them. But none of them have a sophisticated understanding of *repressed* emotions, or psychodynamically dissociated emotions—in short, shadow material.

Although Cleaning Up and Growing Up are two very different processes, I have found that each major stage of Growing Up (as well as most states of Waking Up) can produce its own types of shadow material. Thus, corresponding to the spectrum of levels of development (in both Growing Up and Waking Up), there is a spectrum of shadow elements. There are crimson shadows, red shadows, amber shadows, orange shadows, green shadows, and turquoise shadows, along with shadows of each of the major stages of Waking Up. In this chapter, I'll focus on shadows from Growing Up, since few people are engaged in Waking Up; but the principles are the same in both. Each level of development has a different structure, contents, and tools of awareness, and therefore uses its own elements to create different defense mechanisms, as well as provides the material that will become the shadow material of that level itself.

So, if you really want to work on shadow material and a full Cleaning Up process, you'll want to look at each of these levels of shadow material and adjust the therapeutic process to specifically address each of them, with their own fine differences and nuances and the different defense mechanisms involved at each level. But—the good news—there are also some very general practices that work with shadow material no matter what level it comes from. I will now give a very general overview of shadow material and what causes it—how it is created—so that you'll be familiar with the overall process itself; and then I will present a very general technique—the 3-2-1 process—that works with virtually all types of shadow material. I will explain this technique, and then I will directly apply it and also give you the tools to continue applying it in your life, if you want.

THE SHIFTING SELF-BOUNDARY

One of the central keys to understanding defense mechanisms in general—and thus to understanding how shadow material is created—is that the self-boundary (that is, the line between what we feel to be our "self" and what we feel to be "not-self" or "other") is incredibly plastic. It shifts easily, and development itself is a continuous redrawing of the self-boundary to include more and more territory. We've already seen one example of this: development goes from egocentric to ethnocentric to worldcentric to integral—that is, the self shifts from an identity with just itself, to an identity with just an ethnocentric group, to all groups worldcentrically, to a global village. That's an extraordinary self-boundary expansion. And it can continue to expand, shifting from all humans to all life forms, a type of ecological Web-of-Life systems identity (a shift from worldcentric to integral Kosmocentric). And in Waking Up, it can expand even further to a complete Oneness with the entire universe, a so-called Kosmic consciousness or ultimate Unity consciousness.

So we can see how plastic that self-boundary is. And at any one of those stages of the expansion of the self-sense—including any of the 6 or so major stages of Growing Up—any aspect, component, or element of the self at that stage can be repressed, or denied and disowned, split off and dissociated. When this happens, that disowned self-material becomes shadow—it is banished to the repressed unconscious, where it is no longer experienced as part of the self or "I" but as part of the not-self—it is experienced as alien, as other, as not-me, as an "it." And typically such shadow material is then projected onto other people, things, or objects. I no longer have any of that nasty shadow material, but my neighbor, boss or spouse is loaded with it! I know *somebody* has a lot of this shadow material, but since it can't be me, it must be somebody else—anybody else, just not me. Shadow.

We already gave an obvious example of this, the zealous antihomosexual crusaders, who, when shown images of homosexual pornography, had much more sexual arousal than the average straight male did. They themselves had a significant amount of homosexual desires, but they repressed those desires as shadow elements and then projected that shadow material onto gay men, and then they tried to get rid of their gay shadows by getting rid of gay men. This is indeed classic shadow projection and the shadowboxing that results.

But here's the hard part—the really hard part. It's not just that if you project your shadow material, then you will end up being threatened by—and dramatically overreact to—anybody or anything onto which you project your shadow. It's much worse than that. It's that anybody or anything that you emotionally overreact to—that you exaggeratedly despise, hate, or loathe—is almost always your own shadow material that has been projected. And that makes the entire concept very hard to accept. Do you mean that the stuff out there that I hate is really part of me?

Well, yes. Let's say that you start working for a company and find that you can't help it, you just hate your new boss because he is so unbelievably controlling. Now very likely, not everybody has this intense emotional reaction to the boss; why are you one of the ones who do? Isn't it very possible that you yourself have a fair amount of controlling tendencies, and yet you despise those qualities, and disowning and pushing them away from yourself, you end up projecting them onto your boss and thus despise your boss? *If you were really comfortable with your own controlling tendencies, you would be comfortable with your boss.* But no, you must have first enormously disliked and thus dissociated and disowned these qualities in yourself, and then having projected them onto your new boss, you now despise and loathe him. And notice, he might himself be quite controlling—*but only if you despise this tendency in yourself will you despise it in him.* And because you have projected your own controlling tendencies onto him, he has a *double dose* of controlling qualities—he has all his own, but now he has all yours, too—*and it's that double dose that is driving you crazy.*

So welcome to the very simple, almost foolproof, way of discovering what your own unconscious really contains—you don't need a complicated test or a consultation with an expert. Those things that merely inform you about the world are likely not your shadow material; but those things that upset you, that greatly annoy you, that you truly despise are almost certainly your own shadow material. And this, as I said, is a hard realization, because it means that all of those things in the world that you most loathe, despise, and find despicable are most likely qualities that you yourselves possess but have denied, disowned, and projected. That's not an easy realization, is it? (It's especially not easy for social justice activists. "I'm not racist; they are." Really? Try again. . . .)

What did you think was in your unconscious? A bunch of angels, sweetness and light, sugar and spice? No, it contains the things that you hate about yourself, things that you judge most harshly, things that you simply cannot stand. Those are the things that are actually in your unconscious, and they are in your unconscious because you despise them, you cannot stand to have them in your own awareness, so you shove them into the basement. That's how they became shadow elements in the first place.

You can also completely lose track of incredibly positive things about your self—your beauty, goodness, strength, and virtue—and project those onto other people as well—the so-called golden shadow. You then spend your time not shadowboxing but shadow hugging, enormously admiring all those superheroes around you who are so amazing.

Although both are very common, right now we're focusing on the negative shadows because they are usually the most easily recognized forms. You push those out of your self-sense by simply moving them to the other side of your self-boundary, where they appear to belong not to you but to the "other." Then all you have to do is find an appropriate other (or "hook") onto which you can hang (or totally project) the hated quality, which will usually be somebody or something that already has a good deal of the hated quality. The antihomosexual zealots, after all, had to find real gay men to despise and protest.

Thus, for that little narcissist in you that is constantly self-aggrandizing, dominating, and controlling people—Donald Trump makes a perfect hook, and onto that admittedly clinical narcissist goes your own bit of self-aggrandizement. Since yours is the one you first loathed and deeply despised, you will find people like Trump to be not just morally wrong but deeply disturbing and upsetting. You might have ongoing nightmares about them, scour the newspapers for indications of their activities, join political organizations that seek to eradicate them, and otherwise dedicate a good amount of your time to shadowboxing. Now that might be a very good thing for the world, to be working like that to get rid of somebody like Trump. But if he really is a hook for some of your own deepest projections, you can see how utterly clever defense mechanisms are—they know you perfectly because they are, after all, basically you. So they know exactly what irritates you most, what you most want to deny, and then they simply shuffle the boundaries of the level from which these despised qualities originate, push the hated qualities on the other side of your self-boundary, and you end up denying them, projecting them, and shadowboxing them.

Many media reporters demonstrated this hatred of Trump almost daily, reporting on all his activities without mentioning a single positive thing, and it became obvious to many people that if these reporters had indeed discovered Trump's deep narcissism, they were themselves displaying an equally deep, self-generated, pathological hatred of the man. But virtually all the Democrats—or approximately half the population of the United States—had gone mad and loathed every single thing the man did, and I mean absolutely every single thing. Well, you have to admit, whether you admired Trump or not, he was an excellent hook onto which to project one's own narcissistic and self-aggrandizing shadow. Virtually every sentence out of his mouth was about how something he was involved in was the "greatest thing in history," the "best best results anybody's ever gotten," the "highest scores we've ever seen," or "I got the highest ratings on that job that anybody thought was possible." I used to somewhat eagerly watch him just to see how somebody could be so unrelentingly narcissistic—I mean, demonstrating clinical levels of pathological narcissism—it was just stunning.

But, love him or hate him, Trump gave to the United States four years of the most narcissistic hook for national projections that any president has ever offered. Almost anything he did invited projections. And since virtually everything he said was antigreen or anti-political correctness, he was especially despised by green (the media, academia, entertainment). The media, in particular, dedicated itself to reporting only negative news about Trump. There were even objective studies done about this. The *Los Angeles Times*, for instance, reported on one of these studies, which found that, for the last five presidents (both Republican and Democrat), the media had used a positive tone in reporting about them an average of 70 percent of the time; in contrast, the media used a positive tone with Trump only 12 percent of the time. This green media backlash turned the *New York Times* into a gossip rag, with its front page carrying not news but editorial opinions (all of them, of course, anti-Trump). This contra-Trump attitude contributed enormously to a great increase in national polarization and a "woke" green leading edge of culture. So, to ask the obvious, if leading, question: which part of Trump did you hate the most?

Trump is, admittedly, a bit of an extreme case, although he does demonstrate how shadow projections can catch hold at a national level. (The shadow material that was most often projected onto Trump included narcissism, fascism and Nazism, sexism, racism, and xenophobia.) The United States became so intensely polarized because the projections themselves were so big and intense (because the hook was so big and intense). Trump had such an exaggerated, narcissistic personality that the people who disliked him *really* disliked him. This dislike was so extreme that it was often called

"Trump derangement syndrome" (TDS). *Whatever* Trump was in favor of doing, those with TDS were massively against it. This is why the Democrats went mad. Trump was such a huge monster that they were allowed to react in equally huge ways, no matter how insane these ways were. This is why otherwise very level-headed people in this country started supporting moves that were clearly exaggerated to insane proportions and were something that they would never have previously engaged in. They would adopt these outrageous positions simply because they were the opposite of something that Trump wanted. For example, if previously they were in favor of allowing all undocumented immigrants (sometimes referred to as "illegal aliens") to be given U.S. citizenship—which was already a quite controversial position—under Trump, they came very close to wanting fully open borders altogether (which was clearly and obviously something Trump did not want at all). This exaggeration went for protesters, too, who began adding burning and looting to their previously less aggressive and more nonviolent approaches. Shadowboxing became shadow burning.

But in your own case, your shadow material is probably less huge. It's more likely to be some bit of your own envy, anger, jealousy, greed, sexual desire, controlling tendencies, or adulterous impulses. But the same process will occur. For example, when you find somebody to project your own adulterous impulses onto—say, your partner—they will seem to possess the projected trait and you will seem to be completely lacking in it. Then you will begin to uncontrollably suspect your partner of wanting to fool around. You might even accuse them of doing so. Even if they deny it, if you keep suspecting and accusing them of it, this might actually contribute to them being unfaithful, or at least thinking really hard about it. ("My partner is already punishing me for doing this, I might as well really do it.") This underscores another deeply irritating aspect of the way defense mechanisms work: defense mechanisms bring about that which they are meant to ward off—which is another reason they just don't work well. Most arguments and fights between partners come from one or both of them projecting some shadow material onto the other and then shadowboxing away. The negative trait that one partner sees "out there" is something that actually belongs to them.

So this is the incredibly hard lesson of shadow research and why it's so unbelievably important to include some form of Cleaning Up in any path of self-understanding: the things that we most despise in the world are exactly the things that we possess and most despise in ourselves. This is so hard because we are convinced that we have none of those horrid traits; we're free of them (just as we were with Trump's). Of course, the reason that we think we're completely free of this hated quality is that we've denied, disowned, and projected all ours. We're not really free of it; we've simply repressed it. And so out it goes into the world, where we loathe and despise this quality with a self-righteous indignation and hatred that we think is altogether morally justified, because this quality is inherently so utterly evil. As the *Pogo* comic strip used to say, "We have met the enemy, and it is us."

And yes, watch for golden shadows too. We can completely lose track of the truly positive and admirable qualities in ourselves—our compassion, strength, shining brilliance, beauty. We project them onto other people and then see people everywhere who seem to be real heroes, at least compared to the wretched mess that we are. Today, the most commonly stated self-orientation is, as Whitney Houston sings, "The greatest love of all is the love I have for me." But not many people actually feel that, because they're too busy projecting all their lovableness onto others, leaving them with the feeling that deep down they are wretched and worthless souls. They're not shadowboxing with others, they're shadow hugging them. There are indeed people in the world who are truly deserving of admiration; just don't forget the parts of you that also are.

We definitely see this positive projection in almost all cases of what is called "romantic love," which is noted for its intense, obsessive, highly driven nature. In intense romantic love, one (or both) of the partners project some deeply positive aspect of themselves onto their lover, and are then excessively attracted to them, which is an attempt to re-own their own projected material—a case of real shadow hugging. They project a good deal of their own lovableness, beauty, brilliance, kindness, self-esteem, or strength, and see all of it fully existing in their loved one—which throws their own being into an overpowering desire to regain that quality, resulting in an intense energy of overwhelming, overworked, obsessive love. They can't sleep, can't eat, can't think. Nothing goes through their minds except thoughts of their totally beloved partner, who is overflowing with the qualities that have been projected onto them. (Men often project their own appeal, attractiveness, or beauty onto women, and women often project their own power, resilience, or strength onto men—but it really can be any deeply positive trait or quality.) Again, their lover might already have, and probably does have, a large amount of the quality that is being projected onto them, which is what invites and leads them into such an intense projection in the first place. But when such a person loses track of their own positive quality and projects it onto somebody else who already has a great deal of it, the double dose of that quality drives them into an intensely overinflated love for the person. That is, romantic love is so totally overinflated because the beloved seems to have a double dose of some positive quality—the normal amount of some positive quality plus the extra quality that is being projected onto them. That double dose of lovableness drives the person in love into an incredibly overexcited romantic love.

Precisely because it's a double dose of love—which doesn't exist anywhere in the "real" world—this romantic love usually wears off within a year, or sometimes much sooner. Even if the partner who is doing the projecting doesn't fully re-own the projected shadow material, they will start to realize that no human being—including their partner—can be as great as they once imagined. Nobody can be that beautiful, that brilliant, or that strong as they imagined their partner was.

This realization often comes when the two lovers begin to live together and are exposed to the full human-beingness of their partner—they eat, go to the bathroom, apply makeup, and so on—going through all of the processes that a normal human being goes through and are not the superidealized version of a human being that they had previously been imagined to be. (This is why almost all love novels end precisely at the point that the two lovers finally come together—the romantic and projected lovableness that's driven the novel so far cannot withstand the lovers actually living together or being together full-time; it's only downhill from there. Imagine Romeo and Juliet actually moving in together, and in the next scene Juliet wakes up with curlers in her hair and cold cream all over her face. How's Romeo going to like that? "Romeo, Romeo, wherefore art thou, Romeo?" "I'm up here, throwing up.")

Romantic love can die very abruptly and with a great deal of disappointment or even anger. But often it can be replaced with a less intense love, and sometimes with an enduring friendship. But in either case, shadow projection has come to an end. (If they haven't re-owned their shadow, they will likely begin a series of affairs, still pursuing their shadow and still shadow hugging away, which will generally continue until they really do re-own their shadow—or, if married, until they get caught.)

If they have re-owned their shadow, their own self-sense grows, because it has taken back some aspect of itself that was previously split off and projected, which decreased the size of their self. Such diminishment moves in the opposite direction of a genuine evolution, which always moves toward increasing and expanding awareness, self-identity, and thus the size of the self. In other words, in the process of awakening to a genuinely true reality, Waking Up, Growing Up, and Cleaning Up are constantly working in the direction of evolving and expanding our awareness, increasing the size of our self-sense, and stretching from an identity with just our isolated individual organism to a Supreme Identity with the entire Kosmos, a oneness with absolutely everything that is arising moment to moment—a stunning increase in the real size of our self.

And the creation of shadow material is a major process that completely works against that evolution, that actually diminishes self-identity and narrows consciousness. And a real problem with shadow material is that the process of Cleaning Up shadow material is not at all the same as that of Waking Up or Growing Up, and the techniques that work for either of those processes have no real impact on shadow material. And so a core addition to any self-transformation process is to include Cleaning Up with both Waking Up and Growing Up—and this is something that any genuine process of working to awaken a Big Wholeness will do.

As we just saw, the problem with all defense mechanisms is that they tend to bring about exactly what they were meant to ward off. Which is to say, defense mechanisms don't really work. This is why they leave, in their place, not just a blank space (which they would leave if they succeeded in actually deleting and projecting the offensive material); what they actually leave is a painful neurotic or even psychotic symptom—and these symptoms are always symbols of the repressed shadow material. This is why, if you know how to interpret symptoms correctly, they will tell you exactly what shadow material is hidden within them. So simply look around: what do you exaggeratedly most hate, and most love, in this world? This is the world of your shadow. And this is the world that all of us will have to re-own if we want to truly be "one with everything."

The idea that we have to take back our shadow material is not all bad news. There is, after all, the golden shadow. You can repress and project anything across the spectrum from very positive to very negative—and thus end up either shadow hugging or shadowboxing. When you project negative and despised material—anger, power drives, controlling tendencies, dominating qualities—you tend to loathe and despise those onto whom you project those qualities. But, as we saw, it is also quite common to lose track of your truly positive and admirable qualities—your courage, beauty, talent, kindness, lovableness, or moral idealism—and when you project them, you usually end up hero-worshiping, falling into romantic love, or getting caught in slobbering overadmiration.

In either case, negative or positive, we need to re-own and reintegrate the disowned and repressed material, converting it from an "other" (or an "it") to a re-owned aspect of one's own self (or "I")—"Where it was, there I shall become"—hence making the self a little bit bigger, and the not-self a little bit smaller, thus heading in the direction of evolution itself.

So the path of Cleaning Up lies before us. I recommend using the 3-2-1 therapeutic shadow-work exercise to start taking back your own shadow and start Cleaning Up the mess. So let's look at this practice, which is a process that can, if you wish, help incorporate a truly effective Cleaning Up of the shadow material in your life.

THE 3-2-1 PROCESS

In *The Religion of Tomorrow*, I run through twelve of the most central structure-stages of Growing Up (including 1st, 2nd, and 3rd tier) and point out the types of shadow material—negative and positive—that are most common at each stage. In other words, there are a dozen levels of shadow material, all of which are very real and most of which are commonplace. It is very important to be aware of these levels of shadow material because the practices of Cleaning Up are distinctly different from the practices of both Waking Up and

Growing Up. (But don't worry; we'll be working with the 3-2-1 process, which works with shadow elements at all of those levels, and thus is a great simplification. It's still crucially important that you work with your own shadow, but this will greatly simplify things.) If you're in a self-realization program, you are pretty much on your own in figuring out these shadow problems because it's very likely that the self-realization program will tell you nothing about them. But they are indeed real problems, and they are very, very common, and few self-realization or growth systems take them into account. It is almost certain that you already have one or more of these pathologies and shadow issues because everybody does, including spiritual teachers. If you don't know how to spot these shadows, then they will simply continue to plague you, because, again, nothing in either Growing Up or Waking Up will directly help you Clean Up. And if the shadow issues are bad, they can completely derail your progress in both Growing Up and Waking Up. Plus there's the simple fact that they hurt, they cause enormous suffering, and you want to be able to effectively address these issues whenever they arise.

Instead of going through every level of development and its possible shadow problems—again, please see *The Religion of Tomorrow* if you want that kind of detail—we are going to go over a very general type of therapeutic process that works for almost every major shadow issue. There are, of course, specific practices for each type of shadow, but this process has a therapeutic effect on all of them. I call it "the 3-2-1 process."

It gets its name from the very mechanism that underlies the formation of a great deal of shadow material—namely, the process of dissociating, denying, and repressing shadow elements—in other words, the general form of most defense mechanisms. If you look closely at the *perspectives* that consciousness takes with each of the steps in the process of creating shadow material, you find that the shadow generally starts as a 1st-person trait. (For those of you who are a little rusty on grammar, "1st person" means "the person speaking"—I; "2nd person" means "the person being spoken to"—you; and "3rd person" means "the person or thing being spoken about"—he, she, it.)

So, as I was saying, the shadow generally starts as a 1st-person trait, something that is fully part of the individual's conscious self, the central and core self-identity at whatever stage—it's an "I" or a "me" or a "mine"—me and my desire, my anger, my self-controlling tendencies. Then there is some sort of dissociative activity—some sort of negative judgment, denial, disowning, disavowing, or repressing—and the shadow material is isolated, avoided, and pushed against as it is denied and disowned. This repressive pushing against moves the shadow material from being a 1st-person quality to being a 2nd-person quality. That is, it is no longer an "I" or "me" or "mine"; it now belongs to something that is "not-me," that is "other," as if it were actually a different person right inside my psyche—a "you." It becomes a 2nd-person reality, often called a "subpersonality" because it is indeed like another person, a subject, included within the larger personality. It might do some damage from there, because this can already be a pathological fragmenting, but often this degree of repression is not enough, because you can still be aware of a 2nd-person entity and the nasty characteristics that they contain (it often appears as a "you" in your own internal dialogue). So you push it even further, into a 3rd-person reality, which means that it gets treated as a completely separate "it"—this is Freud's "id"; that is, "it." And that is something that can actually be shoved on the other side of the body-boundary entirely, so this "it" belongs to some 3rd-person reality out there—it belongs to "him," "her," or "them." In any case, in my own being, this 3rd-person shadow remains as a totally alien "it," which is now completely disguised as a symptom that seems to be a totally foreign thing or an "it" beyond my control, and it is usually described in those 3rd-person terms: "The anxiety, *it* is stronger than me"; "The depression, *it* just comes over me"; "This obsession, I can't control *it*." These symptoms make no sense to me at all; they're "all Greek to me."

So this shadow material has gone from 1st-person to 2nd-person to 3rd-person—from "I" to "you" to "it." The 3-2-1 therapeutic technique simply reverses that process. Since almost all shadow material—no matter what level—goes through this 1-2-3 process in its creation, reversing that process—the 3-2-1 practice—works with shadow material regardless of which level it comes from. Each shadow level will still have its own specific defense mechanisms, its own cognitive tools, its own drives and desires, and each of those can be dealt with specifically. But virtually all of them go through this general 1-2-3 process during their creation, and reversing that process—the 3-2-1 practice—will therefore work in a significant way with pretty much any shadow material.[1]

PRACTICING THE 3-2-1 PROCESS

As for a typical shadow issue, let me give an example that I often use, since it's very simple. Let's say that you have a significant amount of anger, and yet, for some reason, this anger becomes taboo for you—it might be due to your upbringing or various traumatic experiences in your childhood, or it might be due to the influence of friends and peers, or perhaps the influence of a religious belief that you have. Your self-system, in the translative processes that it uses to organize its world, will start to interpret its world with a negative judgment about anger, which, if significant, will create an operation that whenever it detects anger, will push it through the 1-2-3 process of dissociation. You will start to actively disown your anger in an attempt to get rid of it. Every time anger arises, you will shove it on the other side of your self-boundary, making it appear as "other," and hence removing yourself from any guilt or shame about you yourself possessing this quality.

Of course, this anger is still yours—it's still in reality a 1st-person trait—but now you are pretending that it is not you, and you are actually perceiving it that way. So you convert it from a 1st-person "I" or "mine" to a 2nd-person "you" or "yours," as if it were another little personality in your psyche. That might be enough, but since that subpersonality is constantly yacking in your ear (as a subconscious voice in your own internal dialogue) about how you should notice it (it is, after all, a 2nd-person subpersonality), you will likely go one step further and toss it out completely—you will shove the shadow material totally outside of your system and thus perceive it as belonging to somebody or something else. You've now managed to completely convert this material from a 1st-person "I" to a 3rd-person "it" (or "him," "her," or "them"—"I'm not angry; they are"). Whenever anger arises in you, you will not see it as your own anger; rather it's disowned, denied, dissociated. But since you know somebody definitely has a lot of anger, and since it clearly cannot be you, it has to be somebody else—anybody else—and so you look around for a person, thing, or group onto which to project your anger. It's no longer a 1st-person anger, it's now a 3rd-person anger—it belongs to him, her, them, or it.

Once they have your anger, that anger will be aimed at you, because you are, after all, its real source and owner. Thus for no reason that you can tell, the 3rd person onto whom you've projected this anger will start to seem to be very angry at you. Normally, if somebody just got mad at you for no reason, you might get angry right back at them, but now you can't, because you've denied this anger; you are *not* allowed to feel anger. Since you can't feel any anger yourself, you very likely will feel something like fear or anxiety instead, with all of this negative hostility aimed at you. Fear of, and anxiety about, this 3rd person will arise, but this fear makes no sense to you—you have no idea why this person is so mad at you. All you know is that this "other" makes you extremely uncomfortable, fearful, anxious. The reason why you are getting so anxious or fearful around this 3rd person is that they now have a double dose of anger—they have all their own anger plus all yours.

If you want to be cured of this dissociation, then "where it was, there I shall become." In other words, you need to re-own this material by turning the 3rd-person "it" shadow back into its 1st-person "I" reality. So from 1-2-3, we go to 3-2-1.

Let's say that you have projected your anger onto a gang of local hoodlums—a local teenage gang that has a reputation for causing a lot of trouble—a good hook for the projection of anger. Since you now lack any substantial amount of anger yourself (or so you think), this gang now has a double dose of anger (their anger plus all yours, and your anger has your ear). Since the anger you project onto this gang is really yours and is really tied to you, the gang will now seem to really be after you, to have it in for you specifically. Now you might directly notice this and become unglued anytime this gang gets anywhere near you. Or you might not think that this gang is any more angry at you than a gang would normally be at anybody, but for some reason, you start to have nightmares. Maybe you have recurrent nightmares that you are being chased by a huge monster who is enraged at you and keeps shouting that it's going to kill and eat you alive. You don't feel anger at this monster—since you have repressed your anger—so you feel only a great deal of fear. Consumed with fear, you spend your time in the dream running away from this monster until it's about to catch and eat you, and then you wake up in a cold sweat and breathing hard.

With these particular shadow symptoms in mind, we perform the three basic steps of 3-2-1, which are *locate* (and describe) *it*, *talk to it*, *be it*.

First, *locate* (and describe) *it*. What exactly is your issue, your problem, your neurosis, your symptom—what is your major shadow complaint? If you already suspected that you had projected your anger onto the local gang and were now experiencing fear, then we could work with that. But you probably don't suspect that you have projected your anger onto this gang—you probably think that the enormous terror you feel about this gang is simply what everybody feels, so you might not even mention this as a complaint; you think it's normal. So we look at your complaints, and one of your major concerns is this recurrent nightmare where you are being chased by a monster that wants to kill you. If you were keeping a journal and recording things that were serious problems in your life, even if you didn't mention the gang issue, you would almost certainly mention this nightmare, especially if it is a recurrent one. If the same nightmare had awakened you three or four times in a cold sweat, you would make note of it in your journal. So we would take that nightmare as a likely shadow issue. Thus we've *located* a major problem as being this recurrent nightmare of a monster who wants to devour you, which awakens you in fear and a cold sweat.

Look at that monster carefully; *describe it* in as much detail as you can—all in 3rd-person "it" terms. That's part of step 1. Really look at this monster carefully, and describe it as completely as you can; again, in "it" terms ("The monster looks like this; it's this color; it's this tall; it smells like this; when it's chasing me, it does this," and so on). Really get to know this monster, and give as complete a description of it as you can.

Step 2 is to *talk to it*. Start to address it as an actual 2nd person, as a "you." Using a technique borrowed from Gestalt Therapy, sit in a chair, place an empty chair in front of you, and then imagine that the monster is sitting in that empty chair. If the monster is really frightening, this will be relatively difficult. So always pay attention to the fact that the fear you feel in the presence of the monster is the same fear that you originally felt when you judged the shadow material as being negative and something that you had to get rid of. You became fearful of that material remaining yours, and so you tossed it out. The fear you feel as the monster sits in front of you is exactly that fear.

Begin talking with this monster as an actual 2nd-person "you." Literally have a conversation with it. If you don't want to use a real chair, you can do this in a notebook or on an iPad (or you can simply do it in your head). As yourself, talk to the monster, and when it responds, change chairs. Start asking it questions: Who are you? Why are you here? Why are you doing this to me? To each question, respond as the monster, switching chairs when you do so. Really get to know it as best you can. Go back and forth in conversation. That's step 2.

This is where you will start to get a real understanding of why you repressed this material in the first place. "Why are you doing this to me? you ask the monster. "Because you're worthless. You can never do anything right." But why am I worthless? "Nothing you've ever done has been right. You're a complete mess." As you continue talking with the monster, you're getting closer and closer to your original shadow material, and it will slowly become more and more obvious to you that this material is actually your own anger. This is where you want to be very careful, because you will start to feel your own anger the more you talk with the monster—that is, your own fear will start to give way to your own anger, and it's the anger that you want to accept and re-own.

It might also dawn on you that, for example, this monster is starting to sound a lot like your father, who always seemed to judge you negatively no matter what you did. And you always got mad at him, and let him know it, too, right up until the time he totally lost his temper and punched you really hard in the stomach, which doubled you up on the floor. And you never got angry at him again. In fact, you never really got angry again, although you did start having nightmares.

Now most shadow elements are not created by a onetime big trauma like that (your father punching you really hard in the stomach) but instead involve a series of repeated minitraumas (for example, for months or even years, your father repeatedly told you how worthless you were). Many shadow issues often have their genesis in something that occurred during the early stages of Growing Up (involving the first three chakras of food, sex, and power; or the archaic, magic, and mythic stages), between the ages of three and twelve, and that usually means that something went wrong with relationships with parents, siblings, teachers, or peers.[2]

At the second step of the 3-2-1 process, you repeatedly take some 3rd-person, alien shadow material and directly address it as a 2nd-person you (thus moving it from 3rd person to 2nd person). As you continually playact being the monster, you experience more and more of what the monster actually is. And that monster is really angry at you. In fact, it wants to eat you alive, it's so enraged. The more you role-play this shadow material, the more you will start to feel into what the shadow actually is, what it is really made of. In this case, it is made of anger—*your* anger. As you try to play a monster who really wants to eat somebody, you realize just how angry this figure is. You're starting to make this subject object; you're starting to make this shadow conscious.

As that starts to happen, you will likely feel some apprehension (some of the original fear), combined with a genuine understanding that this monster represents your anger, and your fear will start to clearly give way to anger. You'll actually feel the transformation of your fear into anger.

At this point, you may or may not have images or memories about when and why this material was first denied, repressed, and disowned. For example, you might remember your father hitting you in the stomach. Some therapeutic techniques, such as psychoanalysis, think that memory recovery is crucial; others, such as cognitive therapy, think it's totally unnecessary. But in either case, it is crucial that you recognize that this shadow material—in this case, this anger—is *yours*. You need to feel that in your bones. This step is, after all, the point where you begin to accept and re-own the shadow material. At this point, you take the third and final step: from talking to it to *being it.*

Thus far in the Cleaning Up process, you've been talking to this angry monster as if it were another person within you who was angry; now simply be that anger. Take it back as an "I," "me," "mine." "*I'm the monster; I'm angry; I have anger; I own this anger—it's MY anger.*" Thus, you've converted the dissociated and disowned anger from being a 3rd person (when you fully described "it," in its shadow-form, as the frightening monster), to a 2nd person (when you talked directly to this monster as a "you"), to its original 1st-person form (when you identify with it as "I," "me," or "mine"). It's no longer your *shadow* anger, it's your own *real* anger. To the extent that your nightmares were generated by this disowned anger, when you truly re-own it, the nightmares will stop, no question. You will also notice that the local gang doesn't seem nearly as frightening as it used to. So that's the 3-2-1 process—locate it (3rd person), talk to it (2nd person), then be it (1st person).[3]

SUMMARY

This therapeutic technique is a good example of shadow work in general, the overall Cleaning Up process.[4] It's especially important that we do some Cleaning Up as we continue to Grow Up and Wake Up. As we develop, newly emergent territory is added that we are meant to identify with. Development and evolution, we have seen, is always to "transcend and include," and the *transcend* part means that we are going beyond the present stage to add a new and larger stage or to add new and novel material to our awareness, and we need to own that material responsibly—we need to *include* it fully in our awareness (it is, after all, "transcend *and include*"). As we grow (and transcend) from red to amber, we are adding (and including) the larger territory of amber to our awareness; and as we grow (and transcend) from amber to orange, we are adding (and including) the larger territory of orange (along with amber) to our awareness, and so on at every stage—until, at the end of Growing Up and Waking Up, we have expanded our identity from the narrow, finite, skin-encapsulated ego to a Supreme Identity with the entire Kosmos.

If at any one of those evolutionary stages of "transcend and include," we have any major problems or issues with including or assimilating that new material, then that material will become shadow. We will fail either to adequately transcend or to fully include, and if we have problems with the "include" part, this new territory will be deflected out of our awareness and into the wide world of "not-me" and "other." Not only will we not fully identify with and assimilate this new territory, we will replace it with a painful series of symptoms, neuroses, pathologies, and dysfunctions. Our self will not get bigger but smaller. It will be headed in exactly the wrong direction, throwing more and more material out of awareness and making ourselves less and less instead of greater and greater, which is what evolution wants to bring about.

If we have problems with any of this newly emergent territory—the new territory of red, amber, orange, green, or turquoise—then we contract against it and freeze in fear. We are not moved by love but instead are driven by fear. We self-contract in the face of this newness and toss the novel and emergent territory out the door of our awareness, rejecting this step closer to Wholeness and choosing instead a painful limitation and repression. We become less than we were meant to be, and deep within our own souls, we know this.

All in all, I think we can see that Cleaning Up does indeed offer a new and very real type of Wholeness, helping us go from a small, fractured, inaccurate self-image to a whole, full, and healthy psyche. Shadow issues are so massively common and enormously problem creating in almost every field of human activity, that it's astonishing that there isn't more conventional wisdom about how to deal with them. In any event, my hope, as usual, is that even if you disagree with the details of how I have presented the shadow, you will clearly see that Cleaning Up shadow issues is a truly important part of any sort of holistic search for a genuinely Big Wholeness.

Big Wholeness includes Waking Up, Growing Up, Opening Up, Cleaning Up, and Showing Up. So far we've covered Waking Up, Growing Up, and Cleaning Up. We'll eventually get to all of them, but coming up next, I want to introduce Showing Up. Showing Up is another example of striking it rich when it comes to aspects of our own being. It is also one of the easiest ways to see the importance of an Integral approach to our reality. Showing Up means to fully show up for all the basic dimensions and perspectives to which human beings have genuine access. Let's see what that means and the enormous effect that it can have on your own life, shall we?

11

Showing Up

Showing Up is not only an incredibly fundamental and important part of any Big Wholeness, it is also one of the easiest ways to understand the importance and significance of taking an Integral approach to our problems. You can see this immediately in the diagrams placed in this chapter; see figures 11.2 and 11.3 below. Let's have a look. . . .

THE 4 QUADRANTS

Probably one of the most common and mundane examples of Showing Up appears as the 1st-, 2nd-, and 3rd-person pronouns found in every mature language the world over. These pronouns represent three very different perspectives on reality that anyone can take. The fact that these 1st-, 2nd-, and 3rd-person pronouns are so universal and ubiquitous suggests that they refer to very real, very important, cross-cultural realities. Here's how these pronouns are defined (the dimensions or perspectives included in Showing Up): the 1st person is "the person speaking" (I, me, mine); the 2nd person is "the person being spoken to" (you or thou); and the 3rd person is "the person or thing being spoken about" (him, her, they, them, it, or its).

So what do these perspectives refer to? These cross-cultural realities are as follows: (1) the *subjective* dimension, which is the 1st person, with pronouns such as "I," "me," "mine"; (2) the *relational* dimension, which is the 2nd person, with pronouns such as "you" or "thou," and since there needs to be a mutual understanding—or "we"—in order for a "you" to be understood, this relational dimension is often referred to as the "you/we" dimension, and because this involves two or more subjects, this dimension is often called "intersubjective";[1] (3) the individual *objective* dimension, which is the singular form of the 3rd person, with the pronouns "he, "him," "his," "she," "her," "hers," "it," and "its"; and (4) the collective *objective* dimension, which is the plural form of the 3rd person, with the pronouns "they," "them," "theirs," and "its"—which is a *systemic* dimension, often called "interobjective." In short: the words "I," "we," "it," and "its." This is a common example of the 4 quadrants, the four basic dimension/perspectives that all humans have access to. I call them "dimension/perspectives" because they are real dimensions that possess real perspectives—thus, for example, the *objective* dimension possesses a genuinely 3rd-person perspective.

I often summarize these 4 quadrants as the "Big Three," because I often treat the two objective quadrants (the singular "it" and the plural "its" dimensions) as one—as the objective "it" world—so we have "I," "we," and "it" as one version of the quadrants. We've already seen that these fundamental dimensions ground the use of 1st-, 2nd-, and 3rd-person pronouns. They're such fundamental perspectives that they appear even in the 3-2-1 process. These four (or three) perspectives are everywhere. For example, notice that Jesus Christ spoke *about* God (3rd person), he spoke *to* or *with* God (2nd person), and he spoke *as* God (1st person). That Trinity is exactly the Big Three of "I," "we," and "it."

For an Integral Spirituality, for a genuinely comprehensive understanding of Spirit itself, you will definitely want to realize a full relationship *about*, *with*, and *as* Spirit. You might not like the Christian version of these three, and you certainly do not have to accept a patriarchal Father, Son, and Holy Ghost. In other words, you want a relationship that includes concepts *about* Spirit as a 3rd-person, objective, truly existing reality (such as a Ground of All Being, a Great Chain of Being, or a Great Web of Life); you want a relationship that includes relating *to* or *with* Spirit, so that Spirit also embraces a 2nd-person, vibrant, relational reality (as exemplified in Martin Buber's beautiful writings on the I-Thou relationship; that's perfect Spirit in 2nd person); and most important, you want a relationship that includes a 1st-person view *as* Spirit, where Spirit is seen *as* your own True Self (I AMness, the great I-I, your Original Face, or what the *Nirvana Sutra* calls *mahatman*, the "Great Self"). I call this the "1-2-3 of Spirit"—looking at Spirit through all the quadrants to make sure we're Showing Up for all the important bases.

The Christian Trinity—and the three universal pronouns—are only the barest beginning of what the quadrants cover. (I'll go over more of them in a moment.) In order to Show Up, you can't leave out any of these perspectives when it comes to your own approach to Spirit or Reality in general—in other words, you want to Show Up for all of these major perspectives and the very real dimensions that they disclose. If these realities are there, why on earth would you not include them? And not only when it comes to Spirit, but when it comes to all your life itself. Over sixty human disciplines have been fully reinterpreted using an AQAL Integral Framework—giving everything from Integral Business to Integral Education to Integral Medicine to Integral Art to Integral Politics to Integral Psychotherapy to Integral Architecture, and, yes, Integral Spirituality, among others. Those approaches are made integral by including all 4 of their own quadrants.

I didn't discover the 4 quadrants by studying the universal pronouns. Rather, I discovered them as I was preparing to write my book *Sex, Ecology, Spirituality*. I had laid out various developmental schemes from a large variety of branches of knowledge, and although there were always intriguing similarities, they together did not fit into any obvious basic framework. For example, the sequence quarks, atoms, molecules, cells, organisms is obviously a nested hierarchy (or holarchy) of development, where each stage transcends and includes its predecessor. So is Jean Gebser's sequence of the development of worldviews: archaic, magic, mythic, rational, pluralistic, integral. So is Gerhard Lenski's techno-economic development sequence: foraging, horticultural, agrarian, industrial, informational. All three are examples of developmental or evolutionary holarchies. Yet none of their levels seemed to match up very well. They seemed to be almost totally different. But surely they must be related somehow. How do they actually fit together?

Although the solution seems very obvious today (at least if you're familiar with Integral Metatheory), it took me quite some time to figure it out. Whenever I found a developmental sequence or evolutionary holarchy, I would write it out on a sheet of paper from a legal pad and lay it on the floor. I eventually had well over one hundred sheets of paper completely covering the floor. So I had examples of linguistic development, stellar development, biochemical development, numerous grades and clades of biological evolution, stages of human development for almost every type of intelligence, evolutionary developments of forms of government, various technological developments, evolutionary levels of worldviews, value systems, and cognitive developments—and on and on. And every day I would walk through the house and stare at these yellow pages all over the floor.

Eventually it dawned on me—it was a big "aha" moment—that about half of these sequences seemed to be focused on interior or subjective realities, or realities in consciousness (for example, Maslow's needs hierarchy). The other half were devoted to exterior or material realities (like Lenski's techno-economic stages of development). Dividing them into subjective and objective (or interior and exterior) worked very well. Then a bit later, as I kept staring at them, it suddenly became obvious that about half of them were focused on an individual (for example, the evolution of an atom to a molecule to a cell to a multicellular organism is a holarchy of individual holons), and about half were focused on collective or group development (for example, individual holons come together into groups to form, respectively, stars [atoms] to planets [molecules] to a biosphere [cells] to a particular ecosystem [organisms]). And this worked quite well, too.

When I put them all together, this gave me four major, very distinct groups—namely, the subjective and the objective realities of both an individual and a collective/group. I wrote these out on a single large diagram, which gave me four boxes or 4 quadrants; on the original diagram, the two Left-hand quadrants were the interior, inside (or subjective) quadrants and the two Right-hand quadrants were the exterior, outside (or objective) quadrants. The two upper quadrants were the individual or singular views (Left-hand and subjective or Right-hand and objective), and the two lower quadrants were the collective or group or plural views (Left-hand intersubjective or Right-hand interobjective). See figure 11.1. So we have the inside (interior, subjective) and the outside (exterior, objective) of the singular (individual, personal) and the plural (collective, group). And it very much looks like they all arise together, evolve together, and "tetra-enact" each other. They turn out, in fact, to be four simultaneous dimensions of every holon in existence.

	Interior	Exterior
Individual	Upper Left	Upper Right
Group	Lower Left	Lower Right

FIGURE 11.1. The 4 quadrants.

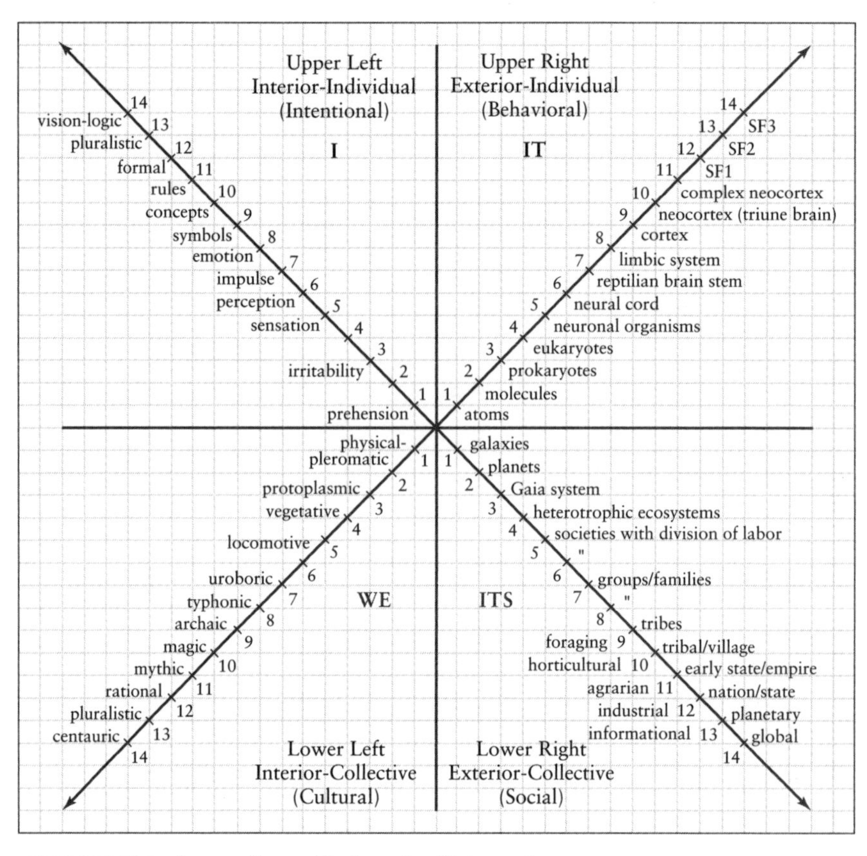

FIGURE 11.2. A sampling of holons in all 4 quadrants.

Figures 11.2 and 11.3 are two examples of the 4 quadrants. Figure 11.2 is a sampling of holons from the lowest to the highest in each quadrant, and figure 11.3 is a sampling of holons in the quadrants as they appear in humans.

These dimensions are about as basic as you can get, and they seem to be based on fundamental distinctions (subject versus object and singular versus plural), and these dimensions are exactly what gave us the 1st-, 2nd-, and 3rd-person pronouns.

What's so amazing about the 4 quadrants is the number of other quite well-known classifications that these quadrants seem

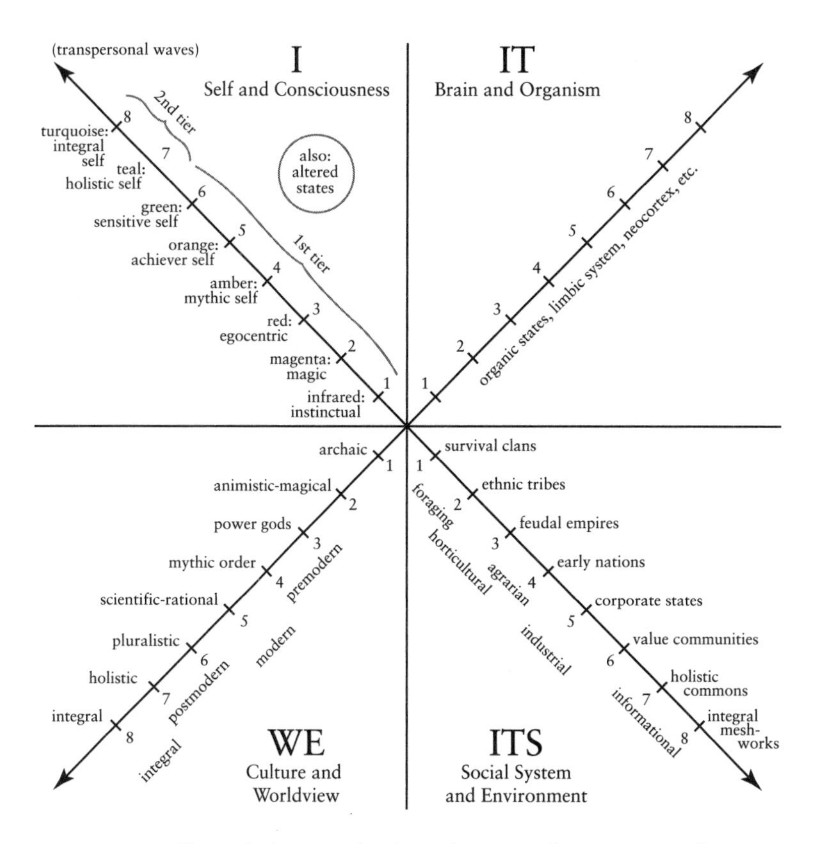

FIGURE 11.3. Some holons in the 4 quadrants as they appear in humans.

to support. We've already seen that this includes the 1st-, 2nd-, and 3rd-person pronouns and the Christian Trinity, but it also includes the Good, the True, and the Beautiful; Buddha, Dharma, Sangha; Habermas's three different validity claims; Popper's three worlds; Kant's three Critiques (of Pure Reason, Practical Reason, and the Power of Judgment); and so on. The quadrants seem to be the original foundation of all of them. All of those classifications, in other words, seem to be variations of the quadrants, which are their prior ontological principles. Again, the quadrants appear to be tapping into some extremely fundamental dimensions in the creation of this universe. It's hard to think of any other pairs of opposites more prevalent or irreducible than the subject/object and the singular/plural—they really are incredibly fundamental. And thus "Showing Up" for all of them seems to be a very good idea indeed.

4 QUADRANTS OR THE BIG THREE?

So which is it, 4 quadrants or the Big Three? Notice that, almost from the start—and even in the objective natural sciences—there has been a recalcitrant argument about what is the "really real" reality in the objective, 3rd-person, material world—is it the whole system (the Lower Right) or just its individual parts (the Upper Right)? Atomists look at a wheel and all they can see is a bunch of individual parts. (And since the same must be true of the parts as well, all we end up with is a load of the most fundamental "atoms" or "ultimate particles" that are thought to be real.) Systems theorists, if anything, err in the opposite direction: the only thing that is really real is the whole system itself. All individual parts or elements are just abstractions or fragmentations from the actual underlying reality of the whole system.

As to which of these quadrants is "really real," Integral has always said "Yes." And if you say, as systems theorists usually do, that *both* objective, 3rd-person, or Right-hand quadrants are real (so that you include both individuals and whole systems, both the Upper Right and the Lower Right quadrants, which together comprise the sum total of the *objective* universe), then you get 4 quadrants (two Right Hand and 2 Left Hand); if you say, with the atomists, that only one of the Right-hand quadrants is real (namely, the Upper Right quadrant of individual atoms), then you get 3 quadrants (the Big Three). All 4 of the quadrants are, of course, real, although it is quite common to reduce them to the Big Three. Even Habermas—considered by many (including me) to be the world's greatest philosopher—in his three validity claims, collapses what I call the Upper Right and the Lower Right into one, single, 3rd-person, objective world. So keep that in mind.

As thorny as these questions about the relation of the individual and the collective can be (the relation of the upper and lower quadrants), the more difficult question has always concerned the relation between the subjective or interior and the objective or exterior quadrants (the Left Hand and the Right Hand quadrants). Again, Integral has always said "Yes" to the irreducible reality of all 4 quadrants, but let's take a little more detailed look at the subject and object—often known in the West as the "mind-body problem," and more recently as the "mind-brain problem," which is often called "the hard problem" and is considered the most difficult problem in Western philosophy.

THE HARD PROBLEM OR THE MIND-BODY PROBLEM

Because the 4 quadrants turn out to be such fundamental aspects of reality, they end up solving (or explaining) a huge number of recalcitrant problems. This seems to include the mind-body problem, which, as we noted, is said to be the most difficult problem in Western thought. But it is a difficult issue only because there is a constant attempt to try to reduce one quadrant to another, and Integral maintains that's not possible. Fundamentally, the mind (or consciousness) is simply the Upper Left quadrant—what you see when you look at an individual organism from within, in a 1st-person or subjective stance—while the brain, on the other hand, is indeed part of the body, the Upper Right quadrant—which is what you see when you look at an individual organism from without, in an objective or 3rd-person stance. So only you (having access to your own 1st-person perspective) can see your mind, but a surgeon regularly cuts open a skull and can directly see the brain (and so can anybody else, or any

3rd person, watching the operation). The brain itself looks something like a crumpled grapefruit, but your mind doesn't look anything like that. Mind and brain are clearly two different things in at least some important ways. And in reality, neither 1st-person mind nor 3rd-person brain can be reduced to the other without totally destroying it. (And there are not just these two dimensions that are interacting—the subjective and the objective; there are always 4 major dimensions, including the intersubjective and the interobjective, that are always tetra-enacting, which we'll explore below.)

Nowadays, the mind-body problem shows up especially as the mind-brain problem (where "brain" replaces "body" in the formulation, because the brain is found in the body, so the mind-body problem becomes the mind-brain problem). Because there has been so much research showing that all states of consciousness or mind register as some sort of brain neurophysiology, there is a great temptation to simply see the mind or consciousness (which inherently is a 1st-person perspective) as being the same thing as these brain states (objective body states, which are a 3rd-person perspective). Thus hidden materialists will often reduce the mind to the brain and then say that, because the brain is simply part of the body or organism, the mind-body problem is solved—when, of course, it's nothing of the sort. The fact that you have reduced the 1st-person (Upper Left) quadrant of consciousness to the 3rd-person (Upper Right) quadrant of brain neurophysiology does not mean you have explained 1st-person consciousness; it means you have destroyed it. The 1st-person dimension is no longer the 1st person; you haven't explained it— you've explained it away. Wherever you saw a 1st-person mental event you simply replaced it with a 3rd-person neurophysiological event, but that doesn't explain 1st person; it deletes it.

However, the mind-body problem, in its most fundamental aspects, does not just start with humans. Because it is essentially about the relation of the Left-hand and the Right-hand dimensions, this "split" is most centrally between the interior and the exterior perspectives, and that split goes all the way back to the Big Bang, when a manifest universe first appeared, and as such, there was a differentiation between, for example, the interior of an atom (its proto-feeling or prehension) and its exterior (its visible matter/energy form). In just a moment, I will go over exactly what the interior (or prehension) of an atom means; for the moment, note that, as you can see in figure 11.2, the Left-hand (interior) and the Right-hand (exterior) dimensions of existence accompanied every major level of evolution from the start—from the interiors and exteriors of quarks and atoms all the way up to a human mind (interior) and its material brain/body (exterior). These represent two different perspectives on the same underlying and whole holon.

Since this occurs at each level, where the interior and the exterior are basically two different dimensions of the same underlying Wholeness (or Nonduality), when they are manifest, they each appear as a partialness. And this partialness is what makes the body/mind problem so hard to solve for a human awareness: the problem itself cannot finally be solved (in a way that "feels" right) until the primary dualism between subject and object, interior and exterior, is dissolved, and that occurs only with a genuine Waking Up or One Taste awareness, whereupon the underlying Nondual reality is itself actually and truly realized. Cartesian dualism cannot finally be solved by any amount of logic, reasoning, or evidence (which is why it's the most difficult problem for Western logic to solve); it yields only upon a direct Waking Up to the ever-present ultimate Reality of Nondual Suchness. At that point, the inside and the outside—as the sky turns into a big blue pancake and falls on your head—are finally seen as "not-two," and that Realization finally (dis)solves the mind-body or mind-brain problem. However, in the relative world, there are still a staggering number of correlations that need to be mapped—what are the major correlations between Upper Right brain states and Upper

Left mind states? But the duality itself is resolved through the realization, revealed with a genuine Waking Up, that both dimensions are partial perspectives on the same underlying Wholeness.

In this regard, I should mention that you don't need a major Waking Up in order to begin Showing Up. In order to Show Up, it is only necessary to realize that, at whatever level of Growing Up you are at, you have all 4 of these major dimensions available. This realization can indeed happen at virtually every level of Growing Up because the quadrants do indeed go "all the up, all the way down"—they're fully present at all levels, as you can see in figures 11.2 and 11.3. We'll continue to explore what that means, why it is so important, and how it can make such a significant change in your life.

To sum up: all 4 quadrants are manifestations of a genuinely nondual Reality. Moment to moment, nondual Spirit *manifests* the entire relative world, and when it does, *it does so as all 4 quadrants simultaneously*. It arises as a subject with various objects, and in an individual holon inextricably interwoven with a group or collective holon. As we'll explore in more depth just below, you can't have subjects without objects, and individual holons always exist in various groups or collective holons—the 4 quadrants arise together, evolve together, and tetra-enact each other.

THE REAL MEANING OF MATTER

There's another reason why the 4 quadrants tell us something very important and why they are especially significant when it comes to spiritual realities—it really changes the very core of how we view spirituality itself.

In all the Great Traditions, *without exception*, when something like the Great Chain of Being is presented (which the vast majority of the Traditions embrace), what they call "matter" is *always* on the very lowest rung of the Great Chain. A typical Christian version of the Great Chain of Being, for example, runs from matter to body to mind to soul to spirit (where "matter" in this scheme means just dead matter, while "body" means the living body of feelings and desires; in other words, matter is the physical world that existed before any life forms evolved, which themselves began with the emergence of the body level). Everything above matter, or the physical dimension of reality, is indeed claimed to be "meta-physical," "supernatural," or "trans-material"—that is, all of those higher levels (body, mind, soul, and spirit) are thought to be totally beyond matter and can exist fully without any sort of material aspect. And notice, in this scheme, that the feelings of a worm's living body exist on the second level, or the body level of feelings and desires; and the human triune brain, considered just in its material form, exists on the first level, the matter level. (But a real human brain exists at least on the third level, the mind level.) So a worm's feelings are higher in reality than a human brain—and something is clearly not quite right about that scheme. It is for these kinds of reasons that both modernity and postmodernity completely rejected almost all the ideas that have come from the premodern Wisdom Traditions and their silly Great Chains.

An Integral analysis suggests instead—an insight that also allows science and religion to clearly fit together—that matter is not the *lowest* level of reality but rather the *exterior* dimension of *every level* of reality (it's the Right-hand reality of every Left-hand occasion). Thus, when my mind has a *logical* thought in the 1st-person, interior Upper Left, my *material* brain is producing electrical impulses in the 3rd-person, exterior Upper Right. Even Upper Left *spiritual* states (such as a Zen satori) have correlative Upper Right *material* brain states (a satori causes a change in brain physiology). An enormous amount of recent research has found specific brain patterns accompanying major mystical states, including those of a feeling of oneness with the entire universe. Some researchers even refer to the area or pattern of the brain that lights up with a mystical experience the

"God-spot," which some laboratory wags have called the "G-spot." These Upper Left mystical events in consciousness cannot be reduced to those Upper Right material brain correlates, although they always occur together, precisely because all 4 quadrants are always tetra-enacting and tetra-arising.

So what the Traditions thought of as being beyond nature, supernatural, or beyond the physical—and thus literally "meta-physical"—turns out to really be intraphysical: it's not a view from beyond matter; it's a view from within matter, from the interior consciousness that is always correlated with an exterior form or material dimension.[2] Likewise, the supernatural is not beyond nature, it's within nature. Nature is not being left behind—but neither is Spirit being exclusively identified with Nature. Rather, all Left-hand consciousness events are not beyond matter or nature but are the interior or Left-hand quadrants of the Right-hand or exterior quadrants, as you can see in figures 11.2 and 11.3. Thus matter is not the lowest level of existence but the exterior dimension of all levels of existence.

This is a major change in how we see the relationship of consciousness and matter, or spirit and matter. And most importantly, it allows a truly spiritual perspective to legitimately exist in a world that also has material correlates everywhere (that is, it can happily exist *alongside* a world of scientific materialism, since it covers the interior, subjective quadrants, while scientific materialism covers the exterior, objective quadrants). Scientific materialism is mistaken when it reduces the entire world to matter, but we don't have to deny that there are these material correlates—as we've seen, they are indeed there, they are real. No 3rd-person, objective perspective of a scientific materialism will ever—by definition—be able to be a 1st-person, subjective perspective, and thus no 3rd-person reality will be enough to explain (let alone deny) the existence of 1st-person realities. Therefore, no amount of scientific research can dislodge a spiritual perspective—it is totally beside the point because 3rd-person, exterior science can neither prove nor disprove 1st-person, interior consciousness and spirit.

One of the simplest ways of thinking about this second meaning of matter—the exterior reality of any holon—is that these material exteriors can always be seen, videotaped, photographed, or otherwise detected by the human senses or their extensions. Of course, in some cases, we might need a videotape smaller than any we now possess, but if we had a videotape small enough, we could see any exterior that exists (including those of, for example, quarks and strings). If you look at figures 11.2 and 11.3, all of the Right-hand or exterior holons can be seen or photographed, but none of the interior or Left-hand holons can.

The only reason that almost none of the Great Traditions realized this (and therefore they all put matter on the lowest level of the Great Chain) is that none of them had the tools to see material dimensions at much smaller or much larger dimensions (microscopes or telescopes), so they had no way of seeing that these correlations where always occurring. They were having satoris all the time, but none of them could see the corresponding physiological brain changes that were also occurring. Likewise, when modern science emerged with the Western Enlightenment, and tools were developed to see these correlations, the tendency was to dismiss all the spiritual traditions that weren't "smart" enough to see these correlations. In other words, ever since science and religion began to emerge and exist together, they have each denied the existence of the other.

At the same time, we can fully acknowledge the reality of those 3rd-person correlates without completely collapsing and reducing everything to them. That is, we can fully accept the existence of Right-hand realities without having to completely trash and deny all Left-hand realities at the same time. And notice that this does not mean that some of our subjective truth claims must go without any corroborating evidence at all. Although objective science cannot prove, disprove, or otherwise dislodge a spiritual reality, a higher stage of Growing Up can dislodge inaccuracies in spiritual intelligence found in a lower stage (just as, with the modern Enlightenment, rational spiritual intelligence dislodged much of mythic spiritual intelligence). And a higher state of consciousness in Waking Up can dislodge or sublate inadequacies of a lower state (as a 5th state can dislodge or move beyond a 2nd state). But none of those interior, 1st-person realities can be proven or disproven by the merely 3rd-person views of a scientific materialism.

So any spiritual states in the Left-hand quadrants will have material correlates in the Right-hand quadrants (even a satori lights up the brain). And thus matter becomes not the bottom rung on the Great Chain but the exterior dimension of each and every rung on the Great Chain. Even the lowest level of reality (or "matter" in its first meaning) has an interior in addition to its exterior. Whitehead called the interior, at this lowest, most fundamental level, "prehension" (see fig. 11.2). Whatever this lowest level's *exterior* turns out to be—which can be seen or videotaped with some form of objective detecting instruments: subatomic particles, photons, quarks, ten-dimensional strings—it will also contain the lowest level of *interiors* too—namely, some sort of prehension (Whitehead called prehension "the atom of experience"). We can think about prehension starting on the lowest level and then continuing in increasingly complex forms as it moves up the spectrum of consciousness (the Left-hand dimensions).

As that material level continues to evolve—with increasing complexity and increasing prehension—it eventually brings forth a dimension of reality that actually is living, starting with the earliest living cells, such as prokaryotes—whose interiors include what biologists call "irritability" (its form of prehension), which means that, for example, if you poke a living cell, it reacts. The collective form of the first or insentient level is broadly known as the "physiosphere," and the second or living level is called the "biosphere."

The biosphere is still material in its *exteriors* (as all holons are)—a living cell can still be objectively seen and photographed (using a microscope)—using "matter" in the second sense, that which is the exteriors of all interiors. But the biosphere is not material in the first sense, which refers to the nonliving, insentient physiosphere. The exteriors of a living cell (such as you would see by looking at a cell through a microscope) are clearly visible matter (an observable form existing in mass/energy spacetime and, therefore, something you can see, photograph, videotape, or otherwise objectively detect). As matter continues to evolve into even more complex material forms (in the Right Hand), by the time the material triune brain has emerged, a level of reality known as the "noosphere" has emerged and the interiors (Left Hand) have evolved to a level of consciousness that can create images and symbols. (Consciousness is on the way to developing concepts, rules, meta-rules, and higher—starting with level 9 in the Upper Left of fig. 11.2; the biosphere itself starts with irritability at level 3, and the lowest or earliest form of prehension starts at level 1.) All the interior levels are complex forms of prehension, the inside, feeling-awareness aspect of holons (as contrasted with their exterior forms, or matter).

In this simple example, we see three major realms of being—the physiosphere, the biosphere, and the noosphere—each of which has an interior (various forms of prehension) and an exterior (various forms of matter). The Left-hand quadrants include interiors that range from the first form of prehension (in the physiosphere) to forms of prehension that include the irritability of living cells (in the biosphere) to mental symbols and concepts (in the noosphere). The Right-hand quadrants include exteriors that run from strings and quarks and atoms (the physiosphere) to the forms of biological organisms (the biosphere) to a complex triune brain (the noosphere). "Matter" can continue to refer to the lowest, insentient, dead level of reality (which still has an interior with the first forms of prehension), but it can also refer to the exterior of any level of reality (not just the dead or insentient).

This view is sometimes called "panpsychism," a term I'm not fond of, although many major philosophers have been identified with that label (for example, Whitehead, Leibniz, and Spinoza—Einstein famously said that "I believe in the God of Spinoza"). My qualms with the term is that psyche (as in *pan-psych-ism*) is too complex an entity to be found in the interiors of, say, quarks or protons (or the nonliving physiosphere in general). At this very early level, the feeling that is present—its prehension—is much too simple to be considered psyche. The lowest capacity that a psyche (meaning "soul" or "mind") is usually taken to possess is the capacity to use images and symbols, and these are much too complex to be *pan*, which means "all" or applicable to "everything," that is, found in even the most elementary and fundamental holons in existence.

I prefer the term *pan-interiorism*, because one thing is certain: if these lowest (or physiosphere) holons have something called an "exterior," they definitely have something called an "interior." Like all opposites, the two terms don't make sense without each other. Physicists seem to have no trouble giving a fairly detailed description of physical holons as seen from the outside (all the major quarks, for example, have now been detected or "seen" by particle accelerators—as we noted, everything in the Right Hand can be seen by some sort of "videotape"). But if they have exteriors, they also have interiors (as some form of prehension). We wouldn't even understand what it meant to say that "we can detect these quarks as seen from without" if there were not also some type of "seen from within." Why even acknowledge that these are exteriors, seen from without, objective, if there were not also interiors, seen from within, subjective? Wherever there is an object reality (the *exterior* of an individual or collective holon), there is a subject reality (the *interior* of an individual or collective holon). Again, these two—subjective and objective—are opposites because they intimately depend on one another and always arise together.

So I'm a pan-interiorist. Having a world of all exteriors and no interiors would be like having a world of all ups and no downs, all lefts and no rights, all ins and no outs. It doesn't even make any sense.

But we have to be careful not to let this seduce us into a scientific materialism. The levels of increasing being and awareness (or prehension) that show up in the Left-hand quadrants will show up as increasing *material complexities* in the Right Hand. So—to continue using the Christian version of the Great Chain—where in the Left Hand, there is an evolution from matter to life to mind to soul to spirit (all very real interior realities as forms of prehension), in the Right Hand, there are *increasingly complex material configurations* at each of those levels: from insentient atoms and molecules to the first living cells, to more complex multicellular organisms, to more complex organisms with a reptilian brain stem, to yet more complex organisms with a mammalian limbic system, to yet more complex organisms such as humans with a complex, triune brain (which is so *complex* that it alone *has more neuronal connections than there are stars in the known universe*). And actual spiritual experiences—starting with satori at the soul level—have correlates in the complex triune brain, as recent research, we noted, has demonstrated.[3]

The inherent correlation of consciousness and matter (that is, the correlation of Left Hand and Right Hand) is what Teilhard de Chardin called "the law of complexity and consciousness"—namely, the more complex the material housing, the greater the degree of consciousness. When Alan Watts was asked why he was a vegetarian, he said, "Cows scream louder than carrots when you kill them"—same thing. So, while, in the Right Hand, matter is becoming more and more complex, in the Left Hand, consciousness (prehension) is becoming greater and greater. And, as I remarked, we have to be very careful not to let this expanded definition of matter result in a scientific materialism: the fact that matter is the exterior of all levels does not mean that you can just address matter itself and you've covered all the bases. That move completely guts the interiors and gives us "the crime of the Enlightenment," as we'll see.

DEFUSING THE DEBATE OVER TRANSGENDER IDENTITY

The 4 quadrants can also be used to defuse the inflammatory arguments about transgender identity. Let's think about individuals who were identified at birth as males who transition to being female through hormones and surgery. Biologically, their sex (in the Upper Right quadrant) remains male—every cell in their body has an X chromosome and a Y chromosome, and that cannot be changed.[4] This leads many people in the culture wars who focus on this Upper Right scientific quadrant to claim that transwomen are not women because males who have transitioned to female are still completely male in their biological makeup (or XY, which is definitely true). On the other side, there are those who focus on the interior, subjective quadrants, where how one feels about one's gender is found in the Upper Left quadrant and how one's culture defines and constructs norms for each gender is in the Lower Left. (The words *male* and *female* refer to the sex assigned at birth, and *masculine* and *feminine* refer to gender.) From the perspective of the Upper Left quadrant, transwomen are indeed women since they feel that their identity is female.

Gender studies often claim that, no matter the person's sex assigned at birth, gender is indeed nonbinary—there are not just two genders. Facebook, for example, now recognizes over one hundred different genders. Those who argue that only scientific biological sex is real maintain that those who think gender can diverge from sex are clinically delusional, whereas those who argue for the reality of transgender claim that their opponents are nothing but transphobes, expressing a nasty prejudice and bias against this minority. This is a perfect example of a wildly fragmented culture-war argument about which quadrant alone is real. Neither side sees that the other side is discussing something that is equally true but partial. Both of these quadrants actually exist, and taking the perspective of only one of them will give you the viewpoint of just one side of the argument. If you take a 3rd-person perspective and recognize the reality of the Upper Right (scientific) quadrant, you will see that every cell in a person's body is male (XY) or every cell is female (XX), a fact that can never be changed. But if you take a 1st-person perspective and recognize the two subjective (personal or cultural) quadrants—you will see that sexual identity (gender) is indeed nonbinary, with over a hundred different sexual identities possible. Both of those perspectives are true, and both of their viewpoints are indeed simultaneously true but partial.

THE QUADRANTS IN EVERYDAY LIFE

Showing Up means to fully acknowledge, and totally inhabit, all 4 quadrants of existence—to not try to deny, ignore, or reduce any of them to the others but to see all of them as equally real, equally important, and equally tetra-evolving and tetra-enacting. Not only does this end numerous centuries-old arguments about which quadrants are real and which are dismissible, it allows each of us to start acknowledging these realities in our own lives. Although it's probably not yet obvious, virtually any endeavor that you are engaged in right now is almost certainly denying, or reducing, or is completely ignorant of, or is totally confusing, one or more of the 4 quadrants—and this truly is having some very unpleasant repercussions in your life.

Allow me to explain. Every example I have given so far about the importance of the quadrants draws on some very academic and abstract controversies, and it's probably not obvious how directly important the quadrants are in your own life, right now, moment to moment. So let me give you an example that relates directly to your own life. I'll take a common experience—say, having a particular thought, such as, "It's time to watch my favorite podcast." I'll try to show how that thought has immediate correlates in all 4 quadrants, and each of them is crucial in being able to have that thought at all. And further, every time you have a thought (or any individual experience), all 4 quadrants are activated and fully involved.

This thought itself "exists" in the Upper Left quadrant (where *exists* means "primarily manifests as"). This is the perspective of 1st-person singular ("I," "me," "mine"). This thought exists alongside an enormous number of other thoughts (about the past, the present, and the future). Without splitting philosophical hairs, the sum total of these thoughts and other subjective 1st-person experiences is generally known as the "mind" (sometimes "consciousness," sometimes "experience"). Your mind is what you are directly and immediately aware of right now if you look within—you have a 1st-person perception of something inside you, and it is the 1st-person part that makes it *you*, your self, your mind, your subject, your experience. Of course, you can also use this consciousness to look at things outside of you. *But either way*, this 1st-person reality actually exists ontologically (it's a real dimension), and it sees the world from that 1st-person stance (it's a real perspective). That is why we call quadrants "dimension/perspectives"—they are real dimensions with real perspectives.

Right now, if you are reading this or hearing it or viewing it, there is a stream of thought going through your mind, and that stream is attempting to translate what is being said by me into something that makes sense to you. But that translation process could not occur at all unless both you and I were members of a common culture. "Culture," in the Integral Framework, specifically means the collective holons seen or experienced from within—it's the Lower Left quadrant. There are, of course, two quadrants in the Left Hand—the

Upper Left and the Lower Left. The Upper Left is 1st-person *singular* ("I" or "me" or "mine," which is the interior of an individual subjective reality). The Lower Left is 1st-person *plural* ("we," "us," "our," "ours," the interior of a collective or an intersubjective reality). I've previously said that the Lower Left is 2nd person ("you" or "thou"), and that's true. But if I meet you as a 2nd person ("the person being spoken to") and then find out that you don't speak English and I can't speak your language, then neither of us has any way at all to communicate, so we are reduced to being 3rd persons for each other. Each of us might as well be talking to a rock or a hammer.

In other words, for a real "you" and a real "I" to be able to form an actual "we," there has to be at least some degree of mutual understanding or genuine communication. So the Lower Left is indeed a 2nd person "you," but in order for that 2nd person to remain a real 2nd person, there has to be some sort of "we" that is formed. This "we" is often formed through a verbal or linguistic exchange between us (collective language is an important part of the Lower Left quadrant). But if we cannot understand each other in any way, then there is no real 2nd-person "you"; each of us appears only as a 3rd-person "it." This "it" is the exterior ("matter" in the second sense); it's just us looking at our Right-hand exterior realities with no way to gain access to any of our Left-hand interior realities. So although I often refer to the Lower Left quadrant as "2nd person," since any awareness of this demands a "we," I often call it "you/we" or just "we" (notice that "we" is a 1st-person *plural* pronoun, which is exactly what you and I need in order to communicate). This "we" definitely contains an "I" and a "you," but they can't begin to share anything unless a "we" genuinely starts to form. Thus any real "you" that exists implies and demands a real "we."

The quadrants are consistent here. Remember that the two Upper quadrants are singular (or individual) and the two Lower quadrants are plural (or collective). And the two Left-hand quadrants are subjective (prehension or interior), and the two Right-hand quadrants are objective (matter or exterior). So this Lower Left quadrant of culture means that my "I" and your "I"—both Left-hand, subjective, 1st-person *singular* realities—have come together to form a 1st-person *plural*; and that "we" is culture. The Upper Left, 1st-person, singular, or *subjective* dimensions come together to form a Lower Left plural or *intersubjective* dimension—which is how we define "culture." Both of them are interior dimensions (Left-hand); one is singular and one is plural. *Culture in this sense includes an enormous number of shared areas*—such as a shared language, values, meaning systems, ideals, morals, norms, collective agreement on which actions should be rewarded or punished, cultural habits, common goals, and so on.

Unlike the realities in the Right-hand quadrants, *nothing* in the interior dimensions of the Left-hand quadrants can be videotaped or photographed. That is, in themselves, they cannot be seen as material, exterior objects. If they could be, they could be photographed or videotaped, and they would be Right-hand realities. People sometimes get confused here because things like language can be seen in any written document. Very true, but that written document is simply the exterior, 3rd-person correlate of an interior 1st-person experience and understanding. For example, if you and I were both looking at the same page written in, say, Spanish, and you understand Spanish well but I don't speak it at all, then although exactly the same 3rd-person exterior light is hitting your eyes and mine, in our 1st-person minds, the words mean a great deal to you and mean absolutely nothing to me. While the material forms of language can indeed be written down in objective forms in the exterior world (documents that can be videotaped), the understanding of these material forms does not occur in that dimension. That understanding is not an exterior, 3rd-person object such as the body or brain but is an interior experience of the 1st-person subject or mind. For Integral, of course, both of these exist and both are involved; it's just that neither can be reduced to the other.

So the very fact that there is some sort of communication between us means that the thoughts of your "I" are in some sort of "we-space" with my thoughts. That is, you are engaging your "I" and, by taking the role of other, you are trying to see and understand how my "I" views the world. Especially if we were in the same room, it would be very clear that this is happening, and if we were engaging in dialogue, this we-space would be one of *mutual understanding* (which is the core of all we-culture). It's true that if you are reading this material by yourself, and I'm not physically present, then we are not directly and explicitly forming a mutual understanding; but the strong implication is that if you are understanding any of this text, then if we were indeed in each other's presence, we would be able to form an obvious exchange of mutual understanding by talking to each other. To the extent that we were both a real "you" for each other, there would likewise also be a real "we" that had formed—and thus the Lower Left is always a "you/we." Even if you were alone in a cave, to the extent that you are a real "you" ("the person being spoken to"), you are implicitly part of a "we" (actually several different "we's" or sub-"we's" or sub-sub-"we's"). Hence, for example, whenever you think, even if you are totally alone, you are actually thinking using some language, and that language is a genuinely collective entity that exists only as a real we-structure, collective shared meanings and mutual understandings—any real "you" is always a "you/we."

Like everything else in the Left-hand quadrants, this is not an exterior object; hence the "no videotaping" rule. You can videotape, or figuratively "put your finger on," anything in the exterior, Right-hand quadrants. You can put your finger on a single atom (you can see it with an electron microscope) and put your finger on a molecule (see it with a regular microscope), and likewise you can put your finger on a cell, an organism, a plant, or an animal, as well as on exterior collectives such as ecosystems, galaxies, nebulae, and planets, and on exterior artifacts, including foraging, and horticultural, agrarian, and industrial activities (although you would need a big finger). In sum, exteriors exist in an objective, seen-from-without, 3rd-person, material dimension, and thus you can videotape them or put your finger right on them, and in many cases actually touch them.

But can you put your finger on, say, mutual understanding? Can you touch it? Just where exactly does it exist? Can you videotape it? No, that just won't work at all, and it won't work—ever—precisely because 1st-person subject and 3rd-person object are two very different (but always correlated and interwoven) dimensions, and they are detected using very different, very real perspectives. All 1st-person realities can be experienced but not videotaped; you cannot put your finger on anything in your mind (although you can put your fingerprints all over a brain). None of the experiences of love, envy, mercy, care and compassion, fear, malice, hope, jealousy, even the experiences of most of logic and mathematics, can be seen in the exterior world (nobody has ever seen the square root of negative one running around out there in the material world). You can photograph none of those experiences; you can't put your finger on any of them.

The very fact that you and I are now engaged in a communication process means that although there are a phenomenal number of 3rd-person, objective processes that are occurring in both of us—from light waves falling on our eyes to digital data bits being processed in our neuronal circuits—these processes must be converted to subjective understanding through a *different* set of events and conditions: We both have to speak and understand the same language (so that the same language is moving through our 1st-person minds, which is different from the fact that light is reflected from what we each are reading into our 3rd-person eyes). Both of us must have access to and, most importantly, understand how to use computers (so that, once again, the same understanding is moving through our minds, which is different from the fact that light is falling on our eyes from the computer screen). Both of us must be familiar with and share a great deal of background knowledge. Both of us must have a joint interest in this material, and so on. All of these events and conditions require 1st-person, subjective realities in each of us. If so, then we each have—in addition to our 1st-person *singular*, subjective "I," or individual mind—some sort of 1st-person *plural*, intersubjective, shared culture, or "we."

Most important of all, there is not a single thought in the mind that is not deeply interwoven with, and made possible by, a culture of other minds. These individual minds come together into a culture not simply because the same light waves fall on their eyes and move into their brains (a 3rd-person dimension) but because a shared understanding unites their minds (a 1st-person dimension). It is widely agreed that there is no such thing as a "private language," a language that only you can understand. Even if you could create such a thing (and simple forms of this have been created), it would be utterly worthless as a means of communication, since—by definition—nobody but you would understand it. For communication and understanding to occur, you would have to teach somebody else this language, at which point it is no longer private.

So keep this in mind as you think about culture—and about any thought you might have, including "It's time to listen to my favorite podcast." It's not an individual, isolated, self-existing thing. There are an enormous number of cultures (and subcultures and sub-sub-cultures) that you belong to, and all of those individual thoughts have some sort of context and meaning in one or more of those cultures. Put simply, each subjective thought has an intersubjective meaning. And none of them can be videotaped; you can't put your finger on any of them. They are direct, interior, subjective holons, either singular or plural, each of which also has a Right-hand correlate that you can indeed see or videotape; just don't confuse or equate them with those Right-hand realities.

So wherever there's some sort of an individual thought or Upper Left occurrence, there is also some sort of collective Lower Left occurrence as well—especially some sort of language structure, set of norms and rules, or some sort of mutual understanding with one or another groups, and so on. Likewise, the reverse is also true—any group or collective, by definition, always contains one or more individual members, or it wouldn't be a group. In short, when either one of these quadrants (Upper Left or Lower Left) is present, so is the other one. Subjective mind (Upper Left) and intersubjective culture (Lower Left) always go together.

As we've also seen, one *objective* correlate of the mind is generally called the "brain." I don't often discuss the brain in much detail, simply because the neurophysiological study of the brain is indeed an objective, natural, Right-hand science, and thus it will move forward and make progress, come what may. There's a new study every week showing that a particular part of the brain lights up when anger (a mind state) is experienced, or when anxiety (a mind state) is experienced, or even when there is an experience of being one with Divinity—as we saw, it's actually called the "God spot" (or the "G spot"). But these are not reducible to each other. Surely, any sort of real God or Spirit is absolutely not equal to, or the same as, a particular location in the physical brain of a single, isolated organism. What kind of God would that be? A mental satori might indeed have a correlate in the physical, material G-spot in the brain—but what this satori discloses (an absolute Oneness of the entire universe) clearly cannot be reduced to, or exists only as, that itty-bitty G-spot. The entire universe is a bit bigger than a walnut! In other words, there is a huge difference between Upper Right and Upper Left, even though both of them are always arising together and intimately depend upon each other.

Because neurophysiology is a naturally expanding and progressive science—and you can look up its results in any decent textbook—I rarely focus on the details about the brain, except to point out that, like virtually all phenomena, it is holonic in nature.[5] Indeed, like all quadrants, the Upper Right quadrant shows a holistic tendency. There is no question that evolution tends toward greater material complexity and self-organization: from quarks to atoms to molecules to organisms (and carrying on, from plants to fish to amphibians to reptiles to mammals to primates to primates that are human)—holon to holon to holon—and the human brain epitomizes that transcending and including. (Notice that, were it not for scientific materialism, those chains of increasing material complexity would also, and actually do, indicate chains of *increasing consciousness* among each of its ever-more complex holons—"the law of complexity and consciousness.")

Of course, the 3rd-person, *singular*, objective brain is also interwoven with a large number of 3rd-person, *plural*, interobjective systems—the Upper Right is interwoven with various Lower Right ecological systems and techno-economic collectives and their multiple artifacts. These material phenomena are all very real Right-hand exterior realities (or "matter" in the second sense). As I just noted, the individual, 3rd-person brain and its organism is in a constant mutual exchange with an almost unlimited number of 3rd-person plural, collective holons—systems of water, food, oxygen, and all sorts of ecological and techno-economic correlates (from foraging to horticultural to agrarian to industrial to informational systems).

There really are no individual holons without plural forms, without some sort of group or collective or systems form. In other words, every reality in the Upper Right quadrant has some sort of correlate in the Lower Right quadrant, just as every reality in the Upper Left quadrant has one or more correlates in the Lower Left quadrant. For example, take the existence of a frog. There really isn't just one frog anywhere in existence. Even when the frog was first evolving, there had to be at least a male and a female frog. Male and female cannot exist without each other—not to mention their reliance on collectives of surrounding animals and plants. This is why all individual biological realities depend on complex ecological realities. And ecological realities always contain not only living beings but also their artifacts, which are the inanimate products of various animate forms of life, such as a bird's nest, a beaver dam, an anthill, and so on.

Human beings especially produce an enormous number of artifacts, from cars to houses to trains to skyscrapers to computers to information-processing systems. And notice that all artifacts are 3rd-person, inanimate objects (in the Lower Right quadrant). It turns out that these artifacts, even though they are in themselves inanimate, have also undergone stages of evolution—or at least they can always be arranged in evolutionary stages. That is, as human beings underwent various stages of evolution, they produced increasingly evolved the forms of artifacts, and these artifacts can be aligned alongside the correlative stages of human evolution that produced them. For example, there are obvious stages in the development of war machines (bow and arrow, to crossbows and catapults, to airplanes and bombs, to nuclear weapons). Gerhard Lenski looked at these levels of artifacts and discovered a very important series of stages in the techno-economic area, and each of them, like the levels of corresponding evolution in human unfolding, displayed an increasing degree of complexity. These artifacts evolved from systems of foraging (or hunting and gathering) to horticultural stages (agriculture using simple digging sticks or hoes) to agrarian stages (agriculture using heavy animal-drawn plows) to industrial stages (using machines) to informational (using computers). These artifacts are all nonliving, 3rd-person plural realities or exterior, collective objects and, as such, they all exist in the Lower Right quadrant.

The Lower Right also includes systems of living beings, such as families, ecosystems, and nation-states; living beings are, after all, what produce artifacts in the first place. But the artifacts found in those systems are, by definition, *nonliving*, and those systems of nonliving things are found only in the material Lower Right quadrant—"matter" in the second sense. Thus, for example, the Lower Right includes the techno-economic artifacts of foraging, horticultural, agrarian, industrial, and informational, and although all of them are themselves nonliving, techno-economic forms, they include living human beings, along with other living plants and animals in an ecosystem. And as genuine systems, they are taken to be real realities by systems theory.

As we have seen, the real battle in science is between atomism and systems theory (both deal with objective or exterior material realities). But for Integral Metatheory, the parts of a wheel are real, but so is the wheel—both individuals and collectives are real (which is why virtually all phenomena in each quadrant are actually holons, or whole/parts). Then, Integral adds, so are their interior realities; that is, both interior holons and exterior holons are real. For example, brains (Upper Right) go with minds (Upper Left), minds go with cultures (Lower Left), and brains exist in ecological systems (Lower Right). All 4 quadrants are deeply interwoven.

So every time you have a thought ("It's time to watch my favorite podcast"), you are also lighting up some sort of neural network in the brain, which—as a biological body—is itself massively interwoven with innumerable exterior ecological phenomena and system processes. And not only can this exterior collective be looked at from without as a 3rd-person plural or interobjective dimension—a system "its" in the Lower Right—the *same collective* can also be looked at from within as a 1st-person plural or intersubjective dimension in the Lower Left—a cultural "we." That is, not only can the exterior group be videotaped from without, it can be felt, shared, and known from within. This is culture. We've already seen how inextricably interwoven culture is with the other quadrants. Thus, for example, corresponding to the interobjective, techno-economic realities in the Lower Right (in holarchical order: foraging, horticultural, agrarian, industrial, informational) there exist the intersubjective, interior, cultural worldviews that *inherently go with those levels* (respectively, archaic, magic, mythic, rational orange, and pluralistic green) in the Lower Left. All we-spaces are inextricably related to the various "its" systems that go with them (as you can see in fig. 11.2).

Although any given phenomenon often emphasizes a particular quadrant (like culture emphasizes the Lower Left and consciousness the Upper Left), the phenomena in each quadrant have correlates in all the other quadrants. They exist together and arise together—they tetra-enact and tetra-evolve. Thus, when you are having that seemingly individual and stand-alone thought in the Upper Left mind ("It's time to watch my favorite podcast"), you are actually and ultimately plugged into all 4 quadrants.

This is how and why the universe hangs together. And by "what hangs together," I don't mean just objective atoms or interobjective systems, I mean subjective, objective, intersubjective, and interobjective dimension/perspectives—all 4 quadrants. When the universe blew into existence, it didn't involve just a large number of physical forces (for example, gravity, the strong and weak nuclear force, and electromagnetism—all merely 3rd-person realities)—it also involved the fundamental distinctions of individual and collective (singular and plural) and interior and exterior (subjective prehension and objective space/time). These are different ways that the universe—the self-organizing universe—sees itself and is aware of itself. It involves all 4 quadrants. The totally interwoven nature of the entire universe is exactly why you can have a real experience of Unity consciousness or a Kosmic consciousness, and its very existence is indeed "not disputable."

THE IMPORTANCE OF THE 4 QUADRANTS IN BIG WHOLENESS

The importance of all 4 quadrants becomes especially significant when we look at Showing Up, which is defined as "showing up for all the important perspectives and dimensions in the universe," that is, all 4 quadrants. This is easily seen when we look at the different methodologies that humans have developed to gain access to the different realms of reality. For each of these different dimensions of reality—subjective, objective, intersubjective, and interobjective—we have developed different epistemologies about how we come to know them. And although adherents to the method and epistemology appropriate to one quadrant have often gotten into fights and arguments with adherents to that of another about which one alone is real, it's clear that all of these methods need to be included in any sort of truly holistic approach to reality. Further, the very existence of all of these methodologies show us just how real each quadrant is.

For the Upper Right quadrant, we have developed empirical methods and an empiricist epistemology. These methods define reality as consisting primarily of that which can be seen or detected using the five human senses or their extensions (which really means "can be seen by the body in the Upper Right quadrant"; and this means, essentially, anything that can be videotaped). All theories—or simply all statements—about reality have to be backed up with "evidence," which usually means experiential data—data derived from using the five senses or their extensions (that is, the evidence can be videotaped). Among other things, this method is taken as the foundation of any theory that claims to be "scientific." This Upper Right empirical dimension is clearly an important part of any true reality, and it definitely needs to be included.

Of course, this empirical sensory evidence can be extended to include any groups or collections of objects as long as they can be seen by the senses or their extensions (or otherwise provide some sort of experiential evidence that can be videotaped). Thus this collective empiricism also includes wholes that can be videotaped (for example, an entire ecosystem, which is a real collective system of "matter" in the second sense, can be videotaped even though it's not just an individual holon—as Upper Right empiricism requires). In other words, this collective empiricism applies to any Lower Right reality. Systems theory and the epistemology that it has developed is a form of collective empiricism. And, as we have seen, there has always been something of a battle between atomism and systems theory in science, because there is a very real difference between the Upper Right quadrant and the Lower Right quadrant. Both atomism and systems theory have developed methodologies that adequately get at their respective realities (that is, empiricism is aimed at the Upper Right and systems theory at the Lower Right), and clearly, both of them need to be included.

Although champions of the exterior or objective domains have always claimed a dominant or even sole access to any "real reality," there have always been geniuses who have claimed that we have access to incredibly important realities that need to be embraced in the interior or subjective domains. In general, these approaches are often called "phenomenological." Like their exterior, material correlates, they have often been divided into methods that approach the individual interior (Upper Left) and those that approach collective interiors (Lower Left).

Individual phenomenological approaches include the methodologies that have attempted to deal with the human mind, or mental realities. Well known among these are psychoanalysis, structuralism, humanistic-existential therapy, other forms of psychological therapy, and, of course, phenomenology itself. In all of them, some version of introspection or "looking within" is employed (since this area involves the interior of minds), as well as ways for other individuals to reproduce these introspective realities in their own case, so that these results can be checked or verified to some degree. Especially important for any sort of genuine Showing Up is the discovery of developmental structuralism—the discovery of ways to investigate the actual structures of the mind (since they cannot be directly videotaped). We looked at these structures when I outlined the 6 major structures of Growing Up. As I noted, these structures were discovered only around one hundred years ago (since they cannot be seen merely by looking within), but their importance for understanding the mind—and its various approaches to reality—cannot be overestimated. These phenomenological methods, which approach Upper Left minds and their interiors are thus crucial for any sort of holistic access to truth.

We also find phenomenological approaches to collective, intersubjective, or cultural realities as well. These approaches, since they deal with the Lower Left (collectives of subjective minds—that is, intersubjective cultures), embrace an enormous number of disciplines, including cultural studies, ethnomethodology, semiotics, law, and sociology, among others. These intersubjective, cultural, or Lower Left realities are incredibly numerous and include everything from shared values to meaning, language, social norms, customs, habitus (cultural habits), as well as Heidegger's approach to Dasein (cultural being) and Foucault's study of structures of (cultural) power. Since there are various cultural or subcultural contexts for almost every mental phenomenon, the study of these contexts—often called "cultural studies"—is invariably important for any sort of inclusive methodology.

These four approaches to epistemology (empiricism, systems theory, phenomenology, and cultural studies) are indeed so fundamental because they address the inside and the outside (the subjective and the objective) of the individual and the collective (the singular and the plural). In other words, they address the 4 quadrants, which are indeed the 4 major dimension/perspectives of reality. And the fact that each of these four epistemologies has developed a powerful methodology for accessing a different dimension demonstrates the reality of those dimensions.

Precisely because there are different major dimension/perspectives of reality, when different epistemologies latch onto them, people often get into fights about which dimension/perspective is the most important, or which is the only real one—for example, the battle between atomism and systems theory (individual versus collective) in science, not to mention the battle between subjective and objective (which includes mind versus brain). Given this tendency of partisans of one quadrant to deny the reality of the others, it is especially important that we include a genuine Showing Up for all the quadrants. Especially if we are talking about a Big Wholeness, we want to make sure that each area of that Big Wholeness (Waking Up, Growing Up, Opening Up, Cleaning Up, and Showing Up) is as complete and whole as it can be. And this means that we should make a thorough study of each of those areas, so we will know all the aspects that need to be included in each of them. Think of Growing Up, for example, and the care that was needed to discover all the various structures of the mind's development that must be included—and once we had them, we needed to embrace them all. The same is true with Showing Up. We need to carefully include all the various aspects of Showing Up (all 4 quadrants), and given the warfare between partisans of a particular quadrant, this can take a bit of work.

Hopefully this chapter has given you a broad understanding of the various areas that need to be included in an authentic and inclusive Showing Up—and that especially means the inside and the outside of both the individual and the collective—that is, the 4 quadrants. We saw how many other realities depend on those quadrants, from the 1st-person, 2nd-person, and 3rd-person perspectives to the 1-2-3 of Spirit, such as Christ's speaking *as*, *to*, and *about* God. The quadrants are so fundamental because they involve two of the most fundamental oppositions in all of existence—inside versus outside (or subject versus object) and individual versus collective (or singular versus plural). We can't find one of those pairs without its opposite—subjects always arise and exist with objects, and individuals always arise and exist with collectives. This is why the 4 quadrants go "all the up, all the way down," and why so many other systems depend on or even include them.

Now you can more easily understand why every single thought that you have is plugged into all 4 quadrants of your own being. Every time you have a single subjective thought (in your Upper Left mind)—such as "It's time for me to watch my favorite podcast"—you are also activating some aspect of your objective brain physiology (in the Upper Right). And further, not only does every Upper Right object have a correlate in the Upper Left subjective quadrant (every brain state has a corresponding mind state) but it also occurs in the context of a Lower Right collective or system of objects—every Upper Right object has a Lower Right interobjective correlated context. And furthermore, every Lower Right interobjective system has one or more correlates not just in its own Upper Right object domain but also in the Lower Left, intersubjective, cultural domain (as we saw with Lenski's research on the evolution of artifacts). In other words, every phenomenon in the real world always involves all 4 quadrants, perfectly tetra-enacting and tetra-evolving.

And while all of those realities might appear to be separate and all by themselves, each of these 4 perspectives are deeply interwoven with, and lean upon, all the others. So, in every moment of your life, you are plugged into the entire universe at its most basic and fundamental dimensions and perspectives. No matter how alone you might feel, at every moment of your life, you are truly and actually at home in the universe.

And—to move directly to our next topic—you can directly know this fundamental "at-home-ness" not through just one intelligence but through many types of intelligence. You are, in fact, at least a dozen times smarter than you ever thought.

So let's now look at how you can engage in Opening Up to all of these many intelligences—what do you say?

12

Opening Up

OUR MULTIPLE INTELLIGENCES

We have seen that it is necessary to study each quadrant fully, so that we know all the elements that need to be included in each of them in order to Show Up for all of them. One of the things that happens when we do this with, for example, the Upper Left quadrant, is that we discover that our consciousness undergoes an evolutionary development through various stages of Growing Up. And further, there are pathologies that can develop at each of these stages, and dealing with them is the process of Cleaning Up. A thorough study of the Upper Left also discloses the extreme importance of Waking Up. Finally, including all of those areas (Waking Up, Growing Up, and Cleaning Up) is necessary for a full Showing Up—which moves us very close to a full-fledged Big Wholeness.

There is one other area that a complete study of the Upper Left also gives us, and that is what we call "Opening Up." This involves becoming aware of our multiple intelligences and fully Opening Up to all of them. As human beings, we don't just have one basic intelligence, often called "cognitive intelligence," the one measured by the all-important IQ test. Rather, recent research (by, for example, Harvard psychologist Howard Gardner) suggests that we have up to a dozen different intelligences. In addition to cognitive intelligence—which is still important—we also have emotional intelligence, moral intelligence, musical intelligence, aesthetic intelligence, intrapersonal intelligence, kinesthetic or bodily intelligence, mathematical intelligence, social or interpersonal intelligence, values intelligence, and spiritual intelligence, among others. These are additional intelligences that we all have available to us.

There is a good deal of argument and debate in developmental circles about the total number of intelligences we have (some others that have been suggested include linguistic, psychosexual, faith, self-concept or ego, gender, worldview, willpower, and motivation or needs intelligence, among several others). But the eleven intelligences that I just listed are widely agreed upon.[1]

I now want to briefly go over this process of Opening Up, since it does provide a new and very important type of Wholeness to our awareness. I will do this fairly quickly, however, since it's not that hard to see and understand. But don't let this brevity confuse you into thinking that Opening Up is not an important area of Big Wholeness, since that would be a very mistaken conclusion. Next to Growing Up and Waking Up, Opening Up is easily as important as any area of a Big Wholeness.

EVOLUTION AND OUR MULTIPLE INTELLIGENCES

One of the basic reasons why we apparently have multiple intelligences available to us is that as we evolved over hundreds of thousands of years, life constantly presented us with several fundamental questions—What is real? What is the right thing to do? What do I find attractive or beautiful? What is that other person thinking?—that, as a species, we found ourselves attempting to answer, over and over again. As we gained skill in answering a particular type of question, we evolved an intelligence for doing so. We developed not only cognitive intelligence (What am I thinking or aware of right now?) but also emotional intelligence (What am I feeling right now?), aesthetic intelligence (What do I find attractive or beautiful?), moral intelligence (What is the right thing to do?), and spiritual intelligence (What is the most important and ultimately real thing for me right now?). Whether you look at them as a Lamarckian or a Darwinian inheritance, humans developed and passed on around a dozen of these intelligences, which they used any time that one of those major questions came up. (See table 7 for a list of basic intelligences and the fundamental questions they evolved to answer.) We still have those intelligences available to us, and Opening Up to them is realizing this fact and stepping into our own larger awareness.

TABLE 7. Our Multiple Intelligences and the Life Questions They Address

Intelligence	Life question
Aesthetic intelligence	What do I find attractive or beautiful?
Cognitive intelligence	What am I thinking or aware of right now?
Ego intelligence	Who am I?
Emotional intelligence	What am I feeling right now?
Intrapersonal intelligence	What am I internally aware of?
Kinesthetic or bodily intelligence	What does my body feel?
Mathematical intelligence	If I get two apples from one tree and three apples from another, how many apples do I have?
Moral intelligence	What is the right thing to do?
Motivational needs intelligence	What is it that I most need right now?
Musical intelligence	What does that music say to me?

Intelligence	Life question
Social or interpersonal intelligence	What is that other person thinking?
Spiritual intelligence	What is the most important and ultimately real thing (of ultimate concern) for me right now?
Values intelligence	What do I value most about this situation?

Your thinking capacity—or cognitive intelligence—is not the only type of intelligence that you possess. Making room for these other intelligences is indeed to Open Up to the rich variety of intelligences that you have available, as well as the many different capacities that you possess because of these intelligences (capacities for cognitive, emotional, moral, aesthetic, and spiritual growth and learning opened up by these intelligences).

I think that with this new inclusion to our Big Wholeness, we are starting to see just how truly "big" this Big Wholeness can be—and just how high and deep and wide our awareness genuinely is, or certainly can be, if we know where to look.

So gaining this Big Wholeness is certainly something that we should want in our lives. What would be the opposite of this full Wholeness? How about global suicide, which is now a possibility?

13

Very Dark Shadows Today

The human species is the first species in existence capable of fully committing suicide—that is, of completely destroying itself on a global scale. Literally, the *total* destruction of humanity: this became possible only in the modern Industrial Age (orange), and the point at which this became glaringly obvious marked the official beginning of the postmodern Information Age (green).

MUTUAL ASSURED DESTRUCTION

The first very concrete example of the possibility of global suicide was MAD (mutual assured destruction), which was the intentional military/political stance that the United States and the Soviet Union took toward each other during the Cold War. Both sides believed that the Cold War could be kept "cold" and could be prevented from becoming "hot" because no matter who fired its atomic weapons first, the other side could retaliate with enough nuclear power that both parties to the conflict were guaranteed to be totally and mutually destroyed (thus "mutual assured destruction"). Either the atomic blasts themselves or the nuclear winter that would follow would result in the death of essentially all humans, and much of the rest of life on earth. This was an absolutely insane attitude, of course; what's more insane was the relentless logic that showed just how inevitable such an approach was.

This all came to a head—and first became very obvious—with the Cuban Missile Crisis, which could be said to inaugurate the Postmodern Age. Here, during the "thirteen days that shook the world"—in 1963—the United States and the Soviet Union were driven relentlessly toward an actual nuclear conflict, a crisis that started when the Soviet Union moved intermediate-range nuclear missiles into their satellite state Cuba—which is merely a few miles from mainland United States. President John F. Kennedy was charged with deciding how to respond.[1] What's so telling about this crisis—and what makes it arguably the official beginning of the postmodern world—is that, no matter that each side wanted desperately not to pull the trigger that would cause both sides to go up in a globe-engulfing mushroom cloud, nonetheless each step they took to prevent this destruction drew them inevitably closer and closer to a world-destroying conflagration. This crisis is such a postmodern-defining event because both sides fully knew that this was happening, and yet that didn't matter. They both knew that they wanted above all else not to start World War III (with its guaranteed MAD), and they both took the very best steps they could to help prevent it—and they both watched as each of those steps nonetheless kept taking them closer to mutual destruction. What on earth do you do when each step you take to prevent something actually brings you closer and closer to that which you are trying to prevent—and you're perfectly aware of that, and that doesn't help?

Another thing that makes the Cuban Missile Crisis arguably the official beginning of the Postmodern Age is that it was relentlessly negative in tone, whereas virtually all modern thinkers were relentlessly positive and progressive. Adding to the formation of the postmodern world were poststructuralism, from such French philosophers as Derrida, Foucault, and Lyotard), and the creation of digital/computer technology (and the development of Artificial Intelligence, which many experts felt would lead to the end of humanity), but the Cuban Missile Crisis was the first time we were immediately threatened with the destruction of the entire planet, making it as negative as negative can get.

These thirteen days of insanity indeed marked the transition from the modern world to the beginning of the postmodern. Modernity—the orange, rational, achievement-oriented stage, enthusiastically dedicated to progress, profit, excellence, and meritocracy, grounded in verifiable truth and dedicated to the proposition that people everywhere should have equal opportunity to life's bounty—collapsed as the official philosophy of the leading edge of cultural evolution. The leading edge shifted at the beginning of postmodernity to the green, postrational, truth-uncertain, relativistic, egalitarian, multicultural attitude. Green was dedicated not to equal opportunity but to equal outcome, and hence wedded to a wish for justice for all victims (a wish created by a heart of gold but with the unintended consequence of making victimhood sacred and something to be actively sought). In the modern world, only winners were rewarded; in the postmodern world, only victims are. Where the general attitude of modernity was freedom, profit, achievement, and happy progress in truth, the general attitude of postmodernity is VUCA—volatility, uncertainty, complexity, and ambiguity. Where modernity introduced advancement, growth, antipoverty wealth, and an avalanche of progress in almost every area it touched, postmodernity saw the downsides of each of them and was left to pick up the pieces (something that it, or any other 1st-tier stage was ill-equipped to do adequately).

Thus the enthusiastic optimism of modernity gave way to the pessimistic downturn of postmodernity, anchored not in truth, beauty, progress, or profit but in an awareness of death, decay, inequality, and power and the resultant demand for social justice. (And the social justice demanded was not the freedom of equal opportunity, which orange offered, but the forced equality of a guaranteed equal outcome, which green wants, and which nccessarily must be forced because human beings are vastly different from each other, and thus any extensive equality is the denial of diversity and demands social force.) As we saw, these two—freedom and equality—are opposites. Precisely because people are extraordinarily diverse, you can have freedom or equality, but you can't have both. 2nd-tier Integral will carefully integrate these two values, but orange and green are fated to simply fight it out, guaranteeing that there will be culture wars until a tipping point puts global Integral into place as the new leading edge.

Where modernity pioneered progress in a stunning number of areas—and almost no one saw or understood the unintended consequences of this progress, some of which were, in fact, globally suicidal, such as industrial pollution—postmodernity was faced with incontrovertible evidence that the bill had come due, and the bill was global in scope (from military MAD to collapse of the biosphere to rampant capitalistic greed to nuclear disaster to the realization that Artificial Intelligence itself would possibly, even likely, destroy humanity).

The fact that humanity could, and very likely might, completely destroy itself—literally!—was a shocking realization, *radically new in all of humankind's history*. Never before had any of humanity's actions resulted in the possibility of a *totally* global self-destruction, and never before had such a possibility even entered humanity's awareness.

This realization began to seep into the world at large, drenching it with death. And this marked a profound change in human nature itself. Humans were now the species that could become extinct—at their own hands—and they knew it. How do you live with that?

Thus, where most of the leading-edge thinkers of modernity spent their time pondering ways to advance their field to ever greater excellence, most of the leading-edge thinkers of postmodernity spent their time desperately thinking about how to correct the actions introduced by modernity. If, with modernity, humanity started smoking, with postmodernity, humanity discovered that it had lung cancer. And what made it so deeply shocking was that there was no cure for cancer.

What all of these elements have in common is that they represent the very first emergent realities of an evolution that, with orange, finally reached a global, universal level—and, with green, became aware of the costs of doing so (many were the unintended consequences of orange but nonetheless were devastating). Humanity itself, starting, perhaps over a million years ago, with a social reality that embraced no more than around forty people in a small, local hunting clan or a tribe (crimson archaic), evolved through ever-larger social holons, from extended hunting tribes of several hundred people (magenta magic), to large multitribe villages of several thousand (red magic-mythic), to beginning megatribe military empires of millions of people (amber mythic), to late military empires and globally interconnected, early modern nation-states with millions of people worldwide (umber mythic-rational),[2] to a universal, scientific Enlightenment originally touching millions and eventually everybody on the planet (orange rational), to a postmodern global village of a stupendous 7 billion people (green pluralistic).

Each of those transitions marked major evolutionary leaps; but particularly profound was the leap from *ethnocentric* (and lower) to *worldcentric* (and higher)—that is, the leap from traditional amber mythic to modern orange rational—because this marked the first time that human evolution had reached *global* universal dimensions, where each human's being and identity was inextricably tied to that of every other human on the planet (not to mention the life of the planet itself). The emergence of these global levels (the worldcentric universal stages beginning with orange and moving to green) marked a stunning shift in human evolution itself. At first, especially with worldcentric orange, humans mostly saw the major advances of such a leap. This indeed was the beginning of modernity, particularly marked by the Western Enlightenment with its cognitive advances seen in things like the invention of almost all the modern, universal sciences (for example, physics, astronomy, chemistry, and biology), its moral advances seen in things like the end of slavery and its emphasis on universal rights for all humans, and its economic advances seen in things like capitalism, which for all of its problems, did involve a massive increase in profits for the owners. These were the beginning stages of a development now going global and universal. There were downsides to all of them, of course, as there are downsides to every level of development (the dialectic of progress), but for the most part, none of these downsides were seen or understood at first—and certainly they were not believed to mark the possible end of everything.

The reason I compare this to cigarette smoking is that the downsides of modernity usually did not show up at the start. It took centuries to see some of the truly alarming and mostly unintended consequences of the awesome leap of global modernity. That realization, I'm suggesting, marked the official start of postmodernity—the very name itself, "postmodernity," was as much a deep wish-fulfillment as anything else: "My god, look what we have done!—and how can we correct this modern nightmare? We can't just get rid of modern, so we'll go postmodern!"

For example, none of the ugly ecological effects of industrial capitalism were initially obvious. If the direct link between, say, carbon dioxide production and global warming (with its potential ultimate downside of a complete biospheric collapse and the end of humanity and most life on earth) were fully seen and understood right from the start, the actual unfolding of industrialization might have gone very differently. No matter how ugly capitalism is pictured by its critics, no CEO is demented enough to take actions that they know will directly kill their children and grandchildren.

But it is only recently—deep into a postmodern world—that we have sufficient scientific evidence to clearly establish the dire consequences of global warming. That is why I say that if, with modernity, humanity started smoking, with postmodernity, it discovered it had lung cancer. And the real shocker is, again, there is no cure for cancer, as the Cuban Missile Crisis came one small jot away from decisively demonstrating. But it did manage to sear this awareness of our global mortality into the human mind indefinitely, a place very soon to be taken by the threat of a population bomb, then global ecological devastation, and then the possibility of humanity's suicide through Artificial Intelligence, among others. Welcome to the Postmodern Age.

This brings us directly to the point that we have been discussing about modernity and postmodernity—namely, both are in the range of a development that for the first time in human history had gone global and worldcentric, and that now many of humanity's problems are being created by this global scope itself. The global reach of the progress of modernity created global problems. When human awareness went from ethnocentric to worldcentric not only did humanity start to benefit from the amazing advances and positive benefits of a global awareness but also its major problems became global in scope.

And for the first time in history, this meant that humanity now had the means to destroy itself on a global scale. Not only is the modern and postmodern world more evolved than that of our archaic tribal ancestors but it also can be suicidally sick in ways that our ancestors literally could not even imagine. You can kill only so many other human beings with a bow and arrow; but the red nuclear button is a "global delete" button: push that once and humanity itself disappears. Is this good news or bad news?

Well, both of course. The good news is that the average person now possesses a greater amount of being, awareness, and identity due to a continuing and evolving Growing Up, as well as the advances and gains that have resulted in, among many other things, an increase in average human life span from less than twenty-five years in the first tribes to close to seventy-five years in people everywhere today. (Are the critics of modernity ready to give up those extra fifty years of their own life? Whenever an adult critic of modernity asks me, "Do you know where we'd be today if we were still at a tribal level?" I usually answer, "Yes, we'd be dead.")

But there are indeed downsides to modernity, and the bad news is, welcome to the Cuban Missile Crisis, MAD, global warming that can potentially lead to biospheric collapse, and an advance in Artificial Intelligence that might be the death of us all. Truly, no era prior to orange modernity could have produced anything remotely like this.

I've spent a fair amount of time going over this point about humanity becoming global, because there is one thing that is just as catastrophic as any of the downsides of modernity—and that is to look at this issue (and its many problems) *only* from the Right-hand or exterior quadrants, where we find those things that can be seen with the human senses or their extensions—that is, "matter" in its second, extended meaning, which is anything that can be videotaped. Notice one important truth about all this: although we can track the increase in the size of human societies by looking at their exteriors alone (their objective dimensions and their measurable quantities), *we can also track their development by looking at the equally real interior realities*, which unfold, as we have seen, from archaic to magic to mythic to rational to pluralistic to integral—or from egocentric to ethnocentric to worldcentric to integral (which is truly global—what we'll call "global-Integral" or "global 2nd tier").

Now human beings commonly and typically track these issues only by looking at exteriors. They look at population growth, or they track particular cultures in their geopolitical locations, or they track the size of the culture, the amount of its money in circulation or its annual birthrates, and so on, and all too often they completely ignore the correlative interior development that is also occurring. Or, at any rate, that should be occurring. But all too often interior development does not keep pace with exterior development, and the *real* problem is that we don't even track this interior development at all; we simply ignore the interiors altogether and can't even see the problem—and thus we have no effective solutions.

We have abundant evidence that just because today every human being is born into a global village, this does *not* mean that every human being starts with a global awareness. We know that is not true at all. A genuinely global capacity in awareness is the product of about six major stages of human development (6-to-8 on average—which we have also summarized as four stages—selfish or egocentric, care or ethnocentric, universal care or worldcentric, and integrated or integral). To say "Everybody alive today is living in a global village" tells us absolutely nothing about where any given person's consciousness is actually located. Is it at one of several stages of a largely selfish and power-driven egocentric, or at one of several stages of a culturally imperialist or jihadist ethnocentric, or is it starting to move into truly global worldcentric stages with modern orange, and even more global ones with worldcentric green, or finally a comprehensive and integrated global with turquoise global-Integral?

We saw that part of any global problem today is the fact that some 60 to 70 percent of the world's population are living at ethnocentric or lower stages of development—in other words, their consciousness is considerably less than global. Their exteriors (technology and artifacts) might be global, but their interiors (consciousness and culture) definitely are not. These 60 to 70 percent may be living in a global village, but they are not living in a global awareness. (And even worse, the percentage of the population at turquoise global-Integral, a 2nd-tier stage, is less than 8 percent, and yet these stages are the only ones that can actually start to solve some of the problems created by 1st tier.) And none of this is to mention that leaving out all Left-hand interiors also cuts out any approach to Waking Up to any Enlightened states of consciousness. Usually these realities in the Left-hand interiors are ignored when researchers examine planetwide problems; nothing but Right-hand exteriors are taken into account.

Humanity, in other words, is suffering from a profound failure to Show Up.

The central problem that human beings face today is not due primarily to the fact that we exist in a global village, with its economics, finances, trade, technology, education, and politics all being globally interwoven, of 7 billion people. The central problem is that the capacity to inhabit a level that fully embraces this global reality is the result of several major stages of interior human development, and at this time, less than 30 percent of the population have developed to the worldcentric stages where this can be done.[3] For those of us who are not yet able to adequately inhabit a global level of awareness, this means that, as the title of one of Robert Kegan's books puts it (with exactly this problem in mind), we are "in over our heads." Kegan's research indicates that three out of five people do not make it to the modern worldcentric level. In other words, 60 to 70 percent of our planetwide population cannot adequately respond to the level of complexity and sophistication that is now present in, and fundamentally defines, the worldcentric contours of the world. In short, the vast majority of the world's population is "in over their heads."

But the real problem is even worse. The real problem is that we are not even tracking this interior evolution; and so we have no idea that there is even a problem, let alone what to do about it. We are not Showing Up authentically. We are not inhabiting all the major dimensions of our own being, especially the Left-hand dimensions—

which is, at bottom, a truly cowardly stance (laced with a genuine fear of the realities that we have denied existence).

Why is this such a problem? Where cultures have reached an orange worldcentric level of development, they truly wish to treat all people fairly, regardless of race, color, sex, gender, ethnicity, or creed (that is, without an ethnocentric, racist, sexist, homophobic, or xenophobic prejudice). Nonetheless some 60 or 70 percent of the world's citizens have exactly that ethnocentric or lower awareness, with its inherently narrow drives, limited values, and imperialist and jihadist views (often slipping into their more extremist versions, from ISIS to Hamas to Hezbollah). And yet these interior levels are not being tracked at all, and thus the path forward from ethnocentric bias to a more widely shared worldcentric fairness is barely known or understood.

People who do manage to be at one of these more developed (orange or green) levels assume that everybody else can think the way that they do (after all, we're all equally members of the same global village), and yet the vast majority of people cannot do so—but that is not taken into account at all, and the results are seriously disastrous. And that is not because there is something intrinsically wrong with any of these lower stages—being five years old is not an illness—but because it fails to track these realities, our culture contains no information or wisdom on how to advance through these stages to a person's own highest worldcentric potentials and greatest global possibilities, leaving everybody to flounder in this deserted wilderness.

So, in the worldwide population, while the exterior, Right-hand quadrants have reached global orange levels in, for example, their technology and almost all their artifacts, in the interior, Left-hand quadrants, reaching a global level in awareness is mostly only a possibility, a potential, a maybe—and something most people have to discover for themselves (since their cultures are not Showing Up for them). Worse, even in cultures whose leading-edge governing bodies originate mostly at orange or green, many of their major social problems stem from populations that, through no real fault of their own, are still stuck at the pre-worldcentric stages (crimson, red, amber), and form huge pockets of poorly developed subcultures at those earlier levels of development, with all the crime, poverty, and destitution that implies.

A real part of the problem here is that government, as well as many other national and international organizations (including businesses), often operates at an ethnocentric level. Although the science and technology that they use are indeed global and worldcentric, their own interior motives are often red power-tribal or amber jihadist-traditional (and this applies also to military organizations, financial systems, international politics, and transnational businesses; while their technology has reached global worldcentric levels, their leaders often have not). Humanity, in other words, is not living up to its own profound interior potentials. And this is compounded by the fact that we are not even tracking this interior dimension at all! We have no idea that this arrested development is occurring because we don't acknowledge this development in the first place.

We have thoroughly—but thoroughly—refused to Show Up. And it gets worse . . .

THE REAL SINS OF MODERNITY

Any individual in the Upper Left, as well as any collective culture in the Lower Left, who is at an orange worldcentric (or higher) stage of development, really does try to treat all people fairly—regardless of race, color, sex, or creed. At such an interior level of development, slavery, for example, is simply unthinkable: there is absolutely no way that you can treat a person with worldcentric fairness *and* enslave them. That is why it was only when humanity reached the orange stage of its development that slavery was, for the first time in history, outlawed in every orange country on the entire planet. Slavery began with the first humans themselves (according to Lenski's data, around 15 percent of the first tribal societies had slavery). From that red magic-tribal start, slavery dramatically expanded during the amber ethnocentric era (with a stunning 90 percent of some clusters of amber cultures having slavery). One-third of the population of Athens itself, vaunted home of democracy, were slaves.

In the very early phases of orange modernity, slavery started to become global in scale. Modern transportation systems (from ships to railroads) made worldwide slavery a hot trade. But at the same time, the Left-hand quadrants (of consciousness and culture) produced a significant number of individuals whose interiors were also starting to reach orange worldcentric stages, and those individuals drove an increasingly powerful abolition movement that succeeded in every country around the world that had begun to be moved by orange values of freedom. So, as usual in human history, it wasn't just a global *economic* system that drove slavery but also less-than-global levels of moral development (which is also why virtually every preglobal and premodern country had slavery at one time or another). And thus again, we see a modern problem created when modern global technologies and systems in the Right Hand were used by people who were motivated by less-than-global premodern drives and values in the Left Hand.

And notice that making slavery illegal doesn't fully address the existence of racist activity in a culture. Thus, as we saw when we examined the culture wars in the United States, we have made it illegal to engage in any activity that is explicitly racist. But there was a time when not only was it legal to create hotels that were different for white people and black people but there were actually Jim Crow laws mandating them. There was, at that time, legal, systemic racism embedded in the Right-hand quadrants. But all of those laws have now been removed—there is no longer a legal systemic racism in the

United States. But as social justice advocates remind us, there is still an awful lot of racism in the United States, because erasing racism from the Right-hand legal system does nothing to change a person's Left-hand, interior value structure. You can make an exterior *behavior* illegal, but you cannot make *thinking* in racist terms an illegal act (you can't outlaw forms of thinking).

And the people who enforce the Right-hand legal system will still be enforcing the law according to their own Left-hand interior value system; and thus, for example, although there is no law that tells police to arrest blacks more often than whites, that racist act still often occurs. And a police officer whose interior development is at an ethnocentric level is more likely to engage in this behavior. So, we will never get rid of racism until we've addressed the 60 percent of the population who are still at ethnocentric or lower stages of development and still think in racist terms. The same is true for sexist (or patriarchal) thinking, homophobia, transphobia, and so on. That's why we need to consciously track interior or Left-hand development in each culture and why a merely Right-hand approach will never be able to accomplish this.

So we've fixed the problem in the Right-hand quadrants (moving our exterior, Right-hand technology and artifacts to global worldcentric levels), but we haven't touched it in the Left-hand quadrants. I want to suggest that the same is true for almost all our troubles today that are globally problematic, even globally suicidal. These globally suicidal problems are due primarily to a strong imbalance between progress in the Right-hand quadrants, which has reached at least an orange worldcentric level, particularly in technology and artifacts, and progress in the Left-hand quadrants, where some 60 percent have not reached a worldcentric level—and that imbalance is likely to kill us all.

This is why such a special effort has to be made to help the interiors of consciousness and culture keep pace with their exterior technology and artifacts. All too often, as we have seen, development in the average Right Hand runs far ahead of the average Left Hand that is using it, and when that happens, much lower—and much less caring, less compassionate, less loving, and more domineering, more oppressive, and more exploitive—drives and values in the Left Hand end up inhabiting and using those Right-hand technologies. Thus, when, on any sort of large scale, the Right-hand technology and artifacts are orange modern-global (or higher) and the Left-hand motivation and drives using them are premodern and less than orange, the result is the classic global (and usually suicidal) problem of the contemporary world.

This is where we especially see the potentially catastrophic problem with human artifacts. Usually a genius, or several of them, at the leading-edge level of Growing Up, will conceive and help create a version of a very sophisticated artifact in the Right Hand (for example, an automobile, airplane, computer, or the internet), but once the artifacts are created, almost anybody, at virtually any level of Growing Up, can use them. You yourself don't have to be able to conceive and manufacture a computer—once it's there, it's yours to use no matter what your level of Growing Up. That is why exterior, Right-hand technology and artifacts can run so far ahead of the degree of consciousness and culture in the Left Hand. (Marx created virtually all his theory based on this tension.)

Our planet is being assaulted and crippled by people who have access to orange Right-hand worldcentric technology and artifacts, but who themselves are at pre-worldcentric and pre-orange Left-hand levels of development and either can't see or don't care about global realities. This is killing all of us.

Next, I will take some examples of modern, global suicidal problems and demonstrate how each of them is the result of a Right-hand science and technology development that is at orange worldcentric (or higher) coupled with a Left-hand development that is at pre-worldcentric, pre-orange, and preglobal levels. I'll start with the climate crisis as an obvious example.

It's not that we don't know enough about global climate to be able to spot the problems that are occurring here. Very clearly, the Right-hand results of orange modernity—particularly the industrial revolution and its polluting byproducts—have put too much of the greenhouse gases into the atmosphere, which has increased the earth's atmospheric temperature. But our Left-hand response to this problem has been atrocious. There is some disagreement in scientific circles about the degree of severity of the climate problem, but no argument at all that it is very real and extremely threatening. (A recent poll of experts around the entire world showed that almost a full *half* of them think that global warming will kill *all of humanity*—all of it!).[4]

But many people doubt that there will be any catastrophic consequences at all—or worse, they think that global warming is a "joke." These tend to be people who are at ethnocentric levels, or lower, of cognitive and moral development. Somebody who thinks worldcentrically and can understand science will have no problem looking at the evidence of universal weather patterns and making up their mind. But since 60 percent do not make it to that modern, worldcentric level in the Left Hand, we're going to have some real problems responding adequately to the issue. The Right-hand component of global warming is obvious (it is clearly due to an orange worldcentric technology that affects the entire planet); what is not so obvious is the component of the problem that stems from interior Left-hand development being at pre-orange, pre-worldcentric, and pre-universal levels of development. But then, how would we even know that, since we don't track interiors at all?

Another global problem is the modern business system. Almost the entire material artifact system of modern business—built and put in motion as an orange Right-hand system anchored in material money (though itself largely conceived by global modern geniuses such as Adam Smith)—could nonetheless be owned, used, and run by people whose interiors were, for instance, deeply egocentric red, and who believe that greed is good and survival of the fittest rules the day. When this happens, the entire orange Right-hand business system is run by people with pre-orange Left-hand barbaric motives, and as a result, the system spews toxic waste (emotional to environmental) everywhere. Or, at a notch slightly better but still deeply problematic, orange business can be run by people at amber ethnocentric with its intense "us versus them" drives, and who believe that it's a "dog-eat-dog" world. They have a "fight-to-the-finish" attitude, and they are out to conquer the planet (or at least their own market) and are dedicated to embedding an overly aggressive competition into the world at every point (and to hell with the environment).

We should take time to notice that most critics of modern capitalism talk as if capitalism itself were nothing but a massive source of "greed," which they claim to be inherent and unavoidable in capitalistic business itself—whereas it is inherent only in businesses run by management who are at preglobal red or amber. This is the major reason that capitalism has been disliked by so many intellectuals for such a long time. When business management and culture reach to orange, and especially green, the moral stance of business changes to things like fostering sustainability and increasing benefits to employees, proving that such egocentric and ethnocentric vulgarities are not inherent in business or capitalism itself. The problem has the same structure as that of all modern crises—a set of orange economic and global artifacts in the Right Hand being driven by people whose needs and values are at premodern red and amber in the Left Hand. Again, it is easy for this situation to develop, given how simple it is to evolve Right-hand artifacts quite ahead of Left-hand realities. The only real problem here is the grand disjuncture of Right-hand artifacts and Left-hand wisdom. When we see the work being done by Robert Kegan and his DDO (deliberately developmental organization)—which we'll investigate in just a moment—we see that this disjuncture can be overcome and businesses can start behaving with genuine wisdom. When the interiors of a company are all at orange or green (or higher), it starts to have a truly balanced culture, and capitalism finds its real home.

Cybercrime, which the 2019 World Economic Forum listed as one of the top three acute risks to the world, has an analysis similar to that of climate crisis and the ills of capitalism. Cybercrime involves the use of a quite sophisticated (orange or higher) level of Right-hand computer technology by mostly egocentric-criminal (red) minds or by ethnocentric, nationally obsessed, military minds (amber). Again, once the artifact is in existence—in this case, super-sophisticated computer hardware—anybody can use it, including those with very nefarious ends in mind. I mention this example not only because it is so obviously a case of the typical suicidal situation that I have been describing (Right-hand artifact development running far ahead of Left-hand consciousness and wisdom) but also because most people are unaware of the grave risks that it poses. Suffice it to say that a clever cyberattack on the United States, for example, could easily shut down the electricity to the entire country for days on end. Various degrees of these types of attacks are already occurring all over the world on a daily basis. The fact that the World Economic Forum rates cybercrime so highly in its ranking of serious world threats (it's in the top three, right after the climate emergency and nuclear threat) should alert us to this situation.

The same thing is obviously true of MAD (or the nuclear threat in general). If ever there was a situation driven by global, worldcentric, Right-hand science and artifacts coupled with a preglobal, pre-worldcentric, Left-hand interior motivation (amber or red), MAD is it. Somehow, in the intervening years since the Cuban Missile Crisis, we managed to operate—at least temporarily—from an interior level of worldcentric development that was high enough to prevent World War III (the collapse of the Soviet Union in 1989 also helped prevent nuclear war). But what will happen when, say, Iran develops nuclear technology in the Right Hand but remains driven by its ethnocentric and fundamentalist religious interiors in the Left Hand? Or what if North Korea, which obviously has a Right-hand global nuclear capacity and a Left-hand idiot for a ruler, decides to pull the trigger? No wonder the World Economic Forum rates the nuclear threat as the second-greatest threat to the world's existence, right behind the climate crisis as the greatest.

The major point in this section is that Right-hand material realities, artifacts, and technologies often run far ahead of the Left-hand morals and wisdom needed to use them appropriately and responsibly—which is compounded by the fact that we aren't even tracking the Left-hand realities. That is especially important, since it explains why the global level of development brings with it the capacity to destroy humanity on an equally global level. I've gone over some of the threats that could bring this about—including climate crisis, cybercrime, and the doctrine of MAD (or nuclear weapons in general). In each case, we glaringly see the results of Right-hand global technology racing far ahead of Left-hand wisdom.

DELIBERATELY DEVELOPMENTAL CULTURE

The 2019 World Economic Forum's global risk report lists five basic areas of general risk and the top three acute risks. The five general areas are (1) economic vulnerabilities, (2) geopolitical tensions, (3) societal and political strains, (4) environmental fragilities, and (5) technological instabilities. The three acute risks are (1) the climate emergency, (2) the nuclear threat, and (3) cybercrime. Notice that every one of them involves nothing but the Lower Right quadrant—the 3rd-person plural exteriors of collective systems—the dynamic, interwoven systems of collective "its." Among many other problems with this list, it suggests that with all the major problems facing humanity, 1st-person dimensions ("I," "we") or 2nd-person dimensions ("you," "thou," "all of you") have contributed nothing to them—they are all just 3rd-person realities. So from "I" and "we" and "you," nothing has been taken; to "it" and "its," all was given. As always, there are partial truths in this view; but that it is the complete truth is one of the most reductionistic, fragmented, broken, flatland worldviews that can be imagined—and a pure example of the deep failure of humanity to Show Up.

Developmental studies has added another perspective to the problems facing humanity—namely, the distinction between 1st-tier stages of development and 2nd-tier stages. The definition of a 1st-tier stage is that it is marked by the belief that its truth and values are the only real truth and values; all the others are mistaken, childish, or just plain wrong. But then there is the leap to 2nd tier. The stages starting with 2nd tier (such as global-Integral) intuitively understand that each and every previous level is significant and fully needed, if for no other reason than that each of them is a stage in human development, and thus none of them can be skipped, bypassed, or deleted. Just as in the sequence atoms, molecules, cells, and organisms, you cannot go from atoms to cells and skip molecules, likewise in human development you can't go from red to green and skip amber or orange. Starting with the stages at 2nd tier, this profound truth becomes intuitively clear, and thus stages such as global-Integral are the first truly holistic, inclusive, and comprehensive stages in human history.

Thus, the 2nd-tier global-Integral stages make the failure to fully Show Up harder and harder to get away with. And because of this, they will very likely instigate a stunningly profound worldwide transformation that is finally Integral—which means that they will be the likes of which humanity has never, but *never*, seen. Given the above definitions of 1st and 2nd tier, wouldn't you agree?

Robert Kegan and Lisa Laskow Lahey, in their book *An Everyone*

Culture, show what happens when businesses include in their corporate culture an awareness of developmental stages and tie the exterior growth and profits of the business to the interior developmental growth of its employees. They found that when businesses do this, almost every measure of the business's success increases dramatically, including staff happiness, reduced employee turnover, and degree of profits. Kegan, professor at the Harvard Graduate School of Education, has spent his lifetime working with organizations to help them become developmentally conscious, and he concludes that the evidence overwhelmingly shows the importance of an organization becoming a DDO (deliberately developmental organization). A DDO pays attention not just to interiors but also to the *actual stages* of the interiors, the actual levels of Growing Up, and they include that knowledge (of the Upper Left) in the corporate culture (of the Lower Left)—both of which are interior, Left-hand realities. When they do that, the real growth in their human capital—as well as the real growth in the business itself—becomes obvious to all concerned, and things begin explosively to improve.

Notice that Kegan and Laskow Lahey are fully aware of the necessity to track realities and development not just in the Upper Left interior of an individual, but in all 4 quadrants fully. In their book *An Everyone Culture*, they explain that, during a particularly fruitful period of working with several high-powered organizations to help them become DDOs (including companies like Bridgewater, which *The Economist* pegged as "the most successful hedge fund in human history"), they noticed that because they had been focusing almost entirely on just the interior dimensions, they were leaving out several other truly important dimensions, especially the exterior ones. They had overcome the Western materialist bias of taking exteriors alone to be real, but only by going to the other extreme and focusing only on interiors (consciousness and culture). So they deliberately undertook a course of Showing Up. As they explain, "Our colleague

Ken Wilber has created a four-box model, which has been a valuable heuristic for a more comprehensive view of any complicated psychosocial phenomenon.... The four-box heuristic invites people who are thinking about moving in the direction of a DDO to keep their eyes on all four boxes, what Wilber refers to as an 'integral,' or more adequately holistic, perspective."[5] In other words, to fully Show Up. And Kegan and Laskow Lahey know, from experience, that this is actually something that takes some effort and practice—as they say, in regard to Showing Up, "We are works in progress."[6]

Any truly Integral approach to our problems would maintain that our society needs to become a DDC (deliberately developmental culture). And this fits with what I was saying about human beings reaching global stages of development—which, we noticed, means that not only our advances but also our problems are now essentially global. Alan Watkins and I have a term for these especially nasty global problems; they are "wicked problems."[7] There are many things that mark something that we call a "wicked problem"; for example, they are multidimensional, have multiple stakeholders, multiple causes, multiple symptoms, multiple solutions, and are constantly evolving—and today, that basically means that they are global.

Humankind first reached a global stage of evolution with the emergence of its first worldcentric stage—namely, the orange rational-modern stage (beginning, at its earliest, roughly around 1600). This stage brought the first rush of the stunning possibilities and extraordinary benefits of a worldcentric or global level of consciousness. The second major global stage for humankind was the green postmodern stage (beginning around 1960). This stage saw and realized all the downsides of a modern global reality, and thus it relativized everything (and consequently is often called the "relativistic" stage), stumbling into a posttruth world with no way to get out of it. It saw the problems of modernity but could do little substantially to solve them. And both of these stages, remember, are 1st-tier stages.

The green postmodern stage, in fact, is the highest of the 1st-tier stages. The general rule of development is the oft-repeated fact that you cannot solve a problem from the same level that created it. And thus none of the 1st-tier stages can solve the problems inherent in 1st tier itself. They can be solved only by the "momentous leap" to Integral 2nd tier (which, as a stage, is the third and to-date highest global stage for humankind).[8]

Let's take, as a simple example, the major goals of postmodernism and see how that stage itself creates problems that it can't solve—but that an Integral 2nd-tier stage can. Probably the central desires of postmodern social justice can be summarized with the words *diversity*, *equality*, and *inclusiveness*. What green wants, above all else, is to include all beings in a perfect equality—embracing all diversity under an inclusive umbrella of equality. In a certain sense, that's a fine and noble ideal. Unfortunately, it can't be accomplished with only green tools. The way green approaches the issue of achieving equality or equity is to identify the areas in which all people should be treated the same (socially, culturally, sexually, racially, educationally, politically). So it tracks all the exterior measures that seem to indicate that people are being treated unfairly (such as an alleged wage gap for women, or a rape culture on campus, or an epidemic of white privilege evidenced in things like vastly unequal wealth, or transgender bathroom rights, and so on). Unfortunately, because green is still 1st tier and thus is not fully inclusive itself, it takes a totally flatland approach to these issues—it tracks only exterior measures (like equal outcome). And by *diversity* it explicitly means a diversity of exterior things that can be seen—especially one's skin color (racism) and one's biological sex (sexism and the patriarchy). It does not count Martin Luther King's "content of character" but only King's "color of their skin."

Green especially does not track—or is not even aware of—the profound differences in the way *stages of interior development themselves treat these issues*. The desire for social justice as social equality, for example, is a desire that originates *only at green*. And, as we've seen, there are around six major stages of development that an individual must go through in order to even see and want those green values in the first place. Green is really attacking ethnocentric attitudes and practices—that is, ones that originate at amber and are truly racist, sexist, misogynist, homophobic, transphobic, xenophobic, fundamentalist-religious, hyperpatriotic, colonialist, and so on. These are generated by amber ethnocentric and brought together as "identity politics," which actually means "ethnocentric identity politics"—all specific identities are ethnocentric. If you choose a specific identity—being white, black, or female, and so on—you are selecting an ethnocentric group to identify with, which is why all identity politics is generated at amber ethnocentric. As we've seen, up to 60 percent of the U.S. population are at ethnocentric stages (or lower). There is simply no way that individuals at those earlier stages would ever agree to accept values that stem from green (what they would do, however, is elect as president somebody like Trump, who is essentially antigreen and anti–political correctness).

Thus, the central element in any green postmodern social agenda—if it wanted to be truly effective and actually succeed in advancing green values—would have to be to propose and seriously support the ways and means (educational, economic, technological, and cultural) that would help individuals grow and develop *in their interiors* to the higher, worldcentric stages (and green would especially aim for the postmodern worldcentric stage). It would have to work, in other words, to help create a DDC—a deliberately developmental culture. This is the *only* way that support for green can actually be created and enhanced.

But green does exactly the opposite. It views all such ideas of things like "higher" development as being themselves evidence of a horrid power hierarchy and thus riddled with ethnocentrism—racist or sexist or whatnot. In other words, it sees Growing Up only as a dominator hierarchy, not a growth hierarchy—and so no growth is exactly what tends to occur. (Green does this with all hierarchies, because it believes that all hierarchies are power hierarchies—that is, it equates all growth hierarchies with dominator hierarchies, even though the vast majority of hierarchies in the natural world are growth hierarchies—such as quarks to atoms to molecules to cells to organisms. As I previously noted, molecules don't hate and oppress atoms; they love atoms so much that they include and embrace them in their own structure.) We saw that even to mention something like cultural evolution in an Ivy League environment is to get quickly dismissed. So green's course of action effectively prevents exactly what it most wants. It prevents the movement into higher, world-centric green stages by denying stages themselves, and all the ways and means that it proposes for reducing racism, sexism, homophobia, and xenophobia explicitly ignore and deny the most central causes of those prejudices themselves. Thus green spots the problem, but its actions are inherently incapable of solving them.

The global-Integral stage of 2nd tier, on the other hand, is the first stage that is actually and authentically inclusive—green desperately wants diversity and inclusiveness, but Integral actually delivers it. It genuinely includes the real diversity of the interiors (and their different worldviews), as well as their stages of development, and considers carefully how individual growth through those stages can be most effectively enhanced and equally included. Thus, global-Integral includes the real *diversity* of every stage of development, and it finds legitimate ways to *equally* embrace them all in a worldcentric way that is genuinely *inclusive* and that fully encompasses Growing Up and Showing Up (as well as Waking Up, Opening Up, and Cleaning Up).

In short, Integral introduces a DDC and, as does Kegan, it does so in all 4 quadrants—a Growing Up that is authentically Showing Up. And you will probably have noticed by now that the very idea of a conveyor belt is exactly the introduction of a DDC. Of course, the wider point is that we, as a society, should want all our multiple intelligences to be conveyor belts, consciously introduced and fully encouraged and enhanced.

To finish the narrative that we started at the beginning of this chapter, the Cuban Missile Crisis was solved (if *solved* is the right word) by a happenstance occurrence in a meeting that Bobby Kennedy (John Kennedy's brother, whom he had made attorney general) had with Soviet ambassador Anatoly Dobrynin. We will never know for sure what really happened in that meeting, but the upshot was that, through various negotiated actions (including the United States taking their missiles out of Turkey), the Soviets agreed, in turn, to remove their missiles from Cuba and never put them back. We managed to avert World War III (and its mutual assured destruction)—for now.

But the other downsides of modernity were not averted, and they proceeded forward at full steam. And, as we've been saying, since modernity was global in its reach, both the good stuff and the bad stuff it brought were global too. And thus the panic-inducing horror of global suicide switched almost immediately from MAD to all the other downsides of modernity, each of which began to erupt in one form of cancer or another, and each of which carried (often as an unintended consequence) a possible lethal worldwide catastrophe, and each of which kept leading-edge postmodernists (and sane people everywhere) in need of SSRIs (antidepressants). The smallest list of potentially suicidal catastrophes (reaching global or near-global dimensions) was deeply unnerving:

- a massive population explosion (referred to as a population "bomb," given its incredibly destructive possibilities)
- an alarming global warming becoming more unthinkable by the day (and if left unchecked, truly threatening human life everywhere, becoming the latest cause of the paralyzing fear

of global suicide first introduced by the Cuban Missile Crisis)
- a global financial meltdown threatening worldwide economic collapse
- a planetwide terrorist movement that seems to strike almost anywhere with impunity
- nuclear arms threats (and the apparent willingness to use them) in places from Iran to North Korea
- an increasingly planetwide warfare conducted by vicious warlords using orange modern technology yet driven by red religious tribal drives
- serious water shortages everywhere on the planet
- global trafficking and slavery reaching over 60 million people a year
- a staggering fifty thousand children starving to death each day
- environmental instabilities everywhere on the planet
- the creation of an AI superintelligence set to overtake human intelligence with the "singularity," which many experts think will be the real end of humanity
- cybercrime becoming the major form of worldwide warfare, with a capacity to wipe out an entire country's electrical systems
- in one of the closest things to evil that exists on this earth—just five people on the planet owning the same amount as owned by the poorest 50 percent of the world[9]

Because of all of these crises (I'm sure you can think of more), it had indeed become a deeply cancer-ridden planet. And since they were getting hit directly in the face by this, 75 percent of the youngest generation developed clinical-level depression (*Time* magazine reports that 75 percent of Gen Z have had to miss work because of clinical levels of anxiety or depression; 50 percent of Millennials have).

It wasn't the exponential speed of technological development that was primarily causing these disastrous problems. It was the lack of a similar degree of interior development that could keep up with technology and offer some sort of balance, wisdom, and sane judgment to oversee the technology itself. It's been said that democracy is a bet that half of the people are right at least half of the time. Developmentally, this means that democracy will wisely work only if half of the population is at orange worldcentric (or higher) for at least half of its decisions. (What do you think you'll get if a large majority—some 60 percent—are at less than orange worldcentric?)

I repeat, strongly, that nobody at a worldcentric stage of morals (orange or higher) would have anything to do with slavery—or with a Holocaust, trafficking, utterly fraudulent worldwide banking practices, terrorist acts pushing this or that ethnocentric and jihadist fundamentalism, warlords and their standard-practice mass rapes and ethnic cleansing, toxic and biosphere-destroying waste dumping (as long as we make money), or racist, sexist, homophobic, or misogynistic acts. And yet typically, how do we handle all of those problems? We totally and completely ignore the interior stages where those disasters and prejudices primarily originate. This is like treating AIDS by denying the existence of HIV.

From almost the very start of the global levels of consciousness themselves—with both modernity and then postmodernity—humanity was engaged in a colossal failure to Show Up, a deep lack of authenticity. Otherwise how could something so evolutionarily advanced—the leap from ethnocentric to worldcentric—have gone so bad, and virtually from the start? Was it intentional, or was it another unintended consequence? Whatever it was, it marked the darkest of all the dark shadows that the modern and postmodern world would live under for three or four centuries and counting. This deep failure to Show Up, this failure of integrity, represented humanity's abandoning and attempting to delete many fundamental areas of reality itself, at just the time that humanity was making a stunning series of profound discoveries in the remaining areas—interiors were erased, while exteriors were making history-altering advances. How could something so *unbalanced* have befallen the highly developed leading edge of evolution?

And what on earth can we do about this massive failure to Show Up? In order to know how to cure it, it would help to know what actually caused it.

14

The Nightmare of Modernity

The greatest sin of modernity was indeed that, alongside of its stunning advances and progress in the exterior, Right-hand dimensions of reality, it almost fully erased and deleted any reality for the interior, Left-hand dimensions. The official background philosophy of the modern Western world, to this day, is scientific materialism, which considers the scientific exploration of the material dimensions of reality ("matter" in the second sense—that is, any Right-hand dimension) to be the only sure route to gaining any real and enduring knowledge. Philosopher Jürgen Habermas agrees with this assessment. He considers this erasing of the interiors by modern science—which he calls "the colonization of the lifeworld by science"—to be one of the greatest downsides of the modern worldview. The erasure of the Left-hand, interior realities was a cultural catastrophe of the first order. So let us ask again, How on earth did something like that happen?

THE GREAT SYSTEM OF NATURE

We've traced the problem of the complete denial of interior, Left-hand realities to the beginning of global modernity. Humanity had just made a revolutionary leap to orange worldcentric stages of being and awareness. This was truly a leap in evolutionary terms, with a large number of new and emergent virtues, but one that, almost from the start, began to go sour. It was a higher level, yes, but one that was becoming deeply sick. A sick version of a higher level. Was that good news or bad?

A bit of both, it turns out.

Contrary to popular but deeply misguided views of the Western Enlightenment (which marked the beginning of modernity), the central and guiding concept of the Enlightenment was not materialism ("matter" in the first sense—that is, the reduction of all reality to insentient, nonliving fundamental particles), nor was it mechanism or atomism. It is common to claim that it was, and then all the problems of modernity that we outlined are blamed on the rise of materialistic atomism and mechanism. But that is a deeply confused explanation of what truly characterized the Enlightenment, and thus leads us astray when we seek for the true cause of all the problems stemming from the Enlightenment.

Rather, as Charles Taylor clearly demonstrates in *Sources of the Self*, the central idea that explosively drove the Enlightenment was the notion of a totally interwoven and unified order of Nature, what some French philosophers called the *Système de la Nature*—the grand System of Nature. According to this idea, Reality or Nature was a highly interwoven and interconnected system. John Locke called it the "great interlocking order." Every reality in the universe was intimately interwoven with every other one, in a magnificent, interlocking System of Nature. The mythic God was dead; the great interlocking Web of Nature was born.

It's important to realize how widespread and profoundly influential this idea of a deeply systemic and unified Nature was, because inherent in this idea of Unity is hidden the part that gave rise to the profound failure to Show Up that began to plague humanity. I said that this problem was inherent in some part of the System of Nature, but which part?

Because it all started so promisingly. The grand System of Nature was itself said to be based on the Great Chain of Being (which is another element commonly missing from the popular accounts of what constituted the core of the Enlightenment). We've seen the Great Chain (or Great Nest) appear in its Christian form as "matter, body, mind, soul, and spirit." The idea of this chain—with each of its links intimately interwoven with every other link, so that there literally were "no missing links"—was widely accepted decades before Darwin dutifully attempted to supply evidence for it in the biological realm. The belief that there were "no missing links" came directly from the idea of the Great Chain, not from any scientific discoveries, although they would corroborate it.

Arthur Lovejoy's *The Great Chain of Being* is the acknowledged authoritative text on this idea, and as Lovejoy demonstrates, the Great Chain itself was the most widely adopted worldview in history, literally. Versions of it were accepted by the majority of the great thought leaders throughout the world. As Lovejoy himself says, the Great Chain of Being was the worldview that has been the "official philosophy of the larger part of civilized mankind through most of its history."[1]

It was certainly engaged in by the Enlightenment. Says Lovejoy, "Next to the word 'Nature,' 'the Great Chain of Being' was the sacred phrase of the eighteenth century."[2] The Great Chain ensured that no matter how separate or isolated any parts might look, they were actually interwoven parts of a great Whole, and that Whole was the ultimate reality, so that the aim of any true thinker was to demonstrate this Wholeness. Diderot's *Encyclopédie* (the rational bible of the Enlightenment) began its entry on the advancement of knowledge: "Everything in nature is linked together," and "the art of the philosopher consists in adding new links to the separated parts." Small wonder that scientists and philosophers alike "were wont, when they reached the height of their argument, to discourse with eloquence on the perfection of the Universal System as a whole."[3] As Pascal himself put it, "Its parts all are so related and interlinked with one another that it is impossible to know the parts without knowing the whole or the whole without knowing all the parts."[4]

So we have the Great Holarchy of Being—the Great Chain seen not as a series of linear links but rather as concentric spheres, each larger sphere enveloping all the nested smaller ones (which I often call the "Great Nest of Being"). This idea ensured a systems-theory view of a totally interwoven Nature, and this view of a globally universal system was indeed a terrific start for modernity! An idea that had been one of the most prevalent in civilized humanity up to that point—namely, the Great Chain of Being—had slid seamlessly into modernity itself as it shifted up from amber to orange.

At orange, there was also a higher and truly significant emergent that came into being: the increased capacity for differentiation, a differentiation that was an intrinsic part of the increased "differentiation and integration" that evolution brings at each stage of its development, including the leap of modernity. We see this differentiation clearly and directly in Max Weber's academic definition of modernity itself: modernity, he said, was marked by the "differentiation of the value spheres" (a definition accepted by Habermas). By "value spheres," Weber meant the Big Three (the 4 quadrants)—modernity was marked by the differentiation of the spheres of the Good (morals), the True (science), and the Beautiful (art), which allowed wonderful progress to be made in all of them.

At the previous stage—amber, traditional, mythic-religious—the quadrants were largely fused or undifferentiated: whatever the Church proclaimed was taken to be the way it was, whether that had to do with the Good, the True, or the Beautiful. These three spheres had not yet been clearly differentiated and released from Church domination. Thus, the churchmen saw no reason to actually look through Galileo's telescope—the Bible told them exactly what they would see.

But the orange modern stage introduced precisely that differentiation, and thus it allowed artistic Beauty, moral Goodness, and philosophical and scientific Truth to explore their own ways and develop their own means, methods, and logics. This allowed art, morals, and science (the Big Three) to start developing their own highest potentials, which they immediately began to do. The positive result of all this—and the enormous progress made in so many areas—has been called "the dignity of modernity," and it was exactly that, a true and profound dignity, which included, among many other things, the freeing of slaves on a large scale for the first time in history, not to mention the discovery of all the modern sciences—physics, biology, astronomy, chemistry, geology, and so on.

This also meant that there was an exciting new chance to fully Show Up for all these newly released dimensions of reality—a chance not only to see them as being separated and differentiated but also to bring them together and integrate them, as well as to fully inhabit them, embodying an even greater integrity and authenticity. In other words, this new worldcentric, orange stage of Growing Up meant a new and higher way to Show Up—to fully and authentically inhabit all 4 quadrants, with trust, sincerity, and integrity. The quadrants had always been there, but now they jumped into self-conscious awareness. There were now new and higher elements—orange elements—in all 4 major dimensions of humanity's existence; and in ways never seen before, humanity was invited to step up and Show Up. The dignity of modernity, at this new and higher orange global level, was the unprecedented platform on which humankind was now invited to act.

And for around a century or two, that is exactly what humanity did, with results that now collectively define many of the basics of the world in which we still live, usually called something like "the values of the Enlightenment." But somewhere along the line, the *differentiation* of the value spheres degenerated into the *dissociation* of the value spheres. The spheres of science (the Right-hand, exterior quadrants) were elevated to sole reality, and the spheres of the Good and the Beautiful (morals and aesthetics, Left-hand interiors in general) were relegated to the dust bin—none of them were objectively true. They were merely subjective; they weren't important; they didn't really matter; they weren't really real. The officially accepted view of reality drew closer and closer to a purely objective scientific materialism. The disqualified universe was upon us, and the disenchanted world settled around humanity like a suffocating pillow. And what was worse was that the cultural leaders who participated in this didn't even know it was happening.

Whereas the differentiation of the value spheres lead to the dignity of modernity, the dissociation of the value spheres was the disaster of modernity—also frequently called "the crime of the Enlightenment." It would be this disaster that led to virtually all the modern global nightmares (made obvious to postmodernity)—ecological, military, economic, spiritual, transnational. The central ideas of the Enlightenment (the ideas of the System of Nature and the Great Holarchy of Being) were not the sin of modernity. Rather, the sin was the corruption and dissociation of these ideas—which, on balance, meant that humanity was, in some of the most disturbing ways possible, now refusing to Show Up. A scientific materialism settled on the world, which didn't embrace all 4 quadrants but only the Right-hand, exterior quadrants—a realm of nothing but material realities, exterior forms, sensory surfaces, and superficial outsides. The interiors of consciousness, culture, the subjective, the good, and the beautiful were blown away, gone with the modern wind.

THE ENORMOUSLY GREAT AND TOTALLY MIXED ADVANCE OF MEASUREMENT

What exactly happened? Especially given the wonderful start, with modernity's idea of a completely interwoven Great Holarchy and the all-inclusive System of Nature? As background to answer this question, we start to see, over a century or two, the profound change in the meaning of "matter" that we discussed earlier —namely, matter is no longer viewed as the lowest and bottom rung of reality (which meant, for most of history, the bottom rung in the Great Chain); rather it starts to be viewed as the exterior dimension of every rung. That is, matter is the exterior correlate of forms like the living body, mind, and soul, with each of their interior forms possessing an increasing degree of consciousness, and where the levels of increasing complexity of matter in the Right Hand correlates with the levels of increasing degrees of consciousness in the Left Hand.

For example, in the ancient world, people did plenty of thinking, but virtually nobody knew that this also involved hugely complex processes that were occurring simultaneously in the physical brain. As microscopes and other detection devices were invented (various "videotapes") by the modern world, this became increasingly obvious, and many modern scientists began drifting into the notion that 1st-person consciousness was nothing but a 3rd-person, material brain process. The crime of the Enlightenment was slowly emerging.

Integral suggests that the second meaning of matter was being disclosed. It could not have been discovered earlier because humanity had no instruments, tools, or videotapes that could see these material structures. Matter was not being viewed as just the lowest level on the Great Chain but also as the exterior of all the levels of the Great Chain (where its increasing complexity matched an increasing consciousness). But for most investigators, the understanding of the relationship between matter and consciousness wasn't obvious—

matter was matter, and that was that. (It was obvious to many panpsychists that all matter has degrees of mind, as we'll see.)

For the most part, this relationship didn't become a problem for around a century or two. Scientists went about their work of studying these exteriors (the brain, recall, is an exterior, objective, or 3rd-person view of the interior mind of an individual), which was especially made possible by many orange-level technological discoveries, from the microscope to the telescope to photographic plates. The natural sciences, as they focused on these exteriors, started to make utterly amazing discoveries—in physics, chemistry, biology, evolution, geology, astronomy—all part of the great dignity of modernity. Impressive advances were also being made in the other value spheres of aesthetics and morals, but the progress in science was outrageous. By the height of the Industrial Revolution, humankind was set upon the course of building an orange worldcentric, global, objective science and technology and a world of material artifacts in the Right Hand, but it had less interest in, or even awareness of, the interior realities in the Left Hand that were inhabiting this new space. Intensive focus on the exteriors had made the reality of the interiors less and less obvious—and apparently less needed: after all, look at the staggering progress of physics and the sciences of the exteriors! And right here we start to see the classic case of interior wisdom not keeping pace with our exterior technology, and that will turn out to be the crime of the Enlightenment.

It's important to realize that there were things in modern science itself that invited this disaster, and this brings us to what is probably the single greatest contributor to, and actual cause of, the crime of the Enlightenment. Science, in its most basic definition, is certainly not limited to studying only data revealed by the human senses and their extensions. It is definitely true that science is experiential in nature—it wants experiential evidence for its claims—but as William James knew, there are sensory experiences, mental experiences, and spiritual experiences—and all of them can be legitimately investigated with a general, scientific-experiential approach (for more on this, see my book *Eye to Eye*).

If modern science had stayed with experiential data (including the experience of the sensory, mental, and spiritual domains) there would have been few problems. But modern science wasn't just experiential. Of all the experiences that humans can have, modern science valued the most those that could be measured.

Modern science didn't seek just empirical reality, or just experiential reality, or even just evidence. It wanted empirical evidence that could be measured. As Whitehead points out in *Science and the Modern World*, the true core of the modern scientific method was invented simultaneously and independently in 1605 by Galileo Galilei and Johannes Kepler. They both introduced the core idea that the laws of Nature can best be understood by measuring. So Kepler measured heavenly movement and discovered the laws of planetary motion. Galileo measured earthly movement and discovered the laws of terrestrial motion. The megagenius Isaac Newton put both of these measurements together in his universal laws of gravity and motion. Those laws are popularly imagined as dawning on Newton when an apple fell on his head—an image that reflects the reality that Newton discovered that the force that made the apple fall to the earth is the same force that makes the earth circle the sun: namely, gravity. This combined earthly laws and heavenly laws into a grand unity, and once again the great System of Nature was front and center.

But notice that, in this case, that meant the collective exterior realities were seen as a great system—it meant the Lower Right quadrant, insofar as it could be measured. There is no mention of interiors anywhere in the laws of Kepler, Galileo, or Newton—nor, of course, should there be. Centering on exteriors led exactly to these types of discoveries. In looking only at the exteriors, they delivered only the exteriors. The background context for understanding given by the Great Chain—an idea the Enlightenment fully embraced at the start—was that every measurable exterior material reality was nonetheless intimately bound up with all the interior realities (the higher levels, including body, mind, and soul, were all interwoven in the Great Nest). So these original and brilliant scientific pioneers, as they began to measure the world, didn't think that they were leaving out anything important as they simply and solely explored the Right-hand, material realm.

The activity of measuring, adopted on a wide scale, was indeed quite new, and this activity is what marked the modern sciences as indeed being modern, or truly new and novel. Previously, science researchers brought only a heightened observation of nature or an aggressively empirical approach to studying nature. And many earlier scholars had indeed followed that approach to science and had examined nature in an empirically aggressive fashion. Aristotle, for one, had already looked at nature in as empirical and as far-reaching a manner as can be imagined.

But none of them had measured anything. They had been employing something of a scientific method, which intensely observed and empirically classified nature, but they had not been using a modern scientific method, which added measurement of nature. Thus none of them came up with anything near Galileo's, Kepler's, or Newton's laws—none of them came up with modern science. Part of Whitehead's genius was to point out that, yes, empirical science had been around in various forms at least since the Greeks; but *modern* empirical science emerged only in 1605 with Galileo and Kepler and the discovery of the vast importance of measurement.

Of course, it is much easier to measure exterior matter than it is to measure interior mind. In fact, it is notoriously difficult to measure mind or mental realities, and it's considerably easier to measure matter or exterior physical realities. Thus, if you are following the rule that the laws of nature are best understood by measurement, then you will be open to reducing Nature to just the material, Right-hand quadrants. And since you still believe in the great System of Nature, you will reduce Nature to the Lower Right quadrant, the systemic material quadrant. Thus, none of the equations of the newly discovered sciences (chemistry, biology, physics, astronomy, geology, and so on) had equations that applied to any interior reality at all—they applied only to exterior matter (in the second sense), and since they referred to the great System of Nature, they were referring to the collective or systemic forms of matter, the Lower Right quadrant.

Integral suggests that the "great interlocking order" was quickly becoming nothing but the Lower Right quadrant. This was still a great System of Nature, still fully interwoven and completely interlinked, but only as it could be seen and measured with the human senses or their extensions. The great interlocking order was seen only through a 3rd-person plural perspective, which saw only the Lower Right or collective material dimensions of the System of Nature. The dissociation of the value spheres, the "disaster of modernity," the disenchanted world—this was fast becoming the dominant reality.

This new approach was most impactfully applied by James Watt who, in the 1760s, had an idea that arguably would affect more human beings than any other single idea in history: he conceived the principles of a truly workable steam engine. And that changed everything, absolutely everything. Along with a few other important if secondary inventions, this marked the beginning of the Machine Age, the start of the Industrial Revolution, the beginning of modernity itself.

The first modern philosopher—by almost all accounts, René Descartes—would characterize this new reality by maintaining that the mind (the interiors or Left-hand dimension) possessed *intention* and matter (the exteriors or Right-hand dimension) possessed *extension*. Extension meant extended in space, time, and quantitative aspects—and this tended to mean categorically, as we just noted, that only the exteriors, the objective dimensions of matter, possessed extension and thus could be measured. (Interior intention can be measured, but it is much harder and trickier, and combined with the fact that interiors seem to be "private," almost all the interiors were originally dismissed when it came to measurement.) And thus, when science maintained that measurement was the key to reality, it almost automatically meant that only the objective, 3rd-person exteriors were to be taken to be real. As a result, the new scientific method very quickly led people to embrace scientific materialism. And this meant a deeply earnest and official promise from the modern West that, from this time forward, it sincerely would not Show Up.

So it came about that Nature was conceived as a great interwoven and interlocking system but composed of nothing but physical elements, sensory surfaces, and material realities. In other words, all quadrants were reduced to the Lower Right quadrant. I call this "subtle reductionism"— "subtle" because it's easy to miss the reductionism because it still covers all the interwoven Web insofar as it contains the material correlates of all the quadrants, although it leaves out the interior quadrants themselves. It still believes in the great System of Nature but only in Nature that can be seen (that is, videotaped) with the senses or their extensions—that is, 3rd-person evidence. (Gross reductionism goes even further and reduces those wholes to their atomistic parts—reduces the Lower Right to the Upper Right. This started to occur during the Enlightenment and is often confused with the main "crime" of the Enlightenment, although it was really just a byproduct of it.)

But this subtle reductionism wasn't that obvious at the start. After all, it was originally believed that the measured material realities were still fully interwoven with all the levels in the Great Nest, so everything was being included; they're all fully interlinked and interconnected, so there's nothing to worry about.

Although matter was indeed the exterior dimension of every interior dimension in reality, by definition those exteriors are not the interiors themselves, nor can they replace or substitute for them in any way. Among other things, the interior realities include values, such as better and worse, right and wrong, more valuable and less valuable, good and evil. You can't find any of those Left-hand value distinctions anywhere in the exterior, Right-hand realms. A tree is bigger than a frog, but it is not better. A mountain weighs more than a forest, but it is not more moral. A male peacock's tail is more colorful than a female's, but it is not more valuable. Interior worldcentric identity, on the other hand, is better than a sexist or racist ethnocentric identity. In other words, values are found in the Left-hand, interior realms, and as those realms continuously lost more and more ground, the universe increasingly became truly valueless—it became a "disenchanted" and "disqualified" world.

Gone are interiors, gone are virtues, values, purpose, the good, and the beautiful—the interwoven world of holistic frisky dirt is all that remained. It was a world of dynamically interwoven "its," but with no real "I's" or "you's" or "we's" anywhere. Since none of those interior realms had any objective truth, they were only subjective and could be totally rejected. This can be called a "naïve ecology"—it is definitely interlocking and interwoven, but it is composed only of surfaces, exteriors, and objective dimensions. It's what you see if, right now, you simply look at the total picture in front of you and imagine it all as being a single, interwoven system. It sees an ecological wholeness or system but only in its exterior or superficial components. That is exactly the Lower Right quadrant—it contains trees, grass, frogs, dogs, cats, and humans (plus their artifacts) but only in their objective, exterior, material surfaces, all of which can be seen or videotaped. And there is literally nothing else, not a single interiority anywhere in sight.

But that is the view—supported by an empirical science with measurement at its core—that was taken as supreme by the Enlightenment and then moved forward into modernity. Strenuous rebellions against this restricted and collapsed view were already starting. The Romantic and then the Idealistic movements railed against this reductionistic view. As one of its critics exclaimed, "You would have to be insensitive or dead to accept this much reductionism." But these objections couldn't overcome the official endorsement of scientific materialism with its instrumental rationality. The truly holistic System of Nature, with its fully interwoven interiors and exteriors, was collapsed into a materialistic holism. That is, the total and perfectly interwoven System of Nature was indeed recognized but only in the Lower Right quadrant, or its exterior collective dimensions—a completely flatland holism. This is indeed a holism, but a holism that lacks authenticity, a holism that refuses to Show Up.

This flatland form of the great interlocking order is the real sin that stemmed from the Enlightenment; and to this day, this scientific materialism is the official background philosophy of the Western world. If you want to know what's "really real," you no longer ask religion, you ask science.

The worst part of this crime of the Enlightenment wasn't just the reduction of all reality to the Lower Right quadrant; it was the official erasure and disappearance of the Left-hand quadrants. Consciousness, culture, mind, and subjects in general were cut out entirely, because they were not able to be scientifically measured. And we have seen that almost all of modernity's and postmodernity's problems stem from cutting off and failing to follow these now deleted interior realities. And this derives not from the Enlightenment itself but from the crime of the Enlightenment, the reduction of the great System of Nature, the interlocking order of all 4 quadrants of existence, to the Lower Right quadrant.

The final aspect of this problem was that even though science itself reached global, worldcentric levels of development, our interiors did not reach these same levels of global development, because they weren't even being tracked anymore or even considered to be real.

Because of this enormous imbalance between our exterior science, technology, and artifacts and our interior levels of consciousness, culture, and wisdom, our problems became globally suicidal—and there is where our modern world still stands today.

The *disaster* of modernity had become modernity itself.

ATOMISM VERSUS SYSTEMS THEORY: A NEW PARADIGM?

As we just noted, ever since the emergence of modern science, there has been, within science itself, a heated battle between subtle reductionism, which claims that reality is ultimately composed of systemic wholes made of dynamically interacting material elements and processes, and gross reductionism, which claims that reality is composed of nothing but those isolated material elements themselves—a battle, in short, between various forms of dynamic systems theory and various forms of materialistic atomism. All of this infighting has occurred solely within the Right-hand, exterior quadrants, of course—none of the interiors are included in this battle (systems theory doesn't even pretend to deal with the phenomenal realities of beauty, morals, love, goodness, value, or 1st-person consciousness as 1st person). It is a battle strictly between proponents of the systems (or collective holons) of the Lower Right and proponents of the atoms (or individual holons) of the Upper Right.

This certainly happened during the Enlightenment, where the great interlocking order began as a reflection of the Great Nest of Being and ended up as nothing but the interwoven material systems of the Lower Right. And, of course, there were those who carried this reductionism even further and went straight to gross reductionism, giving strongly reductionistic accounts of the universe as merely "atomistic," or "physicalistic," or "mechanistic." The terms associated with these gross reductionisms are often taken to represent the core of the Enlightenment itself, but we've seen that these types of gross reductionism all depended upon a distortion and corruption of the truly core ideas of the Enlightenment, which were the Great Holarchy of Being and the totally interwoven System of Nature. And what's most telling is that the only thinkers who were vehemently denying gross reductionism were the subtle reductionists.

Thus systems theory (which I *fully* embrace—but only for the Lower Right!) will give extensive arguments that it includes all the reality that can and should be included and that it sees everything as being fully interwoven with absolutely everything else. But, as I began to say, these accounts don't even mention aesthetics, ethics, morals, virtues, vision, purpose. There is nothing whatsoever about stages of Growing Up or states of Waking Up or ways to Clean Up or the importance of Opening Up and Showing Up—nothing from the interiors or Left Hand at all. This is simply the great interlocking order, the Web of Life, reduced to its collapsed form of exteriors alone—without even any awareness of what the real problem is.

Proponents of a systems approach can get very fired up with how inclusive they are. They hold up atomism as the great enemy and maintain that they, in contrast, are arguing for a reality that is completely whole, that is mutually interwoven, that consists of intricately interlinked and interactive dynamic processes, where everything is connected to everything else and the universe is a great harmony of systems within systems. They invite you to join them in this great crusade for unity and wholeness. And the thing is, they are entirely right about their view—in it, reality is indeed an enormously interwoven system. The problem is that their interwoven and "holistic" system actually leaves out fully half of the universe. It is a thoroughly 3rd-person view of nothing but the Right-hand exteriors, which completely deletes and erases the Left-hand, interior dimensions in their own 1st- and 2nd-person terms. Thus, for example, 1st-person consciousness and awareness of the Upper Left are reduced to 3rd-person bits and bytes of information running through neural networks and brain systems in the Upper Right. Likewise, system theorists, armed with a plethora of "New Paradigms" (which they maintain will "transform the world"), claim that the leading edge of the most advanced natural sciences now points to a fully and completely unified world (very like, they claim, the one that mystics throughout history have advocated).

For example, "quantum entanglement" is taken as proof that "everything is interwoven." Quantum entanglement refers to the fact that when two subatomic particles whose characteristics determine each other are split apart, no matter how far apart they travel, whenever you determine the characteristics of one particle, those of the other are instantly and simultaneously determined. Since even information traveling at the speed of light could not do this, the interwovenness ("entanglement") of the two particles has to be built into their very existence. That's fine. But the quantum laws applying to those two subatomic particles tell us almost nothing about any higher or more complex dimension of reality, not even within science itself. Quantum physics doesn't explain or predict anything much about biology, psychology, ecology, or sociology. It tell us nothing about the functioning of DNA and how genetics works, nothing about most forms of biochemistry and the complex interaction of molecules, nothing about ecology or about how a possible biospheric collapse is occurring, nothing about shadow material and how to clean it up, absolutely nothing about Growing Up or Showing Up or anything like that. Even if the laws governing these two subatomic particles applied equally to all other physical particles (and they come nowhere close to doing so), they certainly don't apply to any higher levels of reality. To claim they do so is itself the ultimate in reductionism.

And we have already seen this truly embarrassing fact: if quantum mechanics actually revealed the very same interwoven reality that a Zen student sees with a satori (ultimate Unity consciousness), then every professional physicist would have had a major satori, whereas virtually none of them have. Study physics all you want, you'll never have a Waking Up experience as a result.

The New Paradigm theorists are giving—again, with a heart of gold and the very best of intentions—yet more arguments in favor of the (collapsed) great interlocking order, the (broken) System of Nature. Ironically, virtually all of them loudly claim that they are overcoming the nasty Enlightenment paradigm of atomism and mechanism, whereas they are really presenting yet another view of the Enlightenment's collapsed and subtle reductionism. The advanced natural sciences—the "new sciences" that the New Paradigm embraces—do indeed often present the holistic nature of some area of nature, but again, only in its exterior, objective, material form, a dynamic "its." They are nothing more than variations on *traditional* systems sciences—and so of course, as orthodox sciences, they give us the latest on new forms of scientific materialism. But a traditional science that covers a web of reality is still a traditional science—that is, a scientific materialism. And like all of the other new scientific materialist theories, the New Paradigms argue strenuously that the real enemy is atomism. It is atomism, with its focus on hyperindividualism, that drives the world toward greedy capitalism, catastrophic environmental destruction, and the continued power of dominator hierarchies. Only a unified systems view—which these New Paradigms are showing us—can reverse this horrid situation and usher in a new life on this planet.

And thus the reductionistic form of the great interlocking order—"the crime of the Enlightenment"—lives on. It embodies the same disaster of modernity, and it continues to crush and mutilate the interiors while claiming to embrace the whole world. This is textbook subtle reductionism. These New Paradigms claim that the solutions to humanity's globally suicidal crises all depend upon embracing this great interlocking order, while in fact, as we've seen, that claim involves reducing all 4 quadrants to their 3rd-person forms—which are, yes, plural, collective, and interlocking—and this is exactly the problem. These approaches are actually symptoms of the illness for which they claim to be the cure.

So this is what it all comes down to. In any approach to life, first and foremost, simply Show Up. Show Up for life. Do not inherit the downsides of modernity that have resulted in every major modern suicidal catastrophe. Especially as you begin to look for more unity, more harmony, and more Wholeness in your life, don't make the mistake of looking only at the surfaces, only at the varnish and veneer. Especially don't fall into a collapsed and reductionistic version of the great interlocking order, the grand System of Nature, and let the fact that all its surfaces and exteriors are fully interwoven, interlinked, and entangled distract you from the devastating fact that the collapsed great interlocking order is an order of dynamically interwoven "its." There are no "I's" or "you's" or "us's" or "we's" anywhere in it. It's a colossal failure to Show Up—and the worst problem of all is that it doesn't know, or even suspect, that it's not Showing Up. So be careful when you apply this great "Web of Its" to your own life (unless you want to become nothing but an "it" yourself).

THE WORLD OF TOMORROW: A GLOBAL TRANSHUMANISM?

Although you can engage in all of these practices of Big Wholeness right now—Showing Up, Growing Up, Waking Up, Opening Up, and Cleaning Up—by the time such an Integral approach becomes a full and significant part of a future society, that society will be one in which robotics has almost fully replaced any and all sorts of human work. We will exist in a leisure culture that allows us a life span of literally several hundred years to do pretty much whatever we want. And a large measure of what we will want will be ways to Wake Up, Grow Up, Clean Up, and Show Up—if for no other reason than that they will be almost all that's left for us to do with our time. No robot will be able to do them for us, and thus we will be doing them for ourselves—happily. And so we will eagerly engage in the journey and adventure of finding ourselves growing, expanding, and evolving from an identity with just this single, isolated organism to an identity with every single thing and event in the entire Kosmos—a Kosmic consciousness that is our own deepest and truest Nature, our own Original Face.

As for technological predictions, it's the widespread faith of Silicon Valley that we are moving into a future of "transhumanism"—where human beings will be able to download their consciousness into computers and thus will be able to live indefinitely, live basically forever. Just be careful—you'll live forever as long as nobody drops your computer and shatters it. No materially constructed computer is guaranteed to be completely indestructible and therefore to persist forever—and thus nothing that depends upon it will be either. How embarrassing would that be—to have your everlasting life ended today by somebody dropping the computer that you were staring out of? A silly accident?

And consider this: what level of consciousness do you want to be at when your consciousness is downloaded—and remember, this is basically for ever and ever? Do you want to be able to Wake Up, or just spend the rest of everlasting time in an illusory, egoic state of awareness? It looks like transhumanism equals everlasting ignorance (nonenlightenment). Do you really want that—to continue to be stupid forever?

And what about evolution itself? Apparently your awareness will not grow, develop, or evolve one inch beyond the point when it is downloaded, so that you get to spend the rest of everlasting time in a relatively but pervasively idiotic condition with no chance to evolve. How would you like to spend the rest of your life on earth in, for example, a mythic ethnocentric state of awareness? Really, how truly disastrous is that?

You can instead, starting right now, choose a future that refuses flatland. You can choose to Show Up right now, step into the fullness of your own being, and radiate its Source and Suchness to one and all. You don't have to accept the disaster of modernity. You don't have to embrace the New Paradigms that sing the glory of the great interlocking order but leave your interiors gutted and splayed out and left as roadkill on the path to your own supposed future glory. You don't have to delete your Left-hand interiors and collapse your realities into nothing but the Right-hand exteriors of superficial surfaces and shiny varnish and veneer, devastating any hope of Growing Up, Waking Up, and Cleaning Up and left with nothing but a surface shell of being and a hollow core of consciousness, which is all that will remain of your authentic awareness after it suffers a complete and total "colonization of the lifeworld by science."

What you've seen in this book so far is what is hopefully some fairly convincing evidence that there really is a Growing Up (and you can engage in it effectively right now); there truly exists a Waking Up (which you can directly taste, also right now); and something called Cleaning Up is a definite possibility (bringing with it a certain wholeness and peace of mind), as well as a genuine Opening Up (to multiple potentials lying directly inside you)—and all of those can be embraced and effectively embodied this moment in an authentic Showing Up, allowing your life to radiate in all directions, even to infinity and back.

I've been focusing, in the last few chapters, on a genuine Showing Up, looking at what it means and how we as a culture have, on the whole, lost track of it and what we can do to regain it. I want to shift now to a serious look at Waking Up—both what it is and how you can gain a genuine access to it. I introduced the topic of Waking Up early in the book, but now I would like to go into more detail, because it is so important as part of a genuinely true and complete realization of a Big Wholeness. And I also want to give some pointing-out instructions, as well as introduce some practices to help you authentically Wake Up, including the practices of an Integral sexual Tantra, where you'll learn how to be on a path to a real Awakening every time you have sex.

So I invite you to accompany me on a journey to your own Real Self, your own

True Nature, the core Condition and Reality of your own being. It's a path without date or duration, on a road without aim or goal, toward a realization without beginning or end. I don‘t think you'll be disappointed.

15

Waking Up

OVERVIEW

First, a word about what we will be doing as an approach to the fundamental process of Waking Up. I think you're going to find this interesting, because we'll be focusing on the two highest states of consciousness: turiya (the Witness or pure Awareness) and turiyatita (ultimate nondual Unity consciousness, One Taste, or simply Suchness). We will also be exploring the immediate feeling tones that accompany both of those states—in other words, the feelings of Enlightenment, or how the Enlightened state actually feels.

With the Witness, for example, you have shifted from identifying with a small, finite, limited, *seen* self (usually known as the ego), to the vast, infinite, ever-present Witness, the pure Seer (not anything seen), pure Awareness itself (not any content of Awareness)—and this is marked by a sense of radical Freedom or profound Release and Liberation. The Witness can truthfully report, "I see that mountain, but I am not that mountain. I have sensations, but I am not those sensations. I have feelings, but I am not those feelings. I have thoughts, but I am not those thoughts." The Witness is not anything that can be observed or seen; it's the pure Seer. It's not any content of Awareness;

it's pure Awareness itself. So it's radically free of the binding nature of any content at all—it's *neti, neti*, "not this, not that."

As you go in search of this True Self ("I'm not this; I'm not that"), *you won't find it by seeing something*—if you see anything, that's just more objects, more content, more stuff. Whatever you see is fine; you're just not identified with it. Rather, you will start to sense a vast Freedom from all of this, a vast Openness and Spaciousness, not as an object but as an atmosphere. As the Witness of all objects, it is profoundly Free of all objects—this is known as the Great Liberation. The Great Liberation is inherently free of all dukkha, or all suffering, and is altogether free of the constant presence of anxiety, depression, and angst. It's no longer the victim of Life; it's the Witness of Life, itself radically Free. This sense of vast Freedom is something you can directly discover as you recognize the true Witness in yourself, in this very moment.

Now, the *feeling* of this infinite Freedom is many things; it's a feeling of Liberation, a feeling of ecstatic Release, a feeling of profound joy, and a feeling of deep happiness, which many of the Traditions summarize with one word: *bliss*. So the Witness exists as a radical Freedom, the feeling of which is bliss. In Sanskrit, bliss is known as *ananda*; and ananda is a core metaphor of Spirit itself. And here almost all the Traditions are very careful to distinguish between "ultimate Spirit," about which, à la Nagarjuna, literally nothing can be accurately said, and a qualified Spirit, about which something can be said, at least metaphorically. Ultimate Spirit is sometimes referred to as "nirguna Brahman," where *nirguna* means "totally unqualifiable." In other words, it's a real Emptiness (empty of all thoughts and all things). In contrast, "saguna Brahman" means "Spirit with metaphoric qualities," or qualities that are true only in a metaphoric sense. Everything I am saying about Spirit right now, needless to say, applies to saguna Brahman. You can directly understand nirguna Brahman only if you yourself have a direct Waking Up, which I will discuss later in this section.

Saguna Brahman is defined in the Indian tradition as *satchitananda*: *sat* means "being"; *chit* means "consciousness"; and *ananda* means "bliss." Being-Consciousness-Bliss: the metaphoric core of Waking Up. And just as the Witness is an ever-present reality (it is fully present right now, whether we realize it or not), so its Freedom and Bliss are likewise ever-present, fully existing in this moment, right now—whether we recognize them or not. So as we do exercises that will help us recognize our True Self and its sense of radical Freedom, we especially will be looking for this ever-present Bliss—this Bliss, after all, alerts us to our Real Self's ever-present Presence, which is something we can directly experience, right here, right now.

So, put simply: the radical Freedom of the Witness is Felt as Bliss—and that's one of the major things we'll be looking at.

As we continue exploring these highest states, we'll move from turiya to turiyatita, which is said to be the very highest and ultimate state of consciousness. This 5th state (so-named because it follows the 4th state of turiya) is not so much a Self that does the Witnessing but a simple Suchness or Thusness of pure undivided Presence (or One Taste). Here, I no longer Witness the mountain, I *am* the mountain. I no longer see the stars, I *am* the stars. I no longer watch the clouds, I *am* the clouds. I no longer feel the earth, I *am* the earth. The sense of Self that stands back and witnesses the world dissolves into a pure *unity with* the entire world—and I am That. There is still a sense of Freedom in this, but even more so there is a sense of *Fullness*. There is literally nothing that is outside or separate from me. There is only me, but it's not a "me," it's just *this*—the Suchness, Thusness, Isness of this and every moment, no inside and no outside, no past and no future, just *this*.

Freedom is always a sense of *freedom from* something (even the freedom to do something depends upon a freedom from any restraints). For the Witness, its radical Freedom is a Freedom from the entire manifest realm, a Freedom from all of samsara, a joyous

Freedom from all of its suffering, anxiety, depression, torment, and terror. It is Free from that because it is none of that—it's *neti, neti*, "not this, not that." But the *Fullness* of One Taste is not separate from all manifestation—rather, it's radically *one* with all of it (hence, *One* Taste—or pure Nonduality). This is a type of freedom, but it's a freedom that comes not from excluding All but from being radically One with All. Because One Taste is one with everything that is arising—an ultimate Unity consciousness—there is nothing outside of it that could limit it, threaten it, hurt it, or torment it. The feeling that One Taste has comes from this superabundant Fullness.

So, the feeling of this radical Fullness is not so much Bliss as it is *Love*. (Although, of course, both of them are present in the Ultimate state.) Love itself is the sense of being one with something, and the radiant warmth of that oneness is what we call "love." In this case, it is an infinite and ultimate Love because it is a oneness with the entire universe, a One Taste with everything that is arising. I am literally one with—or nondual with—the entire Kosmos, a Kosmic Consciousness, fully embraced in the Suchness or Thusness of this present Now-moment. And I do not experience this Now-moment; I am the totality of this Now-moment, in all its radiant Love.

The recognition of these two highest states—the pure Witness and One Taste—is simultaneously the recognition of a radical Freedom and a profound Fullness, and these are directly felt as a genuine Bliss and an all-embracing Love. This Loving Bliss (or Blissful Love) is the actual texture of each and every Now-moment that we will ever have, reflecting the ultimate Freedom and radical Fullness that is our deepest and ever-present Nature. In this part of the book, we will be looking for the pure Witness and nondual One Taste with their radical Freedom and pure Fullness, felt as an ongoing Bliss and all-encompassing Love.

Starting in this and continuing into the next chapter (chapter 16), I will be going over the highest two states of consciousness (turiya and turiyatita) and giving some pointing-out instructions to help you realize the ever-present Presence of both of them. Then, in chapter 17, I will be working with the feelings of Enlightenment (Bliss and Love) and giving several pointing-out instructions to help you recognize their ever-present Presence in you. As the final part of our adventure in Waking Up, we will be exploring a sexual Integral Tantra. Tantra itself is many things, but most centrally it is a way to use the blissful and loving feelings that naturally arise in sex as a pathway to the Bliss and Love of ultimate Spirit itself. We've already seen that Bliss and Love are the two most fundamental feeling tones of authentic Spiritual Awareness. Tantra is a direct way to use the temporal, finite feelings of sexual bliss and love to remember, evoke, and enhance the ever-present infinite Bliss and Love of our own True Nature. In short, sexuality can be used as a means of Waking Up—so that every time you have sex, you will be directly plunged into divine Spirit itself, and put face-to-face with your own deepest and truest Self and Suchness. In chapters 18 and 19 on Integral sexual Tantra, I will be going into specific exercises and practices to do exactly that—and this will very likely change the way that you see sexuality forever.

THE HISTORICAL FORGETTING OF WAKING UP

Waking Up is surely one of the most profound areas of Wholeness that the modern world has forgotten, ignored, or outright denied. It was largely denounced by modernity. Why did it do so? We have seen that there is an important distinction between spiritual *intelligence*, which is an indirect "knowledge by description" that occurs in Growing Up, and spiritual *experience*, which is a direct "knowledge by acquaintance" that occurs in Waking Up. Particularly in the West, as humanity was evolving and Growing Up from amber traditional-mythic to a more orange modern rationality ("The Age of Reason"), the leading-edge elite were increasingly impressed, for many good reasons, with the type of knowledge that a rational science could generate, and they were also increasingly more likely to speak out against the disastrous undersides of a merely mythic religion. Indeed, modern Europe (from 1700 onward) had just undergone several decades of truly barbaric religious warfare—"My God is better than your God"—whereas modernity itself believed that "God is dead." (And the amber mythic God was indeed dying as any sort of leading-edge view.)

As the scientific worldview of orange rationality continued to gain momentum, the religious worldview of a largely mythic dogmatism steadily lost ground. A century or two into this, most leading-edge thinkers had put their reliance in rational science, not mythic religion. Today, the official cultural philosophy of the modern West is still scientific materialism (we traced the historical rise of this situation in the previous chapter).

However, when modernity tossed out religion altogether, it totally confused spiritual intelligence (which is a line in Growing Up) with spiritual experience (which is a direct state of Waking Up). Now in the various religious systems themselves, this was always a dicey distinction. The founders of most of the major religions around the world had themselves experienced some degree of a profound Waking Up, but you could not say the same for their followers. The essential aim of the particular religion itself was generally recognized to be a state of consciousness similar to its founder's, and many of its religious practices were aimed at those higher states. While some people attained those higher states of Waking Up, most of them did not. But all of them, without exception, had attained some stage of Growing Up (mostly mythic), and thus had some level of spiritual intelligence. During the Middle Ages, the most common level of spiritual intelligence was indeed amber mythic, and thus this was the typical dogma ensconced in the various creeds that defined Christianity at that time (for example, the Nicene Creed and the Apostle's Creed, which have strongly amber mythic-literal and ethnocentric cores). Christianity also embraced, in much smaller numbers, those who practiced meditation or contemplation or something like the Cloud of Unknowing, which aimed for a genuine Waking Up (usually of turiya, which is indeed a *neti, neti*, a form of apophatic mysticism). These were often monks, and of those monks, a small number would actually have an authentic Waking Up. For the rest of the population, their spiritual intelligence was mythic-literal.

Very few people at the time understood the distinction between spiritual intelligence and spiritual experience. For one thing, the stages of Growing Up had not yet been discovered. For another, the percentage of the population who had had a genuine Waking Up was quite small. The result was that, in general, there was no consistent line drawn between spirituality as it appeared in Growing Up and as it appeared in Waking Up—they both looked "religious" to the untutored eye. The vast majority of people who said they believed in a Christian God were expressing some sort of mythic-literal belief. Thus when science threw out religion, it threw out all of it. It tossed out the religion of amber mythic, but it also tossed out any spirituality of Waking Up. God was dead, period. That is why the Western world has forgotten about Waking Up.

So I want to resurrect Waking Up and recommend it to you very highly.

THE WITNESS VERSUS ONE TASTE

People often have difficulty distinguishing between, or least remembering, the difference between Witnessing and One Taste. The difference between Witnessing Awareness and One Taste Awareness is simply a difference in your relationship with the totality of the Painting of All That Is. In the former (the Witness), you stand Free of the totality and simply witness it as object, with the Witness itself (as Absolute Subjectivity, pure Seer, or True Self) remaining completely and radically Free of all objects whatsoever (*neti*, *neti*). In the latter (One Taste), you go one step further and dissolve the Witness into the Total Painting itself, and thus drop any sensation of being separate from anything that is arising—a pure One Taste awareness. There is now not so much a sense of Freedom from the All but a sense of Fullness *with* or *as* the All—not *Freedom from*, but *Oneness with*.

For both, the Total Painting is the total of all things and events that are arising in your awareness right now—with no avoidance, no denial, no resistance (whether you Witness all of it or become One with all of it). So the fundamental first step in both cases is to actually rest in the most total of the most total of the most total Totality that you can possibly be aware of. *Simply experience everything you're experiencing; avoid nothing.* Start by resting in a fully all-inclusive Witnessing Awareness of the totality of the Painting of All That Is. And this totality is every single thing and event, sensation and impulse, feeling and desire, that is arising in your experience right now—the Painting of All That Is (the entire world for you).

A helpful key is to notice that, in every case, our normal or typical awareness is driven by a fundamental avoidance, a primordial fear, a contraction. In each moment, there is something *that we don't want to look at*—some idea, thought, perception, impulse, sensation, thing, or event. We therefore turn away, look away, move away—and that fundamental avoidance is the cause of the entire misery of humankind. In a chain reaction, it creates one dualism after another, one fragmentation after another, one brokenness after another—and a synonym for *brokenness* is *suffering*.

One of the most common manifestations of this Primordial Avoidance is the sensation of a type of vague but very noticeable tension, a type of self-contracting, a tightening in experience. There is not a full *Awareness* of all experience but a narrowed *attention* to just some of it, a focusing, a constricting. But notice that even though there is this self-contracting tension, you can be aware of it—and that which is Aware of this self-contraction is itself free of it. Your Awareness is not identified with the contraction; it is the Witness of it. And in that pure Awareness, everything is arising easily, fully, and totally. That Awareness can include the self-contraction as well, if it arises in this moment along with everything else, and primordial Awareness is spontaneously, easily, and naturally Aware of All of That—the birds are singing, the cars are honking, people are chatting, clouds are floating by, and all of that is arising in this vast, open Clearing that is Awareness itself.

So the key to all genuine mindfulness training with both the Witness and One Taste is to recognize an ever-present, primordial Witnessing Awareness that is *not* caught in avoidance but rather is always letting absolutely everything (every single thing, event, and occasion) arise in Awareness and spontaneously manifest itself just as it is. This everything is exactly the totality of the Painting of All That Is. And like all paintings, all of the present moment's qualities are needed for the full Painting to even make sense. We need the ups and downs, the light spaces and the dark, the mountains and the valleys, the good and the evil, the pleasure and the pain, the happiness and the sadness, in order for any of these qualities to manifest at all. If we got rid of all evil and chased only good, got rid of all pain and pursued only pleasure, got rid of all sadness and grasped only happiness, this would be a world of all ups and no downs, all ins and no outs, all lefts and no rights. When the Great Traditions unanimously say that Enlightenment is being "freed from the pairs," they mean the pairs of opposites—ALL of the opposites. Spirit is not just good; it's beyond both good and evil. And it isn't just pleasure; it's beyond both pleasure and pain. Nor is Spirit light, bliss, liberation, release, salvation, or any other concept that makes sense only in terms of its opposite (remember that was Nagarjuna's point about Emptiness).

It's what the Christian mystics call the *coincidentia oppositorum*, "the coincidence of opposites" or the unity of opposites. To realize this is not to be caught in seeking only one-half of any pair of opposites, which would rip the universe right down the middle as we try to get rid of half of it. (Alan Watts wrote a terrific book about the coincidentia oppositorum called *The Two Hands of God*—God always has a left hand AND a right hand, and they always go together, get it?)

Thus the first step with both the Witness and One Taste is to start by resting in an all-inclusive Witnessing Awareness of the totality of the Painting of All That Is. The key is to allow a Mirror-Mind Awareness to function without any contracting, avoiding, looking away, or turning away—*experience all experience; allow all experience to fully arise, just as it is, right now, and let all of it totally wash through you with no contracting and no denial. Face everything; avoid nothing.*

If you do find yourself avoiding something, or contracting, then fine—simply notice that avoidance as well; simply let it be, and let it also arise in Awareness just as it is. You don't want to deny anything, but if you do, fine, simply notice that denial. You don't want to turn away from anything, but if you do, fine, notice that as well. *You can't get this wrong*. And you can't, because some part of your Awareness is always already getting it exactly right. So merely notice what is already arising in your Awareness, and notice that this Awareness itself is an all-embracing Mirror Mind: it spontaneously and easily notices or witnesses everything that is occurring moment to moment. Simply notice that present Awareness, that pure Witnessing, and rest as that.

TWO STEPS IN THIS PRACTICE

The first step is the same in practicing both Witnessing and One Taste (namely, simply Witness everything). You can tell the difference between these two practices by seeing—as the *second step* in the practice—exactly what relationship you are then supposed to take in relation to this Total Painting.

The Total Painting, again, is the totality of all the phenomena that are arising in any present moment—the totality of your present experience (including any thoughts of the past, arising Now, and any thoughts of the future, also arising Now—let them all arise as they wish). If you attempt to become fully aware of this Total Painting by relentlessly Witnessing each phenomenon that arises, without identifying with it, avoiding it, or turning away, then those phenomena will appear as objects to the Witness and the Witness itself will be completely Free of all objects. You will be a True Subject, Absolute Subjectivity, and these objects will all appear "in front" of you. If that is what you are doing, then you are doing a turiya practice (a Witness practice), using a Mirror-Mind Awareness to fully Witness the Total Painting.

If, on the other hand, you go one step further and dissolve the Witness into the totality of the Total Painting of All That Is, then you no longer Witness the Total Painting, you ARE the Total Painting.[1] You are no longer standing back and Witnessing whatever is arising, you are fully one with it—you *are* it, you are in One Taste. When this realization matures, it represents a final realization beyond all dualisms whatsoever, a fully Awakened Nondual Suchness. You no longer feel that you are a separate self, different from everything, but you actually feel that you are one with everything—a total Kosmic consciousness. As a Zen master exquisitely put it, "When I heard the sound of the bell ringing, there was no bell and no I, just the ringing."

In most cases, you still want to enter the Witness fully before you go on to recognize One Taste because, by completely being the Witness and disidentifying with all the objects in the Total Painting—"I am not this, not that"—you completely strip away any attachment to, any fixation on, and any identity with any thing or event in manifestation. And because you have disidentified with every single thing—

"I'm *not* this, *not* that"—you can then more readily become one with ALL things—"I *am* this, I *am* that—I'm one with absolutely everything." This can't fully happen if you still have any hidden identities with any *particular* thing or event, because that prior, hidden identity with that thing will prevent a full and equal identity with ALL things.

You want to move from being identified with just a select few items or a group of items (including a bunch of *objects* that you have made into a *pretend subject* that you call your "self"—which is the typical ego condition, at any of its stages of Growing Up) to not being identified with a single thing or event anywhere, which happens as you stand fully Free as the empty Witness. And from this, you can then move into being one with absolutely EVERY thing everywhere. The practice is quite literally to move from something (the ego), to nothing (the Witness), to everything (One Taste). Something to nothing to everything.

(Again, in the following chapters, we will carefully go over various exercises and pointing-out instructions that will show you exactly how to recognize the states of the Witness and One Taste.)

POINTING-OUT INSTRUCTIONS

There are, to speak very generally, two fundamental types of activities for getting one's awareness into the higher and highest states of consciousness. These can be called "practice" and "recognition." In a practice type of meditation, you take up certain exercises and practice them, attempting to get your awareness from a point where it is not in the higher state to a point where it is in the higher state. The result of this practice is an accomplishment, an achievement, something that you have attained—you have moved your awareness from a lower state to a higher state. This is probably the most common type of meditation, and it definitely works.

It works, that is, for getting into *higher* states, but not for the *highest* state. You can get into *higher* states, because they are relative; they are not ultimate states. They are not the *highest* state because the highest states are absolute and ultimate, which means that they are eternal or timeless, which means that they are ever-present, which means that they are fully the case right here, right now, and there is no way whatsoever that they can be entered, attained, or achieved. The very highest states are instead *always already the case*—it is simply impossible to enter them, or move from a point where they are not to a point where they are, because there is no point where they are not. They are ultimate, absolute, all-pervading, all-embracing, all-inclusive, unborn (they have no beginning in time), undying (they have no ending in time), always already the case, and fully ever-present.

These states in their true nature are not so much like states as they are like ever-present conditions. Maslow called them "plateau experiences," which are essentially permanent, instead of "peak experiences," which are temporary. Relative states are different from other relative states, and as one state comes to be, other states are pushed out—you can't be drunk and sober at the same time; you can't be straight and high at the same time; you can't be in a deep dreamless state and a dream state at the same time; and so on. Relative states alternate with each other; they take turns.

But ultimate states are not different from other states; they are something that is present with all states, underlying all states as a constant background reality. This is true of the Witness, which is always fully present and changeless as all states come and go. The Witness does not come or go, it ceaselessly Witnesses all states as *they* come and go. (And when you realize or recognize the Witness, you will also notice that it has always been present even though you didn't recognize that it was. You are Witnessing right now, whether or not you are aware of it.) The same is true for One Taste—it doesn't come or go, and it doesn't alternate with states; it exists underneath all states and fully embraces and enfolds all of them. This is why both the Witness/turiya and One Taste/turiyatita are always listed as the two major *ultimate* states of consciousness. The gross, subtle, and causal, by contrast, are *relative* states; they come and go in time, last a while and then shift, but none of them are ever-present, timeless, or ultimate.

So the action that is needed here, for these ultimate states, is not practice but simple recognition or realization—that is, the teacher points out this highest state, often by simply talking about it, until you recognize something that is already there. And when you recognize that always already state, you will also realize that it has, indeed, always been there, fully present and fully functioning, but you simply did not notice it. Thus, you have not really entered this state—you have always been in it—and you are simply recognizing or realizing something that is always already the case. (As we just said, you might notice this with the Witness. Whenever you "get in" it, you can notice that it has always been the case, and you are simply recognizing this in yourself.)

Zen famously calls this your "Original Face," which is "the face you had before your parents were born." That doesn't mean that it existed at a point in time before your parents were born but rather that it simply doesn't enter the stream of time in the first place; it is prior to time altogether. Your Original Face, your Real Being, is prior to your parents' birth, prior to the birth of the solar system, and prior to the spacetime created by the Big Bang simply because it is prior to time, period.

To see what this means, start by relaxing into a Witnessing Awareness and simply witness the present moment. Notice that this present moment arises, exists for a second or two, and then fades into the past, as a new present moment arises and comes to your Awareness and the old moment becomes a memory. The new moment lasts for a brief second or so, and then it fades into the past as well, and a new moment arises. And this movement is constant, it just goes on and on and on. The Christian mystics call this the *nunc fluens*, "the flowing present," or "the passing present."

But notice the Witness itself. Notice the Awareness of this passing present, a passing present that moves continuously from present to past. The pure Witness of this moment does not itself change; it's just a constant Presence, a pure unmoving point of being Aware, a true constant Mirror Mind. It merely watches the passing present arise, stay a bit, and pass; arise, stay a bit, and pass. The Witness remains completely unmoved and unmoving, a pure, unending Present or timeless Now—what Daniel P. Brown calls a "Boundless, Changeless Awareness."

The Christian mystics call this unchanging Present the *nunc stans*, "the standing present," or "the unmoving present," or "the timeless Now." According to them, the real Present, the eternal Present, the Divine Present, is this Standing Present, not the passing present—the nunc stans, not the nunc fluens. It exists fully as this never-ending Present. This timeless Now does not come into being or fade into the past—it is an ever-present, unchanging, pure Present. The passing present, your thoughts of the future, and your memories of the past all arise in this unending Present. As Schrödinger put it, "The present is the only thing that has no end."[2]

The Witness is always aware in this timeless Now. It is from this unchanging, timeless, motionless Present Awareness that the Witness sees everything that arises. This Standing Present is Aware of the passing present and everything in it—present experiences, past memories, future thoughts—all of them arising in this ever-present timeless Now. The Standing Present, which is unchanging, is fully aware of the passing present, which does nothing but change.

In other words, this pure Witness or Witnessing Awareness is always existing in the ever-present timeless Now. Usually, if you are given a mindfulness practice, you will be told to focus your attention on the immediate present moment, and pay no attention at all to past or future events. This is called "being aware of just the immediate present." But all this will get you is the nunc fluens, the passing present; it will not get you the real nunc stans, the timeless Now—and that timeless Now is not hard to attain but impossible to avoid.

To see this—and to see that the Witness is always fully existing in the timeless Now (your "Original Face")—I will ask you to repeat the experiment that we first performed when we were discussing the meaning of *eternity* as a never-ending, timeless Now. Think about some event that you believe exists in the past. Picture this past event as clearly and as vividly as you can. Notice that all you are actually aware of is a memory and that memory exists only in this Now-moment. And when that event actually occurred, when it really existed, it was itself a Now-moment. In either case, all you are ever actually aware of is the Now-moment. Likewise, think of something you believe will exist in the future. Notice that is just a thought and that thought only exists right here, in this Now-moment. And if it ever becomes a real event, it will then occur only in a Now-moment.

In other words, the only time you are ever really aware of is the Now-moment and that Now-moment is not hard to attain but impossible to avoid. It's always already the case; it's absolutely ever-present (or eternal).

So the Witness—because it deals only with Realities—is always operating fully in this Now-moment, and the passing present moves through the Space of that unchanging, ever-present, timeless Now. The *contents* of Awareness exist in time; the Awareness itself does not. Awareness itself is operating in a constantly present, ever-present, timeless Now. And this is all happening whether or not you realize it. But hopefully, with some pointing out like this, you will start to recognize this ever-present, timeless Now, which does not exclude the past and future but fully embraces them and is not a narrow slit of passing, present awareness but a vast, all-inclusive, all-embracing Awareness.

This is your Original Face. It exists prior to your parents' birth because it exists prior to time, period. Another way to say this is that it's prior to time because it is indeed eternal—as long as we remember that eternity does not mean going on in time forever; it means a point without time, fully existing in the timeless Now. We saw that Wittgenstein absolutely nailed something that pretty much every mystic the world over agrees with: "If we take eternity to mean, not everlasting temporal duration, but a moment without time, then eternal life belongs to those who live in the present."[3]

There will never be a future time where it will be more present than it already is right now. Never. Whatever comes into existence tomorrow but is not present Now is strictly temporal, not eternal. This is why Shankara, the major founder of Advaita Vedanta, said that Self-Realization could not be attained, because if it were attained, it would have a beginning in time and thus be strictly temporal, not eternal—and thus not a genuine Self-Realization.

Its utter Simplicity is one reason we can so easily miss it, not notice it, not realize it. An example of this utter Simplicity is your own I AMness (which is the Witness existing in you right now). We saw that this is exactly what Christ was talking about when he said, "Before Abraham was, I AM." This sense of I AMness, like the Witness, is always ever-present, but we almost always miss its profundity because (precisely due to its Simplicity) we quickly identify it with something more complex. Then it's not just a pure and immediate I AMness, just as it is, but I AM *this* or I AM *that*—I AM a doctor, lawyer, student, or actress; I AM this tall and I weigh this much and I go to this school and I work at this job—and on and on. We never realize the timeless, ever-present, pure I AMness for the *simple feeling of Being* that it is.

AWAKENING TO I AMNESS

The simple feeling of Being can become especially obvious if you do some sort of dream yoga, where you will learn to keep Awareness, or stay awake, even in various dream states. You start out, in the waking state, identified with hundreds or thousands of things—especially things from the gross or physical state itself—for example, your profession; your wealth; your gross desires, wants, and wishes; your car; your house. In the waking state, your I AMness is identified with your relationship to all of these gross objects, and thus you do not recognize the simple feeling of Being—you are always I AM this or I AM that, where "this" and "that" are a network of mostly gross or physical objects. You never realize I AMness itself.

Then you pass into the dream state, but because of your meditative practice (and yes, this is a practice), you remain aware that you are dreaming—that is, you lucid dream. Now you are no longer identified with any gross objects because they are all gone (there is no nature, no Gaia, no physical reality). You are now aware of subtle objects in the dream state: luminous images, impulses, and vibrant visions. And you—your I AMness (your Witness)—now identify with various subtle objects and images and get lost in an awareness of them. Once again, you do not recognize the utter simplicity of an ever-present Presence, your True Self. You remain identified instead with some sort of separate-self sense, albeit now a subtle self-sense.

Then you pass into the deep dreamless state—the causal state—the very end limit of which is a pure, formless, unmanifest nothingness, a vast emptiness, an infinite abyss. And yet, due to your meditative dream-yoga practice, you remain tacitly aware in this state (and there is considerable research that uses EEGs to investigate brain activity during sleep that shows that these states are indeed possible—that is, an awareness in the deep dreamless state is definitely possible). Yet now, in this dreamless state, there are no objects of any kind—there is literally nothing to identify with. And yet you are still aware; and you notice that the one thing you are still aware of is the only thing that still exists, and that is the simple feeling of a witnessing I AMness that is still present, because it is ever-present, always already the case, and fully present in all states, including the deep dreamless state.

Here, at the end limit of the causal—where there is nothing left to identify with, nothing left to confuse your I AMness with—you might suddenly recognize this ever-present I AMness just as it is. You have recognized the pure turiya state beyond the causal, the 4th state of the pure Witness or pure I AMness.

Thus you come to realize that all the things that you had called yourself in normal life were not your True Self but were just some gross, subtle, or causal objects that existed in time, were relative, and came and went in the temporal stream, and thus were finite, mortal, and inherently suffering. This isn't who you really are at all. You are the infinite, eternal, vast, and unbounded Ground of Being that is Unborn and Undying.

Everybody has some degree of this ever-present I AMness, because, for example—as Ramana Maharshi himself would often point out—even when they go to sleep, let go of their gross ego, and pass through states like dreaming and deep sleep, they still wake up in the morning and say, "I slept great!" They know that there is something in them that doesn't change.

As you recognize this ever-present I AMness, you will also recognize that this is the same feeling of Being that you have always had. As far back as you can remember (which is as far back as time goes in your own individual case), you were always this basic I AMness—you can never remember a time when you weren't *you*. This fundamental Witness was always the knowing aspect of your present Awareness, the "who" of your consciousness, existing in the Standing Present, but you never recognized it because you almost immediately identified it with something that was known in the passing present—with this or that object, with some thing, quality, trait, or characteristic (your ego), and thus you always missed the simple feeling of Being itself and got lost in the world of separate things and events, suffering and torment, and illusion and destitution.

The gross (waking), subtle (dreaming), and causal (deep sleep) states are all *relative* states. They all exist in the stream of time, the stream of the passing present; they all begin, they stay a while, and they go; they all can be practiced, attained, and achieved—therefore they all can be objects of a practice type of meditation (such as dream yoga). The 4th state—turiya, the Witness, or I AMness—and the 5th state—turiyatita, Suchness, or One Taste—are both absolute or ultimate states: they are timeless, ever present, always already; and they are infinite, all-inclusive, and all-embracing.[4] They are always already fully present and fully functioning in the timeless Now, so they cannot be entered into, attained, or achieved; they can only be recognized or realized. The timeless Now or Standing Present easily and fully embraces the past, the present, and the future—it allows all past thoughts, all present thoughts, and all future thoughts to fully arise right now in the ever-present Standing Present, which is thus truly all-inclusive and all-pervading.

And unlike the passing present, which excludes thoughts of the past and the future, the Standing Present fully includes all of them and allows all of them to arise as they wish—they're all equally arising in the timeless Now and fully embraced by it. (This is why the Christian mystics maintain that only the nunc stans or Standing Present is the Real, True, and Divine Present, whereas the nunc fluens or passing present is the core of the temporal and illusory world.)

So this is the "nonpractice" of recognition. It is not entering a state that you were not previously in but have, through practice, brought about; it is the simple and immediate recognition of a state that has always been present but which you have not fully noticed.

There is a slight paradox here, in that it could be said that although this state has always been present, the noticing or recognition of it has not, and therefore there is some sort of beginning, entering, or achieving here. And from one perspective that is true. This is why Zen will say paradoxical things like, "If in the Tao there is any discipline [or practice], then the completion of that discipline marks the destruction of the Tao. But if there is no discipline, one remains an idiot." Fair enough. But the recognition itself, in virtually every case, carries with it the realization that not only was the state always present, you also *always* knew it. This is Zen's "gateless gate"—on this side of the gate (the gate to Enlightenment), it looks like there is a real gate. But when you pass through it and turn around and look back, you can't see any gate at all—there isn't a gate, and there never was one. Welcome to the paradox of instruction: you need a satori to realize that you don't need a satori!

These kinds of paradoxes ultimately occur, as we've already seen with Nagarjuna, because we are forced to discuss these issues using concepts that make sense only in terms of their opposites, so we are using fragments to try and explain the Whole. So until we explore some pointing-out instructions for actual Realization—which we'll do in the next chapter and where you can directly see for yourself—the closest approximation to reality is to take both sides of this paradox as being equally true.

However you want to split that difference, make no mistake on the fundamental issue: what you are ultimately attempting to realize is a state that is indeed fully present right now and cannot in any sense be attained or achieved. If the Ground of All Being were not fully present right now, then you would simply cease to exist. Be as clear about that as you can be. The *Prajnaparamita Sutras*—the fundamental texts of Mahayana Buddhism—repeat over and over again that if you would only understand that Enlightenment itself is absolutely *unattainable*, then you would be fully Enlightened. That's the word they use—*unattainable*. And Enlightenment is indeed unattainable—it cannot be attained—because it is already fully present; you can no more attain Enlightenment than you can attain your lungs or acquire your feet. So what are pointing-out instructions? You come to the teacher and innocently look them in the eyes and maintain that you're not Enlightened but really want to be. And a real teacher—who sees you saying that you have no feet and could they help you attain your feet—does not give you practices that will help you pretend to attain your feet; instead they just start stomping on your feet until you yell, "Okay, I see them! And yes, I've always had them!"

That "stomping" constitutes the pointing-out instructions for a real "gateless gate." And that's what we're going to be doing here. Over the years, there have been dozens—probably hundreds—of pointing-out instructions that have really struck home for me and made utterly obvious that which I had always known. Let me tell you two that meant a great deal to me.

One was very simple, one sentence from Sri Ramana Maharshi: "That which is not present in deep dreamless sleep is not real." This was enormously disturbing to me, because by then I had been practicing Zen meditation for almost a decade and had had several confirmed *kensho* or satori realizations. It was simply pointing to that ever-present I AMness that is not a relative state different from other states, or one that comes and goes and exists in time. Rather, it's something that is present in all states, an ever-present Mirror Mind that is aware of, and fully present in, ALL states and that does not come and go with any state but is indeed an ever-present Witnessing of all states. It's a constant consciousness, and as far as temporal states go, this means it is present twenty-four hours a day—including in deep dreamless sleep. Ramana's statement pointed out something ever-present that I had, at least to some degree, not fully recognized until that point.

The other one has to do with my root teacher in Dzogchen Buddhism (which is often claimed to be the very highest of the Buddha's teachings). During winter retreats, he sometimes kept his door open, and students could come in and ask him questions anytime they wanted. If you were quiet, you could often sit in the corner and listen. And one thing kept happening over and over again. Students would come in and say variations on, "I finally see it! I can't believe it! About an hour ago I was sitting there, meditating, and all of a sudden I became one with everything, and I disappeared and became the all. Why didn't I see this before?!"

And he would always say, "Did this have a beginning in time?" And the student would say, "Yes, like I said, about an hour ago." He would respond, "That's very nice. But I want you to come back when you can show me that which does not have a beginning in time. Come back when you see that."

He wanted them to recognize that which was ever-present, always already the case—something that did not have a beginning in time but rather was always Now. And 100 percent of that Enlightened Mind is in your own awareness, right here and right now. Not 90 percent of it, not 95 percent of it—100 percent of it. You will never attain that. So start looking around in your own Awareness, the way it is arising right now, moment to moment, just as it is—and prepare to be surprised.

And I will be using some pointing-out instructions to help you do just that.

The fundamental ideas that we will be working to recognize in the next few chapters on Waking Up are the major states of the Witness and One Taste (the 4th and 5th states, the two ultimate states that cannot be attained but only recognized), with their primary characteristics of Freedom and Fullness, respectively, and their predominant feeling tones, which are, respectively, Bliss and Love. The Freedom of the Witness is felt as Bliss, and the Fullness of One

Taste is felt as Love. The core of them are present right now, whether you know it or not—and if you don't, I'll be stomping on those feet, especially as we get into Integral sexual Tantra. We'll simply be talking about those things, going over the same points with minor variations, and repeating central themes once or twice in the main presentation, until you recognize these ultimate ever-present states in your own awareness.

Shall we begin?

16

Pointing Out the Witness and One Taste

So let's start by going back and reviewing the two major states themselves, Witnessing and One Taste. Recognizing either (or both) of those states is your direct introduction to that which is *Ultimate* in you—and thus your introduction to your own Realization, Awakening, Enlightenment, Waking Up.

THE WITNESS, ROUND 1

We said that, allowing Awareness to be conscious of the sum total of the phenomena of the Total Painting of All That Is, if you then attempt to stand Free and Witness all of these phenomena—Witness all your present experience with no avoidance of anything—then those phenomena will all appear as objects to the Witness, a Witness that itself is pure Subject or Absolute Subjectivity. Resting as the Witness, a Boundless Changeless Awareness, you will be in the timeless Now, the Standing Present, and all experience, things, and events will be arising "in front" of you as the passing present, and you will be fully, easily, and equally Aware of all of this. All phenomena will appear as objects that arise in front of the Witness, and as the Witness, you are not identified with any of them—in other words, you are truly Free of absolutely all of them, free of manifestation itself—the Great Liberation.

In completely Witnessing the Total Painting, which arises in front of the Witness, you discover primordial Freedom, radical Release, infinite Letting Go. The Witness, if it spoke, might say, "I see the mountain, but I am not the mountain; I am Free of it. I have sensations, but I am not those sensations; I am Free of them. I have feelings, but I am not those feelings; I am Free of them. I have thoughts, but I am not those thoughts; I am Free of them." Hence, this is indeed the Great Liberation, Enlightenment as radical Emancipation. This is a nirvana absolutely free of all samsara.

Suppose I were to ask you, "Who are you?" Get a sheet of paper, and write down your answers to that question. You might include things like my name is such-and-such; I'm this tall and weigh this much; I graduated with a degree in such-and-such; I make this much money; I live in a house whose address is such-and-such; I have a romantic partner whose name is so-and-so; I like these types of movies; I read these kinds of books; I enjoy video games; I have several pets including two dogs; my hobbies are such-and-such; I enjoy this kind of food, and so on. Notice, however, that as you were thinking of all of those characteristics, you were seeing them as objects—all of them are objects of awareness—none of them are a true Subject or your true Self. Those objects are, in other words, exactly what you are not. They are all illusory, pretend selves or pretend subjects; none of them is your true Subject. They are all things that can be seen; they are not the true Seer, not your true Self. Everything that you think is your true Self—and that you wrote down on the sheet of paper—is exactly what you are not. Your true Self is *neti*, *neti*—not this, not that—radically Free of all objects. It is a pure Subject or Absolute Subjectivity.

Proceed with this type of radical disidentification until you can truly recognize the basic and profound Freedom at your very core. That realization is central to the mature forms of any spiritual Realization and Enlightenment and is your introduction to a truly Ultimate state, that of turiya. This practice is particularly helpful with negative, frightening, or intensely uncomfortable states. Simply practice Witnessing them directly, with the understanding that "I am fully aware of this state of pain, anxiety, or depression; I have this state, *but I am not this state*"—and truly get that "therefore I am Free of it." Right now, if you are aware of your body, you immediately *know* that you are not your body (you're seeing it as an object, so it's not your True Subject). Likewise, if you are aware of your mind (or thoughts), it will be just as obvious that you are *not* your mind (it's just another series of passing thoughts, perfectly seen objects, so it's not your True Subject). "I have a body and mind, but I am not my body or mind." You should feel a genuine release, a letting go, an opening, a clearing, a freeing—and a type of happiness or joy at being that Free.

The True Self is the pure Seer, which itself can never be seen. So when you go in search of this True Self, *you won't see it.* Whatever is arising is just fine; simply let it arise, with the awareness that "I am not this, not that." Rest as the true Witness of this and every moment, simply relaxing in the pure Present and not identifying with anything that is arising, letting it all go. All that you will be aware of is a genuine sense of vast Freedom, deep Release, radical Letting Go. Instead of being identified with some isolated self-image, self-concept, or egoic contraction, you are an all-seeing atmosphere of pure Awareness, a Mirror Mind that effortlessly reflects every single thing and event in experience but identifies with, or gets stuck to, none of them. You are a pure Mirror Mind of *neti, neti*, an effortless, easy Awareness that is not identified with any of its contents but simply rests as an infinite and completely released Freedom, totally beyond any of the self-contracting torment, torture, agony, and pain that haunts all things, objects, and events of the manifest world—a torture your ego knows all too well, and a torture the Witness is radically Free of. And it's not that various sorts of torments cease entirely to arise; it's rather "Who cares if they do?"—they're just more transitory objects that come and go and are simply Witnessed like everything else. Some things might even hurt more, but they bother you less.

The entire objective world is arising, and you are Free of all of it, including all the objects that you can see by looking within—ideas, desires, needs, motivations, goals, images, and concepts. All of those interior objects, like all the exterior objects that you see, are exactly what you are not. None of them are your True Subject. In place of an identity with some set of ideas, things, and images—with some sort of ego—there is simply this vast Openness, Emptiness, Spaciousness, and radical Freedom. When you realize that you are truly *neti*, *neti*, the whole sense of being a self-contraction, a skin-encapsulated ego, gives way to being radically and totally Free, Liberated, Unbound. This is your Original Face, the face you had before your parents were born, the face you had before the universe itself was born, before the stream of time came rushing into existence to bind us with its nightmares and tortures. I am no longer the victim of Life; I am the Witness of Life.

This True Self is your own fundamental I AMness. This sense of I AMness is, like the Witness, an ever-present, timeless Reality. When Christ said, "Before Abraham was, I AM," he intuited this fundamental and timeless turiya. You, too, can say exactly the same thing as Christ did—your own I AMness carries that same timelessness and real eternity.

Think about what you were doing a week ago at this time. You probably can't remember any details of your thoughts or behavior, but one thing is certain: the sense of I AMness was there. Think about what you were doing a month ago—and again, even if you can't remember any details of what happened, you know that I AMness was there—and it's the same sense of I AMness that you have now, because I AMness, as the pure Seer, has no qualities or characteristics (it's pure Openness or Emptiness) that could change over time. It has nothing that moves in time.

So think back even a year ago—the same I AMness was definitely there. What about a decade ago, what about a century ago, what about a millennium ago? There is the same timeless, ever-present I AMness, which does not enter the stream of time and therefore exists prior to your parents' birth, prior to this solar system's birth, prior to the Big Bang, and prior to the stream of time altogether.

Erwin Schrödinger tells a beautiful story about a person who, he says, *many centuries ago* sat on the same spot that you now do; like you, this person looked with longing in their heart as they watched the sun set; like you, they were born of woman and suffered pain; like you they had wishes, goals, desires; like you they had dreams and visions and yearned mightily. And then comes the extraordinary punchline: "Was this somebody else? Was this not you yourself?"

Incredible. In that person's pure I AMness, they were the same I AMness that you now are ("Was this not you yourself?"). The Traditions are unanimous here: the number of I AM's is but one—one Self, one Spirit, one Reality. Or, as Schrödinger gorgeously puts it, "Consciousness is a singular the plural of which is unknown."[1] This is why, when you deeply realize your own I AMness, you realize that you will never die—you truly are timeless and eternal (and you *know* that the deepest part of you won't die, don't you?—and that's a close realization of eternity). This does not mean that your physical body won't die. It means that there is a deeper part of you that doesn't touch the stream of time at all—and that part of you is Unborn (it has never entered the stream of time) and Undying (and therefore it will never leave the stream of time, either). As the one and only I

AMness, you are present in all sentient beings and look out through their eyes at the world that you have enacted. Above and below, you are the Only One. And it's in this Onlyness that your infinite Freedom shines.

Because the Witness is totally Free of all objects—not attached to anything in the passing present—it is itself a real Emptiness (empty of all thoughts and all things). This also means that the true Self can never be made an object—the real Seer can never be seen—it metaphorically is what Zen Master Shibayama calls "Absolute Subjectivity"—which is a "Big Subject" or "Big Self" beyond any small subject or small self, not to mention beyond all objects. This is the I-I, the Knower that can never be known; the cognitive Blissfulness that cannot itself be cognized; the ever-present I AMness that cannot be objectified or made into a specific identity with anything. Thus, it can never be bound or limited and is truly, profoundly, and always Free—precisely as you are in your own deepest core. And realize it or not, this is always already the case.

ONE TASTE, ROUND 1

Notice that this True Self, as turiya or the 4th state, is not quite the ultimate, nondual Reality (which is the final and 5th state). This True Self is very real; it's timeless and eternal; it's ultimate and not disputable—but (paradoxically) it's not quite the most ultimate. If we take *self* to mean any sort of sensation that sets itself apart from, or is different than, some sort of "other" (and all selves do), then this True Self could not possibly be a radically nondual Ultimate state, because the Ultimate state is not divided and split into a self versus an other or a subject (not even an Absolute Subject) versus an object. Remember that, to the Witness, the entire world does appear as "other"—it appears "in front." This is why the Witness is indeed an Absolute Subjectivity—it is, in the final analysis, a subjective or a self condition, not a unified or nondual condition. This is exactly why Daniel P. Brown, who names this 4th state "Boundless, Changeless Awareness," also maintains that it is the penultimate state (it is the 4th of his 5 major states), and he says that the illusory part of this state is what he calls "individuality." In other words, turiya introduces the very beginning of the dualistic condition, which is that of a subject versus an object (or individuality, which is accompanied, in Integral Metatheory, by the duality of single versus plural, which gives the 4 quadrants, which are the actual beginning of duality, which if seen apart from ultimate Spirit, is the beginning of illusion). So this True Self is both the very highest reality in the dualistic realm and the final barrier to the ultimate nondual realm. It is the highest pointer and the final obstacle.

This is why, even if you are established in a profound and ever-present Witnessing state, you still have one more (very small) step to go in order to realize your truest and deepest Reality. We saw that both the Witness and One Taste are perfectly Aware of the totality of the Painting of All That Is (and so both of them are correctly referred to, *in the final analysis*, as "ultimate states," so don't let that part confuse you). The Witness has managed to step back from that Total Painting and to Witness all of it with perfect equanimity and an evenly hovering Mirror-Mind Awareness, tacitly and blissfully thrilled with its utter Release and Freedom from all that is, remaining in a condition of radical Emptiness or vast Spaciousness (in itself, a pure nirvana free of all samsara). The Witness is witnessing the entire world as object, and its own Emptiness is the cognizing aspect of each moment, the aspect that "sees," "looks at," or "knows" each and every phenomenon, thus converting them to objects "in front," while the Witness stands Free of them in its own Emptiness.

The required final step into the 5th state of One Taste is to continue Witnessing all of the Total Painting, remaining as an unperturbed Seer who is Looking at each and every thing, and then to gently but fully relax this Witness into everything that is being witnessed. So you go from merely Looking at the mountain to simply *being* the mountain; you no longer see the clouds, you *are* the clouds; you no longer feel the earth, you *are* the earth; you no longer see the sun, you *are* the sun. This nondual Oneness means that the very sensation of being a Looker (or Witness) actually turns out to be utterly *identical* to the sensation of that which is being looked at. In other words, if you feel the Witness or Looker right now, then focus directly on the feeling of what you are looking at—it could be a tree, a car, a building, a computer screen—they turn out to be *one and the same feeling*. Suddenly, "out there" and "in here" both evaporate into "just this"—this single present experience of Thusness or Suchness—One Taste.

There's actually a very easy way to fully realize this nondual state of Oneness. Following Douglas Harding's simple exercise, I often call this One Taste Awareness the "headless" state.[2] Harding's description of this headless state is an incredibly effective pointing-out instruction for getting into One Taste. As Harding himself puts it, notice in this moment that "you can't really see your head"—not directly. If you focus on the area where your head is, all that you will see are two fleshy blobs, which is your nose. But as for your complete head itself, it's just not there; you can't see it. You might feel that you are looking out of your head at the world around you, but your head itself is not something you can see. You're actually "headless."

So here are the pointing-out instructions. While looking out at the world, pick an object that you can clearly see—a mountain, a building, a car, a tree, the book in front of you. Try doing that right now—select an object and look directly at it.

While looking at this object, focus on the area of your head. You will notice that, instead of seeing a head just sitting there on your shoulders, you actually see the object itself—for example, the building—sitting directly right there, on your shoulders, right where your head used to be. The building isn't "out there," on the other side of your face; it's actually arising "right here," on *this side* of your face—the building, in fact, is arising *within you. It is arising in the empty space where you thought your head was.* In fact, *everything* you're now looking at is arising right in the space where you thought your head was—there's no separation at all. If this insight clicks, then you'll realize that, no matter what you are looking at, there isn't an "in here" that is separate from an "out there" that it stands back from and looks at—there is "just this" single experience, which is the object arising on this side of your face right where your head used to be. This is such an obvious experience that "out there" and "in here" actually start to lose any meaning. When we say that "the mountain is appearing on this side of your face, right where your head used to be," all that really means is that there is no separation between subject and object; there is just a single present-given experience, and you are the totality of that single experience (since it is arising "on this side of your face," right where your head used to be, although "this side" and "that side" start to lose all meaning). In other words, moment to moment, *the entire universe is arising within you* (and there is no separate "you"; there is just *this*).

And when everything that seemed "out there" is realized to be arising "on this side of your face," right where you thought your head was, then the very feeling of the space on "this side of your face"—since it is now perfectly one with *everything* "out there"—explodes to include or embrace the *total expanse* of all that is "out there." It expands to include the vast spaciousness of All Space, and you are now totally one with every bit of that All Space (which is arising where your head used to be—except your head, and your own Being, is now EVERYTHING—and Everything is arising exactly where your head used to be). This is the subject/object duality collapsing into a single Nondual unitary experience—One Taste.

I like to quote Trungpa Rinpoche in this regard. He nailed the description of the experience of enlightened One Taste. While explaining what the experience of the final stage of the path, *maha ati*, was like, he said, "The sky turns into a blue pancake and drops on our head."[3] That's very funny, but that's also exactly what it feels like. What you thought of as a "sky" that was "out there" or "up there" is actually a big blue pancake that is sitting exactly where you thought your head was—there's no separation between you and the entire sky—you *are* that sky, and it's sitting right where your head used to be. You can actually *taste* the sky, it's that close.

This simple metaphor—"having no head"—turns out to be a very easy, very obvious pointer to an ever-present Awareness that is a pure turiyatita, a pure One Taste Awareness. By using the gimmick of seeing that we have no head—and that the entire world is actually arising "in here," right where our head used to be—we are plugging into a profoundly deep reality where there is no subject versus object and the world is not idiotically split up into one state that sees and one state that is seen. Instead it is arising as a single totality that is seamless but not featureless. If you feel your "self" ("located" in your head) and then feel this "totality," they are exactly the same feeling (the big blue pancake has fallen on your head)—and thus you no longer witness the world, but you *are* the world. The entire universe is arising within you, where there is no "within" and no "you"—just *this*, just Thusness or Suchness, exactly as it is arising, which is right where your head of "individuality" used to be.

When what Daniel Brown referred to as "individuality" dissolves—because it has become one with everything—then you are indeed in One Taste, the highest and most ultimate state there is. The dissolving of individuality is what I meant by saying, just above, "where your head of 'individuality' used to be." The feeling of being an individual self versus an other marks the 4th state and keeps you out of the 5th state. It is the last barrier to a pure Nonduality, and it happens because you identify with the space right behind your eyes and feel that you are looking out at the world from there, imagining that that is where your individual self resides (your "individuality"). But when the entire sky has turned into a big blue pancake and falls on your head, suddenly there's no room left "in here" for your individuality (because there's no "in here" left at all). The place where your individuality once existed—your head—has now disappeared as a separate something, and so your individuality likewise disappears. It dissolves into a oneness with the sky (and everything else), leaving room for nothing but the unity of the 5th state of One Taste—a Kosmic consciousness or ultimate Unity consciousness. You are One with everything that you perceive—a true One Taste experience. Welcome home!!!

THE WITNESS, ROUND 2

For some different pointing-out instructions, let's go back to the start and take a different approach to both of these Ultimate states.

We begin by resting in our own pure Witnessing Awareness, which is not any content of Awareness. It is an Absolute Subjectivity, which is not an object or a small subject. It is nothing that can be specifically seen; it is just a vast, pure, open, empty Witness or Spaciousness, an Opening or Clearing in which everything is arising moment to moment.

This means that I am also resting in the timeless Now, the Standing Present; and this is not the immediate, passing present, which is different from the past and the future and hence is merely the passing moment, but rather is the timeless Now, which recognizes that all past memories and all future thoughts are both fully occurring in this Now-moment. And so the boundaries to this Now-moment explode, and it embraces all time—all past, all passing-present, and all future occur in, and move through, this timeless Now, this Standing Present. I easily and fully Witness everything from the point of this ever-present, all-embracing, timeless Now-moment, which—

itself Boundless, Changeless, and Unmoving—watches the entire moving world move through the Spaciousness of this timeless Now. As the Standing Present, I watch the passing present. The passing present is in constant motion; the Standing Present does not move.

Thus I disidentify with any and every thing that can be seen, felt, or perceived—resting in my own pure I AMness, where I AM *not* this, *not* that. I am just the simple feeling of I AMness before I am anything in particular. I am pure, free, open, spacious, clear, and empty Witnessing Awareness, and I am Aware of the totality of the Painting of All That Is—while being utterly Free of All of it.

At this stage, I want to emphasize the *all-inclusive* nature of the Total Painting. We want to be aware of everything, to avoid nothing. Our practice should focus on not allowing the slightest avoidance, contraction, grasping, or turning away. If any of these occur, then fine, be aware of them. *Do not avoid any experience whatsoever. Face everything, avoid nothing. Experience all your experience. Let everything freely arise, as it is, just as it is.* This requires no effort at all—on the contrary, it is an entirely *effortless* endeavor. And remember, you can't get it wrong.

Then, as we already noted, you can pursue one of two different paths (namely, you can continue Witnessing, or you can move on to One Taste; we'll pursue continuing Witnessing first, and then One Taste). Here, I want to emphasize that, as a Mirror-Mind Awareness of the Total Painting, you are standing back from all experience, while allowing *all* experience to arise as it wishes. And while standing back from all experience, you simply Witness it. You are not pushing it, pulling it, avoiding it, desiring it, grasping it, judging it, or identifying with it. (And again, if any of these arise, that's just fine, you simply Witness them.)

You are already fully cognizant of this I AMness right now—you are easily aware of the simple feeling of Being. In other words, *you have a clear sense of being you* right now—and that simple sensation of I AMness is the full I AMness; that's it, you're already home. Just remain with that I AM–Awareness, in an ongoing, moment-to-moment fashion, in the Standing Present. This means Witnessing the entire Total Painting as being "not me," as something that my I AMness is not identified with in the slightest—"I have feelings, but I am not those feelings; I am Free of them. I have thoughts, but I am not those thoughts; I am Free of them." All the phenomena of the entire Total Painting become not just "phenomena" but actual "objects." They appear "in front" of the Witness, and the Witness itself is felt as a True Subject, a Real Self, an Absolute Subjectivity, a pure I-I.

The phrase *I-I* is Sri Ramana Maharshi's term for one's Original Face, one's True Nature, one's Real Self—and he used that term because, as the Witness, the pure "I" is, right now, aware of the little "I" or the ego. You can be self-aware right now—that is, you can see the ego, the little "I," because it's not the True Seer, the Real Self; it's just another object that can be seen. The True Self is the Real Subject, which sees all objects, including the little ego or "I," so it's experienced as a pure "I" that is Witnessing the small self or false "I." It's an "I-I"—a pure I AMness aware of the small ego-I, and it is itself felt as a radically unending Clearing, Freedom, Vastness, Spaciousness, and transparent Openness.

There's a very simple test to see if you are doing Witnessing practice correctly. You will know you are doing it right if you find that the relationship that you have to your own thoughts is no different than the relationship you have to exterior objects. That is, the relationship you have to the thoughts that are arising "in you" right now is the same as the relationship you have to that building, that car going by, that tree, those stars, or that computer screen. When you Witness thoughts and you Witness that building, the Witness is aware of each of them in a perfectly equal way—one of them is not "more you" than the other. The inner thoughts arising now are *not* "more you" than the building or the computer screen—they are both equally objects arising in front of your Witnessing Awareness, and you are neither of them. This Witnessing Awareness itself is neither inside nor outside, but *equally Witnesses both inside and outside*. Thus, be aware of inside, then be aware of outside—now equally Witness them both, identified with neither.

In other words, I am not a separate-self sense locked inside my head and existing in a close relationship only with the thoughts, ideas, and images that arise there—and that I often think of as my "self." All of those thoughts and images are simply objects that have pretended to be real subjects, and with which I have therefore inadvertently identified. But I now realize that I can see all of them, so they are actually objects, and I have reverted to the real Subject, the pure Mirror-Mind Witness of them. When I look at any interior thoughts or feelings and when I look at any exterior things or events, the Witness has exactly the same relationship to both of them—they are all equally objects of my Witnessing Awareness—no more, no less. And again, this Witness is neither inside nor outside—it is equally aware of both of them, while itself remaining simply Free, which generates a blissful or joyous release from everything. I check this by going back and forth, back and forth, looking at objects that are "inside" and looking at objects that are "outside," making sure that they are all equally objects of my pure Witnessing—equal reflections of my Mirror-Mind Self.

ONE TASTE, ROUND 2

If you are specifically doing a turiya recognition, then simply continue practicing that Witnessing state, resting in the Standing Present. If you decide to move on to a turiyatita or One Taste recognition, you will want to see the Totality of the Painting not as arising in front of you or outside of you but rather as arising *within* you, *within* your Awareness, *within* your Being—"on this side of your face, where your head used to be." Then you are not Witnessing the Painting; you ARE the Painting. The Totality of it is fully arising within you as this single, unified present moment—it's not outside of you as an object but within you as Awareness. *You are not in this room; this room is in you—this room is arising within your Awareness.* And this means also that you are no longer Subject (even with a capital *S*). You are not Subject or Self; you are simple Suchness, a One Taste unified experience. The sky has turned into a big blue pancake and has fallen right on your head and is now totally one with you, sitting right where your head used to be. It's "within" you, and you fully include both "within" and "without" as One Taste.

This One-Taste Awareness will help stop the acquired habit of standing back from each sensation and hovering over it and instead will recognize the deeper background that enfolds each sensation, so that the world doesn't idiotically exist twice—once as given, and then again as reflected in my awareness. It is given only once, and I do not see that object; I am that object (it is arising right here, right where my head used to be). To repeat how the Zen master put it, "When I heard the sound of the bell ringing, there was no bell and no I, just the ringing."

One of the easiest ways to begin this One Taste recognition is by doing the headless exercise. I'll run through this one more time, quickly, but with some variation, so please don't mind the repetition.

You start by noticing that, typically, you feel like you are "in here," on this side of your face, and the rest of the world is arising "out there," on the other side of your face. Now there is a certain relative truth to that—there is a relative self and a relative other. But underlying both of them is a background, unified state that is not split in two but is unitary (or more technically, a nonduality). When you are aware only of the split between subject and object, that is the *self-contraction*, the restricted, broken, and narrowed entity that is dualistic attention; it is the basic form of Primordial Avoidance itself (because you have to contract against the unity of the present moment in order to split it into an "inside" versus an "outside"—it never starts that way).

So instead of contracting, take some object in your awareness—maybe that tree, or that car, or the clouds out there—and while looking at it, get the feel of "this side" of your face, the immediate feel of the "in-here-ness" that seems to be the location of the sense of yourself as a watcher or looker (we often feel that our "self" exists in our heads, looking through our eyes at the world out there). Steadily feel that "in-here-ness" space for a minute or so. Then, instead focus on the feeling of the objective tree "out there." Feel the sensation of "treeness out there." Next go back and forth a few times between the sensations of "self-in-here" and "tree-out-there," and then suddenly, simply *identify* those two sensations (that is, recognize that in the immediateness of present Awareness, there is only one sensation). Recognize that the "out there" object is actually arising as one with the subject "in here," right where your head used to be. Or, recognize that the object and the subject are *one single experience*, arising right here, right where you thought your head was. Get into this headless state, and then notice that the entire world "out there" is actually arising "in here," right where your head used to be—so that both "in here" and "out there" disappear into "just this," the single, presently arising experience of One Taste.

To help you do this, notice the awareness of what seems to be the *distance* between those two sensations: there is the feeling of "in here," and then—apparently separated from that by a long distance—there is the feeling of the tree "out there." Simply allow that feeling of distance *to disappear*. Allow the distance itself to collapse, so that the tree literally is sitting directly on your shoulders, right here, right where your head used to be, with no distance or separation whatsoever between "tree" and "in here." The tree feels like it is arising "in here," on this side of your face, right where your head used to be. Then simply stay with that oneness, moment to moment, in the Standing Present.

To the extent that there is still a remnant of the feeling of there being an "in here" space, a sense of "on this side of your face," the tree will be arising in that space—that is, the tree will exist "in here," on this side of my face. The tree is arising *within you*. Fairly quickly, that sense of there being a separate "in here" will evaporate and what you feel as "you" (that "self in here") will literally and immediately expand to the entire world of "out there"—these two will no longer be separated. All of a sudden, not just the tree but the entire world that you are looking at *is arising within you*. There is no sense of "within," nor is there a separate-self feeling of a set-apart "you"; there is only the entire world arising moment to moment, and YOU ARE THAT. You are ALL of it. The whole universe is arising within you (and there is no "within" or "you"). In other words, you are one with the entire Painting of All That Is.

So, when the space out there is seen to be arising right here, right where your head used to be, and when those two things become one sensation, one single, present experience (the big blue pancake has fallen on your head), then the space "in here" explodes into a *vast Spaciousness* that includes or embraces the total space out there. It expands to embrace All Space, and what used to be your "self in here" expands to include a vast headless Spaciousness of All That Is. The entire sky is arising where your head used to be, and your head is now where the entire sky used to be. The world does not arise twice—once as "out there" and then a second time when you "in here" look at it, so that you feel that there are two worlds. Rather it arises just once in a single experience, and you are That—a single Suchness, Thusness, or Isness that embraces Everything that is arising. There's no longer a "self in here," because "in here" and "out there" are now directly a headless One Taste. If you are anything, you are All Space; you are All of This, with no inside and no outside, just This—a One-Taste Suchness.

With that, there is no subject versus an object, there is only the presently arising singleness or Suchness of experience, and you embrace absolutely all of it. You do not feel this world; *you-are-the-world* feeling itself. The world is arising not twice but as One Taste.

One of the easiest ways to do this, if you are reading this in a book or on a computer screen, is to practice the headless state as you are reading this. As you are reading this, recognize that you don't really have a head; rather, the reading material is arising right here, right where you thought your head was, and you are actually one with the material itself, it is actually arising in a single space, and you are fully one with that space (this is truly a very real One Taste experience). Then practice reading in that unified headless One Taste state. This might take a little bit of time and practice, we're so used to reading with our head. But stay with it, it's really an amazing experience.

This sense of Oneness is also quite easy to realize while listening to music. Try it. Start by playing one of your favorite songs, let's say, on the radio. Close your eyes. Notice that the music initially sounds like it's coming from "out there," from the radio. Then notice that you can also hear the music as if it's coming from "in here," from deep within your own brain. Then think about everything you have learned about the nature of the Oneness experience, and apply that directly to the sound of the music. Start by dissolving the distance between the music and you—simply dissolve into the stream of music itself, erasing any difference between you and the sound of the music, and hear it as if it were just one single stream of all-pervading music, pushing out any sense of your being a separate self, and uniting fully with the stream itself. There are not two experiences—the sound of music coming from the radio and your listening to it. There is just one experience—you *are* the music in a single stream. (This will be the same experience as you have when you do the "headless" practice.) To paraphrase the Zen master, "When I heard the sound of the music coming from the radio, there was no radio and no I, just the music."

In this state, do a quick experiment. Allow this One-Taste Awareness to expand to infinity. That is, let your Awareness get bigger and bigger, starting from where you are and expanding to include the entire planet, then the entire solar system (the sun, moon, and planets), then the entire galaxy, with billions and billions of stars, and then expand again to include all galaxies, the totality of galaxies. Your Awareness is expanding past all of them and embracing and enfolding all of them as it does so. Then allow your Awareness to completely expand to infinity itself—let it expand to the point where there is an endless beyond, yet your Awareness is aware of even that endless beyond—that utter infinity. Simply throw your Awareness out as far as it can possibly go, to the utter ends of the universe.

Notice, at some point, that the outward movement of Awareness will stop, will come to some sort of an end that seems to be infinity. Why does it stop? How does it even know to stop? How does it know that it is at infinity? And the answer is that it was already there. You know when infinity has been reached because your Awareness is always already infinite. It was already at infinity, and thus it simply recognized itself.

That is just a simple visualization technique that might have clicked, but it also represents a genuine reality—which is that your own primordial Awareness, your own pure Consciousness, is always already absolutely infinite and eternal. There is simply nothing outside of it. This is your Supreme Identity, and that infinite, eternal Reality that your Awareness is is one with Spirit itself. This is ultimate, nondual Unity consciousness, your Original Face, Who and What you really are, always and already. When you practice a simple exercise like the "headless" state, you are plugging into this radical Big Mind, which not only is the unity between you and the tree or you and the music but also contains within itself the entire universe.

Supernovas explode inside your mind; the stars are the sparkling neurons of your brain; lovers everywhere arise within your heart; sentient beings all over the world are in your pure consciousness; your own sense of Being is the limit of infinity itself, which is your own Supreme Identity. At that point, it feels like absolutely everything is arising within your own Being. The entire universe is arising within you, and then "within" itself simply fades away and there is only All This, spontaneously arising, self-manifesting, and self-liberating, and you directly touch and easily embrace each and every single thing that is arising in this and in all of the worlds, now and literally forever (being ever-present at every present). And the entire universe could disappear entirely, and you would still be you, the pure Essence of Being, and nothing ever happens.

This is a colossal Wholeness. Being eternal, a totally timeless and ever-present Now, 100 percent of this eternity is fully present at every point of time. Being infinite, or a totally spaceless Here, 100 percent of this infinity is fully present at every point of space. BE HERE NOW is an old cliché, but it points directly to the fact that you are an infinity underlying and embracing all finite space ("Infinity is in love with the productions of space"), and an eternity underlying and embracing all temporal time ("Eternity is in love with the productions of time"). This is the stunning Wholeness of your Supreme Identity.

And yet, indeed, there is more.

17

The Feelings of Enlightenment

The central point of this chapter is that although Enlightenment has no subject or object, no feeler or thing felt, it does have feelings, Nondual feelings. In other words, there is not just Enlightened Awareness, there is also Enlightened Feeling. We are going to explore those feelings of Enlightenment. I'll mostly use Bliss and Love, but any roughly synonymous terms will do (for example, Joy and Compassion, or Happiness and Care). Not only can you follow your own awareness to Enlightenment, you can also follow your own feelings to Enlightenment.

A BIG BLISS BEYOND BLISS

The release from being confined and suffocated in an isolated, finite, contracted self will open—starting with a pure Witnessing Awareness—to Bliss (*ananda*), all-pervading Joy, deep Happiness, or simply a profound, seemingly infinite well-being. But notice that this is not a bliss that is merely a separate emotion that comes and goes, that has a beginning, middle, and end, and that has an opposite like anguish or misery. This bliss has no opposite but is radically all-embracing. It's not a relative, temporal state but an aspect of an ultimate state, a timeless or ever-present state. It is a capital *B* Bliss that is beyond small bliss and its opposite, misery, and it underlies and persists through both ordinary bliss and misery as they come and go. This big Bliss is simply the feeling aspect of the radical Freedom of the Witness, and like the Witness, it does not come and go but is literally ever-present.

This Bliss beyond bliss and misery is an ever-present quality of the Freedom of the transcendental aspect of primordial Awareness (it's what the radical Freedom of the cognizing Witness feels like), and like the Witness, it is itself ever-present, Unborn, Undying. To put it simply, *this Bliss is the Feeling of the Freedom of the Witness.* Just as the Freedom of the Witness is fully present as it unreservedly and freely Witnesses everything that is arising, this Bliss is equally and fully present in each and every experience as what that Freedom feels like. It's the ecstatic release from all narrowed, broken, and suffering small selves, and it is as ever-constant and ever-present as primordial Awareness itself, never going, never coming, never arriving, never leaving, ecstatically thrilled with every experience that arises anywhere in the universe, since all of them are always already primordially Free. (This involves both a "Freedom from" all manifest constraints and a "Freedom to" Witness anything.)

Freedom—especially in the sense of freedom from something that is constraining—always generates some sort of joy or happiness. When it's Freedom from the entire manifest world, this happiness can be intense indeed, and that is simply Big Bliss by whatever name.

As we stand genuinely Free as the Witness, neither inside nor outside, and allow ourselves to feel into that radical Freedom, we will start to notice—not as an object but as an atmosphere—a profound Feeling of what the Traditions call "Ananda"—that is, Bliss or Joy—the sense of an ecstatic release from this painful realm of tortured and self-contracted fragments. As I am aware of the totality of everything that is arising right now, I realize that I am absolutely

Free of all of it. I am *neti, neti*—I am not identified with any of it, not attached to any of it, not bound to any of it. I have let go of it all; I am utterly Free of any pain, suffering, or torment that it can cause. I am instead this Infinite Space of total Freedom, and simply feeling that vast Spaciousness and its utter Freedom is an enormous Release, an ecstatic Letting Go, a cognitive Blissfulness.

Realizing this ecstatic or joyful Release means that I understand profoundly that even if, say, pain arises, it arises in an Awareness that no longer *is* pain but rather simply Witnesses pain. Pain is no longer *me*; it is *mine*. I have disidentified with it; *it is a subject that I have made object*. And when all subjects have been made object, so that all that remains cannot be made object at all, what remains is Absolute Subjectivity—and as such I am bathed in a radical Freedom that drenches me in a genuine Release and Blissful Joy. So when I am resting in the Witness, I am resting in Freedom, the Feeling of which is Bliss—simply because all freedom elicits joy.

People who have experienced this say that it is a "bliss that can be felt in every cell of the body." Maslow beautifully described this as follows: "One can learn to see in this Unitive way almost at will. It then becomes a witnessing, an appreciating, what one might call a serene, cognitive blissfulness."[1] I really like the phrase "a witnessing, a serene, cognitive blissfulness"—that's exactly it, the serene Bliss of the cognizing Witness. It so nicely puts together the two basic ingredients—the cognizing Witness and its blissfulness. And remember, this came from Maslow's empirical research, so we know that this "cognitive blissfulness" has a grounding in empirical studies.

When I rest as the empty, open Witness—the vast Spaciousness of not this, not that—because there is Nothing left to bind me, and because all Freedom is inherently Joyous/Blissful, I am resting in a boundless expanse of Blissful Freedom. So when I am aware of that tree, that tree is directly arising in the vast, open Spaciousness that is cognitive Blissfulness itself. Bliss sees the tree. Bliss feels the dog.

Bliss thinks this thought. Bliss sees that car. That's the texture of the Witness—a radical Freedom that elicits deep Joy, an infinite Letting Go and Release, a real cognitive Blissfulness.

In the East, it is common to define ultimate Reality as *satchitananda*, which means Being (*sat*), Consciousness (*chit*), and Bliss (*ananda*). Both Being and Consciousness are purely Empty (or Unqualifiable), and thus this Emptiness generates a very subtle feeling, which is the feeling of Ananda or an ever-present Bliss. Since this involves a feeling of Infinity and Eternity, it is a feeling that is different from all relative feelings. It is a feeling that is indeed infinite and eternal, a serene cognitive Blissfulness, ever present, and thus always present.

If I'm still identified with some object or some small-self sensation, I will be bound by that limited identity to the dukkha, suffering, or original sin inherent in this manifest world. Thus any positive feeling (such as bliss) will be touched to some degree by that suffering, and thus will never be a pure positive feeling (such as Bliss). But if I am truly and deeply a pure I AMness, and I am *fully* not this, not that—not any of this or any of that—then the ecstatic Release from the prison of samsara rockets through my Being and a constant background thrill of a genuinely inclusive Big Bliss saturates my state. This Big Bliss is not the small exclusive bliss that exists in time, that comes, stays a bit, and goes, and that alternates with opposites like misery, anguish, and torment, but is an ever-present Bliss that is the very texture of the ever-present Witness. Wherever the infinite and eternal Witness is present, the texture is Blissful. If you are truly Witnessing a torment, pain, terror, or anguish, then not only will it not terrorize you but at its core there will be a constant background Big Bliss, a deep Joy that is the very lining of the Witness itself. To the extent that you recognize the Witness is ever-present, as that Witness, simply look around a bit and you will find—not as an object but as an all-embracing atmosphere—a feeling of deep Freedom, joyous Release, profound Happiness. So it is Bliss that is seeing (or cognizing) that tree—a Blissful Witness is witnessing the World. That is the true texture of an I AMness that has been present for all eternity— Satchitananda—Being-Consciousness-Bliss.

THE FULLNESS OF A BIG LOVE BEYOND LOVE

If the Feeling of the radical *Freedom* of the Witness is a deep, joyful Bliss, the Feeling of the radical *Fullness* of One Taste is an all-embracing Love. This capital *L* Love is beyond ordinary love and its opposite hate; it has no opposite at all but is totally all-embracing. Being ever-present, it is fully present with both small love and its opposite hate. This Big Love underlies and embraces, or truly Loves and accepts, both small love and small hate, and all the other temporal emotions as well. There is an ongoing background feeling of pure Love, which reaches out and enfolds everything in its all-pervading Embrace. While all the other feelings and emotions, whether negative or positive, are running through the passing present with their own dramatic ups and downs, this ever-present Loving background remains steadily the case in the Standing Present. It's how the Oneness of the universe actually *feels*. In short, *this Love is the Feeling of the Fullness of One Taste*. When you are one with the entire World in an ongoing Embrace and Wholeness, you Feel, as a constant background, a total Love, capital *L*. Again, this is an infinite feeling—you are not feeling this because you are loving a particular person or thing but because you are loving *everything*.

This Big Love of the All (*as* the All), with its unifying embrace of everything that is, is a moving beyond all primordial avoidance to a pure undivided or nondual Wholeness. That Wholeness is felt as a pure Love, straight from your own Heart, in a radiant Unity or pure Oneness with absolutely everything that is arising, and everything that is arising is always doing so in a boundless Fullness, an unbroken Wholeness, a genuine expression of pure Love in One Taste.

Big Bliss and Big Love are inherent parts of the Wholeness of Waking Up to infinity and eternity. Even when you are looking at something as simple as a tree, the very perception of that tree elicits and reminds you of an ever-present Bliss that can never come or go, that can never get lost or cease to be, but is the inside lining of every experience *because you are always Free*. When you plug into the feeling tone of the ever-present Freedom of the Witness and realize it as an ongoing background Bliss or deep Happiness, you'll also see that this Big Bliss has been ever-present as well, and previously it bubbled up as the basic little bit of happiness that allowed you to endure the miseries of this world, a small glimmer of what is really your own deepest Nature. But it can be realized directly and fully, and then its ever-present nature becomes as obvious as the Witness itself, "a serene, cognitive Blissfulness." In the deepest part of you, *you are always Free* and will always be free, joyously released and wondrously liberated. This Freedom shoots through every cell of your body as a deep, abiding, Blissful Joy, because indeed you are always Free *from everything*, which is why nothing ever happens.

In the same perception of the tree, as you push through to its core Oneness, there emerges from your Heart an unlimited and all-embracing Love, flooding with infinite care, kindness, and radical embrace not only this tree but of all beings without exception, all of whom are textures of your own deepest Suchness or One Taste. This in indeed *making room for everything*. If you get into a "headless" state, in which the entire universe, as an infinite Wholeness or Fullness, is arising within you, the very Feeling of that Fullness is this vast, ever-present, background Love. *So, just as Bliss is the Feeling of the Freedom of the Witness, this Love is the Feeling of the Fullness of One Taste*. The more that you recognize that this One Taste is always already the case, the more that you also open yourself, if you look carefully, to recognizing that this infinite Love is an ever-present Feeling as well, the ground of all the lesser feelings that might parade by in time. It fully Loves and Embraces each and every one of them as textures of the Fullness of a radically headless One Taste—Present moment to Present moment to Present moment. So beneath all the conventional judgments about experiences that may indeed be relatively true or false, good or bad, noble or disgusting, right or wrong, there is finally nothing in the entire world that you don't deeply and fully Love.

This Bliss-and-Love, which is the feeling tone of ultimate Freedom-and-Fullness, is the very lining of every perception, impulse, sensation, and experience that you will ever have. As you practice both allowing a Witness Awareness to be recognized and noticing the ever-present nature of your own headless One Taste, begin allowing this deep Happiness, or core Bliss, and this pure Love, or total Embrace, to arise as well. Think of it as a Loving Bliss or a Blissful Love—it doesn't really matter—both of them are radically radiating from the deepest center of the timeless Now. Again, this Blissful Love is not an individual feeling or emotion that comes into being, stays a while, and goes, but is the deep, core background feeling, constantly occurring, truly ever-present, moment to moment, under (or with or as) each and every surface feeling that comes and goes. It is the Blissful Loving deep sensation of the Standing Present as it exists under each and every thing and emotion that moves through the passing present. It is an unshakable, unstoppable, ongoing, background feeling that radiates as a spacious Superabundance flowing out of this timeless Now and embracing the entire world.

This Blissful Love is the very core of the Standing Present because this capital *B* Bliss and this capital *L* Love—this Loving Bliss and this Blissful Love—are not typical emotions like love-versus-hate or bliss-versus-misery, which exist in time, and come, last a bit, and then fade, but rather they are the *ever-present* qualities that come with the *ever-present* Freedom of the transcendental Witness and the *ever-present* Fullness of nondual One Taste.

So you will begin to feel, under all your other feelings, if they remain at all, a constant background sense of a whole-bodied Blissful Loving shooting through your entire body from head to toe and smoothly radiating from your own Depths and embracing the world at large. And to the extent that you feel anything, from now on, it is indeed some variation of the basic big Bliss and deep Love of the Witness and One Taste. And both of them are occurring together, because One Taste and its Love transcends and includes the Witness and its Bliss. (For those of you who were impressed with Adi Da, remember that he chose as his spiritual name the words he felt best represented ultimate Reality: Love-Ananda, or Love-Bliss.)

The more that a recognition of the Witness tends to give way to One Taste and stops arising as its own separate reality, the more its Bliss will tend to merge with an all-embracing Love. The Blissful or deeply Happy feelings of the Witness arise precisely because the Witness is radically Free from the entire manifest world. But with the emergence of One Taste, a complete *Freedom from* the entire world has given way to a radical *Oneness with* the entire world. The move from turiya to turiyatita is in one sense a sharp break—Zen says that "the bottom of the bucket breaks." The sense of there being a bottom to the bucket—that is, a solid bottom to Awareness, any sense of there being a subject or witness in awareness at all, any sense of there being a solid self in here that looks at the world out there—acts as the primary dualism that prevents the truer Unity or Nonduality of One Taste. When the Witness disappears as its own set-apart Reality and thus becomes one with the entire world through the unity of the "headless" condition, it returns to being the inherent aspect of a pure nondual Awareness that it always is, which is the cognizing or knowing dimension of a Nonduality or One Taste.

Likewise, when that happens, the Blissful feeling of the Witness tucks itself into the Loving Fullness of One Taste—hence the Loving Bliss or the Blissful Love of any ongoing moment-to-moment

Reality. The Blissful Freedom of being *Free from* everything does indeed merge into a Loving *Oneness with* everything. The sense the Witness has of standing back from the world, resting in its own blissful freedom, and witnessing the entire world arising "in front" of it, merges into a sense of a radical loving Oneness with the entire world, which is now arising fully, not in *front* of it but *within* it. Especially if you get into a headless unity state, there is still the sense of a Witnessing Awareness, but it's fully *one with* the entire world that is arising *within* its own unitary, headless Awareness. There's no longer a Subject or even an Absolute Subjectivity standing back from everything; there's simply a nondual Suchness or Thusness, with subject and object being fully one, so that the world "out there" is arising fully within your own Awareness (right where your head used to be). There is still a sense of Blissful Freedom, but that Blissful Freedom reaches out to, and embraces, with a huge Loving kiss, every single thing and event that is arising anywhere. Both within and without give way to a single headless One Taste—and that is a Loving Bliss and a Blissful Love, Freedom embracing Fullness with all of its being. You're no longer free from the world, you're headlessly one with the world, whatever that world might be—gross, subtle, causal, turiya, turiyatita, or all of them.

If you have trouble getting the Witness together with One Taste—that is, practicing Bliss and Love simultaneously—I will provide some instructions on how to do that in chapter 19, in the section "The Ultimate Unity of Bliss and Love." In that section, you will learn to get into a headless unity state first—in which all the objects "out there" are directly felt to be arising "in here," right where your head used to be, so much so that "out there" and "in here" are directly felt to be one, singular, a unitary experience of "just this." Then take exactly the place where you feel the tree out there is actually sitting "in here," right where your head used to be, and identify that with an all-embracing feeling of love, so that the entire world is felt to be arising within that headless, unitary Love. Simply feel your headless condition to be fully one with an all-encompassing Loving awareness. Feel this unity of the headless state to be an all-embracing Love for everything that you are aware of. In this nondual, unified, headless state, your Witness will now have collapsed into, and become one with, this One Taste condition, so that the Bliss of the Witness has now also become one with this headless Love. Thus, as you look out at the world, do so through a Blissfully Loving awareness. In other words, you start to feel the Love generated by your own headless One Taste to be fully suffused with Bliss—a truly Blissful Loving headless One Taste.

Now notice that the feelings of Bliss and Love are typically present in the act of sex (at least as finite, relative, conventional bliss and love, but often they explode into their ultimate forms). Sexual Tantra uses those feelings of conventional bliss and love as pointers to an ultimate Bliss and Love. That's the topic that's up next. We'll see that the feelings that usually occur with sex—namely, a blissful ecstasy and a loving oneness (that is, a finite sexual bliss and love)—can be used to recognize, remember, and enhance the ever-present Bliss and Love of your own True Nature. Sex is not a sin against Spirit but a direct road to Spirit. And this will very likely change your relationship to sexuality forever.

18

Integral Sexual Tantra

We now move to a new area that is fascinating and definitely important—namely, Tantra. Tantra involves a series of very effective practices and pointing-out instructions that involve uniting sex and Spirit, and thus evoke an underlying and ever-present Nonduality or ultimate Reality. And we will find that this is directly connected to Big Bliss and Big Love.

There are dozens of different schools of Tantra, and they vary enormously. But it is generally agreed that the very highest schools of Tantra (such as those manifested in the upper reaches of Kashmir Shaivism and Vajrayana, or Tibetan Buddhism) are perhaps the most sophisticated and profound of all of the world's Great Wisdom Traditions. Tantra came to fruition from the eighth to the eleventh centuries in India, especially at the amazing Buddhist Nalanda University, but Tantra itself is not confined to Buddhism. In fact, variations on the major themes of Tantra can be found to some degree in most of the Great Traditions. Tantra was a profound culmination of the defining drive of evolution itself, namely, to transcend and include.

So let's look very briefly at the history of Tantra to see exactly what is involved. Since there are Buddhist forms of Tantra and I have already gone over the history of Buddhism, I will be repeating some things that I have already covered. But this is important in order to see exactly how—and why—Tantra evolved in the first place, and why it transcended and included most previous religions.

Early Buddhism began as virtually all the great Axial-period (or great Mythic-Age) religions around the globe did: with a belief that the entire manifest world is rotten. It is samsara, inherently fallen, drenched in original sin, or what early Buddhism called *dukkha*, suffering. The manifest world of samsara is inherently marked by suffering. Wherever there is a manifest world and a sentient being, that sentient being is suffering, and there's nothing whatsoever that can be done about it. However, one can get out of, or off of, the wheel of samsara altogether. In order to do this, one takes up a specific type of meditation, which is aimed at an exhaustive witnessing of the contents of consciousness, until one directly discovers the source of consciousness or awareness itself—that is, one discovers a pure nirvana, discovers the pure empty Witness, which itself is free of all objects, free of all manifestation, free of all samsara. The discovery of this purely formless, contentless, empty awareness is the discovery of *nirvana*, which is a timeless state radically free of all suffering, all ego, all desire, and all pain, because it is free of manifestation itself in any form. (It's somewhat like the deep dreamless state.)

So the aim of early Buddhism was straightforward: samsara (or the manifest universe itself) is inherently suffering; therefore completely drop any and all activities having anything to do with samsara, take up meditation, and discover the pure witnessing Awareness. Because pure Awareness is radically free of all objects and all manifestation, residing in the emptiness of that state is a pure liberation—the pure Freedom of the Witness—free from all self, all desire, and all suffering. Having realized the Witness as an ever-present part of awareness, one takes up permanent residence in its ever-present Freedom. And that permanent residence in Freedom from all samsara, Buddha called *nirvana*.

And by the way, as I previously pointed out, nirvana is a very real, very profound state of consciousness—a state of pure unmanifest absorption, where one rests so completely in pure empty consciousness that nothing whatsoever even arises in awareness. This state is also called *nirvikalpa samadhi*, and its culmination is the state of *nirodh* (pure cessation or extinction)—that is, nirvana—and it's so real that if you are in it, you literally cannot feel any pain at all. No pain whatsoever, no matter how intense. If this seems hard to believe, remember the protesting Vietnamese Buddhist monk who sat placidly in meditation while he immolated himself. Nirvana is very, very real; and it does exactly what it claims to do—it radically frees you from all pain and suffering.

But is this state of nirvana the highest state? As we saw earlier, the Buddhist genius Nagarjuna answered this question by saying, "No." It is not the highest. It is the highest state in dualistic realms, but they are ultimately laced with illusion. Nirvana is split from samsara; Emptiness is split from Form; Heaven is split from earth. This clearly is not a holistic, unified, nondual state—it's a fragmented, broken, dualistic state. And a broken state cannot give you a real and full Enlightenment.

Looking back on it, we can see that what Nagarjuna was aiming for was not nirvana (as early Buddhism was) but shunyata, a state of pure Nonduality and One Taste, which transcended and included the lesser state of nirvana and did not split nirvana from samsara but unified them in a deeper, nondual Wholeness (although "Wholeness," like all terms, was, strictly speaking, inapplicable). Nagarjuna had himself discovered this deeper state, and so he knew the nirvana state was actually limited and less than ultimate. So Nagarjuna ushered in the Nonduality revolution, and—as a yet greater evolutionary achievement—this state did indeed transcend and include the lesser states of samsara and nirvana in a greater state of nondual Wholeness. There was no longer a nirvana split from samsara but a deeper, nondual Wholeness that fully included both; and there was no longer the world of Emptiness split from Form but a deeper Wholeness that fully included both. The *Heart Sutra* would soon summarize this as "That which is Emptiness is not other than Form; that which is Form is not other than Emptiness." In other words, that which is nirvana is not other than samsara, and that which is samsara is not other than nirvana. Moreover, all the opposites that had been taken to reflect a supposed duality of nirvana versus samsara—for example, infinite versus finite, good versus evil, eternal versus temporal, spirit versus matter, and spirit versus sex—were now unified as well (that is, taken to be nondual, or not-two).

This changed absolutely everything. All of a sudden, the things that were supposed to prevent Enlightenment were unified with (or nondual with) the things that caused it. The very things you had taken to be sinful were in fact one with Awakening; the very things that you had been avoiding were things you were supposed to embrace. All of a sudden, wherever these nondual insights emerged, there was a profound shift in religious practices from ones characterized by puritanical renunciation to ones characterized by transformation. (And most religions at the time were indeed puritanical. As I pointed out above, most schools of Deity mysticism, Formless mysticism, and I-AMness mysticism recommended celibacy and other various forms of puritanical renunciation.)

In early Buddhism, for example, if you had a defiled emotion like anger, you would apply all sorts of antidotes to it, trying to suppress or eliminate it. In Tantra, on the other hand, if anger arose, you simply embraced it with a nondual One-Taste Awareness, and it immediately *transformed* from the defiled emotion of anger to the transcendental wisdom of clarity. It did so because nirvana and samsara are not two—defiled anger and awakened clarity are not irreconcilable opposites fated to fight forever, but they are two aspects of the same underlying reality. Enlightenment comes not from chasing one of those opposites and denying the other—running after half of the universe and trying to get rid of the other half—but by transcending and embracing them both. Instead of a list of hundreds of desires, impulses, images, and ideas that a person was supposed to suppress and puritanically renounce, the primary rule of Tantra is very simple: *Bring everything onto the path.* This is a pure, all-embracing turiyatita practice, and it shook the spiritual world to its very foundations.

Thus, where the goal of the early Buddhist path was to be an *arhat*—a "solitary realizer" who had fully renounced samsara and escaped completely into nirodh, or pure nirvana, totally oblivious to the manifest world and all of its suffering beings, having vanished forever into the pure extinction of nirvana—the goal of the new Nondual path was to become a bodhisattva, whose primary vow was a promise NOT to disappear into nirodh or nirvana, never to appear in samsara again. The bodhisattva vowed to see the unity of nirvana and samsara and thus remain in the world of samsara helping all other beings to see that the reality of samsara was itself not-two with nirvana—in other words, a vow to help all sentient beings Awaken.

The bodhisattva vow is often phrased as "I vow to recognize Enlightenment as quickly as possible so I can help all sentient beings realize Enlightenment as well." It was, at its core, a promise to stay not in nirvikalpa samadhi, nirodh, or pure unmanifest cessation but in sahaja samadhi, or nondual unified One Taste. It was a promise not to get into a meditation that was so oblivious to the manifest world that you could watch the planet decline ecologically and not be concerned (it's just samsara) but to get off your mat and help the planet and those people around you who are in such suffering. And you help them the most by helping them Awaken—and awaken not to nirvana but to the unity or nonduality of nirvana and samsara.

You can probably see how spirituality would begin to change profoundly as a result: from finding a way to get out of this world to finding a way to be fully in it, from finding a Heaven not of this Earth to finding a Heaven on Earth, and from seeking a Spirit that repressed the flesh to a Spirit that fully inhabited the flesh. This, truly, was absolutely revolutionary.

We have already seen that many Indian tantric initiations included what were called "the five *M*'s," which were five items that Brahmanical Hinduism had pronounced sinful and were to be totally renounced and avoided, for example, alcohol, red meat, parched grain, and especially real sex. (The names of these things in Sanskrit all begin with an *m*, hence "the five *M*'s.") But these things were not avoided in tantric initiations; in fact, *all of them* were intentionally and deliberately included and practiced in the initiation—and that definitely meant sex too. You could hardly make the point any clearer: the fundamental belief for any truly Nondual realization is that there is only Spirit; there is only God; there is only the One without a second in all directions, and thus the One is not something hard to find but impossible to avoid—there is nothing that is not Spirit. And thus everything that you thought prevented Spirit is actually an ornament and a direct manifestation of Spirit itself; it is not to be suppressed or denied but embraced and celebrated—"Bring *everything* onto the path, because there is *only* Spirit."

And so, in this regard, Tantra became very well known for the practice of sex as a means of spiritual realization, although that constitutes only a small part of its teachings. But the sexual practices and their direct relation to Spirit that Tantra discovered were indeed revolutionary. These practices included things like the awakening of kundalini, a subtle sexual energy said to be coiled like a snake at the bottom of the spine, which when awakened, travels up the spine and unites with an infinite Light, Consciousness, and Spirit lying within, above, and beyond the head. It helps to remember that these discoveries were a direct result of Nagarjuna's original identification of nirvana and samsara, so that the things that most religions had taken to be diametrically opposed—such as infinite and finite, Heaven and Earth, Spirit and sexuality—were seen to be, in fact, two sides of the same coin of ultimate Reality. Thus you could most certainly use one to realize the other—for example, sex does not prevent Spirit but is a direct path to Spirit. The truth of Tantra stems directly from the truth of Nonduality—Spirit and flesh, infinite and finite, Emptiness and Form, nirvana and samsara are indeed not-two.

Tantra got the reputation, in many places, of being the super fast and super easy (and super fun) path to Enlightenment. The typical path to Enlightenment involved cognition, awareness, and intense willpower. In Zen, for example, you might concentrate on a specific koan, like "Mu," and you would use your willpower to concentrate on that day in and day out. If you do that nonstop for three or four years, at some point you will likely get a satori or realization of Oneness or Nonduality. For some people, with Tantra, you essentially engage in sex and let it take its course. Which do you think is easier? The most fun? (Actually some of the tantric visualization practices are as complex and detailed as you can possibly imagine, but the point is, the ultimate driver is blissful sexual energy or kundalini, not just willpower, and this indeed provides a powerfully easy booster.)

A BRIEF NOTE ABOUT TANTRA

I want to emphasize the special way that I am using the term *Tantra*. Although tantric essentials are basically similar the world over, there are some important differences. I've mentioned the brilliant Buddhist Nagarjuna several times. Well, Shankara is to Vedantic Hinduism what Nagarjuna is to Mahayana Buddhism—namely, a genius of Nonduality, a supreme master of the Nondual in theory and practice.

Nagarjuna was not a tantric practitioner himself—he was a master of Nonduality. So when Tantra—which is Nondual—was first developed in Buddhism, it often drew on Nagarjuna's Nondual insights. The same with Shankara. He himself was not a tantric practitioner—he was a master of Nonduality—and thus when Hindu Tantra developed, it was similar to some of Shankara's brilliant insights. I rely on both of them, as does the Integral view itself.

But I am presenting *Integral* sexual Tantra, so it is an integrated mixture of the Integral Framework and all sorts of tantric theory from around the world. This is not Buddhist Tantra per se, or Hindu Tantra, or Taoist, or Christian. It does, however, draw on an integrated mixture of the best principles from the various tantric schools worldwide (including work from Nagarjuna, Shankara, Chuang Tzu [Taoism], and many other masters).

So keep that in mind, especially if you're an expert on any particular Tantra. I have integrated the essentials of nondual Tantra with the best of Integral Metatheory to produce a super Tantra that combines the best of each.

THE USE OF RELATIVE BLISS AND LOVE IN TANTRA

There are two feelings in particular that are associated with the sex act that Tantra especially focuses on. There are, of course, many feelings associated with sex, but two stand out: (1) There is a warm, loving, embracing feeling—a heightened sense of becoming one with another being, and this feeling of love and loving oneness can be overwhelming at times. And (2), there is, especially with orgasm, a feeling of ecstasy, bliss, explosive joy and release—it will put a grin on your face and is generally taken to be the most fun you can have with your pants off. This love-bliss of sexuality is so overwhelming that there are many thinkers (including Freud) who believe that the sexual drive is the strongest drive that human beings have; and many also claim that it is the fundamental élan vital that moves the entire universe.

But notice, we have already seen that the fundamental feeling tones of ultimate Spirit itself are Love and Bliss (capital *L*, capital *B*). This is no accident. According to the Great Traditions, the qualities of Spirit (that is, qualities in a metaphoric sense—in other words, saguna Brahman) emanate from it and manifest or create stepped-down, lesser versions of themselves in the finite, manifest world—which is the method whereby the universe is created. So both Big Love and Big Bliss, metaphoric characteristics of ultimate Spirit itself, step down into the manifest, finite world and give rise to, and appear as, the lesser love and lesser bliss of sexuality itself. By virtue of Nonduality, they are directly connected. Just as transcendental clarity and small anger are directly connected in ultimate Reality, so Big Love and small love, Big Bliss and small bliss, are two ends of the same stick; or more appropriately, the north and south poles of a single magnet. By plugging into one, you can directly and immediately plug into the other. That is the core principle behind the famous tantric sexual practice.

At this time (2022), I am creating a very detailed course in Integral Tantra, as part of a major presentation of Full-Spectrum Mindfulness. So if you are interested in this practice, please keep an eye out for it (see the website for Integral Life, www.IntegralLife.com). But I'm going to present, in a slightly simpler form, some of these practices in the next chapter, so you can try them out for yourself and see exactly what's involved. And you can easily incorporate these tantric practices into your own ongoing Integral Life Practice (or any other spiritual practice you might have). The fundamental background ideas of this Integral Tantra are fully and faithfully grounded in tantric traditions from around the world, but much of the presentation itself is significantly unique, and some of these practices are entirely new and are generated by the insights that come with the Integral Framework. So with that in mind, here we go.

19

The Practice of Integral Sexual Tantra

RECOGNITION IN TANTRA

There are numerous types of tantric *practices*. For example, and to focus on male sexuality for just a moment—there are practices that separate orgasm from the act of ejaculation, so that it becomes entirely possible for a man to experience several orgasms one after another—without ejaculating. (This was another fascinating discovery made by tantric practitioners, which used bliss as part of their spiritual practice.) Having multiple orgasms without ejaculating could be used to bring about an explosive expansion of bliss from out of the genital region that engulfed the whole body and then spilled out of the body into the entire world—a whole-bodied orgasm with a world-engulfing bliss. These practices (by both sexes) are always coupled with breathing exercises that instead of allowing sexual sensations to orient downward and outward, deliberately refocus and guide them to move inward and upward. That is, with the out-breath, they move them from the genital area to the base of the spine, and from there up the spine to the brain itself, and then even beyond the brain to the infinite Light and Consciousness at and beyond the crown. Then on the in-breath, the entire sequence is reversed. The woman does the same thing, moving any sexual sensations (on the out-breath) from the genital region to the base of the spine to the crown and beyond to the entire Kosmos, and reversing the sequence on the in-breath, bringing the Light and Consciousness down from above and into the crown, then down the face and the body to the genital region below.

Not only is Tantra said to be the fun and easy path, it is, in some tantric traditions, said to be potentially quite dangerous, simply because it is so powerful. I have taken all of these dangers into careful account, and my version of Integral Tantra has few, if any, of them. I have practiced Tantra myself for some forty years, and I know all of these dangererous spots quite well by now, so I knew exactly what to leave out. It's not only that I have deliberately left out most of the dangerous parts but also that the Integral framework provides so much balance that the dangers seem to drop out. All I can say is that I have been teaching Integral Tantra for almost thirty years, and none of my students have had any of these dangerous episodes occur. I take this part of Tantra very seriously, and I can, with a fair amount of certainty, assure you that you have little to worry about.

Typical tantric exercises take at least a month or two to start having any effects; they rewire certain circuits in the brain (via neuroplasticity). And these *practices* or *exercises* take a fair amount of effort. They are complex and do take some time before you will see results.[1]

In contrast, Integral Tantra isolates those aspects of this expanded bliss and loving oneness that are indeed ever-present, which you can realize right now and certainly during any sexual activity that you wish. We're going to focus on those *recognition* or *pointing-out instructions* right now—they are, in any event, the real core of Tantra itself.

One small piece of background information: when you breath out, visualizing awareness moving up the spine, rising above and beyond the crown of the head to an infinite release into Luminous Freedom and infinite Consciousness, is getting in touch with turiya, the infinite Witness, pure radical Freedom, with its inherent Bliss. Then from that stance Above, you breathe in, breathing in that infinite Light and Consciousness from Above down and into the crown, bringing the Bliss with it, and then down the face (with mouth fully closed), into the throat and chest, and then into the abdomen and genital area. Thus the infinite Light Above (which is pure Witnessing Awareness) is brought down and into all of the Life Below—a combination that evokes the unity or Fullness of One Taste, turiyatita, whose Love is available to hug and embrace the entire World.

That combination of Light and Life, Freedom and Fullness, with its Big Bliss and Big Love, provides the specific force and drive of the loving-bliss that is sexuality. That is how they are connected. In other words, the Blissful Freedom of the Witness and the Loving Fullness of One Taste are the ultimate spiritual qualities that directly manifest as the blissful-love of sexuality, which is why the latter can most definitely be used to climb back to the former. Thus, sex doesn't prevent Spirit: it is a direct road to Spirit.

Since this involves the two highest states (the Witness and One Taste), the current of Life-up-and-into-Light and then Light-down-and-into-Life is an ever-present circuit of divine Energy. The Taoists call it the "microcosmic orbit," since it is reproducing currents in the body that are said to drive the entire Kosmos. And this is indeed *ever-present*, this union of Freedom and Fullness, Bliss and Love, and its constant circulation throughout the body-mind.

The relationship between this ultimate Blissful Love (capital *B*, capital *L*) and the relative bliss and love that's found in sexuality is important. First of all, small bliss and small love have opposites: bliss has as its opposite something like misery, anguish, or torment, and ordinary love has as its opposite hatred, hostility, some say fear. But

Big Bliss and Big Love are infinite; they have no opposites; they're nondual—they are a capital *B* Bliss beyond the opposites of ordinary bliss and misery and a capital *L* Love beyond the opposites of ordinary love and hate. And they are not temporal, merely coming and going; they are eternal, that is, ever-present. Since small bliss and small love are finite and temporal, they do indeed come and go; they arrive, stay a while, then fade. They have boundaries, insides and outsides, limits, and beginnings and endings. But Big Bliss and Big Love do not come and go at all; they are the ever-present feeling tones of the ever-present Freedom and Fullness of the ever-present Witness and One Taste. They are feeling tones that underlie (Witness and Unify) and are fully present with small bliss and misery, and small love and hate; in fact, they are fully present with all opposites and emotions as they constantly parade by in the passing present of Awareness. They are among the ultimate realities that are always already fully present, the Bliss-Love that is the texture of this timeless Now.

But how can we truly recognize this Presence?

This is precisely where the experiential practice of sexual Integral Tantra comes in. Integral Tantra uses the relative and finite feelings of sexual bliss and love to remember and recognize the ultimate and eternal Feelings of spiritual Bliss and Love. It uses sexual bliss and love (which come and go) to directly recognize spiritual Bliss and Love (which are ever-present). In short, it uses the *practice* of sex to *recognize* Spirit. So, after all that background, let's start.

USING SEX TO RECOGNIZE THE BLISSFUL WITNESS

I will begin by distinguishing Bliss and Love (since they technically belong to two different ultimate states—namely, the Witness and One Taste), approaching them one at a time, and then I will reunite them (which is their ultimate Reality or Condition anyway). At that point, if you are having trouble practicing them together, I will provide some instructions to help with that. I will start with the Big Bliss (deep Joy or core Happiness)—the "serene, cognitive Blissfulness" of the Witness.

When beginning sexual activity (and this can be straight, gay, lesbian, trans, bi, or any other form), begin by resting in the Witness, since we're focusing on Bliss.

Make sure that, as the Witness, your relationship to your body is exactly the same as your relationship to your partner's body. The Witness, remember, is not more identified with feelings that occur "in here," in your body/brain, than it is with objects arising "out there." The Witness is neither inside nor outside—it evenly and equally Witnesses both inside and outside and is itself merely Free. So you can check if you are Witnessing correctly by making sure that, as the Witness, your relationship to objects arising "in here," in the interior, is exactly the same as your relationship to objects arising "out there," in the exterior—both interior and exterior are Witnessed exactly the same. So make sure that, as the Witness, your relationship to your body is just the same as your relationship to your partner's body—they are both equally objects of your Witnessing Self, and you are identified with neither. You can even see both bodies as being one single body—but in any event, you are not identified with either one. You are the pure Witness in all its Freedom (I am not this, not that—I am Free from this and Free from that). If you cannot get fully into the Witness, get as close to it as possible, and then engage in the sexual practice however you wish.

The one thing you want to do differently is that even though, as the Witness, you are not identified with any objects at all but are merely their pure Witness, *nonetheless*, in this specific *practice*, begin to take any feelings of pleasure or bliss, no matter where they originate, and directly identify them with the Witness. That is, feel the pleasure, then "feel" the Witness, and then identify those two sensations—the immediate feelings of pleasure or bliss and the feeling of the pure Witness. Allow that pleasure to begin to see the world; allow that pleasure to begin to Witness the world. We have already discovered that, ultimately, the Blissful Witness or a serene cognitive Blissfulness sees the world, and that is where this sexual practice is headed.

If you have trouble making this connection between Bliss and the Witness, it often helps to remember that we are aiming for what Maslow called "a serene, *cognitive Blissfulness*"—which points to two aspects of the Witness, its Knowing (or cognitive) part and its Freedom/Blissfulness (or feeling) part. These really aren't different "parts" of the Witness; they are two different names for it when we conventionally look at it from two different perspectives (the perspective of knowing or cognizing and the perspective of feeling). So, in this practice, you start to work toward the "blissfulness" part by identifying any pleasure or bliss that you have with the cognizing or knowing part of the Witness. Even though the Witness is a Cognizing Awareness, not anything cognized, in this practice, you are going to identify any pleasure or bliss that arises with the knowing or cognizing part of the Witness since you are aiming for a "serene, *cognitive* Blissfulness." So, as any pleasure or bliss arises, identify your own Knowing awareness with it, and then "Bliss is seeing the world," "Bliss is touching my partner," "Bliss is making love," and so on. Don't worry, this won't disrupt the totally Free nature of the Witness, because the Witness contains a total Freedom/Blissfulness aspect already, and that aspect is completely Nondual, Empty, and All-inclusive. Identifying it with conventional pleasure is just a beginner's step—it won't affect the infinity or eternity of the Witness; it will simply help to remind you of and evoke the real Bliss underlying it.

Tibetan Buddhists call the Witness an "ongoing knowingness." The "knowingness" is the cognitive part, and the "ongoing" is the always ongoing, ever-present, or eternal part. However, this phrase is used in a very special way by Tibetan Buddhists. They mean that when you are feeling this ongoing knowingness, you separate the feeling of knowing from anything that is known. In other words, you want just the feeling of knowing, not knowing something or knowing this or that—just the pure feeling of knowing itself. After all, *the Witness is a pure Knower, not anything known*. And further, the "ongoing" part doesn't leave any room for knowing this, knowing that, or knowing some object, because no object is ever-present or eternal—all objects keep moving by in the passing present, in the world of time. So an "ongoing knowingness" means an "ongoing, ever-present Witness, which is also an "ever-present cognitive (or knowing) Blissfulness" (especially when we identify the Witness with any pleasure or bliss that arises).

To finish this part of the recommendation, when you are in the pure Witness, you are in an ongoing knowingness—an ongoing sense of knowing, not anything known (anything that is arising is just fine)—except that, for this practice, you are identified with any pleasure or bliss that is arising. Get into this ongoing knowingness, and then start identifying any pleasurable or blissful feelings that arise during sex with the feeling of this ongoing knowingness, since you are aiming for a serene, cognitive Blissfulness, which is what this exercise will evoke in you.

When Bliss is identified with the Witness, one could say things like "Bliss sees (or Witnesses) the world," "Bliss sees that building," "Bliss touches the tree," "Bliss feels the dog," "Bliss is making love," and so on. These are all perfect examples of Bliss being a *cognitive* Blissfulness and thus actually doing the cognizing, knowing, or seeing. In other words, this is Bliss being fully one with the knowing Witness—it's a Witnessing Blissfulness, a cognitive Blissfulness, or a knowing Blissfulness. The idea is simply to get the two "parts" of the Witness together—the knowing (or cognitive) part and the feeling (or freedom/blissfulness) part. We have already spent a lot of time on Freedom as being an inherent part of the Witness, so that part should be easy. Now we're working on the blissfulness part by pointing out that Bliss is the inherent Feeling of the Freedom of the Witness. An easy way to remember these two parts is to recall Maslow's phrase "a witnessing, a *cognitive Blissfulness.*" If you have been practicing a Witnessing awareness, you already have the cognitive part down; now all you need to do is add the Blissfulness part.

And that is just a warm-up for the main event.

As orgasm approaches, relax your body into its present feelings, and prepare to take the intense feelings that arise with orgasm and directly apply them to the Witness. As you feel the beginning of intense orgasmic bliss, feel that the bliss is the same as your Witnessing Self, and look at the world through this Blissful Witness. Feel that orgasmic bliss to be one with the Witness itself; feel that bliss to be the very texture of the Observing Self, the very nature of the Seeing Self, and feel that bliss/Bliss looking at the entire world through the Witness in all directions.

In other words, use the small bliss of sexual release to remind you of, evoke, and even enhance the Big Inclusive Bliss that is already present in the very nature of the Witness itself. You are using the intensity of a small temporal sexual bliss to point to and evoke a timeless, ever-present Big Bliss. Feel that sexual bliss, and feel deeply into the Witness as well, and let that intense sexual bliss remind you of, and point to, an infinitely bigger and larger cognitive Bliss that stretches to infinity. That small bliss will eventually come to an end; that Big Bliss will not. Use that transitory, small bliss to evoke, resonate with, remind, and even bring forth that ultimate Bliss or cognitive Blissfulness that is always already the case.

This is a *practice*, which means you should do it over and over until it starts to click. Use the felt qualities and textures of sexual bliss, and transfer them to the Witness. Feel the Witness as having those qualities of bliss, and then *Witness the world from that Bliss*. Allow I

AMness to become that Bliss—that's a true cognitive Blissfulness. As you identify that bliss with the Witness itself and begin to look at the world through the eyes of a totally Blissful Witness, that bliss will start to evoke Big Bliss, because it is tapping into the qualities of the ever-present, infinite Witness itself—it is actually evoking the ever-present, infinite Big Bliss of the true Witness. And thus, as cognitive Blissfulness, I-I witness my body; as cognitive Blissfulness, I-I am aware of my partner's body; as cognitive Blissfulness, I-I see the bed we are on; as cognitive Blissfulness, I-I am aware of the room arising within my own Blissful Awareness. The radical Freedom of the Witness generates a Bliss that finds even samsara ecstatic. I am not in the bedroom; the bedroom is arising within me, within my own Blissful Awareness. I am not in the bed; the bed is arising within my own Blissful Awareness. I am not lying next to my partner's body; both my body and my partner's body are arising within me, within my own Blissful Awareness. *And I notice that, indeed, all of them are arising in a Field of deep Blissful Awareness.* The bliss of sexual ecstasy has reminded me of, evoked, and even enhanced the ever-present Bliss that is the very core of my true Witness, and so, as the Blissful Witness, as cognitive Blissfulness, I see the entire world. Every sensation, every feeling, every thought, arises within a Field of Blissful Witnessing. The entire World is nothing but a modification of this timeless Bliss. And this capital *B* Bliss, because it does not come and go, continuously underlies the coming and going of all lesser feelings (this is indeed the "ongoing" part—the ever-present part—of the blissful Witness). This is the awareness of an Ecstatically Free and deeply Blissful Witness.

As the temporal, sexual bliss fades, keep that bliss/Bliss in memory and continue to apply it to the Witness. Integral Tantra calls this an "orgasm memory": every time you have an orgasm, identify that bliss with the Witness itself, and when that orgasmic bliss fades, identify the memory of that bliss with the Witness itself. Throughout the day, as you practice Witnessing Awareness, whenever you are in touch with the Witness, immediately apply the memory of intense sexual bliss to the Witness, and allow that cognitive Blissfulness to observe the world. Allow the ecstatic thrill of sexual orgasm to be felt as the very Witness that is watching the world. Directly feel that. You, as Bliss, Witness it all. That's the real meaning of cognitive Blissfulness.

You can do this orgasm memory right now. Get into a Witnessing awareness—or as close to it as possible—and remember the intense bliss of an orgasm. Then apply that blissful feeling to the Witness, and look at the world through that blissful Witnessing, that cognitive Blissfulness. It's fairly easy, yes?

To return to the sex act itself—as the small bliss continues to fade, keep a sharp eye out for that larger Bliss that does not fade. Allow that small bliss to resonate deeply with an Awareness in you that is ecstatic at being liberated from all anguish, suffering, and pain. That nirvanic Release is an ecstatic realization, and it is much bigger than the small bliss of sexuality because it exists ever-presently, eternally, and there are no limits to it—it doesn't just pop into existence, stay a bit, light your lights, and then disappear. It is the eternal core of the infinite Freedom that is your own cognizing Awareness, the Original Face that you had before your parents were born—and that Face has a really Big-Bliss smile.

Now, just as Big Bliss is said to have stepped down from the original quality of pure Spirit into the manifest world, resulting in a temporal, limited, finite sexual drive, so too the original intensity of this Big Bliss has also stepped down by several degrees, so that it is usually felt to be weaker than sexual bliss. Thus, for most people, the intensity of the bliss of conventional orgasm is, at least to begin with, significantly greater than the Big Bliss of the Witness's Freedom. Thus, when you practice transferring the feeling of sexual bliss to the feeling of the Witnessing Self, it will feel like it is enhancing or magnifying the feeling of ever-present Bliss. This will indeed give you a hint of the intensity of Bliss that you will begin to feel as you more deeply fall into the realm of the pure Witness and its (nirvanic) Freedom. As you begin to vibrate more with the Bliss with a capital *B*, its original intensity will indeed eventually overtake and outshine that of finite sexual bliss. And frankly, when that happens, many people stop having ordinary orgasms, because they are such a letdown, and do nothing but waste bioenergy.

In any event, the exercise uses the small, relative, finite bliss of sexual orgasm to remind you of, evoke, and enhance the ever-present Big Bliss of your own pure Awareness—a genuine cognitive Blissfulness. This will directly connect Spirit and sex, and using sexual bliss to recognize, remember, and enhance the Big Bliss of Spiritual Awareness is an application of tantric principles. Notice, too, that, for many mystics around the world and throughout history, by far the most-often used analogy for the state of mystical union is that of sexual union. Mystics claim that sexual union is the closest analogy to mystical union because they are indeed directly connected—sex is not something that prevents the presence of Spirit; it is a direct manifestation of, and a road that leads straight to, Spirit itself. This understanding is the fruit of that original insight that first drove Nagarjuna to the understanding of Nonduality (and similar realizations start to appear in Western mystics as well). The ultimate Reality of sex and Spirit is not-two—and there it is.

USING SEX TO RECOGNIZE LOVING ONE TASTE

The same thing applies, across the board, to Big Love and the loving oneness of sexual union. We want to use the immediate feelings of sexual unity and the warm, caring, loving feelings of oneness that arise during sex to remind us of, evoke, and enhance the Big Love that arises from the radical Fullness of a pure One Taste. These two loves are indeed connected—the love that is present in sexuality is a stepped-down version of the timeless Loving Oneness that is ultimate Spirit.

So get into a stance of One Taste and nondual Suchness, using whatever means work best for you. I recommend the headless exercise for a start, so I'll include some comments on how to use the headless condition in the instructions I'm giving. (See the section "One Taste, Round 1" in chapter 16, "Pointing Out the Witness and One Taste," for instructions on how to get into the headless state.) But you don't have to use the headless experience if you don't want to; just get into a One Taste experience using any means that you care to. If you can't quite get into the state of One Taste, that's fine, get as close as you can, and then proceed with the instructions. The loving feelings evoked during the exercise will themselves act as pointers—concrete pointing-out instructions—that will help you to spot and recognize the deeper, ever-present, radical Loving Oneness that is already perfectly present as a profound background reflecting the utter Fullness of your own One Taste (just as your own headlessness is already happening and is fully present in any event, whether you realize it or not).

As you engage in sex, if you in One Taste to some degree, then everything that is arising will already feel like a texture of your own Being, a modification of your own Awareness, and you are all of that. If you are using the headless exercise, then you will already tend to be one with the entire world, which will be arising right where you thought your head was. But whether or not you are using the headless exercise, be sure to heed the following instructions—they will have important effects on you. You want to pay particular attention, within that all-embracing Big Space, to the feelings of warm connection, deep care, and loving embrace, and particularly to any of the feelings of warm, loving oneness or loving union with your partner. If you are truly in a One-Taste Awareness, then these feeling of loving union will already be arising within the even larger Space of a timeless Loving Oneness. That's fine; at least to start, it may appear that this loving sexual union with your partner is more intense that the ever-present Loving Fullness of your own One Taste, which applies not just to your partner but to everybody and everything. This strong sexual feeling of warm unity will definitely give you a direct hint of the intensity and outrageous Loving Fullness that you will begin to feel almost constantly as you more deeply and directly awaken as real One Taste and pure Suchness.

To summarize, begin by using the small, relative, finite, loving union of sexual oneness to remind you of, evoke, and enhance the ever-present Loving Oneness of your own nondual Awareness. During sex, whenever you feel the intensity of any sort of loving touch, care, tenderness, or, especially, loving unity or oneness, focus on that feeling of oneness and apply it to the Fullness of One Taste.

Even if you have not yet fully accessed the state of One Taste, this practice is still simple: get as close as you can to One Taste, begin sexual activity, and right at the moment that, for example, you feel an overwhelming loving oneness for your partner—"I love you so much I can't stand it!"—take that intense love-feeling of oneness, and allow it to expand and fully apply to the entire World. Even if you are doing the headless experiment and are one with the World, which is in unity with you and your headless state, allow the *intensity* of this feeling of loving oneness to apply to your own unified state with the World. Thus, looking at that vast expanse "out there," feel that "I love you so much I can't stand it!" and throw yourself into a direct unity with the World—"I love you so much I *am* you!" Whenever you wonder exactly what it would feel like to be one with the entire World, just think of your feelings of being one with your partner and then expand those feelings to embrace the entire universe. (And do this even if you are in a headless one state—you want to transfer this *intensity* to your headless one state condition.) Or, use those feelings of loving oneness with your partner to recognize and feel a similar Loving Oneness that is already present in your Heart and already embraces the entire World—this is your own ever-present One Taste.

Either way, allow your feelings of sexual loving oneness to expand to the entire universe. "I *love* it All! Because I *am* it All!" At the very least, start with the first of those two statements, and feel that "I *love* it All!" In other words, take up the stance that you are *making love to the entire world*, and get a hold of that feeling. Thus, as you are making love to your partner, particularly if and as a true feeling of loving oneness with your partner arises, simply expand that feeling of oneness to the entire World.

In short, transfer your feeling of loving your partner to One Taste's Love of (and as) the entire World—*go from thinking and feeling that you are making love with your partner to thinking and feeling that you are making Love with the entire World.* Realize that you're fully One with all of it.

One of the easiest ways to do this is indeed to use the headless exercise: As you are making love with your partner, notice the entire visual field of the whole world arising around you, and then realize that the entire field is actually arising "in here," right where you thought your head was, and that you're one with all of it. Then as you feel the unity of that headless state, take the warm feeling of love that you have for your partner and transfer it to the entire visual field and all of the "objects" that are in it, all of which are now arising right where your head used to be.

The headless experience collapses your subject and object into a unity of awareness by putting the entire world "out there" into a oneness with "in here," right where your head used to be, which is a real version of One Taste. Then, when you take any loving feelings that you have for your partner and transfer them to the total unity that the headless world now offers you, this brings together a real love (for your partner) and a real state of unity (in the headless condition)—which makes it very hard to miss or ignore the Loving Unity of One Taste. And this bringing together often will directly evoke a Loving One Taste in you.

You are bringing together the genuine love that you feel for you partner and a genuine, nondual, headless oneness to provide a Loving Unity of One Taste. You feel the love that is arising right now for your partner, and then, while feeling that, you also notice that in your visual field, you are one with the entire world. This loving aspect—which is the part that is added when you take the present feelings of love for your partner and bring them into the headless state of unity—might have been missing when you practiced the headless exercise by itself. Since that loving feeling and your oneness with the world are now arising together at the same time, this love-plus-unity experience is essentially the same as the Loving Unity of a One Taste, which you will likely start to remember, evoke, and become aware of.

In other words, this will intensify the warm feelings of One Taste—it will increase the amperage of the loving feeling that the Fullness of One Taste generates. Allow these sexual love–feelings to *expand* and apply to the *entire World*, which I am one with and that is arising right here, right where I thought my head was. The Loving Fullness of One Taste is always already doing this right now anyway, and so you can actively search in your awareness for that Loving Radiance that is already overflowing and embracing the entire universe in the Oneness of a radical Love—and hence recognize your own ever-present One Taste, directly arising as your own headless state of Unity, which is now a Loving Unity.

As with bliss, retain a memory of this intense feeling of loving oneness generated during sex, and throughout the day apply it to your Awareness as One Taste (or as a headless One Taste, if you're doing that version). You want to evoke, resonate with, remind yourself of, and yes, enhance your feeling of loving oneness with the entire World—and so allow the feeling of your sexual union to do just that. It is important that the feeling of loving your partner expands to the feeling of loving the entire world. (At least move from "I'm making love with my partner" to "I'm making love with the entire World!")

With tantric practice (whether headless or not), we want to take the feelings of loving oneness that arise during sex and immediately identify them with One Taste itself, so that, even if I am just "looking" at a tree, or reading this material, those things are arising in the field of unlimited and unitary Love that I-I am. The very union that I have when the tree or this reading material is arising where my head used to be—when the big blue sky-pancake has fallen directly on my head—is *felt* as a direct and intense Love, because that is what it is: a fundamental union, and union is the very nature of any type of Love.

And so, right where the tree or the reading material or the sky touches me in a pure Oneness, right where my head used to be but is now a vast All Space containing everything, is infinite Love—intensely embracing, a caring kindness, an utter adoration, an outrageous eroticism of radical Oneness. And this applies even to something as simple as a tree. That Love as Loving Oneness, which is ever-present, is something that I start to recognize and remember.

So when I am making love and I start to feel a oneness with my partner, or our bodies start to merge and fuse together, or the love for my partner becomes so intense that begin to dissolve as a separate self, then I let that love spill out of me and move beyond my partner till it embraces the entire World. I am then fused with the entire universe in exactly the same way as I am fused with my partner. I am applying that sexual union to One Taste, and the entire universe is arising within me, in my headless, unitary condition and my radically Loving Embrace.

Here's another way to think of this practice: I take all my feelings of erotic sexual oneness and disperse them evenly throughout the entire field of present Awareness. I move from "I'm one with my partner!" to "I'm one with the World!"—I am headlessly one with everything. In this way, the texture of One Taste, which is a radical Fullness felt as deep Loving Oneness, is immediately evoked and enhanced by this sexual feeling of love. The very atmosphere of intense sexual embrace is spread evenly throughout my Awareness, and hence the oneness of Awareness with every object that it touches—which is ALL of them—is immediately felt as an erotic, outrageous, loving Oneness—which hugs the entire universe in a state of exuberant Love. And it is the overflowing embrace and startling intensity of an intimate loving Oneness that can't get any closer that is remembered, evoked, and enhanced as I transfer and expand all of those feelings from a sexual embrace to the very atmosphere of One Taste itself.

Thus, where previously a separate "I"-sense would see the distanced "tree out there," in One Taste, the unity of I-see-the-tree is what now *sees itself*, a fully headless condition, with no inside and no outside, "just this"—and this Suchness, Thusness, or Is-ness radiates a subtle feeling of Love in all directions (a love transferred and expanded from my partner to the entire world in a headless unity). This is no longer the feeling of conventional love, where I especially love a *particular* person or thing, but a feeling of infinite Love because I love *everything* with no exceptions. It is, after all, an infinite and eternal Love, which is why it feels so different from conventional love. For the same reason, infinite and eternal Big Bliss can feel things that ordinary bliss cannot feel, which is why Big Bliss, even though it is an ultimate Freedom and is therefore neti, neti, can still be felt as Ananda or Big Bliss. That's an important point worth remembering.

Hence, I no longer simply see the tree; I Love the tree—more accurately, both I and the tree arise in the Field of Love that is Suchness itself, and I am all of that. But "all of that" is becoming warmer and warmer as the ever-present Love that is its true texture is becoming more and more recognized. And this is exactly what happens when I take the sexual feelings of loving oneness for my partner and apply them immediately to the Field of Unitary Awareness. This present moment's Suchness begins to increase, radiate, and vibrate with the Love that moves the sun and other stars. There is literally nothing arising anywhere that I don't deeply Love—not a single thing, anywhere.

Imagine a life drenched with that much Love, radiating in all directions, saturating you and everything else in its all-pervading path! This Love spills out of the union between me and my partner, and precisely because its own Source is nothing less than the all-pervading Big Love that is Spiritual Wholeness itself, that feeling of warm, sexual oneness can literally embrace the All. It can spill out of me and my partner and fill the entire room, spill out of the room and fill the entire building, and expand from the building to the whole planet, the entire solar system, the universe itself—and I am That. I very simply am just That, and I disappear into the all-pervading Love that is Spirit.

As my Awareness touches each and every thing and knows that thing by being it—by being immediately one with it (just like I am one with the big blue pancake sitting directly where my head used to be)—that Oneness itself is increasingly recognized as the subtle embrace of an infinite Love. "I am one with the mountain" means "I Love the mountain, which I am." Also, I Love that building, I Love those cars, and I Love those people walking by; I Love the rain, I Love the wind, and I Love the blistering sun. And—perhaps shockingly—I Love the ozone hole, I Love global warming, and I Love that terrorist attack; I love Hitler, I Love Stalin, and I Love Mao Tse-tung; I Love this anger, I Love this pain, and I Love this agonizing shame. This Love is absolutely *all-inclusive*, embracing every single thing and event in a radiant Field of timeless Love, thrilling me with its ecstatic care, its adoring kindness, and its perfectly felt (headless) Unity.

These things happen because this Love and Bliss are just names for the ultimate Ground of All Being, and absolutely everything that exists—good and evil, right and wrong, Adolph Hitler and all—have this as their Ground, or they simply would not exist in the first place. This kind of Love is often called "unconditional Love"—and it is indeed infinitely unconditional, which means that it Loves everything that arises with a 100 percent acceptance—not 95 percent, not 99 percent—but 100 percent, absolutely everything. Nothing is rejected; all is fully accepted—and that is exactly what a Nondual or ultimate Unity consciousness does. There are no empty spaces left in my heart, because the entire universe has taken up residence therein.

As that realization deepens more and more, as you begin to be drenched in the overflowing Fullness of Big Love, and as the truly infinite dimensions of Big Love become more and more recognized and undiminished, the superabundance of that infinite Love will eventually outshine and overcome the limitations of any finite sexual embrace. When that happens, there is again a major shift in how sex is approached. It is no longer used as a means to some end—whether to express a small personal love or provide release from tension—but instead is seen as a pure ornament and manifestation of that Love that does indeed move the sun and other stars. At this point, some people will stop having ordinary orgasms, because they're so constricting. Others will use orgasmic sex as a pure expression of that all-pervading Love. But one thing is certain: never again will sexuality be viewed as an obstacle to Spirit.

THE ULTIMATE UNITY OF BLISS AND LOVE

The fundamental point is that every time you have sex, you are on a road that leads directly and unerringly to a profound Spiritual realization, a very profound Wholeness. You are being shown an ecstatic bliss and a real love that are connected directly and immediately to the Big Bliss and Big Love that is their own Divine origin. And just as sexual bliss and love are usually intertwined and arise together, so Big Bliss and Big Love are seen to be, particularly as they progress, coemergents of one's own deepest Condition. As a Loving Bliss and a Blissful Love, they resonate deeply and directly with your own authentic Suchness in this Standing Present, textures of this timeless Now.

Notice how Bliss and Love fit together and what each brings to the conjunction. When I add Love to Bliss for a Loving Bliss (or Bliss infused with Love), the sense of Bliss—which includes variations such as a deep Joy or a core Happiness—expands out of itself and begins to embrace the entire world. Usually Bliss is impervious and oblivious to the world, because it is connected with the Witness, which itself is totally detached from the world. So Big Bliss is equally detached—that is, it is equally Happy no matter what happens "in front" of it in the objective world or how it happens—Happy is Happy, no matter what. This nirvanic Release could witness its human form burn to ashes on the ground without even blinking, it's that Free from the exterior and interior world. In other words, the Bliss that is inherent in the Witness is likewise Free from all events happening around it in the world—it is indeed impervious and oblivious.

But when that Bliss (or Joy or Happiness) is suffused by, and united with, Love, it begins to reach out of itself to embrace the world—it wants the world also to be Happy, because now it Loves the world. *Loving* Bliss is a Bliss that embraces, enfolds, and enwraps the entire world, an ecstatic Bliss that is in Love with the whole world and all of its inhabitants and in all of its ups and downs, joys and sorrows, amusements and sadnesses. Bliss united with Love is no longer detached and oblivious; it's absolutely All-Embracing.

So check this out by simply imagining, right now, that you are deeply Happy—you are in a state of genuine Joy, a radiant Bliss. There is no reason for this; you are just overflowing with Bliss—no matter what's going on out there. One with the Witness, you are totally detached from the World, which simply passes by "in front" of you, while you remain overflowing with a Blissful Happiness, totally aware of everything that is happening around you but attached to none of it. You are simply filled with Bliss, and as a Freedom-filled Bliss usually is, it is impervious to the world.

Then imagine the entire world starts to impinge on your blissful Awareness, and you see your own Blissful Happiness reach out and begin to hug, embrace, and enfold the entire world and all of its inhabitants. You spread this infinite Bliss to each and every one of them. All of them, now radiantly Happy, are enfolded in your own all-inclusive Blissfulness. They are all arising as gestures within your primordially Blissful Awareness, and you are all of this—a Loving Bliss happily embracing the All.

The easiest way to do this is to remember the headless exercise. As you begin Witnessing the world—totally separate from it—you then notice that it is actually arising "in here," on this side of your face, right where your head used to be, so that you are actually *one* with the world. Then simply realize—and directly feel—that the unitary oneness of this headless condition is itself the deep feeling of an All-Embracing Oneness or a genuine Love—or, in this example, a Loving Bliss.

And notice that, in this visualization, Big Bliss does not lose its radical Freedom just because it has become one with the entire world. Since this Bliss is one with Love and the two of them are fully joined, they each bring their own characteristics to the union—Love brings its Oneness, and Bliss brings its Freedom.

In short, Love brings to Bliss a sense of radical Oneness, Fullness, or Wholeness—a Bliss-drenched Kosmic consciousness. Think of it as a chocolate-covered universe—the entire world indeed is One Taste, and the taste is deliciously and blissfully Divine—as I said, chocolate.

On the other hand, when Bliss is added to Love for a Blissful Love (or Love infused with Bliss), it's still true that Love starts out deeply in Love with the world and *one with* it as well. When that loving Embrace and infinite Unity becomes a *Blissful* Love, Bliss injects it with an infinite Delight, a radiant Thrill, a smiling Exuberance, Happiness, and Bliss that radiates throughout. Notice that when most people fall in love, at first it is often a wild happiness and blissful delight. But as love continues forward, the more intense it becomes, the more often it can bring feelings of jealousy, anxiety, even suspicion, because love is just a feeling-one-with; it doesn't matter whether that oneness is happy or sad. If you really love somebody, you love them whether they're happy or sad. And sad it often is, since love generates states of worry, tension, upset, and drama. As Woody Allen put it, "Love causes tension; sex relieves it."

In other words, what relieves the tension of love is the *bliss* of sex—that is, the genuine happiness of a real Bliss. So a *Blissful* Love is pushed permanently into the Happy camp. Whether there's sadness in the world or not, the inclusion of Blissful Freedom releases Love from any lingering attachment or grasping and returns it to an equanimity of Loving all equally —and the Joy and Ecstasy that it evokes. This is a Blissful Love, happy to be the ever-present texture of the Fullness of One Taste. And that is what Bliss brings to Love—an ecstatic Joy or Happiness in the midst of it all. There is not just a Wholeness (which Love will provide) but a *Happy* Wholeness of a *Blissful* Love.

SUMMARY

We have the Freedom of the Witness, which is felt as Bliss, and that Blissful feeling is simply the feeling tone of the total transcendence of the world and all its suffering. This is felt as a core Bliss, or as a deep Joy, or as an ongoing Happiness, or as any such similar Ananda feeling. It is the deep feeling of a purely liberated nirvana, totally free from samsara and ready to burn its human form to the ground without even flinching. As the Witness is transcended (but included) in the even greater Wholeness of One Taste—which unifies nirvana and samsara in a nondual Suchness—the Bliss of the Free Witness is increasingly merged with the total Loving Fullness of One Taste. This Loving feeling itself is the profound resonance now arising in a Consciousness that is one with absolutely everything there is—whether manifest or unmanifest, formed or formless, finite or infinite, negative or positive, light or dark, happy or sad, ecstatic or miserable, joyous or wretched. There is nothing outside the radical Fullness of this Nonduality. As long as "feelings" have any sense in this context, Happy Fullness is felt as a Blissful Love, embrace, unity, oneness, spaciousness, and wholeness. The self-contained, impervious feelings of Bliss, Joy, and Happiness, which are the core of nirvana and nirvanic freedom, give way to profound feelings that do not stand back from the Kosmos but reach out and radically embrace it, the most typical of which is a Blissful Love.

And with that, the isolated and set-apart nirvana becomes one with the entire world of samsara in a deeper nondual Suchness or One Taste, and Bliss gives way to a Love that transcends and includes it. Thus there is a Loving Bliss and Blissful Love. You will start to feel Bliss and Love together as coemergent, as together they come to be the most dominant feeling tone of the ultimate, timeless Now of one's own True Nature—the true feelings of Enlightenment.

Pragmatically, this means that whenever you feel Bliss, don't just rest imperviously in its own self-contained delight, but expand that Bliss to a loving embrace of the entire world—hence, Loving Bliss. And likewise, whenever you feel Love, make sure to inject it with a real Happiness, so that you are feeling a truly Happy Wholeness, a Joyous Fullness, a Blissful Love.

This is important, because Bliss and Love are the most common feelings elicited by the two highest or ultimate states of consciousness—turiya and turiyatita—and thus evoking both feeling tones together is an important part of our lives. Or perhaps I ought to say, it should be an important part of our lives.

To bring Bliss and Love together using the headless exercise, do the following: Get into the headless state, where the entire World is arising "in here," right where you thought your head was, and you are totally one with the World. Then take that unity—that oneness that is sitting right where your head used to be—and recognize that it is itself a feeling of deep and all-inclusive Love. You are already in full oneness with the World—it's sitting right where your head once was—so simply feel that unity, all of it, as being a state of pure Love or Loving Oneness. This isn't hard. Because you already feel one with the entire World arising where your head used to be, simply feel that unity as being a Loving Oneness that is in a complete unity with all of that World—you're already one with it, simply feel that oneness as also being a Love-filled Oneness. You're already one with that World, now just fall in Love with all of it. And add that Loving feeling to the already present unity, so that not only do you have a Oneness, you have a completely Love-filled Oneness (or a Oneness that is felt as being a completely pure Love, a Love-drenched unity).

After you establish that Loving Oneness, then bring in the feeling of a happy Bliss, and insert that Bliss into the Loving Oneness. Again, this is a matter of what you are feeling and a matter of your capacity to bring in different feelings as needed. You've already brought in Love to your headless unity; now you also want to bring in a Blissful, Happy, or Joyous feeling as well, and add that to the Love. To the already present Loving unity with the entire World, add a sense of Blissfulness to it. This will give you the sense of a Blissful Love, and you will feel this

Blissful Love for the entire World that is arising "in here," on this side of your face, right where your head used to be.

These are, so to speak, the mechanical aspects of arriving at a Bliss-and-Love of the entire World, by sort of plunking one of those feelings on top of the other. The idea of using Tantra is to help realize and intensify these feelings of Bliss and Love, but by using a more organic Tantra, and using it with real organic sex.

When we do that, we use the passing-present feelings of sexual bliss and love to recognize, remember, evoke, and enhance the ever-present Big Bliss and Big Love. As guiding lights, these sexual signposts are unmistakable and unerring, and they are freely and fully given to you every single time that you make love. (Indeed, it is because these signposts are unmistakable and unerring that mystics the world over use sexual love as a metaphor for Spiritual union.) And you can carry the memory of that blissful, loving sexual state into the practice of the day, where it will continue to remind, evoke, and point directly to the ever-present Loving Bliss and Blissful Love that is your own deepest Condition and eternal birthright. This is given to you every single time that you have sex. SEX! Who just died and went to Heaven? It looks like we all have, with this Tantra.

In short, the Bliss-and-Love of pure Spirit gives rise to the temporal bliss-love of sex; it is a manifestation in the dimension of Life of an infinite radiance in the dimension of Light. Put simply, sex and Spirit are directly connected, and sex, far from being an obstacle to Spirit, is actually a direct manifestation of—and therefore a direct road that leads straight to—Spirit itself. And thus, in Integral Tantra, we use the feelings of bliss and love, as they spontaneously arise in sexual encounter, to remember, evoke, and enhance the Bliss-and-Love that are the ever-present Feelings of our nondual Awareness, or real Spirit itself.

Hence, the feelings of bliss and love that arise during sex are an unerring road to Spiritual realization, and sex itself becomes a true form of prayer. And, along with Integral Tantra, I recommend that you pray often. You really can't pray too much. Pray every day, if you can.

In fact, using Integral Tantra, the more often you pray, the more likely you will be to Wake Up, and Wake Up to a truly spiritual Wholeness.

So pray often . . . live long . . . and prosper.

And once you Wake Up to a true spiritual Wholeness, be sure to include that along with a full Showing Up, Growing Up, Cleaning Up, and Opening Up to uncover a genuine Big Wholeness. The good news is that each of those areas are already present in your awareness right now, and therefore you can, in this very moment, discover a profound meaning and purpose right in the midst of your own life. Engage in making room for everything in your experience and in your world, filling it up completely and totally, and thus be as contented and as fulfilled as you can be. Finding a truly Big Wholeness in the very core of your own being, you will *never again* feel empty, hollow, worthless, vacant, meaningless, pointless, emptied-out, or unfulfilled.

Hallelujah and welcome home! I've very much enjoyed taking this journey with you, and I wish you the very best in your future life, which will be as fulfilling and overflowing with meaning as I'm (now hoping) it will be.

Afterword

It is important to realize that all your various areas of development—that is, your Waking Up, Growing Up, Opening Up, Cleaning Up, and Showing Up—are fully available to you right now. You can achieve a direct realization of each of them in this moment, or, at the least, enough of an understanding of them to know where to look for each of them. This means that you have access to a very real Big Wholeness, right here and right now—if, as I've often said, you know where to look. And after going through this book, I believe that you now do know where to look for each of these components of a genuine Big Wholeness, and thus you can begin to incorporate this Big Wholeness into your own life, starting right now.

I mean, just look at the areas that we have covered. We started with the "not disputable" reality of Waking Up, where you could awaken to your own ultimate Reality in this very Now-moment. Because it's the "biggest" part of a Big Wholeness—aiming as it does for a full Kosmic consciousness or ultimate Unity consciousness—we returned to it at the end of the book and devoted several chapters to it, but we did indeed start with it.

Then we added an understanding of the importance of Growing Up, and the fact that, because the stages of Growing Up were discovered only very recently, there is no Wisdom Tradition anywhere in the world today that includes them. Understanding the stages of Growing Up also let us fully see the main difference between traditional religions, which usually have some portion of their beliefs anchored in an egocentric magic or ethnocentric mythic-literal stage of development, and modern science, which usually is founded in some degree of worldcentric, universal rationality (even if it did tend to reduce everything to a scientific materialism). That also helped us to understand the important difference between spiritual *experience* (which is a direct experience of a genuine Waking Up) and spiritual *intelligence* (which is the spiritual thinking or religious response given by any stage of Growing Up).

We also noted that every stage of Growing Up does indeed contain one of the multiple intelligences known as "spiritual intelligence," which addresses questions in the finite, relative world such as "What is ultimately real?" or "What is of ultimate concern for me?" Most people in the modern and postmodern world think that all spirituality originates in a mythic-literal world, whereas only the magic-mythic forms of religion do so—which is why the approach that we presented is indeed "spiritual but not religious" (where "spiritual" applies not to forms of Growing Up but to forms of Waking Up).

By running through all 6 or so of these major stages of Growing Up, you can see not only at what stage you are at in this evolutionary process but also where you are headed, which is toward some sort of an Integral or systemically unified stage. With your understanding of the wholeness added by each stage of this evolution, you could then add Growing Up to your own Big Wholeness.

We then looked at Cleaning Up the shadow material (or unconscious processes) that you generate at each stage of Growing Up (and Waking Up). This shadow material is made of all the things in the world that you genuinely loathe (or in the case of a golden shadow, all the things that you excessively love), because they represent facets of your own psyche that you have split off and disowned. And then we saw that the 3-2-1 process could be applied to virtually any shadows that you have, thus unifying your psyche with that split-off material—and hence adding the holism of Cleaning Up to your overall Big Wholeness.

We then turned to Showing Up, making room for all the important dimension/perspectives in our world—that is, including all 4 quadrants in our own makeup. There are two Left-hand quadrants (the interiors or subjects) and two Right-hand quadrants (the exteriors or objects), as well as two Upper quadrants (the singular or individual) and two Lower quadrants (the plural or collective), and thus the 4 quadrants provide access to the inside and outside of the individual and the group. By including all of them, we make sure that our Big Wholeness is truly "big" and inclusive.

Next we briefly examined Opening Up to an awareness of all our multiple intelligences, the various *lines* of development that grow and evolve through all our major *levels* of Growing Up. We saw that these lines or intelligences had evolved in human beings over the course of evolution because they addressed the many fundamental questions that life kept throwing at us (for example, moral intelligence addresses "What's the right thing to do?"; emotional intelligence "What am I feeling?"; cognitive intelligence "What am I aware of right now?" spiritual intelligence "What is my ultimate concern?"). Psychologists believe that there are about a dozen of them, but many people are unaware of these multiple intelligences, and thus they don't ever think about using them. But when include Opening Up to all of them in our own makeup, this expanded awareness becomes a valuable part of our Big Wholeness and adds immeasurably to it.

We then circled back to Waking Up, both because it is perhaps the most important and foundational aspect of a genuine Big Wholeness and also because it is, in a sense, the "biggest" part of any Big Wholeness, since it seeks to unify and integrate the entire subjective realm with the entire objective realm for an ultimate Unity consciousness or a total Kosmic consciousness—and that's *really* big.

We also wanted to visit the significant idea that, in terms of multiple intelligences, the state of a pure Waking Up or Enlightenment possesses not only a cognitive intelligence but also an emotional intelligence. That is, there are definitely the feelings of Enlightenment—in particular, the Bliss that is the feeling of the Freedom of the Witness and the Love that is the feeling of the Fullness of One Taste. These are the feelings of the two ultimate states of consciousness (turiya/Witnessing and turiyatita/One Taste), and thus, along with those states, these feelings are ever present or eternal, which means you have access to them in each and every moment, including right here and right now. Hence, you can add them, right now, to your own Big Wholeness.

Finally, in relationship to a genuine Waking Up, we closely examined an Integral sexual Tantra, looking for the eternal or ever-present aspects of that Tantra, which could be realized right here and now. We found that Tantra uses the relative feelings generated by sex—the feeling of a blissful ecstasy and the feeling of a loving oneness—to help elicit and enhance the ultimate ever-present feelings of Bliss and Love. So you can also add them to your own sense of Big Wholeness.

I began this book by pointing out that since there are areas of Wholeness that aren't at all obvious, if you want to be a "holist"—a believer in the complete Unity and Wholeness of the universe—you have to include all of them. But you can include them only if you know where to look. But once you know where to look, they will become very obvious—including Growing Up (a Wholeness that becomes obvious when you include all the important *levels* in your life), Opening Up (including all the important *lines*), Cleaning Up (including all the *shadow* elements), Waking Up (including all the important *states*), and Showing Up (including all the *quadrants*).

I think we've seen enough to understand that those areas of Wholeness are not just sitting around waiting for all and sundry to see and discover them. They really do demand a certain type of active looking in order to find them. But when and if you do that, they can all be included in not just a holism or wholeness but also a very expansive, all-inclusive Big Wholeness.

Incorporating this Big Wholeness into your own life will result in the resurrection of a genuine meaning in your life. This is because *meaning* basically means "wholeness." That is, *to have meaning* signifies to "have access to (or be one with) something significant or meaningful"—and thus a Big Wholeness will give you access to—and deeply connect you with—a genuine Big Meaning. With this Big Meaning, you are, in a sense, making room for everything in your life—all the split-off parts and aspects of yourself are brought together into a vivid and glorious Wholeness, which results in a meaning that is altogether profound and out-of-this-world, if you will. Everything in your experience comes together to pull you into this deep meaning, where you feel in touch not only with all the important aspects of yourself but also with everything in your world. At that point, nothing exists outside of you, and thus everything in your world is deeply embraced in this all-inclusive Big Meaning—and ultimate Unity consciousness—that opens up for you. Everything you see and everything that you touch have a genuine and deeply worthwhile significance and value for you.

And thus gone is the tyranny and misery of a life lived alone, gone the shallowness and terror of a life without hope or value. By making room for everything, everything takes on a real meaning and purpose. And right here, at the core of your own life, being one with the world means that the entire world will take on a new, deep, and profound meaning and importance.

This is a meaning that can be found immediately in the midst of your own everyday life, right here and right now. So never mind the sorrow and the pity that you thought your life was all about, and welcome to a world full of glory and presence, significance and value, splendor and promise, purpose and worth. The entire universe opens up to you as a source of profound meaning and value, because now you have made room for all the world in your own awareness—you are directly touching and embracing all of it. Your life is about making room for everything, because your own existence is made of everything. From now on, you will never run into an experience anywhere in the world that is disturbing, foreign, alien, or frightening, because you have indeed made room for all of it.

This is a radically unprecedented opportunity. It is a tomorrow of infinite possibilities. It is a future of unending potentials. And it is a world that you can step directly into—by starting down a path of Waking Up, Growing Up, Opening Up, Cleaning Up, and Showing Up—and beginning that right now. This is your outrageous destiny, your gorgeous glory, your everlasting horizon, a path without date or duration, on a road without aim or goal, toward a realization without beginning or end.

Please take care.

NOTES

INTRODUCTION

1. Here, I should point out, for technical readers, that I am equating *Wholeness* and *Spirit* very carefully. I do not, for example, mean pantheism (which equates the sum total of the manifest universe with spirit). I am using *Wholeness* in the general sense that Nagarjuna in the East used *Emptiness* and Plotinus in the West *the One*—in either case, the emphasis is on the radically unqualifiable nature of ultimate reality (which would include that definition as well). As Nagarjuna put it, "It can be called neither 'Void' nor 'not Void,' but in order to point it out, it is called the 'Void.'" The point, for both of them, is that words, concepts, and symbols just won't work when it comes to knowing ultimate Reality. Instead, one must have a direct and immediate experience (not an explanation) of it in order to truly know it. There is a general agreement on this by the mystics worldwide, East and West. There is also a general agreement among the most sophisticated mystics that this realization is of a reality that is deeply nondual or "not-two," where the "not two" means—to the extent that it can be put into words (which is not very much)—that there is a nonduality, a "oneness," or a "wholeness" of infinite and finite, subject and object, formless and form, unmanifest and manifest, spirit and matter, heaven and earth, nirvana and samsara, good and evil. This nonduality applies to any other pairs of opposites you want to mention (with ultimate reality remaining "not-two," a *coincidentia oppositorum*, a unity of opposites). They are said to be unified or "One Taste" because we are after a Ground of All Being, and "All Being" means exactly that—namely, all of existence and being *and* nonexistence and nonbeing. Absolutely everything is included, all of it is radically embraced, and that can't be fully known by any words,

no matter which ones we choose, but only by a direct awakening and realization of this radically all-inclusive, nondual "wholeness." This could be called a "panentheism"—except that is just a word or concept also, and thus it also falls into the category of explanation not direct experience (which is also why I put *wholeness* in scare quotes). In this book, we'll be going through exercises together that will directly show you this immediate experience of "wholeness" so you can see all of this for yourself.

CHAPTER 1: INTRODUCTION TO WAKING UP

1. The term *Kosmos* (as in "Kosmic consciousness") is a Greek word that means "the entire world"—matter, body, mind, soul, and spirit—which is what a real Kosmic consciousness is actually one with. After the reduction of the world to matter by scientific materialism, it was replaced by the term *cosmos*, which means just the material world. Since matter was then thought to be the only reality, *cosmos* itself came to mean all of reality. Thus, *Kosmic consciousness* came to be spelled *cosmic consciousness*. I will sometimes use that spelling too—as I did the first time I used that term—especially if I don't have room for a note like this, which explains what *Kosmic consciousness* really means. Needless to say, what we want is Kosmic consciousness, not merely cosmic consciousness.
2. Jordan Peterson, transcript of a YouTube talk, "Biblical Series VIII: The Phenomenology of the Divine," last accessed June 6, 2023, https://www.jordanbpeterson.com/transcripts/biblical-series-viii/.
3. Jordan Peterson.
4. You can find extensive treatments of these stages in the work of researchers such as Daniel P. Brown and Dustin DiPerna, as well as in my own work.
5. Ludwig Wittgenstein, *Tractatus Logico-Philosophicus* (Mineola, NY: Dover Publications, 1998), prop. 6.4311.
6. Erwin Schrödinger, *My View of the World* (Cambridge, UK: Cambridge University Press, 1964), 22.

CHAPTER 2: WHY DO WE NEED GROWING UP?

1. Some psychologists dislike the idea of multiple intelligences. If so, that's not a problem; you can simply think of them as different skills or capac-

ities—which no psychologist objects to—and it doesn't change what I'm saying in any way. The development of those capacities unfolds in stages, and those stages are what I'm describing.

2. Different developmental models track somewhat different sets of intelligences, and many of them focus on a specific intelligence (for example, Piaget focused on cognitive development, Kohlberg on morals, Loevinger on ego development, Graves on values, Maslow on needs, and so on). Depending on which metrics or measuring systems is used, you will get a somewhat different percentage of the population at a given level. This is fine, and it reflects the reality that different developmental lines often reach different developmental levels. The metrics I am using here—although I could have used any one of them—is that given by Robert Kegan, in *In Over Our Heads* (Cambridge, MA: Harvard University Press, 1994). His research indicates that fewer than 3 in 5 people reach the modern (orange) stage of development—that is, less than 60 percent.

CHAPTER 4: SPIRITUAL INTELLIGENCE VERSUS SPIRITUAL EXPERIENCE

1. It is true that some people use the term *spiritual intelligence* in a very broad way, which includes a vague combination of both Waking Up and Growing Up. It is truly fine to define *spiritual intelligence* any way that you wish, and I do not doubt the sincerity or wisdom of those who define it that way. But I say "vague" because although they might be pointing directly to a real Waking Up in Spirit, virtually none of them include any understanding of the stages of Growing Up, which severely hobbles their view. So, in my definition, I am specifically differentiating between the degree of Waking Up (pure spiritual experience) and the level of Growing Up (spiritual intelligence), so that we can clearly and openly include both.
2. And *experience* is not really the best word here, since all experiences unfold in time and most have a subject–object duality, but Awakening has neither. It's more a direct realization or recognition of something that is already fully present in a nondual or unified way—an awakening to a Reality that underlies every experience but is not itself an experience. It's more like the "clearing" in which all experience arises and falls. But I'll

often use the word *experience* for this realization since it at least indicates the immediateness and nonconceptual nature of this awareness.

3. See Ken Wilber, *Quantum Questions* (Boston: Shambhala Publications, 2001).
4. Although these structures exist inside the interior or 1st-person reality of an individual—what we technically call "zone 2"—they still cannot be seen by looking within (which is true of all zone-2 structures). We say that they are objective realities because they are universally true for all subjective individuals (that is, they provide an objective view of subjective structures).

CHAPTER 5: THE EARLY STAGES OF GROWING UP

1. As I noted, different models give a different number of levels or stages (in both Growing Up and Waking Up), depending upon the granularity that they are aiming for. In Growing Up, some models present 4 or 5 levels, others give 7 to 9, yet others give a dozen or more. The most common range, as I've indicated, is 6-to-8. My own Metatheory gives upward of 16 stages, and again that number varies depending upon how much detail is required. To see what's involved in this, take the ethnocentric stage, for example; generally, there is indeed a stage that has the qualities described in the text for that general stage. But that stage can be subdivided into 2, 3, 4, or even more substages; all of these divisions are accurate and all of them are based on evidence. Most often, I will present 8–12 stages. In this book, I've settled on 6 major stages, which represent 8 stages, as I explain below, with 2 of the 6 stages actually being a condensation of 2 stages, which gives in total 8 stages overall. These 6 stages are the most basic and most common, they tally with Fowler's research, and they convey virtually all the important information that needs to be presented in the shortest amount of space. In *The Religion of Tomorrow* (Boston: Shambhala Publications, 2017), I presented 13 stages; in *Integral Psychology*, 16 stages. All of them are accurate, because the stages given exist and have abundant evidence supporting their postulation—it's simply a matter of desired detail.
2. Alfred North Whitehead, *Process and Reality: An Essay in Cosmology*, ed. David Ray Griffin and Donald W. Sherburne (New York: Free Press, 1978), 28.

3. William Blake, *The Marriage of Heaven and Hell* (Garden City, NY: Dover Publications, 1994).
4. Let me get a few technical points out of the way. As I mentioned, I have often combined two stages into a single stage. Thus, Graves finds two stages (magical animistic and egocentric), as does Loevinger (impulsive and self protective), whereas Maslow and Selman both have just one (safety and egocentric, respectively). This situation reflects virtually every developmental model in existence. In Integral Psychology, where I gave a meta analysis of over one hundred developmental models, the total number of stages in those models ranges from 4 to over 20. The average number is around 6 to 8 (my own metamodel in that book gave 16 stages, which is the most I felt there was believable evidence for). My view is that there is a single, very broad morphogenetic field of development, and virtually all of these models are tapping into different aspects or levels of that field. Thus, all of them have some truths to offer—but those truths are "true but partial." Also, most of those models did not address the same line of development or type of intelligence (Piaget focused on cognitive development, Kohlberg on moral development, Loevinger on ego development, Maslow on needs development, Graves on values development, and so on). That doesn't mean one of those models is right and all the others are wrong; it might indeed be that all are "true but partial"; it might be that they are all plugging into this broad morphogenetic field, and this field expresses itself differently in different lines; and even the same line can be looked at in different ways.

   So you should not be too worried that different models give a different number of stages of development. We've already seen a simplified, 4-stage model (egocentric, ethnocentric, worldcentric, and integral), and that simplified model is still very accurate. It still covers a complete spectrum of Growing Up in ways that are quite correct. It's just a matter of detail. For example, take Jean Gebser's stages (tweaked as archaic, magic, mythic, rational, pluralistic, integral). There is compelling evidence, from different researchers, that there are actually major stages that exist between every one of those stages (that is, archaic magic, magic mythic, mythic rational, rational pluralistic, pluralistic integral). I have written about every one of those in-between stages. Nonetheless, I often find that Gebser's 6 stages cover many of the most important points. It's a matter of detail—the more detail, the more complicated the model. The question then becomes how much detail is needed to make the points I am trying to make in a particular book.

I mention all of this because if you are familiar with Integral Metatheory, you know that I have at times presented different numbers of the stages of development (4, 6, 10, 13, 16). The stage we're addressing now (red magic-power) is one that I usually present as two stages, which you can see in the list above (magenta impulsive-magic and red magic-mythic power, which I've also often called "magic" and "magic mythic"). Here, I'm combining them, and just to be clear, I'm using the typical name of one stage (magic) and the typical color of the other stage (red); the actual color of the magic stage is magenta.

But right now, we are simply discussing the 6 most common stages of human development and evolution, or Growing Up in general, and the Growing Up of spiritual intelligence in particular.

5. Note that when I speak of these early characteristics, I mean them to apply to the *original* indigenous populations some fifty to one hundred thousand years ago, and *not* to any of today's indigenous tribes, which have continued to significantly evolve. These early magic stages do apply to individuals in today's indigenous cultures insofar as each individual, no matter what culture they are born in, will experience these magic stages in the first few years of their own early development, since everybody goes through all the stages of Growing Up, starting at square one. But unlike the original human cultures, which were at this magic stage, today's indigenous tribes can continue to grow and develop into higher levels of consciousness and culture—mythic, rational, pluralistic, and so on—which none of the original tribes had access to, because those further stages had not yet emerged. But any individual today—no matter what their culture—to the extent that their awareness remains significantly stuck at this early magic stage, will indeed demonstrate the basic (magical) characteristics that we are describing here. And, as we earlier noted, this may result in some very serious, preneurotic, emotional problems, as well as various purely magical and superstitious religious beliefs.
6. The Kosmic Address of a holon is the coordinates of all its AQAL elements, where AQAL stands for "all quadrants, all levels, all lines, all states, all types," which are, respectively, involved in Showing Up, Growing Up, Opening Up, and Waking Up. These coordinates give the holon's "loca-

tion" or "address" in the overall Kosmos. Since the multiverse has no fundamental center, there is no way to say where any holon is located, except by indicating its relation to all other holons, and that's what the Kosmic Address does.

7. C. G. Jung, *Analytical Psychology: Its Theory and Practice* (New York: Vintage, 1970), 110.
8. Since both states and structures are presented here as stages in development, they are technically "state-stages" and "structure-stages." States do not necessarily appear in stages, since they can be "peak experienced" in almost any order—for example, a person can be in the gross state and have a peak experience of turiya, since all these states are ever-present (everybody wakes, dreams, and sleeps). Structures, on the other hand, always appear in stages, since they have to be constructed one at a time—a person cannot, for example, be at moral stage 2 and have a peak experience of moral stage 5. This explains an enormous amount about spiritual awareness, as we will see.
9. There are a few higher cells available to humans, since there are a few higher stages of Growing Up—briefly indicated by the super-integral row in figure 5.3—and there might also be higher states of Waking Up revealed by evolution down the road, but neither are widespread enough today to affect hardly anyone, which is why I'm not emphasizing them.
10. Roger Walsh, *The World of Shamanism* (Woodbury, MN: Llewellyn Publications, 2007).

CHAPTER 6: THE MYTHIC-LITERAL (OR AMBER) STAGE

1. Clare Graves and Spiral Dynamics describe this stage as "saintly," in addition to "absolutistic." The word *saintly* accurately reflects the religion that comes from the mythic, fundamentalist nature of this amber stage of development. But Graves thought that almost all spirituality comes from this stage because he was completely ignorant of Waking Up as the real core of spirituality. He equated all spirituality with one of the lowest levels of spiritual intelligence, the mythic level of spiritual intelligence (in Growing Up), ignoring the unity of spiritual experience (in Waking Up). Thus he missed the essence of real spirituality, which includes a genuine Waking Up, and a Waking Up interpreted by stages of spiritual

intelligence that are two or three levels higher than the mythic-literal (for example, rational, pluralistic, and integral). In all of these ways, Graves and Spiral Dynamics butcher spirituality.

Now that wasn't Graves's fault. It's pretty much what every educated Westerner believes (namely, all spirituality is a type of fundamentalist religion and therefore comes from this mythic stage), which is the disaster of spirituality in the modern and postmodern world and something that any authentic Religion of Tomorrow would immediately rectify.

But it is true that fundamentalist and the mythic-literal aspects of any religion or spirituality do come from this stage. And Graves correctly called this stage "absolutistic," because this stage is certain that it possesses the absolute truth, whether that truth is religious or not. Most people speaking about religion indeed are talking about this mythic stage, and thus the many varieties of spiritual realities all get collapsed and reduced to just this low level of Growing Up. So it's totally understandable that Graves would also call this stage "saintly." But when we distinguish Waking Up from Growing Up—and recognize the many higher stages of spiritual intelligence (rational, pluralistic, and integral)—we allow each religion to drop its absolutistic fundamentalism and instead expand to its truer, deeper, higher dimensions. Then this saintly stage of Graves's system would no longer apply to all religions but only to those that hadn't continued to grow and evolve past this early amber mythic stage.

CHAPTER 7: THE MODERN-RATIONAL (OR ORANGE) STAGE

1. Mary-Alice Jafolla and Richard Jafolla, *The Simple Truth* (Unity Village, MO: Unity, 1999).
2. This can be a useful exercise. Since every stage of development "transcends and includes" its previous stage, there are some profound "true but partial" truths to be found in the previous mythic stage, and development is a slow addition of the "true but partial" truths of each stage. Each stage of development interacts with and interprets its world in distinctive ways—which is what the mythic stage does when it interprets its world in mythic ways, which indeed are very literal. When these "true but partial" truths are subsequently interpreted by the next stage's rationality, they are, in turn, interpreted in rational ways.

These are indeed interpretations that make sense to rationality, but those truths didn't start in rational forms; they started in mythic-literal forms. Nonetheless, a true-but-partial mythic truth is still a partial truth, and when it is interpreted in higher rational forms, it can be useful (simply because development is the sum total of all the partial truths accumulated at all the stages of development, since each stage "transcends and includes"). Thus, if a higher, rational interpretation of a lower mythic truth is done in a careful, profound, and well-thought-out fashion, it can be useful to individuals who are themselves at that higher, rational level—especially if you don't confuse that rational interpretation with the original form or meaning of the myth itself. This is especially the case when it comes to various "existential truths," truths that tend to be true for all individuals at any stage of development (although they will be interpreted differently at each stage). Thus, a truth such as man is born in the image of God is a profound, existential truth, but it will have the meaning that it had at the mythic stage—that is, the word *God* means a mythic God at the mythic stage. At a rational stage, it is still an existential truth that man is born in the image of God, but *God* now means a rational, universal, worldcentric being, which is not exactly what it meant during the mythic stage. For example, in Genesis, right after God claims that all humans are born in his image, this assertion isn't given a truly universal meaning—in fact, in the books following Genesis, God recommends slavery, murder, genocide, rape, and all sorts of other ethnocentric actions. That's not an orange God; that's an amber God. Thus, there is always some slippage of existential truth between the stages. (Note that rational truth itself will be reinterpreted by higher, vision-logic, integral stages of development and translated into integral terms and will suffer the same problems.) In the text, I am giving an Integral interpretation of the rational interpretation of the meaning of myth.

3. C. G. Jung, *Analytical Psychology: Its Theory and Practice* (New York: Vintage, 1970), 110.
4. Turiya, or the 4th state, is not the highest state, which is the 5th state or turiyatita, and this is for a good reason: turiya is actually not completely unqualifiable. It is the home of the very first dualisms that mark the beginning of the manifest realm, a realm that, if seen apart from Spirit, is nothing but illusion, maya, shadows on the cave wall. The Traditions

maintain that turiya or the Witness is the home of the very first dualism, which is the subject–object duality, and even though it is an Absolute Subjectivity that contains relative subjects and relative objects, it still stands apart from that realm and Witnesses it as a radical Subjectivity or Individuality. Integral Metatheory adds that it is also the home of the second major dualism, the individual–collective duality), and these two dualities give rise to the 4 quadrants. So turiya or the Witness is indeed an absolute or ultimate state, but it is tinged with Subjectivity (and Individuality) and this prevents it from being the highest state—turiyatita, which goes beyond both of those dualities and is purely Nondual. But for most practical purposes, turiya is unqualifiable and is certainly radically All-Inclusive, and thus it is included as one of the two major "ultimate states."

5. That Buddhism is a "rational religion" is the reason why so many smart modern and postmodern people—in Silicon Valley, for example—have adopted Buddhism and its mindfulness practices; there are no embarrassing myths to have to live with. Even the prominent New Atheist Sam Harris, who seems to loathe all mythic-literal religions, has himself practiced Buddhist meditation for three decades and has even written a book about it called *Waking Up*, a fact his admirers always seem to forget.
6. Pantheism is a spiritual worldview that equates the sum total of the manifest universe with Spirit or God/Goddess, often viewed as a "Great Web of Life." This viewpoint is commonly adopted by spiritual intelligence once a mythic view has been rejected—that is, when the mythic God is rejected, a spiritual Nature often takes its place. This also allows believers to use leading-edge sciences (such as quantum mechanics and systems theory) to bolster their spiritual worldview. For pantheism, salvation tends to be equated with holism, and an alienated and "sinful" life is equated with fragmentation and fracture—so to see the totality of Reality as a unified Wholeness is the general aim of pantheism.

   Most theologically oriented thinkers strongly reject pantheism because it makes no reference to the completely unmanifest, infinite, groundless Ground of All Being, where *infinite* for these critics means not just the sum total of finite things but something truly beyond the finite—that is, something truly infinite and transcendent. In short, pantheism has no room for, or no acknowledgment of, causal Formlessness or turiya Emptiness or turiyatita Nonduality. It has no truly transcendental Spirit, only an immanent Spirit. Thus, according to these critics, pantheism has no access to any transcendence of (or freedom from) any of the inadequacies of the manifest universe. Since a pantheistic Spirit is itself the sum total of the manifest universe, it can offer no liberation from it.

In contradistinction to pantheism, those who wish to include both a transcendent and an immanent Spirit often call their view "panentheism," with the added "en" meaning "in." Thus the term means "God in all" or "all in God." I agree with the general points of this panentheistic view, but with one major caveat: one can believe or think that panentheism is true whether or not one has had a real Waking Up to that ultimate Reality. You can be at orange spiritual intelligence and embrace the philosophical view of panentheism without ever having the slightest Waking Up experience at all, and that difference definitely needs to be remembered. Thus, once one has had a genuine Waking Up, then one's spiritual intelligence can use a panentheistic (or evolutionary panentheistic or, even better, an Integral panentheistic) interpretation of that Waking Up reality as a very adequate interpretation, especially when one is oneself coming from turquoise Integral or higher.

Another way to state the difference between pantheism and panentheism is to point out that pantheism has no Waking Up anywhere in it. It includes only Growing Up, Opening Up, Cleaning Up, and Showing Up. They are all relative truths, taken entirely from the finite, relative realm (which pantheism equates with its Spirit). None of them includes an ultimate Truth—which is what Waking Up does. So I fully agree with pantheism when it comes to relative truth; but it has no Waking Up to an infinite ultimate Truth of a Ground of All Being, and that's where I (and most critics) have to get off. In other words, I agree with its partial truth; it just doesn't go far enough for a more complete, and indeed more whole and comprehensive, Truth—that is, panentheism.

7. Alfred North Whitehead, *Process and Reality: An Essay in Cosmology*, ed. David Ray Griffin and Donald W. Sherburne (New York: Free Press, 1978), 28.
8. Peirce was a contemporary of William James, and after he invented the philosophy of pragmatism, James immediately borrowed the term and became one of its leading champions. Peirce wasn't exactly happy with how James was handling this, however, and he was a little upset with

James's"borrowing" his ideas, so he changed the name of his own philosophy from "pragmatism" to "pragmaticism," which he said was "a word so ugly as to discourage theft."

CHAPTER 8: THE POSTMODERN-PLURALISTIC (OR GREEN) STAGE

1. Clare Graves said of this transition that "an unbelievable chasm of meaning is crossed" and that it was a "momentous leap," which I in turn paraphrase as "a monumental leap in meaning."

CHAPTER 9: THE INCLUSIVE-INTEGRAL (OR TURQUOISE) STAGE

1. By "leading edge of evolution," I mean two general but slightly different things. First, a stage constitutes the leading edge of cultural evolution when 10 percent or more of the culture's population is at that stage. When 10 percent of the population reach a cultural stage of evolution, a tipping point occurs, and that leading edge's values tend to be absorbed throughout the culture—and so this stage is often responsible for the name given to the era in which this shift occurs. For example, this happened when 10 percent of the culture reached orange reason—"The Age of Reason"—and it also happened when 10 percent of the culture reached green postmodernism —"The Postmodern Age."

   Second, I use "leading edge" to mean the highest stage yet reached by Growing Up itself, which is actually leading evolution before it reaches 10 percent of the population. So in today's culture, green is the cultural leading edge in the first sense (with some 23–25 percent of the population at green), and Integral (as turquoise cross-paradigmatic) is the leading edge in the second sense, with some 0.5–2.0 percent of the population at Integral.
2. Hanzi Freinacht, *The Listening Society—A Metamodern Guide to Politics, Book One* (n.p.: Metamoderna, 2017), 181.
3. Freinacht, 182.
4. Thus, when we say that the only correct answer to "What is Spirit?" or "Does God exist?" is "Get satori and find out," that statement is true enough. When it comes to those questions, for "get satori," we can substitute any number of "pointing-out instructions," since these are descriptions of things you can do in order to directly experience Spirit or

ultimate Unity consciousness yourself (that is, have a direct satori yourself, and thus move from "metaphoric" words to direct experience). This is exactly the approach we will be taking later in this book, when we will be going over a set of pointing-out instructions.

CHAPTER 10: CLEANING UP AND SHADOW THERAPY

1. Let me just mention that there are a few types of shadow material that are not created by the 1-2-3 dissociative process and that therefore are not really helped by the 3-2-1 process. Shadow material formed at the extreme ends of the developmental spectrum are examples of this. For example, some early shadow material doesn't involve material getting pushed to the other side of the self-boundary but rather involves problems that develop in the original formation of the self-boundary itself—for example, borderline and narcissistic disorders. These require specialized and usually professional treatment and isn't something you can do on your own, in any event. But these problems are also relatively rare; the chances are very high that any significant shadow issues you have are from the levels for which the 3-2-1 process works quite well. And keep in mind that this is just one technique; you will most likely want to combine it with any number of other shadow-work practices. But this 3-2-1 practice is a particularly effective technique, and if you do only this, it will help enormously.
2. You can also generate shadow material at higher stages of Growing Up, particularly if you have problems with a new level as it is starting to emerge—perhaps orange, green, or even integral. It's fairly common for people to project their orange or green qualities; but in any case, follow the same instructions that I am outlining here.
3. I arrived at this process not by understanding the actual words that Freud used ("Where 'it' was, there 'I' shall become"), although that helped, but by analyzing every published transcript of Fritz Perls's therapy sessions. Perls was a big star at the Esalen Institute, where he held workshops using a therapeutic process that he invented called "Gestalt Therapy." This technique was incredibly effective—and worked unbelievably fast. Perls famously claimed, "I can cure any neurosis in fifteen minutes." The wild thing is, that was close to accurate; even many of his critics agreed—Perls was an absolute genius at therapy.

So I got all of the transcripts of his sessions and went through them, looking for clues. I found that in almost every case, Perls did exactly the same thing: he would have the person describe their complaint in 3rd-person terms (for example, they hated their boss, had problems with their spouse, had huge anxiety, black depression, uncontrollable obsession). Then he had them put the problem in the empty chair and directly talk to it as a 2nd-person "you." Back and forth they would go, and within ten or fifteen minutes, it was apparent to everybody in the room which 1st-person items they were dissociating and disowning to create their neurosis, and in nine out of ten cases, there was an unmistakable and large diminution of their symptoms. I finally recognized the process that he was following (I don't think he explicitly understood it), and I wrote up an academic paper on it as the "3-2-1 process." That was forty years ago; the article was my first published piece in an official peer-reviewed journal. It described a general process, but as general therapeutic processes go, I still have not found a better one.

4. More specifically, it is the negative side of Cleaning Up, where you take something that is broken and fix or heal it; the positive side of Cleaning Up includes "positive psychology," where you don't fix what is broken but you take something that is already working and strengthen it, making it even better. Cleaning Up includes both positive and negative aspects—the negative aspects almost always being the most urgent, and hence the ones we are focusing on here.

CHAPTER 11: SHOWING UP

1. The "we" is actually the 1st person plural. Since it always contains a 2nd person "you," I often combine them. I explain this more fully below in this chapter, in the section titled "The Quadrants in Everyday Life."
2. If this is so, does that mean no form of afterlife existence is possible, including any form of reincarnation, because the material dimension is left behind at death? No, not totally. Remember that virtually all of the traditions maintain that any afterlife state of consciousness is accompanied by a *subtle body*, a body made of subtle energy (or subtle matter/energy—some form of Right-hand quadrant reality). As for subtle energy, it always exists in a spectrum of forms (from gross to subtle to

causal, where *causal* means the "very subtlest of subtle energies"), and all states of consciousness have some sort of correlate in this subtle-energy spectrum and are always accompanied by it (every Left-hand event has some sort of Right-hand correlate). Like its gross-level forms, this subtle energy, at all its levels, is always perceived as being exterior or objective to consciousness. Any transmaterial state of consciousness, such as an out-of-the-body experience, is accomplished in some sort of subtle body. Thus, consciousness is always embodied (at gross, subtle, or causal levels—every Left-hand event has a Right-hand or matter/energy correlate). So if you happen to believe in something like reincarnation, remember that my claim that matter/energy accompanies every state of consciousness can easily mean that some subtle form of matter/energy accompanies it. The diagram of the 4 quadrants can show not only gross matter/energy correlates but all the subtle and causal matter/energy correspondences (at all the different levels of the subtle-energy spectrum). Thus, it's still true that every Left-hand event has some form of Right-hand or material correlate (gross, subtle, or causal).

3. As for ultimate Spirit itself—with a capital *S*—it is not found in any quadrant in figure 11.2 or 11.3 but rather is loosely represented by the paper on which the diagram of the quadrant is placed. The paper metaphorically represents the Ground of All Being, or that Reality that is fully present "underneath" or "in" each and every holon in the diagram. The quadrants are found in relative, finite reality; the Ground of Being is ultimate infinite Reality—or their Nondual Wholeness or Suchness. This will become clearer as we proceed.
4. That is, all the cells in their bodies—except the sex cells—have XY chromosomes.
5. In figure 11.1, you might notice "SF1," "SF2," and "SF3" in the highest layers in the Upper Right. This represents a series of higher "structure-functions" (which are holons) in the brain structure, and is essentially a generalization of the Eros or self-organizing drive of the Kosmos (which itself appears in all 4 quadrants). That is, according to Whitehead, the 3 "ultimate principles"—or what you need to begin with, in order to get a universe up and running—are first, "the One"; second, "the Many"; and the third, which is the most interesting, "the creative advance into novelty." Since virtually all phenomena are holons—a whole/part or a one/

many—the first two principles (the one and the many) both involve the reality of holons, so the existence of holons is covered. Whitehead further maintains that each moment of existence consists of a past moment being prehended by (or included in) the present moment (this is causality in Whitehead's system), and the present moment being prehended by the upcoming future moment—each moment, in other words, transcends and includes the previous moment (the drive behind this transcendence is what Integral calls "Eros"). This is how and why the universe actually hangs together. The SF series is simply a series of brain structure-functions, and like all phenomena, they transcend and include their predecessor, with increasing degrees of complexity. The SF series also represents the idea that there is a subtle energy at work in all living organisms, and so within a single gross-physical brain structure (like the neocortex), a series of many subtler, higher, bioenergies can and will all exist. And finally, the SF series represents an increase in real Wholeness—each of which "transcends and includes"—which is true of the entire sequence of reptilian to mammalian to primate holons—and can especially be seen in things like the hemispheric synchronization of the brain, a holistic state if ever there was one.

CHAPTER 12: OPENING UP

1. Many cognitive neuroscientists see IQ as the only basic intelligence that we have (and that tends to cover two basic intelligences—cognitive and verbal), but even they admit that it covers only 25 percent of overall intelligence. I agree with them on the importance of IQ and that it covers at least 25 percent of our overall intelligence. I also accept that the standard IQ test is the most accurate test found in all of psychology. They often add that if you do a factor-analysis test on the various multiple intelligences that have been proposed, what shows up most consistently is just some version of IQ (or again, around 25 percent of it). This is fine. If you do a factor-analysis test on the dozen or so types of intelligences, you usually get just some variation of IQ (as cognitive and verbal).

   But that doesn't define or even describe the differences between a mental state of aesthetic value and one of emotional value, moral value, or spiritual value, or the differences between any of other multiple intelligences. These cognitive neuroscientists tend to confuse a simple capacity or skill with an actual intelligence (such as a moral capacity with a moral intelligence). Probably they do this because the phrase *multiple intelligences* leads these researchers to believe that these multiple intelligences are directly competing with IQ—and, I agree, if you do that, they will all reduce to IQ when tested. So, as I mentioned, if you have problems with the idea of multiple intelligences, you can simply think of them as multiple capacities, skills, or perspectives. Whatever you take to be the difference between morals, aesthetics, music, emotions, spirituality, and so on—just those actual differences are what I mean when I refer to multiple intelligences.

CHAPTER 13: VERY DARK SHADOWS TODAY

1. For an inside look at this crisis, see Ernest R. May and Philip D Zelikow, eds., *The Kennedy Tapes: Inside the White House During the Cuban Missile Crisis* (Cambridge, MA: Harvard University Press, 1997). A film based on that book was made—*Thirteen Days*—starring Kevin Costner and Bruce Greenwood, which is quite good and highly recommended. It conveys beautifully the brutally nerve-racking insanity of the whole situation.
2. Umber mythic-rational is the name of an advanced ethnocentric stage of development, lying between the amber stage and the orange rational-universal stage. Umber is marked by the fact that mythic ideas, when they are first touched by universal-rational drives, attempt to become universal, usually via military expansion into empires, and it continues its influence as these empires evolve into early nation-states. It is also usually marked by the rationalization of mythic structures, for example, each of the Greek city-states had its own gods (which Socrates was killed for allegedly not accepting). As its name implies, umber mythic-rational is what happens when orange universal rationality starts thinking about amber mythic realities. (In this explanation, I have generally followed Habermas.) Similarly, in terms of "in-between structures," when it comes to magic-mythic—the stage between magic proper and mythic—the red stage is a structure lying midway between magenta magic and amber mythic and is marked by mythic thinking that includes magic realities.
3. Robert Kegan, a brilliant developmentalist at the Harvard Graduate School of Education, has done extensive research that indicates that in the

United States "3 out of 5 people fail to reach the modern [orange] stage of development"—or around 60 percent of the population fails to adequately reach universal-global stages (Kegan, *In Over Our Heads*). That level is slightly higher in the worldwide population, in which 60 to 70 percent do not reach the global levels, than it is in the United States,.

4. Just how serious the climate crisis is depends on which experts you consult. To give an example that is very counterintuitive—at least for people who think that humanity has only twelve more years left to live—if we consult the IPCC (Intergovernmental Panel on Climate Change, the UN panel comprising the very best experts in climate science and that is responsible for the Paris Climate Accords, for example), their published assessment is that, yes, global warming is real, it is caused by humans, and it is ongoing. But how serious is it? According to the IPCC, the actual cost to the world of global warming will be, by 2050, between 0.2 and 2.0 percent of the global GDP. Wow, less than 2 percent. That hardly sounds like a huge catastrophe. But that is the conclusion of the UN's IPCC, which is taken to be the ultimate consulting body for the climate crisis. But even if this means that we have considerably more time than twelve years left to live, the climate crisis is still due to a global worldcentric technology in the Right Hand coupled with a less-than-adequate (less-than-global) response in the Left Hand, which is my major point here.
5. Robert Kegan and Lisa Laskow Lahey, *An Everyone Culture* (Boston: Harvard Business Review Press, 2016), 242.
6. Kegan and Laskow Lahey, 161.
7. See Alan Watkins and Ken Wilber, *Wicked and Wise: How to Solve the World's Toughest Problems* (Chatham, UK: Urbane Publications, 2015).
8. In the cognitive line, the emergence of orange brings the capacity to be aware of systems, and hence this marked the first worldcentric or global stage in humanity's development, with intense interest in things like universal rights and the system of Nature. Green brings a higher stage of "meta-systemic" awareness, or "systems of systems." This gave green the capacity to reflect on the orange systems of modernity and take a critical attitude toward them, which marked the emergence of postmodernity. The emergence of Integral 2nd tier brings the possibility of "systems of systems of systems," which gives Integral its incredible capacities (para-

digmatic and cross-paradigmatic) that include being so widely comprehensive, inclusive, and integrated.

9. I'm not unduly worried by some forms of wealth inequality. For example, when Steve Jobs "invented" the personal computer, he became a billionaire, but he didn't become a billionaire by stealing money from, say, the local farmer—in fact, Jobs likely helped the farmer, by using a computer, make more money. Because people are born with a diversity of capacities and interests, a totally equal outcome for all can be had only by repressing the diversity, so various forms of diversity and inequality naturally come with the territory. But at some point, the sheer size of the thing can take on a life of its own and become, just in itself, an evil. For me, that line was crossed when just five people on the planet ended up owning the same amount as owned by the poorest 50 percent of the world.

CHAPTER 14: THE NIGHTMARE OF MODERNITY

1. Arthur Lovejoy, *The Great Chain of Being* (Cambridge, MA: Harvard University Press), 26.
2. Lovejoy, 184.
3. Lovejoy, 211.
4. Pascal, quoted in Lovejoy, *The Great Chain of Being*, 128.

CHAPTER 15: WAKING UP

1. Technically, you are not actually of the same substance as the Total Painting, because the Total Painting could disappear completely into a purely formless unmanifest state, and if so, then you would be fully one with *that* state, even though the Total Painting is objectively gone. Identifying the Total Painting of manifestation with ultimate Reality is pantheism; this is nondualism. But this Total Painting, since it is always present in the waking state, is where you want to begin—fully Witnessing it is the first step.
2. Schrödinger, *My View of the World* (Cambridge, UK: Cambridge University Press, 1964), 22.
3. Wittgenstein, *Tractatus*, prop. 6.4311.
4. Technically, turiyatita—nondual, awakened Awareness—is the one and only ultimate state, and thus the only state that is always already the case;

but its knowing aspect (or turiya), as an intrinsic dimension of nondual Awareness, is likewise always already the case. If that knowing aspect is taken by itself, it appears as the Knower, the Witness, the True Self—that is, it appears as a separate turiya, the 4th state. Technically that is a minor step down from the 5th state, and it could be conceived as therefore being a relative state, not an ultimate one. But that knowing component is indeed an intrinsic component, aspect, or dimension of nondual Awareness, and it is as ever-present as the nondual Awareness itself, and thus the Traditions always count turiya or the Witness as being an absolute or ultimate state, along with turiyatita. But make no mistake, *taken by itself,* the Witness is not as high as nondual Suchness or nondual One Taste. The truly ultimate state is recognized when any sensation of a "self" (whether a capital *S* Self or a small *s* self) disappears into the seamless unity of a nondual Suchness, the Wholeness of Waking Up. But both the Witness and One Taste (turiya and turiyatita) are counted as ultimate states, since the fundamentals of both of them are indeed ever-present and all-inclusive. The only reason they are separated is that turiya, precisely because it is a Self-condition and not a fully Nondual condition, can be experienced by itself, for example, in the state of the Witness, and most of the earlier, pre-nondual spiritual traditions often took turiya as the highest state that could be reached. When the Nondual traditions arose, they realized—as usually happens—that the turiya state was an intrinsic part of the turiyatita state (the knowing part), but that wasn't realized as long as one was aware of only turiya, which is what happened with all of the pre-nondual traditions.

CHAPTER 16: POINTING OUT THE WITNESS AND ONE TASTE

1. Erwin Schrödinger, *What Is Life? Mind and Matter* (Cambridge, UK: Cambridge University Press, 1967), 89.
2. Douglas E. Harding, *On Having No Head: Zen and the Rediscovery of the Obvious* (Carlsbad, CA: InnerDirections Publishing, 2002).
3. Chögyam Trungpa, *Journey without Goal: The Tantric Wisdom of the Buddha* (Boston: Shambhala Publications, 1981), 136.

CHAPTER 17: THE FEELINGS OF ENLIGHTENMENT

1. Abraham Maslow, *Religions, Values, and Peak Experiences* (New York: Penguin, 1970), xi.

CHAPTER 19: THE PRACTICE OF INTEGRAL SEXUAL TANTRA

1. You can find descriptions of these exercises in almost any decent text on practical Tantra. I particularly recommend the works by David Deida, all of which come straight from David's own deeply realized 5th-stage Enlightenment.

INDEX